Contents

iii

ECDL Foundation

Credits

Editor
Claire Rourke

Original Text
Alan Bourke
Lorna Bointon

Design
Annette Bolger

Proofreading and Formatting
Claire Rourke

Cover Design
Karolina Mosz

Technical Readers
Annette Bolger
Alan Bourke
Adela Fernandez

Line Drawings
Annette Brennan

Website
OpenApp

Blackrock Education Centre is an accredited ECDL Test Centre

Training for E C D L

Syllabus 5

A Practical Course in Windows XP and Office 2007

Blackrock Education Centre

2010

© Blackrock Education Centre 2010

ISBN   978-0-9564074-5-0

Published by
Blackrock Education Centre, Kill Avenue, Dún Laoghaire, Co. Dublin, Ireland.

Tel: (+353 1) 2302 709   Fax: (+353 1) 2365 044
E-mail: ecdlsales@blackrockec.ie   Web: www.becpublishing.com *and* www.blackrockec.ie

Published   2010

References to the European Computer Driving Licence (ECDL) include the International Computer Driving Licence (ICDL). ECDL Syllabus Version 5.0 is published as the official syllabus for use within the European Computer Driving Licence (ECDL) and International Computer Driving Licence (ICDL) certification programme. Microsoft® Windows®, Microsoft® Office®, Microsoft® Word®, Microsoft® Access®, Microsoft® Excel®, Microsoft® PowerPoint®, Microsoft® Internet Explorer® and Microsoft® Outlook® are either registered trademarks or trademarks of the Microsoft Corporation. The use of WinZip and the WinZip trademark is with the kind permission of WinZip Computing Incorporated.

Other products mentioned in this manual may be registered trademarks or trademarks of their respective companies or corporations.

The companies, organisations, products, the related people, their positions, names, addresses and other details used for instructional purposes in this manual and its related support materials on the manual's support website www.becpublishing/syllabus5 are fictitious. No association with any real company, organisations, products or people is intended nor should any be inferred.

Every effort has been made to ensure that this book contains accurate information. However, Blackrock Education Centre, its agents and the authors shall not be liable for any loss or damage suffered by readers as a result of any information contained herein.

Editor's Note

The Manual

Training for ECDL: A Practical Course in Windows XP and Office 2007 for Syllabus 5 will provide you, the student or tutor with everything that is needed to prepare for the current BCS QCF qualifications. Explanations and step-by-step instructions are given in clear English to allow for self-directed learning or tutor-based training.

Written specifically for the United Kingdom by Blackrock Education Centre, this latest study guide covers all seven modules of the ECDL Core including the two new BCS modules, Security for IT Users and IT User Fundamentals.

The section on e-mail has been written for Microsoft Outlook and the internet has been written for Microsoft Internet Explorer on Windows XP. It has been designed primarily as training material for students of the European Computer Driving Licence (the International Computer Driving Licence – ICDL – outside Europe).

The manual has been approved by the ECDL Foundation as suitable for use with the new ECDL/ICDL Syllabus Version 5.

Design

Every use has been made of the knowledge and skills of our trainers in producing this manual.

- Plain English, not computer jargon, is the language of choice.

- Each new topic is explored with detailed step by step explanations.

- Additional information is provided where appropriate to enhance the student's understanding.

- Practice sequences have been added to reinforce the concepts.

- Particular attention is given to ensuring that the content of the manual reflects the view on the screen.

- The format of the manual makes it desktop friendly.

Web Support

Additional resources can be downloaded directly from www.becpublishing.com
A key feature of the web support is the interactive material for Unit 7.

Users of this manual can send e-mails and receive acknowledgements, download sample files, complete a sample online form, handle media files, review different types of links, manipulate online text and review webpage frames at www.becpublishig.com/syllabus5. Access to these particular resources is described in the relevant section of Unit 7 of this manual.

The Editor

Important

In accordance with copyright law, no part of this publication may be photocopied or reproduced in any form.

Before You Begin

Before You Begin

Section 1 The Computer Workplace

1.1   Introduction
The Before You Begin section is designed for those using a computer for the first time or at beginner level. It contains practical information that will help make basic computer terminology familiar and will outline the most common pieces of computer equipment. Spending time on becoming comfortable with the foundation skills mentioned below will help your progression to learn other skills.

Section 3 deals with the use of laptops, in particular the battery power, the mouse pad and keyboard, and the care and handling of the laptop while in use. The remaining sections apply whether a laptop or a desktop PC is being used.

1.2   Getting Set Up

1.2.1 Starting the Computer
The first thing to do to set up is to switch on the computer (see Section 3 if you are using laptop). On a typical desktop computer, there is a power button situated on the system box. Check the computer's power cable is plugged into the wall socket and press the power button. Generally, the various lights will flash and the computer monitor will be activated. If not press the power switch on the monitor.

Text will appear on the screen to say that Windows is starting up. Depending on the way in which the computer was set up, you may need to 'log in' using a password that has been set up for you. If not, the computer will continue to 'start up'.

This takes a few minutes until a screen similar to the one on the right opens.

1.3   Where You Work
When the computer has finished starting up, the screen that is presented is referred to as the desktop. Similar to the way in which a real office desk is used, on a computer desktop you can sort and manage computer files, open and edit documents. The small pictures on the desktop with the text underneath are called icons, and these represent documents or programs stored on the computer.

Icons

1.4   The Mouse

The mouse is the principal means of controlling the computer. It is a small
box device that you move around with your hand. By moving the mouse,
you control the cursor, which is a small arrow that is displayed on the screen.
This enables you to open, close and manipulate computer applications.

The cursor

Generally, a mouse has three basic parts: a left button, a right button and a scroll wheel in the
middle. As you move the mouse on the mat, the cursor, moves on the screen in tandem with the
mouse. Move the mouse to the right and the cursor moves to the right, etc. When the cursor is
placed in a particular position, e.g. over an icon, pressing a button causes the computer to perform
an action related to the icon.

Using the mouse may appear simple at first. Learning how to use it properly takes practise and it
is crucial for confident and easy use of the computer.

Four actions are performed with the mouse – pointing, clicking, dragging and scrolling.

1.4.1 Pointing

You point to an icon or a button that you want to use, by moving the mouse. A white arrow moves
on the screen representing the action of the mouse.

Practice

Point to the **Recycle Bin** icon.

NOTE

Sometimes a yellow box with text is displayed (depending on your computer settings) when
you point to an icon or button. This is known as a **screen tip**, which gives a short explanation
of the button or icon.

1.4.2 Clicking

Left-click and right-click are used to describe which mouse button to use.
To left-click on an object, firstly point to it. Then quickly press and release
the left mouse button. You will hear the button click. Clicking is also
referred to as selecting.

A **single click** either:

- Select an object.
- Perform an action.

Practice

Point and left-click the mouse on the Recycle Bin icon. The icon darkens,
or is highlighted. This shows that you have selected it. To deselect it, move the
cursor to a blank area on the screen away from the recycle bin icon and left-click.

Practice

Point and right-click the mouse on the Recycle Bin icon. This time a
pop-up menu appears. Without clicking either mouse button, move the cursor
to a blank area on the screen away from the icon and left-click to hide the
pop-up menu.

A **double-click** means left-clicking twice in rapid succession.

- Double-clicking performs a different action, e.g. opening a folder, a file or an
  application.

Double click

Practice

- Double-click the **My Computer** icon.
  The **My Computer** window opens.
- Point and click on the **Close X** button at the top right hand corner to close the window.

1.4.3 Dragging

To drag an object means to move it on the desktop from one location to another. For example, point to an icon on the desktop, click and hold down the left mouse button. Then, while still holding down the left mouse button, move the mouse on the mouse mat (this drags the icon on the desktop).

Practice

- Place the tip of the pointer on an icon, e.g. the Recycle Bin, on the desktop.
- Hold down the left mouse button and move/drag the mouse.
  An outline (or ghost image) of the icon moves with the mouse.
- Release the button to 'drop' the icon in its new position. (It may spring back to its original position, depending on how your computer has been set up.)

1. Point on icon	2. Click left button and move/drag the mouse	3. Release the button to drop the icon
	A 'ghost' image of the icon moves with the mouse	

1.4.4 Scrolling

Scrolling means moving up or down to view different parts of a document or window. For example, if you are working in Microsoft Word and have come to the bottom of the page, it is easy to scroll up to view the top of the page.

To scroll with the mouse, do the following:

- Rest your finger on the mouse wheel and roll away from your hand to move up and roll towards your hand to move down.

> **NOTE**
> Scrolling is only possible when working with documents or windows that take up more space than is available on the display screen.

1.5 The Taskbar

The **taskbar** is a bar that appears along the bottom of the desktop. Depending on your computer settings, the taskbar will either remain visible all the time on the desktop or it might be hidden from view. If it is hidden move the cursor on the desktop to the bottom of the screen, and the taskbar will pop up.

> **NOTE**
> To keep the taskbar visible, point and right-click on the taskbar and, from the pop-up menu, click **Properties**. The **Taskbar and Start Menu Properties** window opens. Click the box to the left of 'Auto-hide the taskbar' to uncheck this option.

1.5.1 Taskbar Buttons

The taskbar contains a number of icons in the form of buttons. A button can be clicked to perform a specific action. Some buttons are always on the taskbar while others appear on it from time to time, depending on what you are working on. Think of the items on the taskbar as if they were drawers in a real desk where things can be put away when they are not being used.

For example:

- Click the **Start** button once and then click it again.
- Double-click the time displayed at the bottom right-hand side of the taskbar.
  The **Date and Time Properties** window opens, displaying a calendar and a clock along with other items.
- Point and click the **Close X** at the top right hand corner to close the window.

The taskbar in the illustration shows some more examples of taskbar buttons.

1.6 Cursors

The cursor on the screen changes automatically into different shapes, depending on the action being performed. The cursor shape gives the user a visual indication of what is happening.

- The arrow or normal select cursor is probably the most common. It is used to select objects, to click buttons and to choose options in menus and on toolbars.
- The busy cursor (or hourglass) appears when the computer is engaged in an activity that will take a few moments to complete. You should wait until the action is completed and the pointer resumes its original shape.
- In some windows, a question mark button appears beside the Close X button on the top right of the box. When you click this button and then point to an object or menu, the cursor changes into the help cursor and a pop-up explanation, in a yellow box, is displayed.

1.7 Turning Off the Computer

Turning off the computer is called shutting down.

To shut down the computer do the following:

- Left-click (click with the left mouse button) the **Start** button.
- Move the cursor to the **Turn Off Computer** button.
- Left-click the button.
  A window opens in the centre of the screen showing three buttons.
- Click **Turn Off**.
- The computer will take a few moments to shut down.

Section 2   The Keyboard

2.1   The Keyboard

The keyboard and the mouse are the main 'controls' for interacting with your computer, i.e. for instructing the computer to do something for you, such as, 'go online' to browse the internet, typing a letter, looking at photos from a digital camera.

The keyboard is referred to as a QWERTY keyboard – taken from the layout of the first row of letters. The letters, or characters, of the alphabet are arranged in the centre of the main keys on three rows.

Most computer keyboards have an additional numeric keypad to the far right of the standard keys. There is also an extra row of keys at the top, called Function keys, which are used by some programs or applications.

In addition, there are some extra keys that are frequently used in computer work, mostly located around the edges of the character keys.

Caps Lock key		Backspace key
Shift key		Enter key
Control key		

2.2   Basic Typing Skills

To understand how the keys work, practise and repeat the short keyboard exercise below using a program called **Notepad** – a small application, for creating basic text documents.

To open Notepad, do the following:
- Left-click the **Start button** on the taskbar at the bottom of the desktop.
- Point to **All Programs**.

- Point to **Accessories**.
- Click **Notepad**.
  The **Notepad** application will open in the centre of the screen.

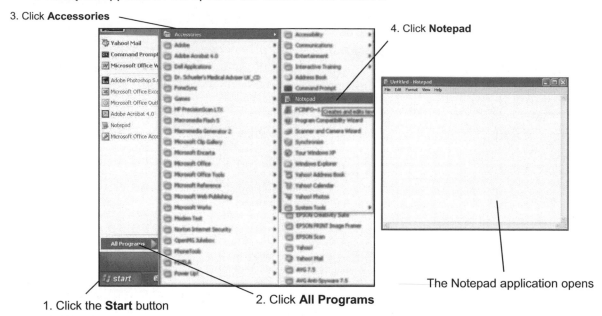

3. Click **Accessories**

4. Click **Notepad**

The Notepad application opens

1. Click the **Start** button

2. Click **All Programs**

Basic typing
1. Type your first name using the **character keys**. Notice how the first letter is not in capitals.

Backspace key – to delete the typed text
2. Delete the text by clicking on the **Backspace key** until all the letters are gone.

Shift key – to create a single capital letter
3. Press down the **Shift key** with one finger and click the first letter of your name with another finger. Release the Shift key. The letter should appear on the Notepad page as a capital letter. Continue to type the rest of the characters of your first name by pressing the character keys.

Space bar – to create a space between words
4. To type your surname you will need to leave a space after your first name. Press the **space bar** once. Then follow instruction 7 to type your surname.

Enter key – to create a new line
5. To make a new line, press the **Enter key** once. Type the first line of your address. (Make sure the first word has a first capital letter and use the space bar to create a space between words.)
6. Repeat instruction 9 to type the remaining lines of your address.

Caps Lock key – to type in all capitals
7. Press the Enter key twice. Press the **Caps Lock key**. (A light should appear on the keyboard indicating that the caps lock key is turned on.)
8. Type Ireland. Notice how all the letters are in capitals.
   Read the text which you have typed to check it.

   If there are any spelling errors, move the cursor to the right of the incorrect letter and left-click. You should see a black line – a **flashing cursor**. Press the Backspace key to delete the mistake and then retype the correct character, etc.

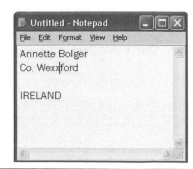

Some of the keys on the keyboard display more than one symbol – one above the other. For example, on the row of numeric keys above the character keys, the number 8 key also has an asterisk, above the 9 and 0 keys there are brackets. (The position of the symbols might vary slightly from one keyboard to another.)

To type these symbols hold down the Shift key (as you do when typing a capital letter).

1. In the open Notepad file, click after the last letter of IRELAND and click the Enter key a couple of times to move down the page.
2. Click key 8, press the space bar, click the key 9, press the space bar and click on the key 0. Press the Enter key.

Shift key – to type the special symbol on a key
3. Hold down the Shift key and, keeping it held down, press the keys 8, 9 and 0 again, clicking the space bar between each. This time the symbols above the numbers will be displayed.

> **NOTE**
> Wherever there is a symbol above another on a key, use the procedure above to type that symbol. The exception to this rule is the euro symbol.

Control (CTRL) and Alt keys – to type the euro symbol
1. Within the open Notepad file, use two fingers to press down the CTRL and Alt keys and, keeping them held down, click the number 4 key. The euro symbol will be typed on the Notepad page.

Practise this drill again. Spend time locating and typing some of the other most commonly used symbols, as shown below.

question mark	?	single and double quotation mark	‘ “
comma	,	sterling symbol	£
full stop	.	dollar symbol	$
apostrophe	’	percentage symbol	%
colon and semi-colon	: ;	underscore	_
ampersand	&	the ‘at’ symbol	@
exclamation mark	!	forward slash	/

2.3   Click and Type

The **I-beam** cursor in Microsoft Office 2007 is associated with the way the text will be aligned on the page. The alignment icons appear beside or under the I-beam to indicate how the text will be aligned.

Left aligns the text

Left aligns the text
and applies a left indent

Centre aligns the text

Right aligns the text

You can place text anywhere in a document by hovering the mouse over the page. This will enable you to view the alignment options. Double-click when you see the alignment option you require and type some text.

This process is known as click and type. Click and type automatically applies the alignment and/or indentation.

Section 3   Using a Laptop

3.1   Using a Laptop

The work undertaken and the way in which the programs work is the same whether you are working on a laptop or a desktop computer. However, there are some specific guidelines for working with a laptop.

Care should be taken when moving the laptop, avoiding knocks, in particular when it is switched on and there are processes running – i.e. applications or background system processes. Any bang at this stage can damage the internal hard drive which will be spinning during this time. While it is a portable device it should remain stable when in use.

3.1.1 Battery Power

A power supply and cable comes with a new laptop. The laptop power – which keeps the machine turned on – differs from the desktop PC in that there is an internal battery which needs to be charged so that the machine can be used without having to plug it into a wall socket (for example, if it is being used in the garden or in a meeting). This battery is charging when the power supply is plugged in. When the laptop is not plugged in, you will need to keep a check on the battery performance to determine how much time you have to work remotely.

A battery power indicator is usually available on the taskbar at the bottom of the screen (see Section 1.5) and an alert as to the remaining performance time is displayed if the power is running low. If you tend to use the laptop a lot outside of an office or the home, it is advisable to invest in a high performance battery.

3.2   The Touchpad

The touchpad is built into a laptop below the keyboard. This is the rectangular shape and the two buttons normally found on a mouse are also built in.

The touchpad might take a little getting used to if you are familiar with using a standard mouse. As you move your finger on the touchpad, the cursor, usually in the shape of a small arrow, moves on the screen in tandem. Move your finger to the right and the cursor moves to the right, etc. Similar to a conventional mouse, the left button is most frequently used to interact with the computer programs and icons. (See Section 1.4 for practice using the mouse.)

Dragging using the touchpad, while the same in principal as using an external mouse, is a little different in practice:

- Move the cursor on the screen to the **My Computer** icon and double-click on the left mouse button on your laptop, to open the My Computer window.
- Move the cursor to the blue bar displaying the title **My Computer**. (Make sure the arrow is in the blue area.)
- With one finger hold down the left mouse button and with the other hand glide your finger across, up or down the touchpad.
  The **My Computer** window will follow in tandem.
- Click the **Close X** button to close the My Computer window.

NOTE
Wherever an instruction mentions to move the mouse on the mouse mat, replace the action with moving your finger on the touchpad. An external mouse can also be attached to the computer and can be used as described in Section 1.4.

3.3 The Keyboard

The keyboard on a laptop is very similar to that which would be used with a desktop computer (see Section 2). The layout has the same QWERTY appearance and the special keys (Shift key, Control key, Backspace key, Enter key, Space bar, Function keys, etc.) will also be in similar positions to those on a desktop computer keyboard.

The main difference in using a laptop keyboard is that there isn't an additional numeric keypad to the right of the main keys. This numeric keypad is incorporated into the main keyboard and is accessed by pressing a function key, which is normally to the bottom left of the keyboard, followed by the required number key. The numbers can be seen in the bottom right-hand corner of the **7**, **8**, **9**, **0**, **u**, **i**, **o**, **p**, **j**, **k**, **l**, **;**, **m**, **,**, **.** and **/** keys.

Numeric keypad is built into the main keyboard

Function key

Section 4   Windows

4.1   Windows

Windows are the visual means with which you interact with the software on the computer, access files and create documents. A window is a panel that appears on the desktop.

To practise working with a window, do the following:

- Click the **My Computer** icon.
  The **My Computer** window opens.

Windows have some common features:

- A **title bar**, which displays the window name.
- A **Close X button** on the top right hand corner, which is used to close the window.
- Windows can be **minimised** – i.e. temporarily hidden from the desktop.
- When a window has been minimised, the title bar is visible as a button on the taskbar. To restore the window, click the button on the taskbar once – the window will reopen to the same size it was before it was minimised.
- Windows can be **maximised** – i.e. enlarged to fill the entire screen.
- To maximise a window click the maximise button.
- Windows can be moved around the desktop and **resized**.
- You can have more than one window open at the same time.

PRACTICE SEQUENCE

1   Ensure the My Computer window is open on the desktop.

2   Double-click the Recycle Bin.

3   Both windows are now open on the desktop.

4   By clicking with the left mouse button on the title bar, move each of the windows, one at a time, around the desktop to reposition them beside each other, one above the other, etc.

5   Note that when you click on a title bar the bar becomes blue in colour. The title bar of the other window becomes grey. The window with the blue title bar is known as the **active** window.

6   To close each window, click the **Close X** button on the top right-hand side.

NOTE

If, when a window filled the screen – i.e. the window was as large as the full screen – when it was opened, its size can be reduced by clicking the **Restore** button. This makes it possible to see other windows that are open (and the desktop).

Restore button

4.2 Scrolling in a Window Containing Folders and Files

When a window is opened on screen, some of the files or folders may be hidden from view. The horizontal and vertical scroll bars are used to access the hidden contents of a window.

To view the full list of contents in a window, do the following:

- Click the down scroll arrow on the vertical scroll bar to scroll to the bottom of the list.
- Click the up scroll arrow on the vertical scroll bar to scroll to the top of the list.
  Alternatively, click and drag the scroll box up or down on the vertical scroll bar.

Left arrow   **Scroll bar**   **Right** arrow

To view the full list of details for files or folders in a window:

- To view the columns on the right-click the right scroll arrow on the horizontal scroll bar.
- To view the columns on the left-click the left scroll arrow on the horizontal scroll bar.
  Alternatively, click and drag the scroll box right or left on the horizontal scroll bar.

4.3 Scrolling in an Application Window

When a document is opened in an application, such as Microsoft Word, the page on the screen represents an A4 page. There may be one or more pages in the document and, therefore, the entire document may not be visible at once. Use the vertical scroll bar as described in Section 3.2 to scroll down or up to view the complete document.

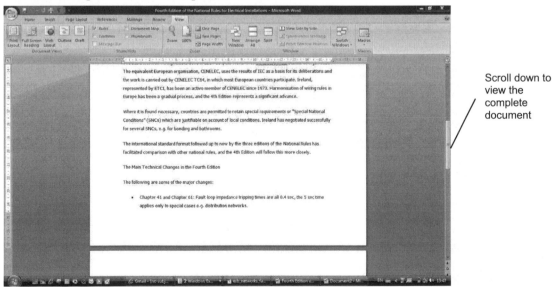

Scroll down to view the complete document

Alternatively, within an application window, use the up and down arrow keys on the keyboard to scroll up and down.

or

Use the **Page Up** and **Page Down** keys.

Page Up/ Page Down keys

Up/Down arrow keys

Section 5   The Ribbon

5.1   The Ribbon

The ribbon is a feature of the Office 2007 applications – Word, Excel, PowerPoint and Access. On opening an application, the ribbon is at the top of the screen. It provides all of the commands that will be needed while working, such as saving a file, formatting, spell checking, etc. The illustrations below show how each of the application ribbons appear on opening a new or existing file.

The ribbon in Word 2007

The ribbon in Excel 2007

The ribbon in Access 2007

The ribbon in PowerPoint 2007

- The ribbon is organised into sections by **tabs**.

Tabs

Related groups of commands

- The tabs are the headings displayed across the top of the ribbon, such as Home, Insert, Page Layout, etc.
- Underneath a tab related commands are grouped together.
- The tab headings indicate a particular category of activity – for example, by clicking the Page Layout tab the various commands required to change the page size, the margins, etc. are displayed.
- Click on a tab to **activate** it or bring it (and the related command buttons) to the forefront of the ribbon.

5.2   Showing Additional Options

Additional options and settings, which don't appear
on the ribbon, are available for each group of related
commands by clicking the title at the bottom of a group.
For example, by clicking Font, the Font window opens
with additional options relating to the formatting of text.

5.3   The Office Button

The Office button is displayed on the top left of the ribbon in each application.

- Click the **Office** button to access a menu for opening and
  saving files, printing, etc.
- You can also easily access the most recent documents
  that you have been working on.
- The Office Button also provides access to the Word
  Options feature which helps users to customise
  applications.

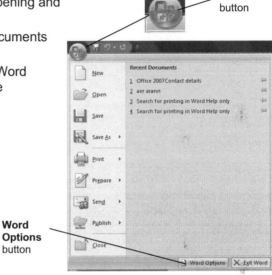

Office
button

Word
Options
button

5.4   Context-Sensitive Tabs

Some tabs, such as the Picture Tools or Table Tools, do not appear on the ribbon until a particular
feature is being used.

For example, if a picture is inserted into the document, the Format tab appears on the ribbon
providing groups of commands to edit the picture. When the picture is no longer selected, the
Format tab will be hidden until the picture is selected again.

The same applies when a table is inserted into the document; the Table Tools – Design and
Layout tabs are available on the ribbon.

5.5   Quick Access Toolbar

By default, the Quick Access Toolbar is positioned at the top of the application window to the right of the Office Button. It is named because the most commonly used commands – e.g. save, undo and open – can be accessed by clicking the appropriate icon. Further options can be added to the Command buttons.

To add further options to the Quick Access Toolbar, do the following:

- Click the arrow on the right of the toolbar.
  A drop-down menu appears.
  The commands that are already on the Quick Access Toolbar will be highlighted with a tick.
- Click any further options required.
- A tick will appear next to the command and its icon will appear on the Quick Access Toolbar.

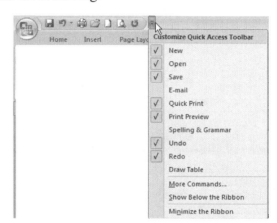

To remove commands from the Quick Access Toolbar, do the following:

- Click the arrow on the right of the toolbar.
  A drop-down menu appears.
  The commands that are already on the Quick Access Toolbar will be highlighted with a tick.
- Click the command to be removed.
- The tick next to the command will disappear and its icon will be removed from the Quick Access Toolbar.

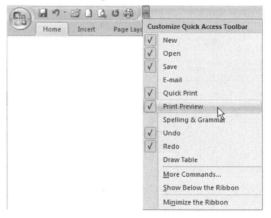

To move the position of the Quick Access Toolbar, do the following:

- Click the arrow on the right of the toolbar.
  A drop-down menu appears.
- Click **Show Below the Ribbon**.
  The **Quick Access Toolbar** will be placed below the ribbon.

The **Quick Access Toolbar** appears below the ribbon

Section 6   Settings

6.1   Default Settings

When the computer has been switched on and the setup process completed, the desktop will be displayed in a particular way, i.e. the icons will be a particular size and arrangement, the cursor size will be a set size, and the colour scheme and graphics of the desktop background will also be preset.

These preset values for the different features are referred to as the default settings. So, for example, when you switch on a new computer, what you see on the screen has been preset in the factory. However, you can change the preset values to suit your individual preferences or needs. You might like to increase the size of the cursor on the screen if it seems too small or change the desktop background to a different picture or colour scheme.

Changing computer settings is covered in more detail in Unit 2, but you may wish to start customising your own workspace to suit your needs, by changing some of the settings below.

To practise changing a default setting, do the following:

Hiding and Showing the Taskbar

The Taskbar will either be temporarily hidden or always visible on the desktop.
To set either of these options, do the following:

- Right-click on a clear part of the taskbar.
- A pop-up menu appears.
- Click **Properties**.
  The **Taskbar and Start Menu Properties** window opens.
- Click in the box to the left of **Auto-hide the taskbar**.
- Click **OK**.
  When the tick appears in this box, the taskbar will be hidden when not in use. When there is no tick in this box, the taskbar will be always visible on the desktop.

Changing the Desktop Background Image

To change the image that appears on the desktop from the default setting, do the following:

- On a blank area of the desktop right-click (click with the right mouse button).
- Click **Properties** from the pop-up menu.
  The **Display Properties** window opens.
- Click the **Desktop** tab.
- The image/background that is currently displayed on your desktop will appear in the computer monitor graphic.
- In the **Background** section, scroll through the list, clicking any items to see how the desktop would appear.
- When you are happy with the selection click **OK**.

  To change the background image again, repeat the steps 1-5 and choose a different background.

Increasing the Size of the Icons on the Desktop

To increase the size of the desktop icons, do the following:

- Right-click on a blank area of the desktop.
- Click **Properties** from the pop-up menu.
  The **Display Properties** window opens.
- Click the **Appearance** tab.
- Note how the choices in the main window change.
- Click **Effects**.
  The **Effects** window opens.
- From the choices presented, click the box next to **Use large icons**.
- Click **OK** to close the Effects window.
- Click **OK** to close the Display Properties window.

Increasing the Size of the Cursor

To increase the size of the cursor, do the following:

- Click the **Start** button and from the **Start** menu click **Control Panel**.
  The **Control Panel** window opens.
- Click **Appearance and Themes**.
- From the list on the left-hand side of the window click **Mouse Pointers** (another name for cursor).

Mouse pointers

The **Mouse Properties** window opens.

- Click the **Pointers** tab and from the drop-down list under scheme select **Windows Standard** (large) or **Windows Standard** (extra large) depending on your preference.
- Click **OK** and see the effect of the change.

Follow the steps again to change the cursor to a different size.

6.2   Application Default Settings

When you open a new document, all the document settings, such as font, text size and page layout, appear with preset values. These are the application default settings.

These default settings can be changed to suit the way in which you work or the documents you create most often. The way in which they are changed, however, varies from one application to the next.

The default font size for a new document in Word is typically set to 12. If you find this too large, you can make 10 the default.

- In the **Home** menu, click the symbol (arrow) to the right of **Font**, to open the **Font** window.

Arrow symbol

- Set the font size to **10**.
- Click the **Default** button at the bottom of the window.
- Click **Yes** in the confirmation window that opens.
  In each new document you open, the font size will be set to 10.

Default button

Section 7 The Help Function

7.1 Online Help

When you are using the computer, there are comprehensive Help systems available to assist you with problems that may arise during the course of your work.

System help assists you with using the computer. It is available in the Start menu.

Application help assists you with a specific application. It can be accessed within each of the Office applications by clicking on the question mark button on the right of the ribbon.

In both cases, there are different types of help available – such as looking up a glossary, taking a tour or tutorial, step-by-step instructions with worked examples, selecting from an index or accessing online help when your computer is connected to the internet.

7.2 System Help

The Help and Support system can be used to access general information about your computer system as well as for specific queries. Information can be accessed using the search facility, an index or a table of contents.

To access the System Help, do the following:

- Click the **Start** button and choose the **Help and Support** item on the menu.
  The **Help and Support Center** window opens.

Forward and Back buttons enable you to move back and forth between articles that have been opened

Assistance is offered via an internet connection to a Microsoft Help website. You may also link up to another computer user who can view your computer remotely

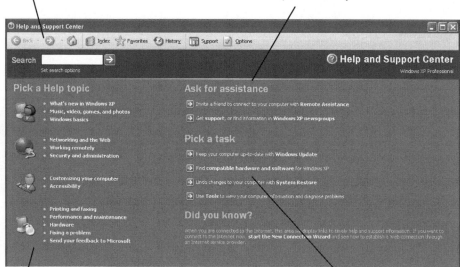

Categories of support under the heading Help topic provide information as well as diagnostic information to locate solutions to problems

Clicking an icon or a piece of text, commonly referred to as a link, in this window activates a link to another Help and Support page which opens on your screen

For example, if information on installing a digital camera is needed, you would use the Help and Support window as follows.

- Click the **Start** button.
- From the menu select **Help and Support**.
- Under the **Pick a Help** topic column, click the **Hardware** item.
  A window opens showing a list of hardware categories.
- By clicking the text link **Scanners and cameras**, the information in the right-hand pane will display a list of help topics specific to scanners and cameras, such as installing a scanner or digital camera, etc.
- Select a topic to answer your query.

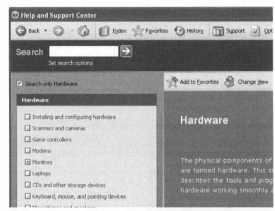

7.3   Using the Index

Another way to access information using the Help and Support window is to use the **Index** option.

- On the **Help and Support Center** toolbar, click the **Index** button.
  The **Index** window opens.
- Type a keyword(s) relating to the topic you are trying to locate in the keyword box, for example, **how to get and print pictures**.
- The computer searches the main categories within the index for the word(s). If a help topic is found, it will be displayed with sub-topics listed underneath.
- Click a sub-topic and then click the **Display** button at the bottom of the window.
  Alternatively, double-click the sub-topic and the information will be displayed in the right-hand pane.

Display button

7.4   Application Help

When you are working in an Office 2007 application, you can get help on a particular problem by searching either the Help content on your computer (installed with the application) or through Microsoft Office Online, when your computer is connected to the internet. The application help feature in Office 2007 is accessed by clicking the question mark button on the right of the ribbon. The example below shows the help system in Microsoft Word, but the process is the same for each of the applications.

To access the help system when working in an application, do the following:

- Click the **Microsoft Office Help** icon on the ribbon.

Drawing Pin button

The **Help** window opens on the Home page, displaying a table of contents in the main section, with the most common help categories.

- If the help topic you are looking for is available in the list on the home page, clicking it will provide a further list of related topics to choose from.

- Click until you find the information you need.
  To keep the **Help** window active or on top of the application window – if you want to refer to the instructions as you carry out a step-by-step procedure – click the drawing pin button will switch between keeping the window on top or behind.

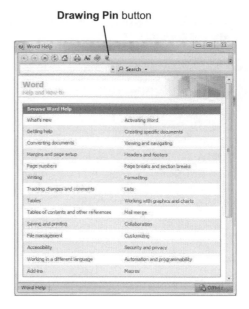

Keep on top

Not on top

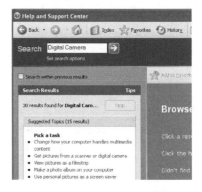

7.5   Using the Search Option

7.5.1 Simple Search

There is a simple Search facility within the Help and Support Center that enables you to type specific search word(s).

To look for help on installing a digital camera, do the following:

- Type a topic into the **Search box**, for example, 'digital cameras'.

- Click the green **Search** box arrow.
  A window with topics related to **Digital Camera** will be displayed in a list under **Suggested Topics**.

- Click the most appropriate text link to access the information you require.

7.5.2 Searching for Help Content Stored on Your Computer: Browse Word Help

There is a simple **Search** facility within the Help window which enables a search on specific word(s).

To find information do the following:

- Type a topic into the **Search** box, for example, **printing**.

- Click the **Search** button.
  The help content stored on your computer is searched for any occurrences of the word 'printing' and the results are displayed in the main section of the Help window.

- Use the **Next** button to go to the next page of results.

- Click the most appropriate text link to access the information you require.
  Typically, background information and step-by-step instructions will be presented.

7.5.3 Searching for Help Content Stored on Your Computer: Table of Contents

You can return to the **Table of Contents** list at any time.

- Click the **Table of Contents** icon.
  The **Table of Contents** list opens in a pane on the left of the main pane.

- Click a topic.

- The help content stored on your computer is searched for any occurrences of the word 'printing' and the results are displayed in the main section of the **Help** window.

- Use the **Next** button to go to the next page of results.

- Click the most appropriate text link to access the information you require.
  Typically, background information and step-by-step instructions will be presented.

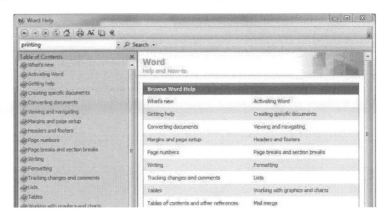

7.5.4 Searching for Help Content on the Internet: Show Content from Office Online

If your computer is connected to the internet, you can include the vast number of help resources in the search, along with the help content stored on your computer.

- Click the **Connection Status** button at the bottom left of the Help window.

- From the pop-up menu, select **Show content from Office Online**.
  A tick mark will be placed beside it and a new search will be carried out displaying results which will include web pages.

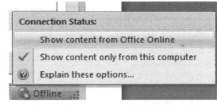

- Click the most appropriate text link to access the information you require.
  If you click a web page symbol, the help topic will be displayed in a browser window (e.g. printing).

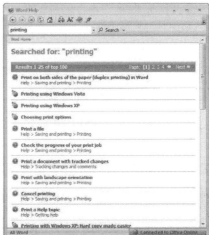

NOTE
When only the content stored on your computer is being searched, the **Connection Status** will display **Offline**.

When the search includes online content, the **Connection Status** will display **Connected to Office Online**.

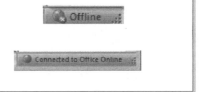

7.5.5 Searching for Help Content in a Specific Location

A specific location or type of help information (such as, visual or audio demonstrations, additional templates, etc.) can be searched for.

- In the **Help** window, click the down arrow beside the **Search** button to display a list of options. The list is divided into two sections, i.e. **Content from Office Online** and **Content from this computer**.

- Click the relevant heading to search in that location.

> **NOTE**
> Selecting **All Word** will search for help content both online and on the computer, when the internet is connected.
>
> Search ▾
> ● Content from Office Online
>   All Word
>   Word Help
>   Word Templates
>   Word Training
>   Developer Reference
> ● Content from this computer
> ✓ Word Help
>   Developer Reference

7.6   Wizards

'Wizard' is a term used to describe a set of instructions that leads you through the steps to perform a task. The wizard asks you various questions about the available options. When you make your choices, the wizard then performs the task for you. Wizards are usually available for complex tasks that involve many steps, such as creating a table or performing a mail merge. (See **Tables** and **Mail Merge** in Unit 3.) The advantage of using a wizard is that it simplifies a complex procedure – you just follow the steps. Automating the task also saves time. The disadvantage of using a wizard is that you may have less control over the final result, as your choice of options may be limited.

Unit 1

Security for IT Users

1

Unit 1
Security for IT Users

1

Section 1   System Performance Security

1.1   Unwanted E-Mail Messages

1.1.1 'Spam' Defined (1.1.1.1)

The widespread use of e-mail makes it a very attractive way for advertisers to reach large numbers of potential customers in a precisely targeted manner. This capability is used by legitimate marketing and advertising companies as well as businesses that are not so reputable.

Unwanted, unsolicited commercial e-mail is known as **spam** or **junk e-mail**. At the time of writing, it is estimated that 80 per cent of the 100 billion e-mails sent daily are spam.

1.1.2 Receiving Spam (1.1.1.2)

Spam messages arrive in a user's e-mail inbox in the same way as normal messages. When the volume of these messages is low, it may not be regarded as much of a problem, however, large numbers can cause a serious inconvenience as the user may have to check each e-mail individually. In addition, the subject lines or content of these e-mails may be of an adult or otherwise offensive nature.

Large volumes of spam also have an impact on computer networks, as they take up storage space, take time to process and eliminate, and place an unnecessary amount of traffic on the internet.

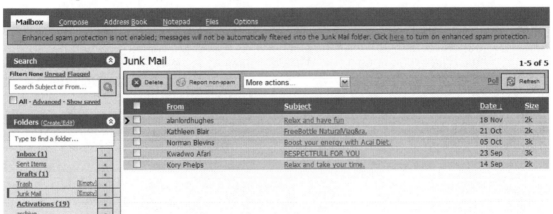

The image above shows a web-based e-mail client with received spam messages that have been moved into a **Junk Mail** folder.

1.1.3 Preventing Unwanted Spam (1.1.1.3)

There a number of measures that can be taken to reduce or eliminate spam.

- Use a number of e-mail addresses, all of which can be received in the same e-mail inbox. One address might be used for business e-mail only, and only given to those people with whom business is done. A second might be a main personal e-mail address used for friends and family. A third could be used when entering personal information on websites.

- Most modern e-mail systems offer sophisticated e-mail scanning and filtering, whether it is installed on a computer with an e-mail package, such as Outlook or Thunderbird, or a webmail service that is accessed via a web browser, such as Gmail or MSN Mail.

- Incoming e-mail is scanned using sophisticated rules and placed in a special junk mail folder. The user can then view the messages and empty the folder periodically. If unwanted messages remain in the Inbox most e-mail packages can be set up to identify spam messages and report them as being junk.

1.2　Malicious Software

1.2.1　Types of Malware (1.1.2.1 and 1.1.2.2)

The term **malware** is used to describe a variety of unsolicited, and usually malicious, software programs. Malware is transferred between computers across networks and the internet using various methods (e.g. from malicious websites and in e-mail attachments) and they infect legitimate program files or exploit security weaknesses in operating systems.

Some types of malware actively destroy data, some steal passwords and private information, and some remain dormant until they are activated to use the computer they have infected as part of a huge attack on a corporate or government network. They are generally grouped into the headings of **viruses**, **worms**, **spyware**, **adware**, **Trojans** and **diallers**.

Viruses

These are small executable computer programs that can attach themselves secretly to other programs. When the infected program is run by a user, the virus hides in the computer's memory. Then, when other programs are run by the user, the virus infects them, thus spreading. Some modern viruses also change themselves constantly to avoid detection. They are called viruses because they behave in exactly the same as a biological virus. Some viruses are relatively harmless and simply exist to spread as widely as they can. Some can be actively malicious, for example they may delete the contents of disk drives.

Traditional viruses can be spread through variety of methods, for example running infected attachments in e-mail messages or pirate copies of software, whether on CD, DVD or downloaded from the internet. For this reason, pirate copies of software, even if they come from a friend or associate, should not be installed on a PC.

It should be assumed that all executable e-mail attachments are infected (i.e. all **.exe** files), even if sent or apparently sent by a known contact. In a business or educational situation where e-mail is received by a central mail server and then distributed to users, any infected attachments should be automatically removed by the server and a message sent to the user to his effect. It is in fact common for **all** executable attachments to be stripped out as a matter of network policy.

In a home situation, good anti-virus software should be able to trap infected e-mails as they come into the e-mail client (e.g. Outlook, Google Mail, etc.) and not allow them to be opened.

Trojan Horses (or Trojans)

These work in the same way as the horse in the classical story. It is an application that, when run, appears to do something useful but will also secretly perform some nefarious action. Modern Trojans usually create a **back door** enabling illegal remote access to the computer and its files if it is connected to the internet.

Trojans often rely on **social engineering** to spread rather than a virus-like infection. For example, a user may receive an attachment containing an executable file in an e-mail which seems to come from a trusted source.

Trojans are commonly used to give hackers access to a remote system over the internet without the owner's knowledge. The computer is then **compromised** and can be used to store illegal files or send junk e-mail. A **keylogger** may be installed, which can record what the user is typing and store it for later retrieval. A hacker can use this information to discover passwords, PINs and other private information.

Worms
These are similar in concept and effect to Trojans but can spread independently across computer networks by exploiting security problems in operating systems and network equipment, rather than requiring a user to do something, e.g. open an e-mail containing an executable file. If one computer on a network becomes compromised, the worm can then copy itself across network connections to uninfected computers without the users involved actively doing anything themselves to cause the infection.

Spyware and Adware
These are types of software that monitor user behaviour and collect personal information when the user browsing the internet. This information is then used to automatically redirect the user to a specific website or to produce a proliferation of 'pop-up' advertising windows which clutter the screen.

Spyware and adware can have other undesirable effects, such as slowing down the internet connection or a computer's performance in general. Most computers become infected with adware or spyware through techniques used on certain web pages that exploit security defects in internet browsers, such as Internet Explorer.

Rogue Diallers
These can use a modem connected to a computer to dial premium-rate telephone numbers, which generates revenue for the owner of the number. Some diallers appear to be genuine and to offer access to content, such as illegal downloads, others operate in secret without the user's knowledge. Because diallers use dial-up modems connected to telephone lines they will eventually disappear as all internet access gradually becomes via broadband.

1.2.2 Anti-Virus Software (1.1.2.3)
Anti-virus software is used to detect and remove all types of malware, not just viruses. The process of removing malware is called **disinfecting** or **cleaning**. To recognise problems, anti-virus applications use definition libraries, which are databases of all known malware.

Because malware can modify legitimate files, it may or may not be possible to remove the problem without damaging the original file. If it is not possible to remove the infection, and the files affected are a crucial part of the operating system, it could be necessary to reinstall the operating system.

Modern anti-virus applications usually have one or more of the following.

- A resident scanner that is loaded into the computer's memory when the computer starts up and monitors files as they are being read and written. If a file is infected, the user is notified and the file either deleted or moved to quarantine.
- Quarantine, a safe area where infected files are stored.
- An on-demand scanner. This will perform a scan of all vulnerable files on hard drives, and can usually be set to run automatically at a specified time.

- A mail scanner, which plugs into an e-mail client application, such as Outlook, and scans and disinfects e-mails as they arrive.
- A pop-up blocker.
- Anti-phishing technology. This will monitor each web page being visited and compare it against a database of known phishing websites, alerting the user if required.
- A firewall.

Most general-purpose anti-virus software will also detect and remove the most common kinds of spyware (i.e. software that collects information about what a user is doing and sends it to the spyware originator, all without the user's knowledge). However, dedicated anti-spyware software also exists which concentrates on this particular problem.

Popular free examples include Spybot S&D and Ad-Aware. They operate as 'plug-ins' to popular internet browsers, and work in the background, detecting and preventing the installation of spyware, and also offer the ability to scan a computer thoroughly for any existing installations that have gone unnoticed by other anti-virus software. Anti-spyware software may have more up-to-date information in its database about what spyware is being used than general-purpose anti-virus software.

An example of the options available within a typical graphical anti-virus application on Windows XP is shown below.

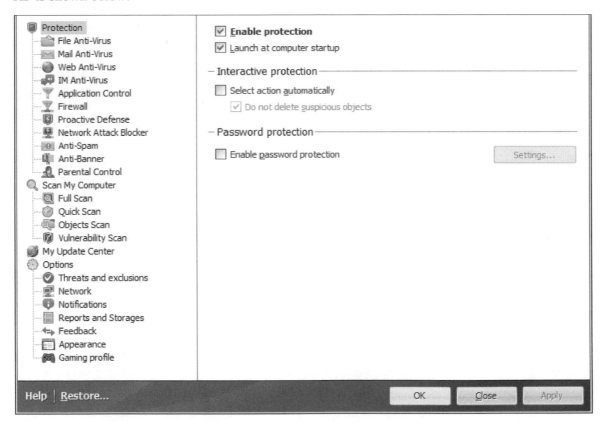

1.2.3 Updating Anti-Virus Software (1.1.2.4)

New viruses, Trojans and assorted other undesirable programs are created every day, so it is important to keep anti-virus software up to date. Companies that sell anti-virus software maintain central databases which are updated regularly, and modern software will keep itself updated automatically, via the internet, without the user having to do anything.

1.2.4 Recommended Practices for Preventing Malware Problems (1.1.2.5)

In addition to the use of e-mail filtering and anti-virus software, some basic rules can further reduce the chances of malware finding its way onto a computer.

- Never open attachments in unexpected e-mail messages, even if they appear to be from a trusted sender.
- Do not download illegal or pirated software from the internet.
- When installing software make sure to read the 'small print' and the EULA (End User Licence Agreement). Some software, for example, may offer a lot of free functionality but at the expense of a user agreeing, often unintentionally, to install adware and spyware alongside it.
- Be alert for any unusual problems with the computer, such as an unexplained slowing down of the computer or excessive disk activity.
- Never reply to junk e-mail messages, even if they provide a link which claims to provide an unsubscription service. Replying will only inform the sender that the e-mail address used was 'live'. The correct course of action is to mark the message as junk or delete it.

1.2.5 Firewalls (1.1.3.3)

A **firewall** is a barrier between a computer and other computers on a network or the internet, essentially making that computer invisible and controlling who accesses it. Firewalls can exist in hardware, e.g. inside a broadband router, or in software and can be configured to provide alerts if someone attempts to intrude.

Hackers often scan the internet looking for connected computers, and when one is found, it, in turn, is scanned for open **ports** which allow remote connection. A firewall hides the computer on the internet and also blocks ports from being used.

1.3 Hacking (1.1.3.1)

In computer security terms, a **hacker** is a person who gains unauthorised access to a computer system for illegal purposes. This may mean physical access or remote access over an internet connection. The access gained might be used to retrieve confidential information, such as credit card or banking details, or to involve the computer in the distribution of illegal material without the owner's knowledge – or simply to harvest working e-mail addresses that can be used as targets for spam.

1.3.1 Hacking Methods (1.1.3.2)

Hackers gain access to systems using a number of methods.

- **Social engineering** is the act of convincing individuals who hold access information legitimately to reveal that information. An example might involve a hacker posing as a technician from a company's IT support department.
- Operating systems and software often contain **flaws** that expose **security holes**. These flaws can be exploited to bypass the normal protection a computer system might have.
- **Trojans** or **worms** (see Section 1.2.1) can create **back-door** access, such as a secret user name and password which can be used by a hacker.

1.4 Hoaxes

1.4.1 Types of Hoax (1.1.4.1)

The unregulated nature of e-mail means it is often used to propagate a variety of hoaxes, scams, chain letters and scares. The instigators of hoaxes prey on the insecurity many people have when dealing with information technology.

Chain letter e-mails work in the same way as their traditional paper predecessors. An example might promise bad luck unless the e-mail is forwarded to five people in the recipient's e-mail content list.

Scams often promise large monetary rewards but only after the recipient's bank details have been forwarded or an initial deposit sent to an address in a foreign country.

Virus creators often use **virus hoaxes** to infect machines. Millions of e-mails will be sent with an infected attachment and a subject line relating to a current event. Many users will not be able to resist clicking on the attachment and their computer will become infected as a result.

Some hoaxes are designed to simply cause annoyance – for example, an e-mail supposedly from Microsoft requesting that users delete a certain file, which turns out to be part of the operating system of the computer.

1.4.2 Identifying Hoax Messages (1.1.4.2)

The best weapon is common sense – if something sounds too good to be true then it is, especially if money is involved.

There are also many websites dedicated to listing current hoaxes, for example:

- **http://www.hoaxbusters.org**.
- **http://www.sophos.com/security/hoaxes/**.

If there is any doubt at all about the veracity of an e-mail then taking a few moments to check it can save a lot of time and effort later.

Hoaxbusters.org recommends using the following five points to check an e-mail. Be aware if the message:

- repeatedly stresses how urgent it is;
- encourages the user to forward it to as many contacts as possible;
- claims that it isn't a hoax;
- warns of dire consequences if instructions aren't followed; and
- the body of the message has a lot of '>' characters, indicating that it has been forwarded multiple times.

Section 2   Information Security

2.1   Identity and Authentication

2.1.1   Usernames and Passwords (1.2.1.1 and 1.2.1.3)

All information stored on computer systems is at risk from unauthorised access. To control access to computers and prevent unauthorised use, all computers should be accessed using **usernames** and **passwords**. The act of accessing a system using a username and password is called **authentication** or, more commonly, **logging in**, **logging on** or **signing in**. This is normally done via a **login screen**.

The following illustrations show the login screens from the Windows 7 and Ubuntu operating systems.

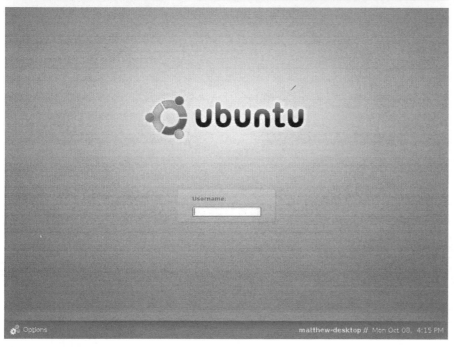

Further levels of authentication may be encountered when a user has logged on. For example, an office worker may use a software application to process a company's accounts. This involves access to confidential information, so the application will have a further login screen where a correct username and password must be entered to gain access. This username and password may be different to those used to access the computer itself or may, sometimes, be linked.

Many online applications and services are accessed using a web browser and can involve their own methods of authentication.

- Online banks and financial services companies commonly require a **Personal Identification Number** (**PIN**) in addition to a separate username and password and possibly other information.
- Buying goods using a credit card requires valid credit card details in addition to a separate username and password.

The screenshot below shows a section of a bank webpage. The user must click the **Login** button to begin accessing their account details.

The user must then provide their PIN and a randomly selected piece of personal information to further confirm who they are.

2.1.2 Levels of Access (1.2.1.2)

Authentication provides a mechanism for controlling access to a computer in the first instance, but it can also provide different levels of access to different users or groups of user.

A common practice in companies and educational institutions, etc. is to restrict normal users from installing new software on their computers, so that only users who are members of the IT department security group can do this. Similarly, a computer in the home may have separate usernames and passwords for children, and rules defined for them which do not allow access to the areas where family documents are stored.

2.1.3 Choosing Passwords and PINs

It makes sense to choose a strong password, containing a lengthy mixture of upper and lower case letters, numbers and non-alphabetic characters, such as underscores. Many systems will now actively enforce the choosing of strong passwords and require users to change their passwords on a regular basis.

Some rules for choosing a good password are:

- **Don't** use words that can be found in a dictionary.
- **Don't** use personal information (e.g. names or car registration numbers).
- **Don't** use sequences of numbers (e.g. 12345) or keyboard letter sequences (e.g. QWERTY).
- **Do** replace letters with numbers where possible and capitalise randomly (e.g. instead of the word **retrovertigo** use **r3tr0V3rt1G0**.
- **Do** use as many letters and numbers as possible.

2.1.4 Changing Passwords and PINs (1.2.1.4 and 1.2.1.5)

Even if a user is not forced to change their passwords and PINs, it is a good idea to change them from time to time. All operating systems provide a method for users to change their password, though the methods used will differ. In a workplace, the user may log in on a particular day and be shown a screen forcing them to change their password. In a home situation the password change must be initiated by the user. See also Section 3.1.4.

For example, under Windows XP Home, the Windows password can be changed as follows:

- Select the **Control Panel** option from the **Start** menu.

  The **Control Panel** window opens.

- Double-click the **User Accounts** icon.

 User Accounts

- Click the icon for the relevant user.

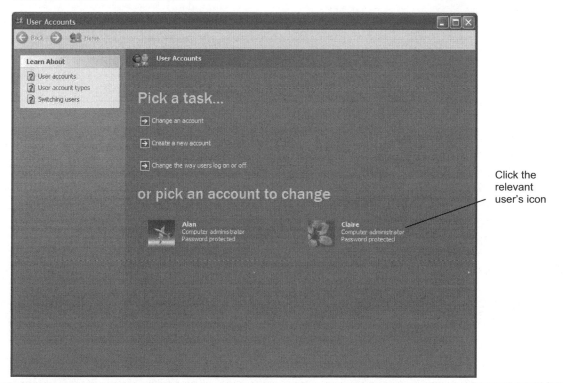

Click the relevant user's icon

- Click **Change my password**.

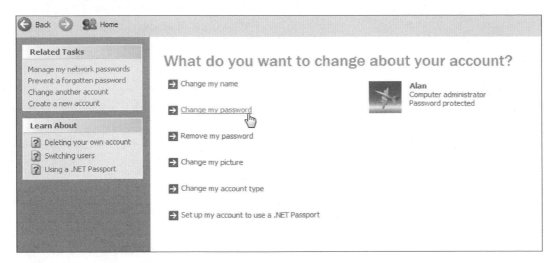

- Complete the form that is displayed.
- Click **Change Password**.

2.2   Confidentiality

2.2.1 Sharing and Writing Down Passwords/PINs (1.2.2.1 and 1.2.2.2)

Writing down passwords and PINs or sharing them with others negates their effectiveness to a large extent and should not be done.

Web browsers can also recognise when a username and password or PIN are being entered and offer to store them so that they will be filled in automatically the next time the site is visited. While the details will be stored in a secure manner, it is still preferable to decline this offer as this practice helps any unauthorised person who is accessing the computer.

2.2.2 Respecting Confidentiality (1.2.2.3)

Access to confidential information brings responsibility – sharing this information with unauthorised persons is usually unethical and often illegal. It should also be borne in mind that in a corporate network, all access to confidential information is potentially monitored and logged.

2.2.3 Physical Security (1.2.2.4)

An unattended computer provides an opportunity for someone to copy information from it, change passwords or perform any number of other unwanted activities.

When leaving a computer unattended, it should be logged off or, alternatively, locked.

To lock Windows XP Professional, do the following:
- Press the **Ctrl**, **Alt** and **Del** keys together.
- Choose **Lock Computer**.

To lock Windows XP Home, do the following:
- Click **Start**.
- Select **Log Off**.
- From the options displayed select either **Switch User** or **Log Off**.
- This will secure the machine as the password must be re-entered to use it again.

2.3 Identity Theft

2.3.1 Identity Theft (1.2.3.2)

Identity theft is a type of fraud whereby a criminal pretends to be someone else in order to steal. Illegally obtained credit card details are increasingly used by criminals to buy goods and services online. These credit card details are harvested using **phishing** (see Section 2.3.3) or automatically via some types of **malware** (see Section 1.2.1) or by **hacking** (see Section 1.3). They are then sold on the black market.

2.3.2 Avoiding the Inappropriate Disclosure of Information (1.2.3.3)

To protect against identity theft, it is important that private information is only disclosed when necessary. The precautions detailed elsewhere against malware, hacking, phishing and spam are also important here.

Caution should be employed when users are online and supplying personal information.

- If the situation legally requires accurate personal information, such as a correct home address for the delivery of goods or a credit card purchase, or when applying for online banking, etc., then accurate information should be supplied.
- In other situations, a particular website may just be harvesting personal details such as address, occupation or age, for marketing purposes and may have no legitimate reason for requesting them. In these cases, enter false details. There is often a requirement to supply a valid e-mail address for verification purposes and this is the perfect place to enter a custom e-mail address used just for this purpose (see Section 1.1.3).
- Never divulge any sort of genuine personal information in internet chat rooms or social media sites, such as YouTube.

2.3.3 Phishing (1.2.3.1)

Phishing is impersonation. A user receives e-mails supposedly from their bank or major online organisations, such as PayPal or eBay, which will give some reason that requires the user to re-enter their username and password, a link to the organisation's website will also be provided. However, the link will actually go to a different website that has been cloned to look like the legitimate website. In this way, any usernames and passwords entered are stored away and used for criminal purposes later.

Some examples of phishing attempts purporting to be e-mails from eBay are displayed at: http://pages.ebay.com/education/spooftutorial/.

Most modern e-mail clients and web browsers can spot phishing attempts and alert the user, however, these are not foolproof and so it falls to the user to employ caution. Some online banks, for example, will ask for a piece of personal information that a third party could not know.

> **NOTE**
> No legitimate online entity, such as a bank, will ever ask for personal details to be resubmitted or supplied via e-mail.

The following images illustrate a phishing scam that resembles the PayPal login webpage. PayPal is an internet-based financial service that enables registered users to make secure transactions online. The phishing scam worked by sending e-mails worded to lure recipients into believing the e-mail was from PayPal. The e-mail also stated that the recipient should go to the PayPal site to update their personal details.

The e-mail contains a link that appeared legitimate.

https://www.paypal.com/us/cgi-bin/webscr?_cmd=_login-run

However, the actual link differed from the displayed link and, when clicked, took recipients to a website designed to resemble the legitimate PayPal login page.

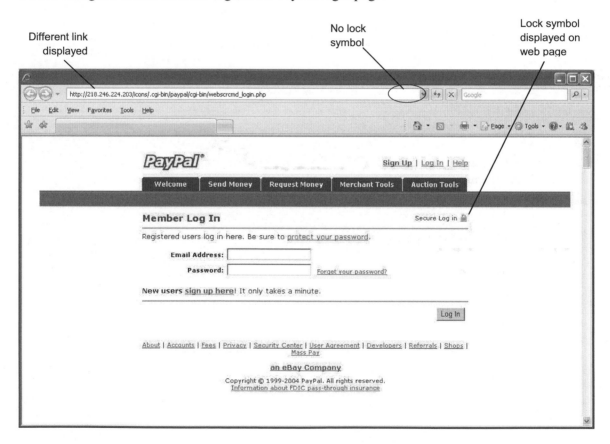

There are two indications that a link or website is a phishing scam.

The first is the **link**.

The displayed link should be the same as the actual link. In the above example, the displayed link is: **https://www.paypal.com/us/cgi-bin/webscr?_cmd=_login-run**. However, the actual link of the website is: **http://218.246.203/icons/.cgi-bin/paypal/cgi-bin/webscrcmd_login.php**.

The second is the **lock symbol**, which is perhaps the most important thing to check. The lock symbol will be displayed either to the right of the address bar or at the bottom of the window, not on the page itself – if the lock symbol is displayed on the page, it is not legitimate.

Lock symbol

Clicking the lock symbol will display the website's certificate which is designed to authenticate the website's legitimacy. The certificate will display the issuing authority, usually VeriSign, as well as the website the certificate is issued to.

Section 3   Technology Security

3.1   Networks

3.1.1 Public Networks (1.3.1.1)
Computers that are connected to each other create a network. If the network can be detected and connected to by outside computers, then the network can be thought of as a **public network**.

3.1.2 Data Security on Public Networks (1.3.1.2 and 1.3.1.4)
Public networks have advantages over closed wireless networks. For example, many public places, such as coffee shops, provide public wireless networks that customers can use for internet browsing. Many home broadband routers have a wireless capability that can be set up to connect various devices in the house, such as computers, phones and game consoles, and provide shared internet access for them.

This openness can also have disadvantages. Computers connected to a public network may make some or all of the data stored on them visible to other users of the network.

3.1.3 Data Encryption on Public Networks (1.3.1.3)
Public networks usually employ **wireless connectivity**. This means the information flowing around the network is broadcast using a special type of radio signal. More conventional **wired connectivity** using physical cables to connect devices can also be used, or any combination of these two methods.

It is possible for a hacker to use readily available hardware and software to construct a **packet analyser** that can intercept and copy data flowing around a network. If the data is **encrypted**, it cannot be decoded by a hacker even if it is intercepted.

A hacker may not even need close physical access to a wireless network as such networks have a range of up to 30 metres, which is why an individual in a densely populated residential area may be able to see the wireless networks from their neighbours' houses.

Encrypting files ensure that they cannot be accessed or utilised except by the person for whom the communication is intended. If there is any attempt to intercept a file as it is being transferred across the internet, the encryption offers a high level of security. Encryption is extensively used to protect information, such as credit card numbers, and sensitive information, such as personal data or company secrets.

3.1.4 Risks when Using Default Settings (1.3.1.5)
Computer operating systems, network hardware (e.g. broadband routers) and computer software all employ usernames and passwords to gain access to them. When initially set up, they will use their **default** settings. It is vital that any defaults are changed as quickly as possible.

For example, a particular type of broadband router will come from the factory with a default administrator username and password, used to access and configure the router's internal settings. It is easy for a hacker on the internet to determine what type of router is in use at a location they are trying to hack into, and for them to look up the default access details. If they gain access, and the default settings have not been changed, then the whole network behind the router may be compromised. See also Section 2.1.4.

3.1.5 Internet Security Settings (1.3.1.6)

Internet security settings should be adjusted from the default settings to, as far as is possible, prevent hacking and identity theft.

In all versions of Windows XP, some settings can be found in the **Security Center** section of the Control Panel.

To change security settings, do the following:

- From the **Start Menu**, click **Control Panel**.
  The **Control Panel** window opens.

- Double-click the **Security Center** icon.

Security Center

The **Security Center** window opens.

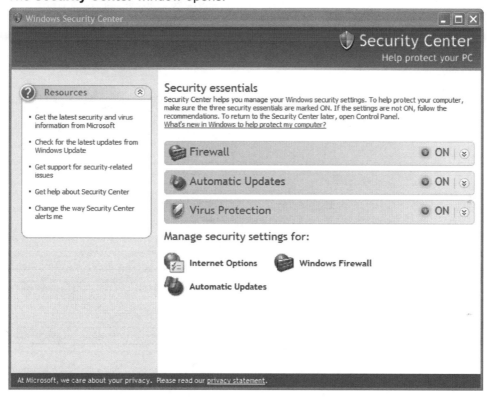

- The **Firewall**, **Automatic Updates** and **Virus Protection** items should all be **on**.
  - o The **Automatic Updates** option is built into Windows.
  - o **Firewall** and **Virus Protection** can be provided by products from a number of third-party companies or by Microsoft.

There are also security settings within different web browsers.

Mozilla's **Firefox** browser settings are accessed as follows.

- Start Firefox.
- Open the **Tools** menu.
- Click **Options**.

The **Options** window opens.

The **Privacy** and **Security** tabs contain the settings for internet security.

Microsoft's **Internet Explorer** has similar settings.

- Start Internet Explorer
- Open the **Tools** menu.
- Select **Internet Options**.

The **Internet Options** window opens.

The **Security** tab has the main options required.

The recommended settings for the internet zone as shown are **Medium-high**.

3.2   Bluetooth Connectivity

3.2.1   Bluetooth (1.3.2.1)

Bluetooth is a wireless technology designed to connect various devices over short distances, creating a **personal area network**. It is intended as a replacement for the cables that would commonly be used to connect, for example, a mobile phone to a computer and in situations where the functionality of a full wireless network is not needed or not possible because of the devices in use.

Common uses of Bluetooth include:

- Connecting a digital camera to a computer.
- Wearing a headset and microphone to enable the use of a mobile phone while driving.
- Using a wireless keyboard or mouse with a computer.
- Transferring files between mobile devices, such as a mobile phone, and a computer.

3.2.2   Bluetooth Settings (1.3.2.2)

One of the main features of Bluetooth is **Discovery**. This means that Bluetooth-enabled devices can discover each other automatically when they come into range without any user intervention. They can then exchange information about their capabilities and become **visible** to each other.

For example, two people with Bluetooth-enabled mobile phones, both of which have Discovery mode on, will potentially have their phones connected to each other and the data on each visible just by bringing them within range of each other.

While this is one of the strengths of the technology it is also a security problem. In general, devices that store personal data, such as phones, PDAs, music players and computers, should not be in Discovery mode unless the user actively wants to transfer data to or from them.

In addition, most devices of this type implement **pairing**, which works as follows:

1

- Both Bluetooth devices are powered up.
- Both devices have Discovery mode turned on.
- When the devices connect, one becomes a **host** and one a **guest**. For example, when connecting a camera to a laptop, the laptop would be the host.
- Each device has a Bluetooth PIN.
- The guest device will prompt for the host PIN to be entered.
- When entered correctly, the devices are **paired** and will now automatically and securely connect when in range.
- Where available pairing should be employed for added security.

Implementing **Discovery Mode** and **Pairing** is different for different makes of device, so the relevant documentation should be consulted to know how to turn on these modes.

3.3   Portable Devices

3.3.1   Using Portable Devices (1.3.3.1, 1.3.3.2 and 1.3.3.3)

The advent of cheap memory and small, powerful processors has resulted in an explosion in portable devices capable of storing personal and confidential data.

These devices include:

- USB Storage Devices (known as flash drives, pen drives, etc.).
- Digital cameras.
- PDAs.
- Laptops, notebooks and palmtop computers.
- Mobile phones.
- Multimedia players.

The compact sizes of these devices means they are vulnerable to loss or theft. As these devices can contain confidential information, in addition to standard precautions (such as employing passwords, PINs and encryption) care should be taken that they are transported and stored securely.

Section 4   Guidelines and Procedures

4.1   Guidelines and Procedures

Guidelines and procedures for the correct and acceptable use of IT, should be provided by all employers and other organisations, such as colleges, to anyone authorised to use their computer systems.

These guidelines are an important because they:

- help to ensure a secure computing environment;
- prevent misuse and overuse of resources, e.g. printers and disk space;
- prevent intimidation and harassment by e-mail and other methods;
- protect the organisation in the event of its computing resources being used for illegal activities;
- provide a legal mechanism for removing offending users from the organisation when necessary.

4.1.1   Learning Relevant Guidelines and Procedures (1.4.1.1, 1.4.1.3 and 1.4.2.1)

An organisation's procedures and guidelines, including its privacy policy, are normally provided to employees when they first join the organisation as part of the standard induction process, for example by the human resources department or college administration office.

They may also be provided directly by the department or individual responsible for information technology within the organisation. Most organisations will also provide a copy of their guidelines on their website.

If necessary, employees should approach their immediate line manager for clarification of any part of the guidelines and procedures that are not clear. In an academic situation, the department or individual responsible for information technology should be contacted.

4.1.2   Adhering to Guidelines and Procedures (1.4.1.2 and 1.4.2.2)

It is important that all stated guidelines and procedures are adhered to at all times, as failure could result in disciplinary proceedings up to and including expulsion from a particular organisation.

4.1.3   IT Security Checks (1.4.1.4)

Guidelines and procedures will often detail checks for which users are responsible.

These include the following:

- Changing passwords regularly, taking into account rules for choosing strong passwords.
- Not sharing login details, as all activity that takes place under a particular login is the owner's responsibility.
- Maintenance of personal accounts to limit disk space usage.
- Encrypting confidential information.
- Performing anti-virus scans.
- Not participating in any activity that would potentially result in a malware incident.

4.1.4   Reporting Breaches of Guidelines and Procedures (1.4.1.5)

Employees should report any breaches of the guidelines, either on the part of themselves or any another individual, that they become aware of. In the workplace, employees should contact their manager and, in universities, etc., the department or individual responsible for information technology should be contacted. If users do not know who to contact, they should report any breaches to an immediate line manager, college department head, etc.

1

Section 5   Data Security

5.1   Physical Security (1.5.1.1)

Computers can be physically secured against theft by using special cables and locks. All computers and laptops have a security slot designed to take one end of the cable. The other end can then be locked to an item of furniture or similarly heavy object.

Servers and other business-critical computers should be correctly mounted in racking units or cabinets and kept in a locked room.

5.2 Data Loss (1.5.2.1, 1.5.2.2 and 1.5.2.3)

Information stored on electronic media is at risk of being destroyed by malware, by hacking or by being physically stolen or misplaced.

There is also other ways that data can be lost.

- **Data can be deleted accidentally**: All operating systems move manually deleted files to a 'trash' area from which they can be recovered, but once they are deleted from this area, the files are usually gone forever. If data is deleted through an action performed by a user when using a particular software application, the files involved will not even go to the 'trash' area. For example, a user may remove their previous year's payroll data in a payroll processing application.

- **Files can become corrupt**: Flaws in operating systems or software, or by a hardware component, such as a hard drive, beginning to fail, can cause files to become corrupted. When a file is corrupt, it still exists on disk but its internal structure may no longer be correct, or portions of the file may not be accessible.

5.3 Backups and Storage Media (1.5.2.4)

Frequent and comprehensive **backups** are vital in light of the many ways in which files can be lost or become corrupted. The act of making a copy of data which can replace the original data if needed is called **backing up** or **taking a backup**.

In an office or academic situation, backups are usually the responsibility of the IT department and users must only ensure that their personal files are backed up to a stated location on a network drive. In the home, the responsibility for backups lies entirely with the users themselves.

> **NOTE**
> When simply copying files onto removable media the considerations already covered regarding encryption and data theft apply.

At a basic level, taking a backup can be as simple as copying and pasting vital files to another location on the computer. Taken a step further, the files can be simply copied to a variety of **storage media**.

- **USB memory sticks** are always increasing in storage capacity and decreasing in cost. They are easy to use because they appear as a new drive in the operating system.

- **External hard drives** can be used in the same way as USB memory sticks, however, they are larger and offer more storage space.

- Optical media, such as **CD**, **DVD** and **Blu-Ray** discs, provide a compact form of storage but have less capacity and must sometimes be written to or **burned** using special software.

- Businesses generally have much more vital data to protect than the home user, and often use expensive **tape** backup systems that require dedicated software to use.

While data can simply be copied to a storage medium, it is better to use **backup software** for the task.

Some advantages of using backup software are:

- The backup can be scheduled to run automatically, so the user doesn't have to remember to do it.

- The backup can be incremental, i.e. only the data that has changed since the previous backup is copied, which reduces the space used and time taken to complete the backup.

- The backup file can be encrypted and protected with a password.

Online Backups

The continued growth and speed of broadband internet has meant that **online backups** are being used more often. In this scenario, the backup is stored in a remote location provided by a commercial online backup company. This storage is extremely secure and failure-tolerant, is often located in armoured underground locations and possibly replicated in several locations. The customer installs **client software** on their systems which can back up their files over the internet to the secure storage location. This sort of facility is also offered to home users by companies, such as www.mozy.com.

Simple backup software can be readily downloaded for any operating system. The following images show some screens from an example of a free application.

5.3.1 Offsite Backups (1.5.2.5)
If backups are on a portable medium, such as a USB memory stick or DVD, it is a good idea to have several available and to keep at least one at a separate location to the rest, in case of fire, etc. Businesses commonly have a **disaster recovery** procedure involving multiple offsite backups which enable them to get back up and running as quickly as possible after files have been lost.

5.3.2 Storing Software and Personal Data Securely (1.5.3.1 and 1.5.3.2)
The CDs and DVDs on which commercial software and operating systems are sold, and the any licensing documents that are associated with them, should be stored securely. A fireproof safe is the ideal method for doing this. However, this type of storage is becoming less of an issue today as software is increasingly delivered as a download over the internet with licences e-mailed to the customer.

When software has been downloaded, the installation files should be kept in their own location on the hard drive, backed up (to DVD, etc.) and stored in a fireproof container, preferably offsite, although most vendors will allow the software to be downloaded again if needed. Licence files or e-mails containing licence information should also be kept safely. It is good practice to print out licence information and keep it securely with the backed up files.

It is important to keep all personal data safe and secure. This means ensuring that data is stored securely where it cannot be accessed by unauthorised users (hackers). Personal data is information relating to you, such as the following:
- Full name and address.
- Details that can be used for security clearance (e.g. mother's maiden name, date of birth, place of birth).
- Bank account details.
- Details of online shopping/ordering (e.g. logins, passwords, credit card details).
- Health and social security records.
- Other sensitive information that could be used to identify or impersonate you.

Personal data can be used for fraudulent purposes, so it is vital that you keep it safe and secure. Hackers can access websites and use credit card details fraudulently to buy goods. If users keep records of their passwords on their computer, hackers may also be able to access the user's bank accounts and transfer money. It is advisable to password protect important or personal data to ensure security.

Be very careful about storing personal data on public or unsecured networks or uploading onto social networking sites. Wireless networks are less secure then wired networks and, due to their accessibility and visibility, are at risk from unauthorised access. A password should be set to prevent unauthorised access to data saved on a network drive. Never disclose personal information on a social network site that could be used to identify you and be used for fraudulent purposes.

Important and valuable information can be stored on small removable storage devices, such as USB memory sticks. Portable devices can be easily mislaid, i.e. leaving them connected to a computer at a college, library or other public place, resulting in loss or theft of valuable data. Ensure that all portable and removable devices are safe from theft by ensuring that they are stored safely and securely (see section 5.1 and 5.3).

1

▶ Self-Check Exercises

1. **There are six main types of malware. True or false?**

   ☐ True.

   ☐ False.

2. **What type of file should never be opened when received as an e-mail attachment?**

   ☐ Word file (*.docx).

   ☐ Executable file (*.exe).

   ☐ PDF file (*.pdf).

   ☐ Excel file (*.xlsx).

3. **When choosing a strong password, which of the following should be included?**

   ☐ Personal information.

   ☐ Sequences of numbers or letters.

   ☐ Non-alphabetic characters.

   ☐ Common words found in a dictionary.

4. **To ensure a website is genuine, where should the lock symbol be?**

   ☐ On the page.

   ☐ At the end of the web address.

   ☐ At the bottom of the page.

5. **Bluetooth can be used to connect a mobile phone to a PC. True or false?**

   ☐ True.

   ☐ False.

6. **Which of the following are commonly used as storage media?**

   ☐ DVDs.

   ☐ Floppy disks.

   ☐ External hard drives.

   ☐ Graphics cards.

7. **How should backups be stored?**

   ☐ In a boxfile near the computer.

   ☐ In a fireproof container in a separate building to the computer.

   ☐ In a fireproof container in a separate room to the computer.

8. **What IT security checks should users take?**

   ☐ Perform anti-virus scans.

   ☐ Share login details with colleagues.

   ☐ Open all e-mails, and attachments, automatically.

Unit 2

IT User Fundamentals

2

Unit 2
IT User Fundamentals

2

Section 1   Basic Concepts

1.1   First Steps

1.1.1   Starting the Computer (2.1.1.1)

The illustration below shows a typical modern computer. Both the screen (**monitor**) and main 'box' (or **base unit**) need to be plugged in and switched on. Most of the other devices that might be connected to the computer take their power from the base unit, unless they are large devices, e.g. printers.

To turn on the base unit and monitor use the **power button** on each. There will be a button with a coloured light on both items. Although they could be in different places on different computers, they will all have the universal power button logo.

When the computer is started, text and pictures will appear and disappear on the screen for a while. Do not use the mouse or keyboard while this is happening, in case the **boot sequence** is interrupted by mistake.

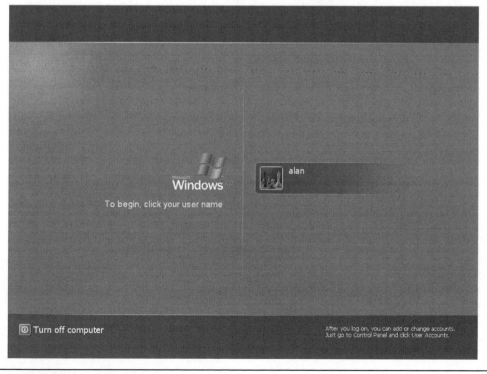

The Welcome Screen, shown above on page 1, is the default in Windows XP Home, and also in Windows XP Pro when it is part of a **peer-to-peer** network. A different screen will be shown when a Windows XP Pro machine is part of an office or educational network, or sometimes in Windows XP Home if it has been set not to use the Welcome Screen. If that is the case then the screen will be similar to that shown below.

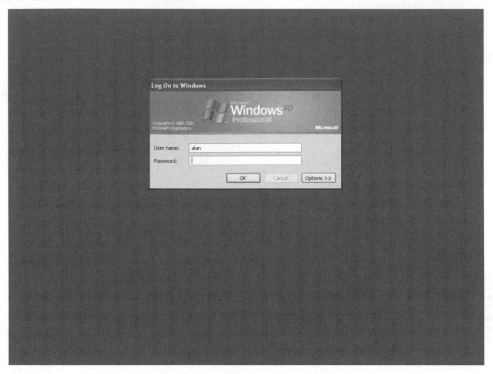

If the **Welcome Screen** is displayed, one of the listed usernames must be clicked and a password must be entered to continue. If the Welcome screen is not being used, a valid **username** and **password** must be supplied to continue. This is known as **logging in**.

The Windows **desktop** will be displayed after a while, which should look similar to the illustration below. (The desktop is covered in section 1.3 and 1.9 of this unit.)

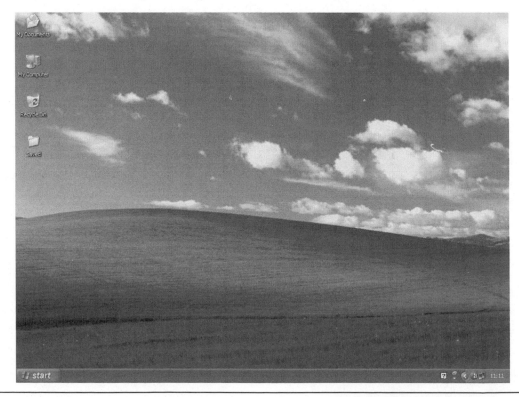

1.1.2 Restarting the Computer (2.1.1.2)

To restart the computer, do the following.

- Click the **Start** button at the bottom left of the desktop.

- Select **Turn Off Computer**.

- The **Turn off Computer** window opens.

- Click **Restart**.

1.1.3 Shutting Down a Non-Responding Application (2.1.1.3)

A problem may arise where the computer appears to 'freeze', and doesn't respond to the mouse or keyboard. In this case, it is necessary to force the computer to end the task it is engaged in.

To shut down a non-responding application using Task Manager, do the following.

- Press the **CTRL**, **ALT** + **DEL** keys simultaneously.

- The **Task Manager** window opens.

- Applications that are currently open are listed on the **Applications** tab.

- Any that have stopped responding will have **Not Responding** in the Status column.

- Click the non-responding application to select it.

- Click **End Task** to terminate the application.

1.1.4 Shutting Down (2.1.1.4)

When the computer is no longer being used, it should be **shut down**. If the computer is switched off without going through the shut down procedure, problems may arise the next time it is switched on. Any work that was not saved prior to switching off may also be lost.

To shut down the computer, do the following:

- Click the **Start** button at the bottom left of the desktop.

- Select **Turn Off Computer**.

- The **Turn off Computer** window opens.

- Click **Turn Off**.

1.2 Getting Help (2.1.1.5)

To get help with Windows XP, do the following:

- Click any empty area of the desktop.

- Press the F1 key.

- The **Help and Support Center** window opens.

- Follow the instructions to choose a topic or type in a topic to search.

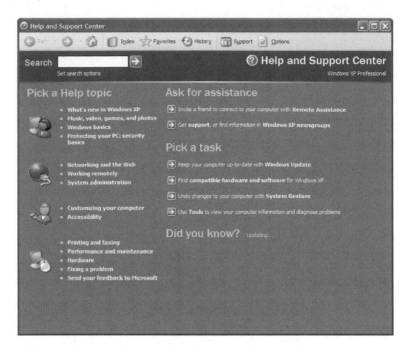

1.3   Using Windows

Everything that can be interacted with – individual applications, messages, prompts, files, folders, etc. – is displayed on the monitor in a rectangular area called a **window**. Windows have common features, such as title and menu bars.

1.3.1 Parts of a Window (2.1.4.1)

The illustration below shows the **My Computer** window. The main part of the window displays a collection of icons – the **Shared Documents** icon in the illustration below, for example. Around the window there are various features that can be used to move and size the window effectively.

A **Border** surrounds the window and defines its boundary. The border can be dragged with the mouse to resize the window.

The **Title bar** displays the name of the window on the left. If the window is displaying the contents of a folder, the folder name will be displayed. On the right of the Title bar, there are three buttons for changing the size of the window and for closing it. (See Section 1.3.3 of this unit for more information on these.)

The **Menu bar** contains drop-down menus that work in the same way as the Start Menu. A sub-menu arrow may appear alongside selected items enabling a further level of selection.

The **Toolbar** displays buttons that can be used to perform different tasks within the current window. In the illustration above, if the **Alan's Documents** folder was double-clicked, the window would change to show the contents of that sub-folder. At that point, clicking the **Back** button would display the contents of **My Computer** again and then clicking **Forward** would return to **Alan's Documents**.

The **Address bar** displays the current location, i.e. the folder that is being viewed. The Address field shows this location in a type of text notation called a **path**. When the computer is connected to the internet, entering a website address in the address field will display that website.

The **Explorer bar** is to the left of the window, and can be set to one of a number of different views. The default view, as shown in the illustration at the bottom of page 4, is to display a series of **panes** containing **quick links** to commonly used applications and locations. For example clicking the **Shared Documents** link in the **Other Places** section of the pane will display the contents of that folder in the right pane of the window. These categories can be 'rolled up' and hidden by clicking the chevron buttons on each.

Chevron ——— (☆)

To change the Explorer bar view, do the following.

- Click the **View** item on the window's menu.

- From the drop-down menu, select the Explorer bar item.

- Select the required option from the drop-down menu that appears.

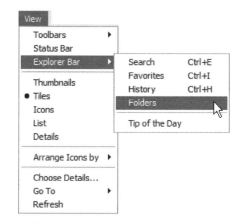

The various options change what the Explorer bar displays, as follows.

- **Search** displays the file and folder **Search Wizard**. This may be displayed as an animated character.

- **Favorites** displays the Internet Explorer Favorites list.

- **History** displays the Internet Explorer browser history.

- **Folders** is the most useful option, and shows the file and folder structure in a clickable tree view.

A **scroll bar** appears when a window is too small to display all of its contents. There can be vertical or horizontal scroll bars, or both. Clicking the arrows at the ends of a scroll bar will shift the contents of window up or down or from side to side so that further items become visible. Holding down the mouse button on a scroll arrow at the end of the scroll bar gives continuous movement. The **slider** in the **scroll bar** gives a general indication as to which part of the window is presently displayed (e.g. beginning, middle or end of a document).

In the illustration on the right, the **slider bar** is at the top indicating that the top-most contents of the window are being displayed. The length of the slider bar relative to the height of the window also indicates how much of the full range of content is being displayed. In this case, almost all the contents are visible. The content that is not visible can be thought of as being 'off the bottom' of the window. Dragging the scroll bar downwards with the mouse would bring it into view.

In contrast, the slider bar in this illustration on the right indicates that only a small part of the entire range of contents of the window is being displayed.

Some windows also have a **Status bar** that appears automatically at the bottom of the window.

The Status bar usually displays information about the contents of the window, such as how many objects it contains, the total size of those objects, etc.

To display the Status bar for a particular window, do the following:

- Click the **View** menu.
- Select **Status Bar** to turn it on.

Some windows, such as the My Computer window, also contain **sub-panes** that appear on the left-hand side. These panes display information or **quick links** to other places or tasks. For example, if you click the **My Documents** link in the **Other Places** section, the contents of the My Documents folder will be displayed in the pane on the right-hand side of the window.

> **NOTE**
> In Office 2007, the application windows (e.g. the main window in Word 2007, Excel 2007, etc.) contain a ribbon with tabs at the top of the window rather than a File menu. The ribbon changes depending on the application, the illustration below shows part of the Home tab on the Word 2007 ribbon, including the Office button and Quick Access Toolbar in the top left-hand corner.

1.3.2 Viewing Windows

The contents of the main part of the window can be displayed in various ways to suit personal preferences.

To arrange icons within a window, do the following:

- Click the **View** menu to display a list of options.
- Click the required option, e.g. **Filmstip**, to select it.

The various options are:

- **Filmstrip**: If Windows XP detects that the folder being viewed contains mostly graphics-format files, such as those from a digital camera, this option will be available. It displays a large preview of each picture and navigation controls for moving from image to image.

- **Thumbnails**: This is similar to Filmstrip view, but displays only the images at a smaller size.

- **Tiles**: This displays large icons for each item in the folder in column format, along with summary details appropriate to the file type, such as its dimensions.

- **Icons**: This view is similar to Tiles but shows just the icon and name, in a row format.

- **List**: This shows small icons for each folder item in a single column.

- **Details**: This is similar to List view but displays multiple columns of details about each item.

1.3.3   Manipulating Windows (2.1.4.2)

Open windows can be manipulated to suit users' working requirements. It is useful when working between two or more windows to be able to move a window, change its size, minimise it or close it.

Moving Windows

To reposition a window on the desktop, do the following:

- Place the tip of the cursor in the title bar.

- Holding down the mouse button, drag the window.
- When the mouse button is released, the window assumes its new position.

Resizing Windows

The size of a window can also be changed. If multiple windows are open at the same time, it may be useful to have the principal window large enough to work in and the others smaller so all of them remain on the desktop with only some of their contents visible.

To resize a window, do the following:

- Move the cursor over the **Resize handle** in the bottom right corner of the window.

Resize handle

- When the cursor changes to the resize cursor, click and drag diagonally to change the size of the window.
- When the mouse button is released, the window will remain at the size it was dragged to.

Resize cursor

It is possible to drag just one edge of a window in a similar way.

Sizing and Closing Windows

When a window is too small to display all of its contents, it can be enlarged or **maximised**, causing it to fill the whole desktop area. This is useful where scrolling would be tedious.

To maximise a window, do the following:

- Click **Maximise** at the right of the **Title bar** to enlarge the window to full-screen size.
- When a window is maximised, the **Maximise** button changes to the **Restore** button.
- Click **Restore** to restore the window to its previous size.

Maximise

Minimise

Close

Restore

If you want to temporarily remove a window from the desktop, it can be reduced or **minimised**. The window disappears from the desktop and a button representing it appears on the taskbar.

To **minimise** a window, do the following:

- Click the **Minimise** button to temporarily close a window, reducing it to a button on the taskbar.

To **redisplay** a minimised window, do the following:

- Click its button on the taskbar.

To **close** a window, do the following:

- Click the **Close X** button.

> **NOTE**
> To minimise all open windows immediately and display the desktop, press the Windows key and the 'D' key together. The Windows key is to the left of the space bar and has the Windows logo.

1.3.4 Switching Between Open Windows (2.1.4.3)

It is common to have several windows open on the desktop at once. Only one can be directly interacted with at a time using the mouse and keyboard, although processes can continue in the other windows. For example, a time-consuming mail-merge operation might be left running in one window (which is called '**running in the background**'), when another window is being used to edit a document. The window currently being used is referred to as having **focus** and is called the **active window**.

The **title bar** of the active window is usually a darker colour than inactive windows.

For example, the **Calculator** window example on the right is inactive and the WordPad window is active.

Clicking a window gives it **focus** and **brings it to the front**. In the illustration on the right, clicking the Calculator window would bring it forward, making it the active window, causing it to obscure part of the WordPad window.

Using the Taskbar

The taskbar, at the bottom of the desktop, displays a button for each open window. A window can be selected and made active by clicking the appropriate button.

When a window is active, its button is darker than the buttons of the inactive windows.

When many windows are open, whether they are folders or applications, there will be many buttons on the taskbar and space may run out. If this happens, buttons representing windows belonging to the same application, or windows viewing folder contents, can be grouped together.

This will happen automatically, when this preference has been set. The number of windows in the group is shown to the left of the button.

When buttons have been grouped you can display one of the windows (files) by doing the following:

- Right-click the grouped button on the Taskbar.
  A pop-up menu opens.
- Left-click the required file to display its window again.

To **close all the files** in a button group, do the following:

- Right-click the grouped button on the Taskbar.
  A pop-up menu opens.

- Left-click **Close Group**.
  All the files in the group are closed.

To **set** this preference and ensure files are grouped together in this way, do the following:

- Right-click the **Start** button.
- Click **Properties** in the pop-up menu.

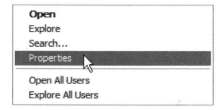

The **Taskbar and Start Menu Properties** window opens.

- Click the **Taskbar** tab, and tick the **Group similar taskbar buttons** option.

Click **Group similar taskbar buttons**

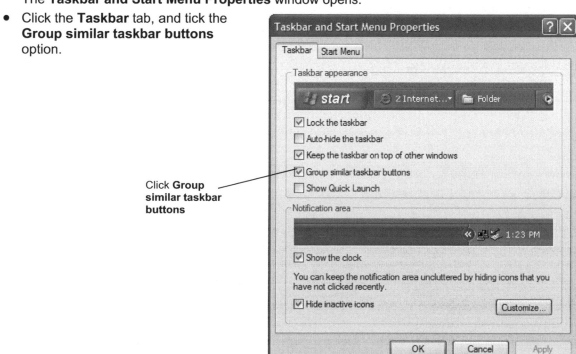

Using the Keyboard

The keyboard can also be used to cycle through open applications.

- Hold down the **Alt** key and tap the **Tab** key.

- A task switcher window opens in front of all the other windows on the desktop with an icon for each open window.

- Still holding down the **Alt** key, repeatedly tap the **Tab** key and note that the selection rectangle moves to each icon in turn.

- When it surrounds the icon for the item to be switched to, release both keys and the selected window will be made active.

1.4   System Information (2.1.2.1)

To obtain information about your computer, such as how much memory there is available, do the following:

- Right-click the **My Computer** icon on the desktop.
- Select **Properties**.

The **System Properties** window opens, with the **General** tab selected.

Under **System:**, the version of Windows XP and its **Service Pack** level are displayed.

Under the **Registered To:**, the name and company name of the registered user are shown, along with the **Product ID** number.

At the bottom, information about the computer itself is displayed.

In the example on the right, the CPU model is an **AMD Athlon 3000+**, it is running at **2.17GHz** and there is **512MB** of RAM installed.

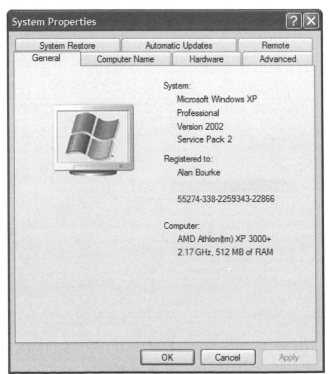

1.5   Changing the Appearance of the Desktop (2.1.2.2)

1.5.1   Themes

A **desktop theme** is a set of icons, fonts, colours, sounds, desktop background picture and other window elements that gives Windows XP a distinctive look. The theme can be changed to suit different users or circumstances. A **color scheme** can then be applied to a theme to further customise the appearance of the desktop.

New themes can be created by modifying the elements of the default set of themes. These modified themes can be saved using a new theme name. The default theme in Windows XP is the **Windows XP** theme with the **Default (Blue)** colour scheme.

To change a computer's theme, do the following.

- Right-click an empty area of the desktop.
- Select **Properties** from the pop-up menu.

The **Display Properties** window opens with the **Themes** tab selected.

The overall appearance of Windows XP is controlled by the selection in the **Theme** drop-down menu.

There are two main preset themes, the default Windows XP theme and Windows Classic, which is very similar to how Windows 2000 looked.

- Select **Windows Classic** from the menu and observe how the Sample changes.

- Click **Apply** to apply the changes.

  The style of the windows, buttons, etc. changes to match the illustration below.

  The locations of items such as menus, close buttons, etc., do not change.

- Open the **Display Properties** window as before.

- Select the **Appearance** tab.

  Note that the Windows and buttons option is set to **Windows Classic Style**. This and the other settings were set automatically when the theme was changed.

Color scheme selection

- From the **Color Scheme** drop-down menu, select **Marine (High Color)**.

- Click **Apply**.

- Do not close the **Display Properties** window.

The colour scheme will change.

- With the Display Properties window still open, select the Theme tab.

  Note that the Theme selection has changed to **Windows Classic (modified)**, as a result of a change in the colour scheme.

- This modified theme can be saved by clicking **Save As**.

Click **Save As** to save the theme

The **Save As** window opens.

- Name the theme file, e.g. BEC theme.

- Click **Save**.

  The theme will then become available in the list of themes in the Display Properties window that can be chosen.

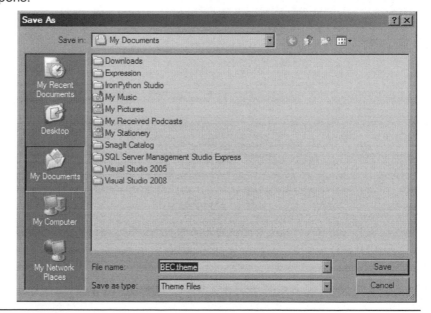

1.5.2   Changing the Desktop Background

The **Background** is what is displayed behind the icons on the desktop. It can be a plain colour or a picture and is part of the desktop theme.

To change the desktop background, do the following.

- Right-click an empty area of the desktop.
- Select **Properties** from the pop-up menu that opens.

    The **Display Properties** window opens.
- Select the **Desktop** tab.

To use a colour as the background, do the following:

- Select **None** in the Background list.
- Choose a colour from the **Color** list.
- Click **Apply**.
- A preview of the colour will appear in the screen in the **Display Properties** window.

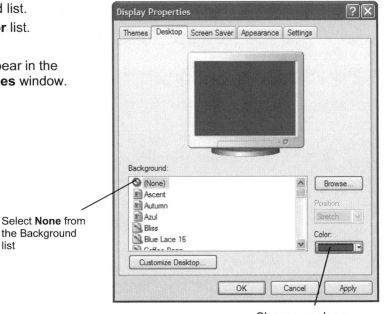

Select **None** from the Background list

Choose a colour from the Color list

To use a picture as the background, do the following:

- Open the **Display Properties** window and select the **Desktop** tab.
- Select a picture from the Background list.
- Click **Apply**.

Select a picture from the **Background** list

If the picture is not listed, or you would like to use a picture that you have loaded onto your computer, do the following:

- Click the **Browse** button.

Use the **Browse** button to locate the picture

The **Browse** window opens.

- Locate the picture using the **Look in:** box.

The **Look in:** box

- The **Position** drop-down menu is available when a background image has been selected, and the selection determines what will happen if the selected image is smaller than the desktop. The options are:
  - ○ **Center**: The image will be centred on the desktop. The rest of the desktop around the image will be shown in the colour that is selected in the **Color** drop-down menu.
  - ○ **Tile**: The image will be repeated in a tile pattern.
  - ○ **Stretch**: The image will be stretched to fill the available desktop space.

> **NOTE**
> If you pick a picture that is smaller than your desktop size, setting the position to **Zoom** will stretch it to fill the screen.

1.5.3   Screen Resolution and Colour Quality

Screen Resolution
The image displayed on the monitor is made up of columns of tiny dots across and rows of tiny dots down, where each dot is capable of being any one of millions of colours. These dots are controlled by the computer to draw the images on the screen.

The number of dots across the display combined with the number of dots down is called the **resolution**. Common resolutions are 1024 across by 768 down, or 1152 across by 864 down. The higher the resolution numbers are, the more dots there are on the screen, which makes the images of the desktop, windows and icons appear more defined.

There are several reasons why it may not be possible to use high numbers to set the screen resolution.

- The computer will have a maximum resolution that it can handle.
- The monitor will have a maximum resolution that it can handle.
- The physical size of the monitor, the distance the user is from it and the user's eyesight are all factors, because while at higher resolutions more windows can be seen, and more icons and text will fit on the screen, everything will be smaller.
- Flat-screen monitors (LCD or plasma) have a **native resolution** which the computer should be set up to match. If not, the monitor will have to scale the images up or down, resulting in much poorer image quality.

Colour Quality

The colour quality, or colour depth, that Windows XP is set to display determines the maximum number of colours that can be used for any image on the screen, including the desktop, icons and windows, etc. All modern PCs are capable of using at least 32-bit colour, meaning that each individual dot on the monitor can be any one of 4,294,967,296 colours.

Changing Colour Quality and Screen Resolution

To change the screen resolution and colour quality, do the following.

- Right-click an empty area of the desktop.
- Select **Properties** from the pop-up menu that opens.

The **Display Properties** window opens.

- Select the **Settings** tab.

To adjust the resolution, do the following:

- Drag the **Screen resolution** slider left or right to the desired setting.
- Click **Apply** to test the setting.
- If the setting is too high for the monitor to display, the screen will blank. If this happens, press the **Esc** key to restore the original settings.
- The **Color quality** can be set using the drop-down menu. It would be unusual to choose any setting other than **Highest (32-bit)**.

Select the Color quality

Screen resolution slider

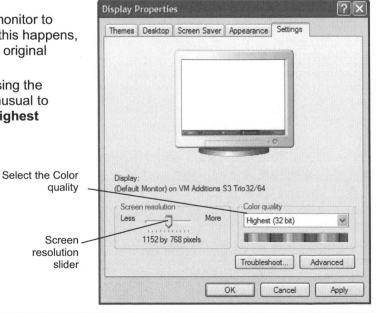

1.5.4 Screensavers

Screensavers automatically turn the screen blank or display a moving picture when the computer has been idle for a period of time. They are useful as a security mechanism as users can choose to require a password to be entered to turn off the screensaver and begin working again.

A screensaver, if enabled, will appear when there has been no activity from mouse or keyboard for a predetermined time. When a screensaver is active, pressing any key or moving the mouse will deactivate it and display the previous contents of the desktop. Windows XP has many built-in screensavers.

To select a screensaver, do the following.

* Right-click on an empty area of the desktop.

* Select **Properties** from the pop-up menu.
  The **Display Properties** window opens.

* In the **Display Properties** window, select the **Screensaver** tab.

  A screensaver can be selected from the drop-down menu.

  The number of minutes that must elapse before the screensaver activates can also be specified.

  If the **On resume, password protect** box is ticked, the Windows password must be entered to deactivate the screensaver.

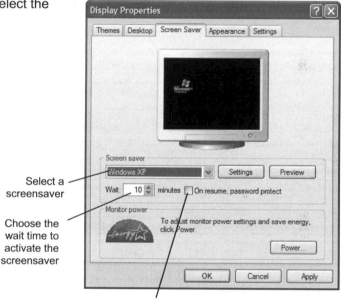

Select a screensaver

Choose the wait time to activate the screensaver

Choose whether or not a password is needed to deactivate the screensaver

1.5.5 The Control Panel

Almost all changes that can be made to Windows XP itself, from adding new applications to changing the time are done via the Control Panel.

To access the Control Panel, do the following:

* Click the **Start** button.
* From the **Start Menu**, select **Control Panel**.

Select **Control Panel**

2

The **Control Panel** can be displayed in either **Category View** (see the illustration below) or **Classic View** (see the illustration on the right).

This text will assume **Classic View** is being used.

Switch to… option

To change from Category View to Classic View, do the following:

- Click the **Switch To Classic View** option in the top left of the window.

Date and Time

Computers have an internal clock – displayed in the system tray at the right of the taskbar – that keeps track of the current date and time.

This is important for many reasons.

- When a file is created or updated, it is stamped with the current date and time. This can be useful when searching for it later.
- The date and time can be easily inserted into Office documents.

To adjust the date and time, do the following.

▷ Click the **Start Button**.

Date and Time

- From the **Start Menu**, select **Control Panel**.
- Double-click the **Date and Time** icon.

Alternatively, double-click the displayed date and time in the **System Tray** at the right of the taskbar.

The **Date and Time Properties** window opens.

In the **Date & Time** tab, the year, month and day can be set using the controls on the left of the window.

The time can be set by clicking the time field below the clock and typing new values or using the up/down arrows.

The **Time Zone** tab makes it possible to change the time zone that the computer is set to by choosing a zone from the drop-down list.

The **Internet Time** tab enables Windows XP to be configured to automatically obtain the correct time from a variety of atomic clocks connected to the internet.

Volume

Computers can have built-in or externally connected speakers so that sound from video clips, MP3 files etc can be heard.

To adjust the volume output from the computer, do the following.

- Click the **Start Button**.
- From the **Start Menu**, select **Control Panel**.
- Double-click the **Sounds and Audio Devices** icon.

Sounds and Audio Devices

Alternatively, double-click the speaker icon in the **System Tray**.

The **Volume Control** window opens.

- Adjust the volume by moving the slider control in the window.

1.6   The Keyboard Layout (2.1.2.3)

The keyboard layout can be changed to suit the language that documents are being produced in. Each language has a default keyboard layout, but many languages have alternate layouts. Even if work is done mainly with one language, other layouts may be useful for typing letters with accents, etc.

1.6.1   Changing the Keyboard Language

To change the keyboard language, do the following.

- Click the **Start Button**.
- From the **Start Menu**, select **Control Panel**.
- Double-click the **Regional and Language Options** icon.

Regional and Language Options

The **Regional and Languages Options** window opens.

- Click the **Languages** tab.
- Click the **Details** button.

Details button

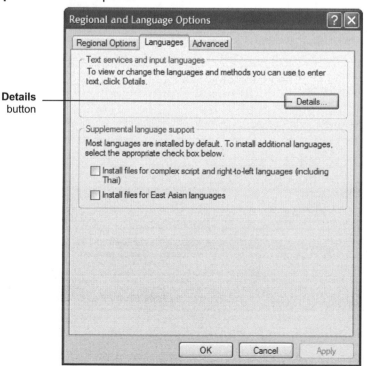

The **Text Services and Input Languages** window opens.

The current keyboard layout is displayed in the Default input language section.

A different layout can be selected from the drop-down list.

Current keyboard layout

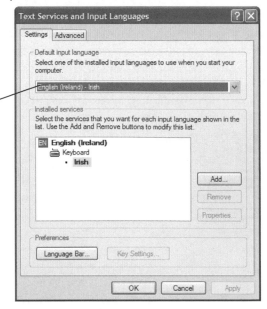

1.6.2   Adding a Keyboard Language

To add a new language, do the following:

- Open the **Text Services and Input Languages** window.

- Click **Add...**.

Add... button

The **Add Input Language** window opens.

- Select a new language from the list.

- Click **OK**.

NOTE

You can switch between different keyboard languages within the different programs that you use on your computer.

Hold down **Left Alt + Shift** to switch the keyboard to US format and **Alt Gr + Shift** to switch to UK format. The language changes are flagged in the status bar of the program you are using.

English (U.K

English (U.S

1.7 Installing and Uninstalling Applications (2.1.2.4)

Applications can be added to or removed from Windows XP to extend the range of functions available to users. Adding a new application is referred to as **installing** and removing an application is referred to as **uninstalling**. Applications that are included with Windows XP are called **Windows Components** and can be installed using the **Control Panel**.

Other software that is not supplied as part of Windows usually comes with a special **installer** utility called **setup.exe** on the supplied CD, or as part of the download, as in the illustration on the right.

NOTE

In office or educational networks, users will often not have sufficient **permissions** on the computer to install or remove applications.

Running this installer will usually start a **wizard** – a series of simple steps that the user can follow to install the application.

1.7.1   Installing Applications

To install a new Windows Component using the Control Panel, do the following:

- Clicking the **Start Button**.
- From the **Start Menu**, select **Control Panel**.
- Double-click the **Add or Remove Programs** icon.

2

The **Add or Remove Programs** window opens.

All the applications that are currently installed are listed here.

- Click the **Add/Remove Windows Components** icon on the left of the window.

From this point, ticking an unticked item in the list and clicking the **Next** button will install the component.

- In the case of Windows XP, the wizard may request the Windows installation CD if it needs to copy files from it.

Tick or untick items

1.7.2   Uninstalling Applications

To uninstall an application, do the following.

- Click the **Start Button**.

- From the **Start Menu**, select **Control Panel**.

- Double-click the **Add or Remove Programs** icon.

The **Add or Remove Programs** window opens.

- Locate the required application in the list, and click it once to highlight it.

Click **Change/Remove**

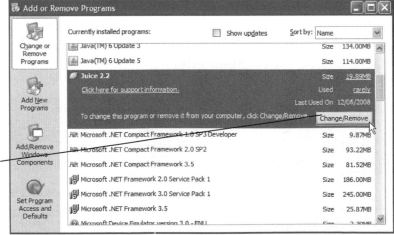

- Click **Change/Remove**.

  A confirmation window opens.

- Click **Yes** to uninstall the program.

1.8 Capturing Images from the Screen (2.1.2.5)

There may be occasions when it is useful to capture an image of the desktop or a particular window and then paste those contents into a file, such as a Microsoft Word document. For example, a user may want to send a colleague a sample of how to complete a particular screen within the Windows XP environment. This can be achieved using the **keyboard print screen** facility.

To capture the contents of a screen or window, do the following:

- Press **Alt + Print Screen** to capture the contents of the active window only.
  Alternatively, press the **Print Screen** button to capture the entire screen as it appears on the monitor.

Print Screen button

To paste the contents of the captured screen or window into a document, do the following:

- Ensure you are working in the document or file where the captured image should be inserted.
- From the **ribbon**, select the **Home** tab.
- Click **Paste**.

To edit the screen capture, an image editing application, such as **MS Paint**, can be used. To access **Paint**, do the following:

- Click the **Start** menu and then click **All Programs**.
- Click the **Accessories** option and then choose **Paint**.
- From the **Edit** menu, click **Paste**.
  The screen shot will appear in the **Paint** window.

1.9 Working with Desktop Icons (2.1.3.1)

Each icon on the desktop represents an application, function, folder or document that can be opened and used. By moving the cursor over an icon on the desktop and double-clicking the left mouse button, the function it performs is activated.

The standard Windows XP desktop has one icon, for the Recycle Bin, but icons will be added in due course through normal use.

Below are examples of the some common types of icon.

An application icon, such as the Microsoft Word icon, can be used to start that application.	Word 2007
A folder icon, such as My Documents, can be clicked to open and view the folder contents.	My Documents

2

This document icon, **Team List.docx**, was created in Microsoft Word 2007. Double-clicking this icon will start Microsoft Word and display the document.	Team List.docx
This is the icon for the Mozilla Firefox internet browser. Other internet browsers include Internet Explorer.	Mozilla Firefox
This is the icon for the Recycle bin.	Recycle Bin
This is a printer icon	hp LaserJet 1320 PCL 6
These are icons for different drives: DVD (F:) drive, removable disk (H:) drive, the C: drive.	DVD Drive (F:) Removable Disk (H:) Local Disk (C:)

1.9.1 Selecting and Moving Icons (2.1.3.2)

The icons on the desktop are usually arranged in a vertical line down the left-hand side, but this layout can be changed to suit user preference.

To **select** a desktop icon, do the following:

- Click the icon.
  The icon will be highlighted and a slight shading will appear around it.

To **move** an icon, do the following:

- Click the icon once with the left mouse button to select it.
- Holding down the left mouse button, drag the icon to another location on the desktop by moving the mouse.

1.9.2 Arranging Icons

In addition to moving individual icons on the desktop, they can also be arranged in a more specific way.

To **arrange** icons, do the following:

- Right-click anywhere on a blank area of the desktop.
  A drop-down menu appears.

- Move the cursor over the **Arrange Icons By** menu option.

  A drop-down sub-menu appears.

- The first section of the sub-menu enables icons to be sorted on the desktop by **Name**, **Size**, **Type** or **Modified date**.

The middle section has two important items:

- o **Auto Arrange** arranges the icons down the left-hand side of the screen.

- o **Align to Grid** means that when an icon is moved with the mouse, it will snap to the nearest point on an invisible grid on the screen when the mouse button is released.

1.9.3   Creating and Removing a Shortcut Icon on the Desktop (2.1.3.3)

It can be tedious to locate the menu item for a frequently used application every time it is needed. As an alternative, a desktop icon can be created as a **shortcut** to open the application more easily and quickly. A desktop shortcut can be removed if it is not used often or if it was created accidentally.

Creating a Desktop Shortcut

To create a desktop shortcut to the MS Paint application, do the following:

- Click **Start**.

- Select **All Programs**.

- Select the **Accessories** sub-menu.

- Move the cursor over the **Paint** menu item.

- Right-click and select **Send To** from the sub-menu that appears.

  A further sub-menu opens.

- Click **Desktop (create shortcut)** item.

  A shortcut for the Paint application will appear on the desktop.

Removing a Desktop Shortcut

To remove a desktop shortcut, do the following.

- Move the cursor over the shortcut icon and right click.

- In the pop-up menu, select **Delete**.

  The **Confirm File Delete** window opens, asking whether or not you want to delete the icon.

- Select **Yes** to delete the shortcut.

- The shortcut will disappear from the desktop.

1.9.4   Using an Icon to Open a File, Folder or Application (2.1.3.4)

An application can be started, or a file or folder opened, using desktop icons.

To do this, do the following.

- Double-click the icon.

  The file, folder or application opens in a new window.

  If a file is being opened, it will open within the necessary application.

Section 2   File Management

2.1   Storage Devices (2.2.1.2)

All user-created files, files that comprise the installed applications and Windows XP itself must be stored on a **storage device** so that they are retained safely and do not disappear when the computer is shut down.

There are two main categories of **file storage devices** for files. These devices are referred to as **drives**. For example, you put DVDs in a DVD drive, tapes in a tape drive, etc.

- **Non-Removable Storage Devices**: Windows XP itself, applications and user-created files are generally stored on a hard disk drive, i.e. inside the computer
- **Removable Storage Devices**: These devices, as the name suggests, are generally used for moving files from computer to computer, installing new software, archiving and creating backups.

Information on a computer is stored electronically. Because of this, there is always a possibility that it can be lost because of a malfunction in the system or through human error. To avoid a total loss of data, it is important to have copies of all important files stored on disks or other removable media, called **backups** (See Section 2.1.4).

2.1.1   Types of Storage Media (2.2.1.2 and 2.2.1.5)

The programs used and work produced on a computer must be stored before it is switched off so that they are available at a later date. The next time the computer is switched on, they can be loaded into RAM and work can continue. This kind of mechanical storage is often referred to as **secondary memory**. Common examples include the following.

Hard Disk Drives (Internal and External)

The computer has an internal, non-removable hard disk drive inside its **base unit**. At the time of writing, the capacity of a typical hard disk in a laptop is 160GB and in a desktop is 500GB, though larger sizes are readily available.

It contains Windows XP operating system, all the installed applications and user files.

More hard drives can be added to the computer if more **disk space** is required. These drives can be fitted internally or connected externally using a USB or FireWire cable.

They are usually made of several metal (hard) magnetically coated disks encased in a sealed metal box. They have one or more rotating **platters** on which data is stored magnetically. Information is read and written by a movable arm that flies slightly above the platters.

The illustration on the right shows a typical hard disk drive with its cover removed.

Rotating platter

Movable arm

External, or removable, hard disks are the same as
internal hard disks but are mounted in a tough casing
and connected to the computer via the USB or similar
port. They are typically used for archiving, moving
large amounts of data between computers and for
backups. At the time of writing, 1TB (1,024GB) units
are available.

USB Drives

USB drives are a convenient storage device that plug into the
high-speed USB (universal serial bus) port that is available on
most modern computers.

They use the same **flash memory** technology that is used in the
memory cards of digital cameras and hand-held video games and
are sometimes referred to as **flash drives**. They are small enough
to fit on a keyring and, at the time of writing, typically have 1GB
to 32GB of storage space.

Portable Digital Devices

Portable digital devices (such as digital cameras, mobile phones and hand-held games consoles)
often use removable **memory cards** for storage. The type of memory technology most often used
on these cards is **flash memory**, and the cards themselves are often referred to as **flash cards**.
There are various card formats and capacities, for example CompactFlash and SD. All the
varieties of card are by necessity physically small.

Capacities at the time of writing range from 128MB to 16GB. Many PCs have inbuilt **card
readers** which can accept a variety of memory card formats. The cards then become visible as
removable drives and files can be copied on and off as normal. Memory cards from digital
cameras can be used in special vending machines to print physical copies of digital photos.

A 1GB **microSD** card is shown on the right at actual size.

CDs (Compact Discs)

While hard disks are magnetic and USB drives use flash memory, CDs use a reflective coating
that can be read using a laser, meaning that CD is a type of **optical storage**. A typical CD can
hold 650MB to 700MB of information.

The CDs that are typically used to distribute copyrighted data, such as commercial software or
music, are read-only – the information on these discs cannot be erased or added to – and they are
more accurately called CD-ROMs.

Listed below are the two main types of **recordable** CD. The process of writing information to a CD is often called **burning**.

- **CD-R**: These can be written to once and read from multiple times.
- **CD-RW**: These can be written to and read from multiple times.

CDs are used in **CD drives**. This will have a front panel with a tray that can be opened to insert and remove the discs themselves. External CD drives are also available.

DVDs (Digital Versatile Discs)

DVDs have largely replaced the CD for optical storage use, and have displaced the videotape entirely in the consumer entertainment world.

DVDs look the same as CDs and use the same technology, but the capacity of a standard DVD disc is 4.7GB as opposed to 700MB for a CD. There are also dual-layer discs that can hold over 8GB. This is important in computer terms because as hard disk drive capacities increase, archival and backup media must keep pace.

In the entertainment world, the capacity of a dual-layer, or high-density, DVD is the only way to distribute films with high-quality pictures and sound. The DVDs that are typically used to distribute copyrighted data, such as commercial software or film, are read-only and referred to as DVD-ROM.

There are many types of recordable DVD disk that can be broadly broken down into the following two groups.

- **DVD-R** and **DVD+R**: These can be written to once and read from multiple times.
- **DVD-RW**, **DVD+RW** and **DVD-RAM**: These can be written to and read from multiple times.

DVDs are used in **DVD drives**, which are identical in appearance to CD drives. All DVD drives can read CDs, and most can write to them as well, meaning that drives that work with CDs only are effectively obsolete.

High-Density DVDs

High-density DVDs are the successor to DVDs. Initially, there were two competing formats, namely **HD DVD** and **Blu-Ray**, but the latter emerged as the standard during 2008. The former could store up to 30GB, while Blu-Ray can store up to 50GB. High-density formats will eventually replace standard DVDs.

Network Drives

If a computer is part of a network, access storage can be used that is physically located on another computer. For example, a network server in an office may have several hard disks of huge capacity that are **shared**, and thus available to other computers on the network. Users can transfer files to and from these shared locations in the same way as they would with the hard disks in their own **local** computers. The files are transmitted over **network cables** or via a **wireless network connection**.

In Windows XP, the icon for a normal folder on a local computer looks slightly different from that for a folder representing a network location.

Tapes

In computer networks, such as those found in most businesses, there is usually at least one **server** (a dedicated computer that provides centralised control and storage). The vitally important data on a server's hard drive is usually **backed up** using removable tape cartridges. These are then often removed from the premises and stored elsewhere as part of a **disaster recovery plan**. This type of storage is beginning to disappear as its traditional advantage of huge capacity at a relatively low cost is eroding in the face of inexpensive alternatives, such as hard disks, which are also more reliable.

Online File Storage

The mass availability of broadband internet access has brought about various types of **online storage**. This form of storage has been around since computers were first networked, but recent examples, such as Mozy (www.mozy.com), provide simple ways to use it. Websites allow registered users to transfer their files to the internet where they can be shared openly or accessed only by the owner. When the file is online, it may also be transferred back to the user's computer as though it were stored on any other device. Online storage is most often used to share files with other computer users, but is also useful for transferring files, which might be too big to e-mail, and for offsite backups This is especially true of digital photos, videos and music. Large files are usually not stored online as they take a long time to transfer to and from the internet.

2.1.2   How Computer Storage is Measured

A computer must be able to 'remember' the information it is working with. The information is 'remembered' by being stored, either temporarily or permanently.

All information processed by the computer is handled and stored in digital form using **binary code**. This code only uses a series of two digits, 0 and 1. In our daily work, we normally use a number system that has 10 digits, 0 to 9, the **decimal system**. Below is how you and a computer count from 0 to 9.

You	0	1	2	3	4	5	6	7	8	9
Computer	0000	0001	0010	0011	0100	0101	0110	0111	1000	1001

2.1.3   Measuring Files (2.2.1.3)

A single digit – **0** or **1** – is called a **bit**. Bits are grouped together, typically in sets of eight, to make **bytes**. Computer memory is measured using the following sequence.

1 Bit	1 Byte	1 Kilobyte (KB)	1 Megabyte (MB)	1 Gigabyte (GB)	1 Terabyte (TB)
A single digit: 0 or 1	8 bits (e.g. can represent the letter A)	1,024 bytes (1 thousand)	1,048,576 bytes (1 million)	1,073,741,824 bytes (1 thousand million)	1,099,511,627,776 bytes (1 trillion)

The size of a file is measured in **bytes** and determines how much memory is needed to store that file. One byte is the basic unit of measurement and is very small. The typical starting point for file measurement is a **Kilobyte (KB)**, which is equal to 1,024 bytes. The next most common file measurement is a **Megabyte (MB)**. One MB is equal to approximately 1 million bytes or 1,000 KB. The third most common file measurement is a **Gigabyte (GB)**. One GB is equal to approximately 1 billion bytes or 1,000 MB. File sizes can increase beyond the measurement of GBs, but are not common and exist in specialist areas, such as computer-generated special effects in films.

2.1.4   Backups (2.2.1.4)

Information on a computer is stored electronically. Because of this, there is always a possibility that it can be lost because of a malfunction in the system or through human error. To avoid a total loss of data, it is important to have copies of all important files stored on disks or other removable media. These copies are called **backups**.

Backups can be made in several ways. Copies can be made to tape, USB drive, external hard disks or burned onto a CD or DVD. The data from some files may also be kept as hard copy. These backups should be kept in a safe and secure place, e.g. locked away in fireproof containers or in a remote location.

At a basic level, taking a backup can be as simple as copying and pasting vital files to another location on the computer. Taken a step further, the files can be simply copied to a variety of types of **storage media**.

- **USB memory sticks** are always increasing in storage capacity and decreasing in cost. They are easy to use because they appear as a new drive in the operating system.
- **External hard drives** can be used in the same way as USB memory sticks, however, they are larger and offer more storage space.
- **Optical media**, such as CD, DVD and Blu-Ray discs, provide a compact form of storage but have less capacity and must sometimes be written to or **burned** using special software.
- Businesses generally have much more vital data to protect than the home user, and often use expensive **tape backup** systems that require dedicated software to use.

While data can simply be copied to a storage medium, it is better to use **backup software** for the task.

Some advantages are:
- The backup can be scheduled to run automatically without the user having to remember to do it.
- The backup can be **incremental**, meaning that only the data that has changed since the last backup is copied, which reduces the space used and time taken.
- The backup file can be encrypted and protected with a password.

The continued growth and speed of broadband internet has meant that **online backup** has become increasingly used. In this scenario, the backup is stored in a remote location provided by a commercial online backup company. This storage is extremely secure and failure-tolerant, is often located in armoured underground locations and possibly replicated in several locations. The customer installs **client software** on their systems which can back them up over the internet to the secure storage location.

2.2   Files and Folders

2.2.1   How Windows XP Organises Files and Folders (2.2.1.1)

It is important that all the folders on a computer's hard disk are stored in a tidy and organised way, and that the basic structure is the same for every computer that uses the same operating system. This is called the **File System**, or sometimes the **Directory Structure** – 'directory' is another term for 'folder'.

Windows XP is itself installed on an empty hard drive, normally by the computer manufacturer. This process creates a standard set of Windows XP **system folders** that is the same on every Windows XP computer. The contents of these folders should never be directly altered and access to them should be restricted.

When users are added in Windows XP, they each get their own **My Documents** folder plus some others. Normally, users can only see their own folder. All user-created files, such as word processing documents, should be stored in this folder.

All drives in Windows XP, except for network drives, are assigned a **drive letter** automatically. The main hard disk drive, upon which Windows XP itself is installed, is given the letter **C**, and can be referred to as **C:** (pronounced **C colon**). Optical drives (CD and DVD drives) tend to be assigned to **D:** or **E:** but this can vary. Further drive letters are assigned to **removable drives** when they are connected. These drive letters disappear when the removable drive is disconnected.

The file system is structured like a tree. The **root** of the tree can contain files and folders. These **folders** can, themselves, contain more files and sub-folders, and so on.

2.2.2   Navigating to a Drive, File or Folder (2.2.2.2 and 2.2.2.3)
Navigating through folders and sub-folders to find a particular location is a very common activity, especially when opening and saving files.

To explore the basic Windows XP file system structure, do the following:

- Right-click the **My Computer** icon on the desktop.
- Select **Explore** from the pop-up menu.

My Computer

NOTE

If the My Computer icon is not visible, open the Start Menu to locate it. It can then be right-clicked from the Start Menu.

Navigating to a Drive

- Right-click the **My Computer** icon on the desktop.
- Select **Explore** from the pop-up menu.
  The **My Computer** window opens.

My Computer

- In the treeview on the left, click the **+** sign beside a drive, e.g. **Local Disk (C:)**. The node will expand to show the contents of the **C: drive**.

  Any item with a **-** beside it has been expanded. Click the **-** to collapse the drive or folder and make the treeview more compact.

  Any drive or folder that has a **+** sign beside it can be expanded.

Navigating to a File or Folder

To view the contents of a folder in the right-hand side of the My Computer window, do the following:

- Right-click the **My Computer** icon on the desktop.
- Select **Explore** from the pop-up menu.
- The **My Computer** window opens.
- In treeview, click the required folder, e.g. **My Documents**, once to highlight it.

  Any sub-folders are displayed in the right-hand side of the window.

- Double-click a folder in the right-hand side of the window to open it.

- Double-clicking any file icon will start the application that the file is associated with.

2.2.3   Displaying Folder Properties (2.2.2.1)

In Windows XP, every file or folder has **Properties**. These are pieces of information that describe that particular item.

To view the properties of a folder, do the following.

- Right-click any folder and select **Properties** from the pop-up menu.
  The **Properties** window opens.

Information about the folder, such as it's size and the number of files it contains can be seen. These figures also include any sub-folders and their contents.

In addition, there are various tabs containing other advanced options concerning security and network sharing.

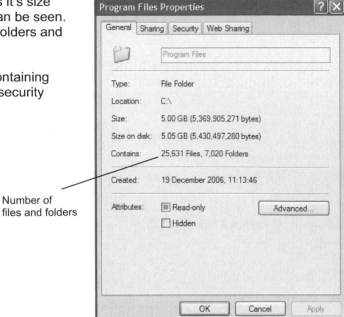

Number of
files and folders

2.3   Creating a Folder and a Further Sub-Folder (2.2.2.4)

A folder is a container in which files and other folders can be stored. Normally, files of a particular type or relating to a particular topic are kept together in the same folder.

Folders should be given recognisable names, such as **Finance** or **Novel**, to indicate their contents. It is also good practice for users to only create new folders within their own **home** folders – security settings in Windows XP will not usually allow folders to be created in many other places anyway.

2.3.1   Creating a Folder

This sequence will describe how to create a folder called **Office** within the My Documents folder. If the My Documents folder is not visible on the desktop, do the following:

- Open the **Start Menu** and locate the **My Documents** menu item.
- Right-click the **My Documents** menu item.
- Select **Show On Desktop** from the menu that is displayed.

Click **Show on Desktop**

To create a folder, do the following.

- On the **desktop**, double-click the **My Documents** folder to open it.
- The **My Documents** window opens, displaying the folder's contents.
- Right-click in an **empty** area of the main section of the **My Documents** window (on the right-hand side).
- Select **New** from the pop-up menu.
- Select **Folder** from the pop-up sub-menu.
  Alternatively, click the **Make a new folder** link on the **File and Folder Tasks** pane.

Make a new
folder link

Right-click in
main section of
window

Select **New** from the
pop-up menu

Select **Folder**
from the pop-up
sub-menu

A new folder will appear. It will automatically be called **New Folder** and the name will be highlighted.

- To give the folder a more meaningful name, start typing and press **Enter** when finished.

NOTE

If the wrong name is entered, see Section 2.4.3 for details on how to rename it.

2.3.2   Creating a Sub-Folder

To create a sub-folder, do the following:

- Double-click the newly created folder to open it.
  It will be empty.
- Repeat the same steps used to create a folder.
- When naming the sub-folder give it a different name to the main folder, see Section 2.3.1.

2.3.3 Creating a Folder from Within an Application

It is possible to create a new folder from inside an application itself, which can save time when working on documents, etc.

As an example, we will create a document in a text editor and then save it to a new folder.

- From the **Start** menu, select **Accessories**.
- Select **WordPad** from the sub-menu. The **WordPad** application opens.

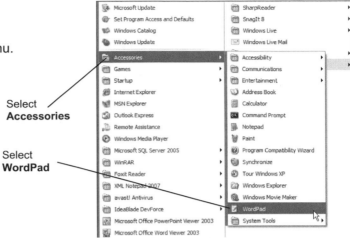

Select **Accessories**

Select **WordPad**

- Type some text into the in the blank document that opens.

To save the document in a folder that has not yet been created, do the following:

- From the **File** menu, select **Save As**. The **Save As** window opens.

- The cursor will be in the **File Name** field.
- Delete the contents of the **File Name** field and type the name for the file, e.g. **test.rtf**.

Give the file a name

New folder icon

Click **Save**

- Click the **New Folder** icon in the toolbar at the top of the window.

- Give the new folder a name.

- Double-click the new folder in the main area of the window to open it.

- Click **Save** to save the new document in the newly created folder.

- Click the Close X button to close the **WordPad** application.

2.4   Working with Files

All files must have a **filename**. In Windows XP, this name can be up to 256 characters in length, containing upper case and lower case letters, numbers, spaces, punctuation marks and almost anything else that can be typed.

Most files have an **extension** to their name, which is a dot (full stop) followed by some additional characters. For example, the filename **My Novel.docx** has the extension **docx**, indicating that it was created using Microsoft Word 2007.

In Microsoft Windows, the file extension establishes the application a file was created in and the icon that is used to represent it, e.g. all Microsoft Word files have the same icon. When a file icon is double-clicked, Microsoft Windows opens the file with the application dictated by its extension.

2.4.1   Recognising Common File Types (2.2.3.1)

Icons in Windows XP make folders and particular types of file easy for users to identify. For example, when an application suite such as Microsoft Office is installed, it takes ownership of all files with particular extensions and tells Windows to use particular icons when displaying them.

Double-clicking a file which has the Microsoft Word icon and the extension **.docx** will automatically start Microsoft Word, if needed, and **open** the file within it. This mechanism is called **file association**.

Below are the icons for files created with Microsoft Office 2007.

My Novel.docx	Lottery Numbers.xlsx	Proposed Mars Mission.pptx
Microsoft Word	Microsoft Excel	Microsoft PowerPoint
Accounts.accdb	Expenses.xsn	Parish News.pub
Microsoft Access	Microsoft InfoPath	Microsoft Publisher

There can be many **formats** for some file types. For example, files containing image data can be **JPEG** format or **PNG** format or **GIF** format or **BMP** format, to name a few. The format describes a method for how the bits and bytes are structured inside the file. In the case of these

image files, JPEG and PNG are more recent formats and are intended to enable large images to be stored in small files, though with some expense to image quality.
Different computers may have different applications installed to handle some file types.

For example, one computer might only have the standard Microsoft Paint application installed, in which case the icon for an image file in BMP format would be like the icon on the right.

Zapotec.bmp

On a computer with Adobe PhotoShop installed, it would probably look like the icon on the right.

Zapotec.bmp

File Type	Example Formats	Icon
Image Files	**.jpg** (JPEG - Joint Photographics Experts)	Boston.jpg
Sound Files	**.mp3** (MPEG Layer 3)	My Last Serenade.mp3
Video Files	**.mpeg** or **mpg** (Moving Picture Experts Group) **.avi** (Audio Video Interleaved file)	AVI
PDF Files	**.pdf (Portable Document Format)**	PDF Adobe
Compressed Files	**.zip** (WinZip)	
Temporary Files	**.tmp** (temporary file – when Word is using autorecovery, it often uses .tmp files to save information temporarily)	
Executable Files	**.exe** (these files are used to install programs, their icons can change, depending on the program being installed)	setup winzip90.exe boot500.exe

2.4.2 Giving a File a Name (2.2.3.5)

Files and folders should be given sensible and descriptive names. It might be easier and quicker at the time to create ten Microsoft Word files called **myfile1.docx**, **myfile2.docx**, etc., but later each would have to be opened individually to discover what they contained.

When collaborating with others, where many users are creating and editing the same files, a file naming **convention** should be adopted. This is a set of rules defining exactly how files should be named that everyone must follow and ensures that structure and control is maintained. For example, it might be decided that all files should have a project code followed by a name followed by a revision date – **0234-Green Valley Estate-05-06-08.docx**.

Take a similar approach to naming folders (file extensions do not apply here, of course). There is nothing to prevent users from putting all their documents into one documents folder, but it might make more sense to create sub-folders for particular projects or type of document. Planning beforehand and then following the plan can save a lot of time in locating files later.

> **NOTE**
> Filenames are **not case sensitive** in Windows. 'My Novel.docx', 'MY NOVEL.DOCX', etc. would refer to the same file.

2.4.3   Renaming Files and Folders (2.2.3.6)

A file or folder can be given a new name as long as that new name is not already being used by another file or folder in the same folder.

To rename a file, do the following.

- Locate the file to be renamed and right-click it.

- In the pop-up menu, select **Rename**.
  The main part of the filename will be highlighted.

- Type the new filename.
- Press **Enter**.

> **NOTE**
> Renaming a folder works in exactly the same way.
>
> To restore the original filename, press **Escape** instead of entering a new name.

2.4.2   Using a Text Editing Application (2.2.3.2)

To practise naming and saving files, in the following sequence, you will create some folders and create a word-processing file to save in one of the folders.

Create some new folders to keep the file in.

1   Open the **My Documents** folder.

2   In the pane on the left, click the **Create a new folder** link.

3   Name the folder **Finance Department**.

4   Open the Finance Department folder by double-clicking it.

5   Create three new sub-folders called **Letters**, **Bank** and **Business**.

6   Double-click the **Bank** folder to open it.

7   Inside the **Bank** folder, create new sub-folders, called **National Bank**, **Finance Bank**, **Bahamas Bank** and **Equity Bank**.

Create a new Microsoft Word document and it in the Equity Bank folder.

8   From the Start menu, select the Microsoft Office sub-menu, and then Microsoft Word from the drop-down menu that appears.

Alternatively, double-click the Microsoft Word icon on the desktop.

The **Microsoft Word** application will start, with a blank document open called 'Document1.

9   Type some text into the blank document.

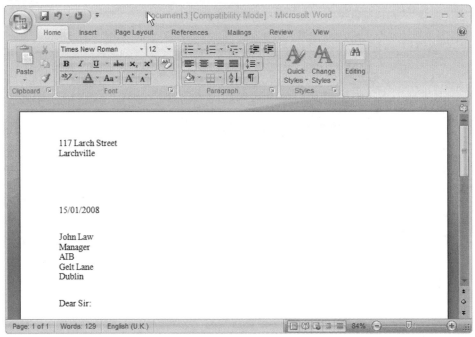

10   To save this short document, click on the Office button within Microsoft Word and select **Save**, or press **Ctrl + S**.

The **Save As** window opens, asking where the document should be saved.

- In the **Save As** window, navigate to the **Equity Bank** folder that was created earlier.

This can be done by clicking on the folders in the main part of the Save As window. The three buttons at the top right can also be used for navigation.
They are:

- o **Back**: Moves back to the previously viewed folder.
- o **Up**: Goes up a level in the folder structure.
- o **Delete**: Will delete the highlighted item in the main part of the window.
- o **New Folder**: A shortcut to creating a new folder within the currently viewed folder.
- o **View**: Changes the folder view (Icons, Details, List, etc.)

11   When the correct folder has been located, the Save As window will look like as the illustration below.

12   Enter **Equity Letter** as the filename.

13   Click **Save**.

> **NOTE**
> If the file already exists, an alert will appear and the existing file can be overwritten, or the save cancelled, or a new filename entered.

2.4.3   Changing File Properties (2.2.3.3)

A particular user's files are normally stored in their own My Documents folder, which most other users set up on the computer cannot access. The exceptions are users with **Power User** or **Administrator** security rights.

Individual files can be made **read-only**, meaning that they can be opened and viewed but the contents cannot be changed. This is useful to prevent accidental deletion.

To view and change the file read-only properties, do the following:

- Locate the file and right-click it.
- Select **Properties** from the pop-up menu.
  The **Properties** window opens.

To make the file read-only, do the following:

- Tick the **Read-only** check box.
- Click **Apply**.
- Click **OK**.

Read-only check box

NOTE
To make the file Read-write so that changes can be made to it, untick the Read-only check box.

2.5 Sorting Files (2.2.3.4)

When viewing a list of files in a window, it can be useful to sort them in a particular way. For example, they could be sorted so that the largest appeared first to make it easier to delete large files to free up disk space.

To sort files by name, size, type or the date they were modified, do the following:

- Open the **My Documents** folder.
- Change the window to **Details** view by clicking the **View** menu and selecting **Details**.

- In **Details** view, click the column header required (i.e. name, size, type or date modified) to sort the list accordingly.

- The small triangle in the column header indicates the direction of the sort. Sorting can either be in ascending order (**A–Z**) or descending order (**Z–A**).

- In the example below, the list is sorted in ascending name order. Therefore names beginning with **A** will be listed before those beginning with **B**. Click the column header again to change the sort direction.

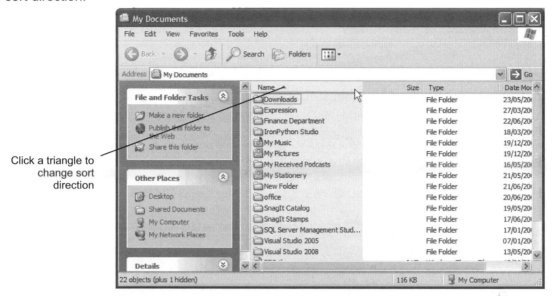

Click a triangle to change sort direction

2.6 Selecting Files and Folders (2.2.4.1)

Before an action can be performed on a file or folder, the file or folder must first be selected. This lets Windows XP know that this is the item (or items) to be acted upon. Selecting a file or folder will cause its icon to change colour.

A single item or a group of items can be selected either on the desktop or in a file browser window. Actions such as dragging or deleting affect all the selected items.

To select a single item, do the following:

- Click it once.

Curriculum
Vitae.docx

When unselected, the file is not highlighted

Curriculum
Vitae.docx

When selected, the file is highlighted

To select several items that are not located next to each other, do the following:

- Hold down the **Ctrl** key and click each item once.

Curriculum
Vitae.docx

My Novel.docx

Loan
Application.docx

To select a range of items that are next to each other, do the following:

- Hold down the **Shift** key, click the first item and click the last item.
  All the items in between these two will also be selected automatically.

To select a group of items that are next to each other, do the following:

- Click anywhere near the items on a blank area of desktop or window background, then with the right mouse button held down drag a selection rectangle (or marquee) around the items.

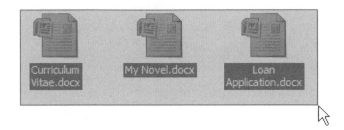

To select multiple groups of items using a selection rectangle, do the following:

- Hold down the **Ctrl** key and then proceed to select each group.

To select all the items in the active window, do the following:

- Hold down **Ctrl** and press **A**.

2.7   Copying and Moving Files and Folders (2.2.4.2 and 2.2.4.3)

Copying and moving files and folders is a common requirement, for example copying documents to a USB drive from time to time for backup purposes.

When a folder is copied or moved, everything contained within that folder (files and subfolders) is also copied.

NOTE
It is useful to check the size of the folder you are copying or moving first and the space available in the location you are copying or moving to ensure there is enough space.

Copying files or folders makes a copy of them in the new location and keeps the original file or folder in the original location.

Moving files or folders removes them from the original location and places them in the new location.

2.7.1   Copying Files and Folders Using the Menu and Keyboard Shortcuts

To copy files or folders using the menu and keyboard shortcuts, do the following:

* Locate the item to be copied in a window and **select** it by clicking it once.
* Right-click the selected item and select **Copy**
  from the pop-up menu.

  Alternatively, press **CTRL + C** to copy the file
  or folder.

* Browse to the **target location** where the item is to be copied to.
* This can be done using the same window (because once the item is copied Windows XP will remember what it is even if you browse to a different location, a different file window or the desktop).
* Right-click an empty area in the target location.
* Click **Paste**.

  Alternatively, press **CTRL + V** to paste the file or folder.

  The file or folder is copied to the new location.

NOTE

If the item is pasted into the same location that it was copied from, Word will generate a new filename or folder name automatically as appropriate – this is normally the original file or folder name with **Copy of** at the beginning.

This is because two items in the same location cannot have exactly
the same name.

Copy of My
Novel.docx

2.7.2   Copying Files and Folders Using Drag and Drop

Rather than copying and pasting, selected items can also be copied by dragging and dropping them. For this method, both the location to copy from and the location to copy to must be visible at the same time.

To copy files or folders using drag and drop, do the following:

* Ensure that both locations are visible.

  This could be two windows, a window and the desktop, etc.

In the screenshot below, there are two windows open, and the copy is taking place from the left window (**Samples**) to the right window (**Copy Of Samples**).

- Select the item or items to copy.

- When the items are selected, press and hold the **CTRL** key.

- Click the selected item (if there is more than one, click any selected item) and hold the mouse button down.

- Drag the mouse to the target location, still holding down the **CTRL** key, this will move the selected file(s).

  Notice that when the cursor is over the destination as in the illustration below, the cursor includes a **+** to indicate a copy is taking place. There is also a 'ghost' image of the file(s) being dragged.

- Release the mouse button and the **CTRL** key to 'drop' the item(s) in the new location.

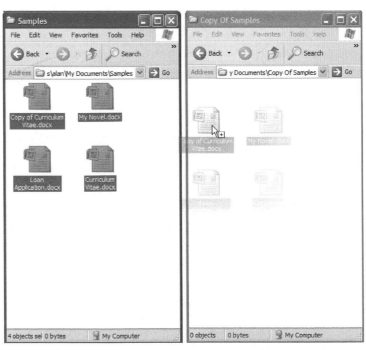

2.7.3   Copying Files and Folders Using My Computer

From time to time, you may need to make a copy of a file or folder. For example, you may want to copy an entire folder to back it up. If you copy a folder the entire contents of that folder and any sub-folders it contains are copied to the new location.

To copy a file/folder using the My Computer window, do the following:

- Select the file or folder you wish to copy.

- Open the My Computer window by double-clicking the My Computer icon.

- Use the **File and Folder Tasks** pane to select **Copy this folder** (if you have selected a folder) or **Copy this file** (if you have selected a file).

The **Copy Items** window opens.

- Select the folder, drive or sub-folder where the copied file/folder is to be stored.

- Click **Copy**.

  If you want to create a new folder in which to store the copied file/folder, click the **Make New Folder** button.

  When a file/folder is copied, the original remains where it is and a copy is placed in the new location. This means that there are now two copies of the file/folder available.

2.7.4   Copying Files and Folders Using Windows Explorer

In addition to copying files/folders using My Computer, you can also **copy** files and folders using Explorer. If you copy a folder, the entire contents of that folder and any sub-folders it contains are copied to the new location.

To copy a file/folder using Windows Explorer, do the following.

- Select the file/folder you wish to copy.

- Right-click the file/folder.

- Click **Copy** in the pop-up menu that opens.

- Right-click the drive, disk or folder where the file is to be copied to.

- Choose **Paste** from the pop-up menu that opens.

2.7.5   Moving Files or Folders Using the Menu and Keyboard Shortcuts

To move files or folders using the menu and keyboard shortcuts, do the following:

- Locate the item to be copied in a window and **select** it by clicking it once.

- Right-click the selected item and select **Cut** from the pop-up menu.

  Alternatively, press **CTRL + X**.

- Browse to the **target location** where the item is to be moved to.

- This can be done using the same window (because once the item is copied Windows XP will remember what it is even if you browse to a different location, a different file window or the desktop).

- Right-click an empty area in the target location.

- Click **Paste**.

  Alternatively, press **CTRL + V** to paste the file or folder.

  The file or folder is copied to the new location.

2.7.6   Moving Files and Folders Using Drag and Drop

Files and folders can also be moved by dragging and dropping them. For this method, both the location to move from and the location to move to must be visible at the same time.

To move files or folders using drag and drop, do the following:

- Ensure that both locations are visible.

- This could be two windows, a window and the desktop, etc.

- In the screenshot below, there are two windows open, and the move is taking place from the left window (Samples) to the right window (Copy Of Samples).

- Select the file(s) or folder(s) to move and keep the mouse button held down.

- Drag the mouse to the target location, this will move the selected file(s).

- Release the mouse button to 'drop' the item(s) in the new location.

2.7.7   Moving Files and Folders Using My Computer

There may be times when you wish to move a file or folder to a different location on your computer. If you move a folder, the entire contents of that folder and any sub-folders it contains are moved to the new location.

To move file(s)/folder(s) using the My Computer window, do the following.

- Select the file or folder you wish to move.

- Use the **File and Folder Tasks** pane to select **Move this folder** (if you have previously selected a folder) or **Move this file** (if you have selected a file).

- The **Move Items** window opens.

- Select the folder or sub-folder where the moved file/folder is to be stored.

- Click **Move**.

- If you want to create a new folder in which to store the moved file/folder, click the **Make New Folder** button.

2.7.8   Moving Files and Folders Using Windows Explorer

In addition to moving files/folders using My Computer, you can also **move** files and folders using Explorer. If you move a folder, the entire contents of that folder and any sub-folders it contains are moved to the new location.

To move a file/folder using Windows Explorer, do the following.

- Click the file or folder you wish to move.

- Right-click the file/folder.

- Click **Cut** in the pop-up menu that opens.

- Right-click the disk or folder where the file is to be moved to.

- Choose **Paste** from the pop-up menu that opens.

2.8   Deleting and Restoring Files and Folders

2.8.1   Deleting Files and Folders (2.2.5.1)

If a file or folder is no longer required, it can be deleted. This might be done to free up space on the hard disk or just to keep files tidy and up to date.

Care should be taken when deleting, if the file or folder is important it is better to be safe and double check before deleting – although Windows XP makes it very difficult to delete something that would damage the operating system itself.

NOTE

An entire application such as Microsoft Word cannot be removed in the same way as files and folders that have been created by users. Instead, the application should be **uninstalled** as discussed in Section 1.5.1.

Deleting items does not remove them completely, but moves them to the **Recycle Bin** folder. The **Recycle Bin** is represented by an icon on the desktop.

Recycle Bin

The item will remain in there and can be retrieved until the Recycle Bin is emptied. The deleted items still take up the same amount of disk space when in the Recycle Bin, so to free that disk space (and delete items permanently), the Recycle Bin must be emptied. When the Recycle Bin is emptied, as far as Windows XP is concerned, the items in the Recycle Bin are gone.

NOTE

Even if the Recycle Bin is emptied, the contents are **still** not necessarily gone forever. The Recycle Bin records that the space used by the files in the Trash is available again for other files to use, but does not necessarily remove the data that comprises the files themselves.

There is **utility software** available that can then **undelete** these files. This software can be invaluable for retrieving important information, perhaps files deleted mistakenly or damaged as a result of a crash.

This also presents a security risk. If an old computer is sold or donated after all the files on the hard disk have been deleted, it may still be possible for a third party to undelete them. There are still other utilities that will securely overwrite the space used by deleted files ensuring that they really are gone forever. This is a common requirement for computers used by the military and governments.

There are various ways to delete an item (or items).

- **Using Drag and Drop**: An item or items can be dragged and dropped into the Recycle Bin. Select an item or items and drag and drop the selection over the Recycle Bin icon.

- **Using the Menu**: To delete an item or items using a menu, select what is to be deleted, right-click the selection and choose **Delete** from the menu.

- **Using the Keyboard**: Select the item or items to be deleted and press the **Delete** key on the keyboard.

    Whichever method is used, a confirmation window will always appear as a precaution.

- Click **Yes** to confirm the deletion.

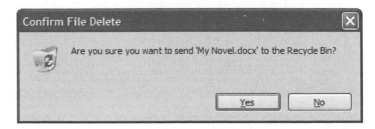

2.8.2   Restoring Files and Folders (2.2.5.2)

Deleting items moves them to the Recycle Bin. Items that are in the Recycle Bin folder can still be restored, or **undeleted**.

To retrieve an item, do the following:

- Double-click the Recycle Bin icon.
  The **Recycle Bin** window opens.

Recycle Bin

- Select the item or items to be restored from the **Recycle Bin**.
- Right-click on the selected item(s).
- Select **Restore** from the pop-up menu that opens.

> **NOTE**
> The item will automatically be restored to its last location before it was deleted.

2.8.3   Emptying the Recycle Bin (2.2.5.3)

To remove items completely, the Recycle Bin must be emptied. Open the Recycle Bin first and double-check that it is safe to delete its contents. Individual items in the Recycle Bin can be deleted or the entire folder can be emptied.

Deleting Individual Items

To delete an individual item in the Recycle Bin permanently, do the following:

- Double-click the **Recycle Bin** icon.
  The **Recycle Bin** window opens.
- Select the item to be deleted.
- Right-click the selection.
- Select **Delete** from the pop-up menu that opens.

To Empty All Items from the Recycle Bin

To delete all items in Recycle Bin permanently, do the following:

- Right-click the Recycle Bin icon.
- Select **Empty Recycle Bin** from the pop-up menu that opens.

2.9   Searching

The Windows XP Search Companion tool enables various search criteria to be used to find files or folders. This is a vital ability as hard disk capacity increases and computers are used to store many thousands of files. It is available on the Start menu and on the toolbar within each open window.

The default Search Companion window looks like the illustration on the right.

This manual will assume that the animated character is turned on.

- Click the **Change Preferences** option in the pane on the left. A preferences menu will be displayed.

- Click **Turn off the animated character**.

In general, the Search Companion works by the user supplying search **criteria** using the options in the pane on the left of the window.

Results, if any, are displayed in the main section of the window when the search is completed or stopped by the user.

The files listed can be manipulated (copied, deleted, moved, etc.) in the normal way.

The files in the search results may be located in different folders.

To open the actual folder that a particular item resides in, do the following:

- Right-click the file in the results list.
- Select **Open Containing Folder** from the pop-up menu that opens.

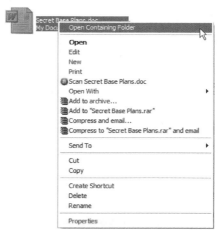

2.9.1   Searching for a File or Folder Using All or Part of Its Name (2.2.6.2)

To search for a specific document or folder, at least part of its name must be known.

- Click the **Start** button and select **Search** from the Start menu.

  The **Search Results** window opens.

  There are several types of file and folder search options on the pane to the left of the window.

- Using these, search options can be limited to **Pictures, Music or video** files, **Documents** such as those produced by Microsoft Office 2007, or **All Files And Folders**. Limiting the search appropriately will complete the search more quickly.

- Click the **Documents (word processing, spreadsheet, etc.)** option.

  The **Search Criteria** window opens.

- Enter the name or part of the name in the **All or part of the document** name box.

- Click **Search** to begin searching the document folders first (i.e. folders such as **My Documents**, etc.).

- When the Search Companion has looked in these folders, it continues to search other areas of the computer.

  The search results are listed in the main part of the window. If the required items have been found, the search operation can be stopped using the **Stop** button.

When a search has been stopped or is complete, the Search Companion window presents another series of choices.

- Select an appropriate option from the Search Companion window or click **Start a new search** to search again if the required file/folder was not found.

- If you have finished using the Search Companion, click the **Close X** button on the toolbar at the top of the screen.

2.9.2   Searching for Content (2.2.6.2)

One of the main criteria used to search for files or folders is by content. In searching for all files relating to or mentioning **Blackrock**, for example, the files would probably all have very different names. In this case searching file content, rather than filenames, would be more likely to locate all relevant files.

To search for file content, do the following:

- Open the **My Computer** window.

- On the toolbar, click **Search**.
  The **Search Results** window opens.

- Click the **Documents (word processing, spreadsheet, etc.)** option.

- Click the **Use advanced search options** link.

- Type the text that will be searched for in the **A word or phrase in the document:** box.

- Select any of the other search options if you wish to refine the search further.

- Click **Search** to begin searching.

2.9.3   Searching for Files by Date, Type and Size (2.2.6.3)

Searching by Date Last Modified

To search by the date a file or folder was last modified, do the following:

- Open the **My Computer** window.

- On the toolbar, click **Search**.
  The **Search Results** window opens.

- Click the **All Files and Folders** option.

- Select **Modified Date** from the drop-down menu under **Specify dates**.

- Enter a date or date range.

- Continue searching in the usual way.

Searching by Date Created

To search by the date a file or folder was created, do the following:

- Open the **My Computer** window.

- On the toolbar, click **Search**.
  The **Search Results** window opens.

- Click the **All Files and Folders** option.

- Select **Created Date** from the drop-down menu under **Specify dates**.

- Enter a date or date range.

- Continue searching in the usual way.

Searching by File Size

Files of a particular size can be searched for. For example, a user may want to find files that are **at least** or **at most** a particular size in **kilobytes (KB)**.

To search by file size, do the following:

- Open the **My Computer** window.

- Click **Search**.

- In the Search Companion box, click the **Documents** (**word processing**, **spreadsheet**, etc.) option.

- Click the **Use advanced search options** link.

- Click the **What size is it** chevron button.

- Make a selection from the available options.

- Be more specific with the size by using the **Specify size (in KB)** boxes.

- Continue searching in the usual way.

Searching by File Type

To search by file type, do the following:

- Open the **My Computer** window.

- Click **Search**.

- In the Search Companion box, click the **All Files and Folders** option.

- Click the **More advanced options** link.

- Click the drop-down arrow for the **Type of file** box.

Scroll through the available list and select the file type to search for.

- Continue searching in the usual way.

NOTE
The various methods discussed above can be combined to refine the search as much as possible, and ensure that it completes quickly.

2.9.4   Using Wildcards in Searches (2.2.6.4)

A wildcard character is a keyboard character – such as an asterisk (*) or a question mark (?) – that can be used to represent one or more real characters in a name. It is a particularly useful tool when a filename cannot be remembered precisely.

Question Mark (?):
The question mark can be used as a substitute for a single character in a name. For example, if **hot?.docx** was entered, files such as Hot1.docx and Hots.docx would be located, but not Hotel.docx.

Asterisk (*):
You can use the asterisk as a substitute for zero or more characters. If you're looking for a file that you know starts with **hot** but you cannot remember the rest of the file name, type: **hot***. This will return all files (Word, Excel, Access, etc.) that begin with the letters **hot**.

If you know the file you are searching for is a Word file, adding the Word extension (.docx) will narrow the search to that file type, for example, entering **hot*.docx** will find all files that begin with **hot** and have the file extension **.docx**, such as **Hotel.docx** and **Hotspot.docx**.

To search for all files of a particular type, the * plus the **file extension** (.doc, .xls, .rtf) can be used. For example entering the search criteria ***.doc** will return all Word files, entering ***.xls** will return all Excel files, and so on.

2.9.5   Viewing Recently Used Files (2.2.6.5)

The most recent documents used can be accessed by selecting the **Office Button** and then selecting a file from the **Recent Documents** list.

Select a recently opened
file from the **Recent
Documents** list

To change the number of documents listed in Recent Documents, do the following:

- Select the **Office Button** followed by **Word Options**.

- Select the **Advanced** button and scroll down to the **Display** section.

- Enter the number of recent documents that should display in the Office Button menu.

Adjust the number of
files to be displayed

2.10   Compressing Files

2.10.1   What File Compression Means (2.2.7.1)

It is possible to reduce the size of some files so that they take up less space on the computer or so they can be transferred across a network, including the internet, more efficiently. The process for doing this is referred to as compressing.

It is important to note that not all files can be compressed equally. Text files may be compressed by up to 90 per cent. Files produced by Microsoft Office 2007, such as .docx files, or graphic image file formats, such .jpeg or .gif, will not normally compress further except by very small amounts, because they are already compressed internally.

A large file attachment that is emailed to a recipient who does not have a fast internet connection can take a long time to download. If the file was compressed before it was sent, the number of bytes to be sent would be reduced and so the time taken to download would be less. The recipient would also need to be able to **extract** the original file from the compressed file using the relevant software.

A very simple example of one type of compression would be as follows.

A file contains the following text: **88888AAA2222222222**.

There are 18 characters present, taking up a certain amount of space. A program is used to **compress** the file, resulting in a **compressed** version containing the following: **8[5]A[3]2[10]**.

2

That file obviously takes up less space – 13 characters. If that compressed file is processed by an **extraction** utility program, that utility knows for example that 2[10] should be expanded back to the original form, i.e. **2222222222**.

There are different methods that can be used to compress files, such as ZIP, RAR and LHA. The standard for compression in the Windows world is the **Zip** format. This format is a **standard**, in the same way as JPEG-format graphic files conform to that particular standard. As a result, there are many pieces of **utility** software such as ZipGenius and WinZip that can work with these .zip files. These utilities are **archivers** as well as **compressors**. In other words, they can be supplied with a list of files or folders and will compress each one individually before then rolling them all up into one compressed file.

Extracting the contents of this file in another location or on another computer will then recreate all the files and folders archived within it. This makes the compression process even more useful for transferring files since it not only makes the overall size smaller, it can also bundle multiple files into one.

For example, this is a **zip file**.

Finance
Department.zip

Opening it with the WinRAR utility shows that it contains compressed files and folders.

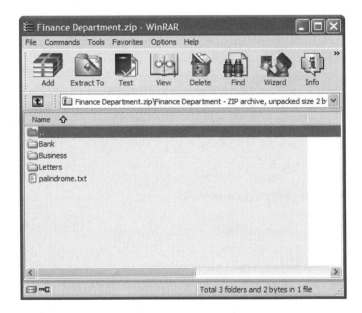

Windows XP has the built-in ability to work with Zip files. One advantage of this is that if Windows is allowed to handle zip files instead of a third-party utility, then those zip files work exactly like normal folders. Double-clicking one will open its contents in a normal window and the contents can be acted upon as with any window.

This manual will use this standard Windows XP functionality in any examples.

2.10.2 Compressing a Single File (2.2.7.2)
To compress a single file, do the following:

- Locate the item to be compressed.
- Right-click the item.
- Click **Send To** on the pop-up menu that opens.

- Click the **Compressed (zipped) Folder** option on the sub-menu.

If the file is large, the compression make take some time. If this is the case a progress window will be displayed.

- The compressed filename will be the name of the file but with a .zip extension.

2.10.3 Compressing a Single Folder (2.2.7.2)

A single folder can be archived and compressed in exactly the same way as a single file. Note that this is a **recursive** procedure – in other words everything inside the folder and any sub-folders will be included.

NOTE

Multiple files and folders can be selected and compressed using the same method as single files and folders.

2.10.4 Viewing the Contents of Compressed Files

Double-clicking a compressed file will open it in a normal window, assuming a third-party utility, such as ZipGenius, has not been installed and is not associated with zip files.

2.10.5 Extracting Files and Folders (2.2.7.3)

To use the files in a compressed file again, they must be extracted. Either everything in a compressed file or folder can be extracted or just selected items.

To extract the entire contents of the compressed file, do the following:

- Copy the compressed file to the location where the files are to be saved after extraction.
- Right-click the compressed file, select **Extract Here** from the pop-up menu.
  The contents will be extracted.
  If there are folders involved, the folder structure and contents will be recreated.

Extracting a single item from a compressed file, do the following:

- Double-click the compressed file to open it in a window.
- Locate the item to be extracted.
- Copy or move the item out of the window in the normal way.
- The zip file will be updated automatically.

Section 3   Maintaining Systems

3.1   Introduction

Before you can perform basic system maintenance on your computer, you need to be able to identify the different components of a computer. This enables you to perform basic checks, such as ensuring that cables are attached securely in the correct ports/sockets.

3.1.1 Typical Components

Typical components of a computer system comprise: the system box (base unit), which houses the central processing unit (CPU) and holds the programs that are used to make the computer function; a monitor to view data and graphics; a mouse to select menu and toolbar options, icons, and objects; a keyboard to input data; and a printer to produce hard copy of monitor output.

The computer can be in the form of a system box which sits beneath the monitor or as a tower which usually sits beneath the desk. The back of the computer housing contains ports to connect peripherals, such as the monitor, mouse, keyboard and printer.

Other peripheral devices may be connected, such as external disk or CD/DVD drive, USB memory drive, microphone, web camera, scanner or digital camera.

3.1.2 Computer Peripherals

Regardless of the type of computer you use – e.g. tower or box – ports will exist to enable the connection of peripherals, such as the basic components of monitor, mouse, keyboard and printer.

Other types of peripheral devices are listed below.

External drives	USB memory drive
Scanner	Web camera
Speakers	
Microphone	Digital camera

3.1.3 Ports and Sockets

Ports are sockets that enable peripheral devices to connect to the computer. On computers manufactured before 2006, the **keyboard** and **mouse** are connected to the computer via PS2 sockets.

 PS/2 ports (purple for keyboard and green for mouse)

Parallel ports are used for connecting printers to the computer. The image below shows the port on the computer; the corresponding port on the printer would have pins. Most modern computers now connect via USB ports.

 Parallel ports connect printers to the computer
(there are two types of parallel ports: LPT1 and LPT2).
These ports have mostly superseded by USB ports

USB ports connect peripherals, such as memory drives, digital cameras, etc., to the computer.

 There are two types of USB connector, A and B.
The A connector inserts into the computer port and the B
connector connects to the peripheral device. **Firewire** connectors
are used for transferring data to and from digital devices, such as
digital cameras, at higher speeds than a USB device.

Laptop computers often need a docking station to provide extra ports,
as well as extra drives. To provide more ports on a personal computer,
a USB hub can be purchased. This is handy if you use many peripheral
devices (camera, speakers, microphone, memory drives, etc.).

3.2 Understanding and Performing Routine Maintenance (2.3.1.1)

A routine maintenance procedure should be scheduled to be performed at set intervals, e.g. daily, weekly or monthly. Regular use of scheduled activities is referred to as 'housekeeping' and ensures the smooth running of a computer system. Simple routines, such as shutting down the computer correctly, can be an important part of regular maintenance – an incorrect shutdown procedure can result in screen freeze and start-up errors. It is important to take safety precautions when dealing with any electrical equipment and routine maintenance should be performed using the manufacturer's guidelines.

Routine and scheduled activities include the following.

- Ensuring that the computer is shut down correctly on a daily basis.
- Making regular backups of data.
- Cleaning components (keyboard, mouse, screen, etc.).
- Using anti-virus software to scan and prevent viruses, adware and spyware.
- Removing old and temporary files and outdated software.
- Setting scheduled tasks, such as check disk, to search for file errors, disk de-fragmenter to speed up file access, running Window Updates and regularly scanning for viruses.

> **NOTE**
> New equipment will come with manufacturer's guidelines for installation and routine maintenance requirements, such as cleaning components to increase the life span of the product. If you don't have the manufacturer's guidelines, for example when buying a second-hand computer, visit the manufacturer's website to download information or find contact details.
>
> It is important that any maintenance is performed using the manufacturer's advice and guidance, particularly if the equipment is still under warranty and/or you are an inexperienced user.

3.2.1 Basic Checks (2.3.1.2)

Basic checks should be performed on a regular basis to ensure trouble-free computer usage.

The basic checks that you should perform at start-up are:

- **Check power**: Is the computer connected to the mains electricity source and is the socket switched on?

- **Ports and cables**: Are all cables connected to the correct ports? If unsure about a connection, remove the cable from the socket and reinsert. Push the connector firmly into the socket/port.

- **Check for lights**: Is the green power light on the computer and also on the monitor lit. If the monitor does not display press the space bar or move the mouse to check this is caused by the screen saver.

- **Check printer**: Is the printer connected to a mains electricity socket. Are both ends of the connector firmly inserted into the correct port on the computer and the printer? Is there a green light on the printer? If a light is flashing (usually amber), this could indicate that the printer is offline, is out of paper, has a paper jam or the toner cartridge is empty and needs replacing.

Some of the common error indicators (and possible solutions) to look for at start-up are listed below.

- Lack of monitor display could be caused by:
    o The monitor not being switched on, in which case turn it on;

  o The cable connecting it to the computer not being inserted correctly, in which case remove the cable and reinsert it correctly;

  o The computer being on standby or being switched off, in which case, switch the computer on;

  o The monitor being faulty, in which case try the monitor with a different computer – if it still doesn't work, the monitor is faulty; if it does work, the problem is with the original computer; or

  o a faulty graphics component in the computer, in which case consult a reputable IT technician.

- Messages display on the monitor when a problem occurs – do not ignore these messages. Make notes of the problem, such as the error name or error code that is provided. Sometimes, an error message will give the solution to the problem but other times it will request that the user contact the software/hardware provider for help.

- If your computer displays an error message within a few seconds of starting, you may have a hardware configuration problem. If the Windows logo displays, you may have a start-up problem which could be due to a new piece of hardware, a new program or a corrupted system file. If you get a non-system disk or disk error message, you have a disk error which means that Windows cannot be found. If you don't even see the start-up screen, you probably have a hardware problem.

- Flashing lights on a printer can indicate a lack of paper, a paper jam, that the printer toner cartridge needs refilling/replacing. Check that the printer is connected to a power supply and that the power is on at the socket, that the cable is secured firmly to the port on the printer and computer, ensure that the power is switched on at the printer, check the paper tray and refill if necessary, check the printer cartridge.

- Beeps can indicate a problem with the computer or with the keyboard; if it is a keyboard problem it may be caused by a stuck key or indicate that the keyboard requires cleaning. If this is the case, just up end the keyboard to shake out any debris and use a wipe to clean between the keys.

- If the computer beeps on start up, it could indicate a Memory Display Read/Write failure. To test where the problem originates, disconnect the keyboard cable from the port at the back of the computer (on computers before 2006 this will probably be a purple coloured PS/2 port; post-2006 it will probably be a USB port) and reconnect to another computer. If the same problem occurs, then the problem is with the keyboard, not the computer. Please note that PS/2 connectors should not be disconnected whilst the computer is on.

- If the mouse cursor is not visible check that the mouse is connected to the port. If using an optical or wireless laser mouse, ensure that the batteries are working and ensure that it is not being affected by other electronic devices nearby. If using a roller ball mouse, ensure that it is clean by opening the back of the mouse and using an alcohol rub to clean the ball and a cotton swab to clean the guides inside the mouse.

3.2.2 Performance and Maintenance (2.3.1.2)

Performance and maintenance of your computer can be managed via the Control Panel. In Category View, these tools are grouped under the **Performance and Maintenance** heading; in Classic View, they are displayed as individual icons.

- Administrative Tools.
- Power Options.
- Scheduled Tasks.
- System.

We will look at each of these options in turn.

Administrative Tools

This window provides options to manage performance and collect and view data.

Administrative
Tools

- **Component Services**: This is used by the system administrator to administer programs or automate administrative tasks. This service is also used by software developers configure routine component or program behaviour.

- **Computer Management**: This is used to manage local or remote computers. This tool combines several administrative tools in one area, providing easy access to computer managers/administrators.

- **Data Sources (ODBC)**: ODBC stands for Open Database Connectivity and is a programming interface that enables programs to access data in database management systems.

- **Event Viewer**: This is used to view and manage logs of system, program and security events on your computer. It gathers information about hardware and software problems and monitors security events. It displays monitoring and troubleshooting messages from Windows and other programs.

- **Local Security Policy**: This is used to configure security settings for the local computer, such as user rights, password policy, audit policies and other security options.

- **Performance**: This is used to collect and view data about memory, disk, processor, network and other activity in a graph or report format.

- **Services**: This is used to manage services on your computer, set recovery actions and creates custom names and descriptions of services so that they can be identified.

Power Options

This enables the user to configure energy saving settings, thereby reducing power consumption of computer devices.

Power Options

Through this window you can:
- Turn off the monitor and hard disks automatically to save power.
- Put the computer on stand-by when it is idle.
- Put the computer into 'hibernation'.

You can set the computer to use your own predefined settings, such as turning off the monitor and hard disks for short periods to conserve power; using stand-by mode when the computer is idle to place the computer in a low energy state; using hibernation to save everything in memory on the hard disk, before turning off the monitor and hard disk and then turning off the computer. Be aware that leaving your computer in stand-by mode during a power failure may result in loss of data. You can also use Power Options to set an alarm when the battery reserve power falls below the critical level you have set.

Scheduled Tasks

This enables the user to schedule computer tasks to run automatically. This can include virus scanning software, program updates or other tasks that should run at a scheduled time. The image below displays virus scanning software scheduled to scan a computer at 20:00 every Friday and provides the Next and Last Run Time. Other scheduled tasks are also listed.

Scheduled Tasks

Scheduled tasks starts each time you start Windows and runs in the background. With Scheduled Tasks, you can also do the following.

- Schedule a task to run daily, weekly, monthly or at certain times (such as system start up).
- Change the schedule for a task.
- Stop a scheduled task.
- Customise how a task will run at a scheduled time.

To schedule a task, do the following:

- From the **Start** menu select **All Programs** and then **Accessories**.
- Select **System Tools** and then **Scheduled Tasks**.
  The **Scheduled Tasks** window opens.
- Double-click **Add Scheduled Task** and follow the step-by-step instructions in the wizard to add a task.
  On completion of the wizard, the scheduled task will appear in the Scheduled Tasks list.

Check Disk

Check Disk searches disk drives, such as the local hard drive (C:), or removable storage areas, such as a USB drive, for disk errors.

To perform a Check Disk procedure, do the following:

- From the **My Computer** window right-click the drive to be checked for errors and select **Properties**.
- Select the **Tools** tab and then, from the **Error Checking** section of the Properties window, click the **Check Now** button.
  The **Check Disk** window opens.

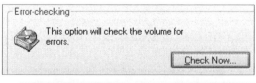

- Check the boxes for the required procedure, e.g. **Automatically fix file system errors** or **Scan for and automatically fix bad sectors**.
- Click **Start** to begin checking the selected disk drive.

Choose a Check Disk option

Disk De-fragmenter

De-fragmenting a disk helps to speed up the process of accessing files on your computer.

To de-fragment a disk, do the following:

- From the **My Computer** window right-click the drive to be defragmented and select **Properties**.

- Select the **Tools** tab and then, from the **Defragmentation** section of the Properties window, click the **Defragment Now** button. The **Disk Defragmenter** window opens.

- Select the drive to be defragmented.

- Click the **Defragment** button.

- Click **Pause** or **Stop** to temporarily or permanently halt the progress of the defragment procedure if required.

Backups

Information on a computer is stored electronically. Because of this, there is always a possibility that it can be lost because of a malfunction in the system or through human error (other causes include flood, theft, fire, viruses, unauthorised entry, hard disk corruption and power surges). To avoid total loss of data, it is important to have copies of all important files stored on disks or other removable media. These copies are called **backups**.

Backups can be made in several ways. Copies can be made to external hard disks or burned on to a CD or DVD. USB Memory drives are known as Solid State Technology (no spinning parts as in a CD/DVD drive), and are capable of storing larger amounts of data, ranging from megabytes to gigabytes. You can add more drives to your computer as required, but you may need to purchase a USB hub to provide extra ports/sockets.

The data from some files may also be kept as hard copy. These backups should be kept in a safe and secure place, e.g. locked away in fireproof containers or off the premises at a remote location. Storage space can be a limitation when backing up data, particularly if the data is being stored off-site. Costs of the removable storage media is another factor to be taken into consideration. A log of backed-up data should be kept to facilitate rotational backup procedures.

Remote backups are now offered by internet service providers over broadband internet connections but these are not recommended for sensitive or confidential data.

Disk Cleanup (2.3.1.6)

Disk Cleanup is used to clear disk space on the computer and delete unwanted files.

Unwanted files could be one or more of the following.

- As you use applications to create documents and files on your computer, temporary files are created and stored.
- Temporary files are created when you browse the internet.
- Unwanted and old program files remain on your computer unless deleted.
- Files deleted from the hard drive are stored in the Recycle Bin until permanently deleted.

All of these files use up space on the hard disk.

To remove unwanted files, do the following:

- From the **Start** menu, select **All Programs**.
- Select **Accessories** and then **System Tools** and finally click **Disk Cleanup**.
- Disk Cleanup will search drives and display temporary files for you to delete.

3.3   Understanding Non-Routine Maintenance (2.3.1.3 and 2.3.1.4)

Non-routine maintenance is a task or tasks not on a list of scheduled tasks that is performed manually by a computer user. Non-routine maintenance may involve opening the back panel of the computer to clean or change components; reformatting the hard drive, partitioning the hard drive and reinstalling the operating systems or dealing with unexpected hardware failure.

Non-routine maintenance can also be maintenance that an inexperienced computer user cannot perform, sometimes involving technical knowledge and practical skill beyond that of a home user or office worker. Some non-routine maintenance should be left to the experts, such as the network manager in a large company or college, or a skilled technician.

The following are examples of non-routine maintenance.

Simple unscheduled tasks within scope of inexperienced user

- A
  ny task not on a scheduled list, such as using the Task Manager to deal with non-responding programs.
- B
  acking up files outside of scheduled tasks.

Complex unscheduled task requiring skilled experienced user or technician

- R
  emoval of the back panel of the computer to change the motherboard or circuits.
- D
  ealing with hardware failure.

It is important that maintenance outside the scope of an unskilled or inexperienced computer user is left to a skilled technician. If the equipment is still under warranty, you should contact the supplier manufacturer before trying to perform non-routine maintenance or resolve computer problems. If the equipment is not under warranty, you should take your computer to a reputable computer repair company or shop, such as PC World.

3.4   Cleaning Components (2.3.1.5)

To ensure the smooth running of a computer system, it is important that exterior computer components, such as keyboard, mouse, screen, peripherals or casing, are kept free from dust and dirt. Maintaining a dust and dirt free environment will help to improve the running of the computer and prevent ventilation areas getting clogged up.

To clean exterior components, do the following:

- Ensure that the cleaning material is free from fluff.
- Ensure that the cloth is barely damp, not wet, when wiping exterior components (**never** wet the insides of a computer casing or the components within a computer).
- Spray cleaning fluid onto the cleaning rag, not the component.
- Use a hand-held vacuum cleaner to clean fluff and dust from ventilation areas.
- Keyboard and mouse can be cleaned by:
  - shaking them upside down to remove loose dirt;
  - using a small brush to brush dust away from keys;
  - using a damp rag to clean spillages;
  - using a small vacuum cleaner to suck up dirt lodged between keys (be aware that if the suction is too great, it could also suck up the keys).
  - removing the back casing from a roller ball mouse and then remove the roller ball. Use a damp cotton swab or rag to clean the guides inside the mouse casing and use an alcohol rub to clean the ball.

3.5   Identifying and Resolving IT Problems (2.3.2.1 and 2.3.2.2)

Before you can resolve an IT problem, you must first perform a thorough check to identify the type of error.

Power

- Check the power supply. If the computer does not power up when turned on, try another electrical appliance in the same socket; if the appliance works then the problem is with the computer not the socket.

Connections

- Check all external connections and sockets. Look for bent pins, stray cables and loosely fitting connectors. Ensure that connectors at each end of the cable are inserted firmly into the port. Remember that the connector that fits into the computer port is different to the connector that will insert into the peripheral device. Look to see if the connector has pins and match it to the correct socket/port.

New Hardware Installed

- Check whether or not new hardware has been recently installed. If so, has it been configured properly? If the problem lies with newly installed hardware, you may need to remove it and reinstall it. Sometimes, new hardware is not compatible and needs to be removed or you may need to restart the computer so that new hardware can be found.

Printing

- Check that there is power at the socket.
- Check the cabling and connectors – is the cable securely connected to both computer and printer?
- Check that printer is on – check for the green light. If an amber light is flashing this could indicate that the printer has a paper jam, is out of paper, is offline, the toner cartridge needs refilling/replacing.
- Check the paper tray to ensure that it contains sufficient paper

- Check that there is not a paper jam – be very careful when dealing with a paper jam. The printer rollers may be very hot and cause burns and fingers may become trapped in the machine parts. First, cancel all print jobs and turn off the printer for several minutes to enable it to cool down. Contact a technician if the paper is jammed between rollers – do not tear at the paper as this may leave bits of paper behind and make it harder to retrieve the remainder.

- Check the printer cartridge – does it need refilling/replacing? Always use gloves to refill or remove a toner cartridge and be careful not to spill contents on bare skin. After handling toner, be careful not to touch eyes, nose or mouth before you have washed your hands.

Non-Responding Program

- If a program is not responding, hold down the **CTRL** + **ALT** keys and press **Delete** to display the Windows Task Manager. Select the non-responding program and then select **End Task**.

Error Dialog Boxes

- If an error dialog box appears check the error message and take the steps provided to resolve the problem or make a note of the error code/name and the problem and report to a technician if outside the scope of your experience.

Storage Full

- If the message is that the storage full, there are too many files stored on a drive and the capacity of the drive is exceeded. Delete unwanted and old files to free space on the drive.

Virus Threat

- Unfamiliar messages, screen freeze or programs slowing down can all mean a virus threat. If any of these occur run a virus scan to check for and eradicate threats.

Network Connections

- If a network connection is lost, the connection to a wireless cable or router may be lost. Go to Windows Network Connections **Start**, **Connect to**, **Show All Connections**. A network connection that is not connected will have a red X on them. If there is no red X, ensure all the cables are plugged in correctly. If the connection is still not available contact an IT technician.

3.5.1 Reporting IT problems (2.3.2.2)

Before reporting an error, check whether or not the error can be resolved by rebooting the computer. Make a note of any on-screen error messages, particularly the error name and code. Also make a note of the computer name, particularly if using a network, and the action you have already taken to resolve the error, such as rebooting. Note the date and time the error occurred and the effects of the error. Also make a note of the action you were trying to perform when the error occurred.

There should be a reporting procedures set up in your workplace, such as a questionnaire/error reporting form or online form, to help resolve errors. You should know who is in charge of resolving computer related problems – this is usually a resident technician, such as the system administrator or network manager.

There is little a home user can do to report IT problems. Microsoft provides an error reporting service for Windows operating systems – the information that they receive is used to track and resolve problems within the software. This may not be of immediate help to you or your particular problem but will help to resolve any further problems in updated software and prevent the same glitches.

3.5.2 Software Updates

Software companies, such as Microsoft, provide updates in the form of service packs (Microsoft provided Service Packs 1 and 2 for Windows XP). Service packs can provide updates on the following:

- Program reliability.
- Program compatibility.
- Security.

Software developers also provided patches that update previously purchased software. These can help resolve problems within some programs.

Visit the software supplier's website to download updates/service packs, or patches. Drivers may need to be installed before certain peripherals can be connected to your computer – drivers can also be found on the supplier's websites. Follow the on-screen instructions carefully to download the updates on your computer. Some updates come via storage media, such as CD-ROM. These will contain program files, called executable files (with an **.exe** extension), which will automatically run on your machine when you insert the CD into the drive.

Again, follow the instructions on screen carefully to load the update. Your workplace may upload drivers or updated software on a network for each member of staff to access – this could be on a Local Area Network within the site, or on a Wide Area Network, which covers more than one site. Updates may also be posted on the company intranet (internal internet system). Ask your network technicians or system administrator for advice on downloading updates from a networked drive as this procedure may be subject to limited access rights and be password protected.

> **NOTE**
> Executable files with an .exe extension can transfer viruses when run on your machine, so be very careful and only download updates from reputable and known sources.

3.5.3 Windows Updates

Windows can be set up to automatically look for and deliver important updates.

To set Windows to automatically look for updates, do the following:

- Select **My Computer** and then click **View System Information** under System Tasks.
- Select the **Automatic Updates** tab and select the **Automatic (recommended)** button.

- Choose a regular day and time for automatic updates to be downloaded onto your computer.
- Click OK.

  Automatic updates include security updates for your computer, so your computer could be more vulnerable if this option is disabled.

3.5.4 Windows Task Manager

Occasionally, a problem may arise where the computer appears to 'freeze' or where it ceases to respond to the mouse or keyboard. In this case, it is necessary to force the computer to end the task it is engaged in.

Using **Windows Task Manager** you can end programs or processes without having to turn off your computer. The Task Manager provides information about computer performance and displays details about programs and processes running on your computer. If you are connected to a network, you can also view your network status and how your network is functioning. Depending on your circumstances and whether or not you share your computer with other users, you can view additional information about those users.

To end a task that is not responding:

- Right-click an empty area on the **taskbar** and choose **Task Manager**.
  Alternatively, press **Ctrl + Alt + Delete**.
  The **Windows Task Manager** window opens. This window will display all open applications, folders and files.
  The Task Manager will display the status of the files (**Not Responding/Running**).
- Ensure the **Applications** tab is selected.
- Click the **Task** name for the non-responding application.

NOTE

In some instances, further choices and/or information may be presented to you by the Task Manager and you may have to progress through a sequence of choices before shutting down the non-responsive application.

- Click **End Task**.
  A confirmation window will open.
- Select **End Now**.

- You have the option of switching to another application by selecting the **Switch To** button.
- Create another task by selecting the **New Task** button and enter the name of the program/folder
  or file that you want Windows to open.
- If you do not know the name of the document, click **Browse** to locate the file.
  The Windows Task Manager menu options enable the user to log off, stand by, shut down or restart the computer.

- The Task Manager can be closed by clicking the Close X button or selecting **Exit Task Manager** from the **File** menu.

3.5.5 System Properties

System Properties enables the user to see information about the computer, change settings for hardware, performance and automatic updates. It helps the user resolve issues by locating any error indicators associated with the hardware.

The following section will help you understand how to access the properties of your computer system and also to differentiate between different storage areas.

System

- Click the **System** icon in the **Control Panel**.
  The **System Properties** window opens.
- Click the **Advanced** tab. This provides access to **Performance**, including visual effects, processor scheduling, memory usage and virtual memory.

- Select **Visual Effects** settings to change the appearance and performance of Windows on your computer (e.g., change how the menus animate).

- **User Profiles** enables you to change desktop settings related to your login. To create new user accounts, select User Accounts from the Control menu.

- **Startup and Recovery** enables you to change settings related to system start up, system failure and debugging information.

- The **Error Reporting** option enables you to send error reports to Microsoft to help improve future software products and prevent the same glitches.

  The user has the option of disabling or enabling the error reporting procedure and also choosing whether or not to report problems occurring in the Windows Operating system and/or programs.

  If the latter option is chosen, the user can choose the programs on which to report errors.

Other options within this window are:

- **System Restore**: This monitors your hard drive and helps to track and reverse harmful changes to your computer. You have the option to disable this tool if you wish.

- **Automatic Updates**: This checks regularly for important updates and installs them onto your computer at a date/time specified by you. This option can be disabled if wished, but please note allowing automatic updates may help protect the security of your computer.

- **Remote**: This enables the user to select ways that the computer can be used from another location, such as allowing users to connect remotely to your computer (user accounts must use passwords to perform this action).

- **Hardware**: This enables the user to see, and change the properties of, all of the hardware devices installed on their computer. There are also options to set up and store hardware configurations and ensure that drivers are compatible with Windows software.

- **Computer Name**: This enables the user to change the name of the computer and set up local user accounts on a network.
- **General**: The information about your computer can be viewed, including the system software name and type (e.g. Microsoft Windows XP, Service Pack 2), the registration details (name of owner or company to whom the operating system is registered), and the computer specifications, such as RAM, etc. You can also access general information about your computer by right-clicking the **My Computer** icon and selecting **Properties**.

The Local Disk is the hard drive or C: drive which is usually installed within the computer. You can also install an external hard drive if required.

To check for errors on the local drive, do the following:
- Right-click the **C:** drive icon in the My Computer window.
- Choosing **Properties** from the pop-up menu.
  The **Local Disk (C:) drive** window opens.
- Select the **Tools** tab.
- Select **Check Now** to scan the surface of the disk for inaccuracies.

3.5.6 Hardware Errors
Hardware errors may prevent access to certain drives. For example, hard drives can become corrupt and fail, due to virus infection or age (mechanical, moving parts wearing out). It is essential that a regular backing up system onto removable storage media is maintained in case of hard drive failure.

The warning signs of hard drive failure are:
- computer freezing regularly;
- losing files;
- computer locking up during start up;
- the hard drive making strange noises.

In the event of hardware failure, contact your manufacturer if under warranty. If your computer is not under warranty, you should take your computer to a reputable computer repair company or shop, such as PC World.

3.6   Identifying Sources of Help (2.3.2.3)
Sources of help for dealing with IT problems include the following.

- On-screen messages display when a problem occurs – do not ignore these messages. Make notes of the problem such as the error name or error code that is provided. The message may give a solution to the problem or it may request that the user contact their hardware or software provider for help.
- The application's Help facility.
- Manufacturer's guidance and advice on website or downloadable help sheets.
- Advice from a skilled technician or from the vendor.
- Forums and chat rooms.

Contact your manufacturer if the hardware is under warranty. If your computer is not under warranty, you should take your computer to a reputable computer repair company or shop, such as PC World.

3.7   Dealing with Expert Advice (2.3.2.4)
It is important that you are aware of your own limitations when dealing with IT problems and be prepared to gain expert advice if necessary.

Before gaining help and advice from a third party ensure you have the following:

- The computer (printer, scanner, etc.) make and model.
- Details of error message (error name or code).
- Computer (printer, scanner, etc.) date or version number.
- A description of the problem and any steps taken by you or other parties to resolve it.

Only act on advice from a reputable source from a skilled and experienced advisor. If in doubt, get a skilled technician to diagnose and resolve the problem.

- Be very careful when working with electrical equipment and take precautions.
- Wear protective gloves when dealing with printer toner or cleaning fluids.
- Turn off electrical equipment at the power socket before opening casings or dealing with cables.
- Ensure that equipment is cool before touching components (e.g. printer rollers can get very hot and burn your fingers).
- Never take the casing from the back of a computer which is still under warranty.

Section 4   Print Management

4.1   Introduction

In the home, it is not uncommon to have a single printer attached to a single computer. However, in an office network multiple printers are usually available to each user's computer. For example, an office might have a black and white laser printer dedicated to large-volume printing and a colour printer restricted to lower volume documents, such as presentations, brochures, invitations or report covers.

Before any printer can be used, Windows XP needs to know how to connect to it and communicate with it.

To enable the computer to operate a printer properly it is important that the appropriate **driver software** is installed. As part of the installation of the driver software, Windows XP also needs to be informed as to how the printer is connected to the computer, for example through a USB port or across a network.

To view the printers that have been installed, do the following:

- From the **Start** menu, select **Printers and Faxes**.

  The **Printers and Faxes** window opens.

  Icons for the printers that have been installed are displayed in the main part of the window.

Icons for the installed printers are displayed in the main part of the window

4.2   Changing the Default Printer (2.4.1.1)

Many printers can be installed in Windows XP, but only one printer is designated as the default printer, which is the printer that is automatically used for printing. A different printer can be specified in the print window when printing from applications, such as Microsoft Word.

The default printer is indicated with a tick in the **Printers And Faxes** window.

A tick denotes the default printer

To change the default printer, do the following:

- From the **Start** menu, select **Printers and Faxes**.

  The **Printers and Faxes** window opens.

- Right-click the printer to be set as the default.

- Select **Set as default printer** from the pop-up menu that opens.

4.3   Installing a New Printer or Printer Driver (2.4.1.2 and 2.4.3.4)

When installing a new printer that is directly connected to the computer, the exact manufacturer and printer model must be known as it is very important that the correct driver is installed. If this doesn't happen, the printer may not work or may produce output of a lower quality than it is capable of.

Windows XP comes with drivers for many common printers from many manufacturers, even older models. It is possible, though, that there isn't a driver available with Windows XP, especially for very new, very old or obscure devices. In this eventuality, the options are as follows.

- Check any CDs that came with the printer for a driver.
- Check the printer manufacturer's website for a driver.
- Read the documentation and see if any **generic** drivers will work – for example, almost all Hewlett Packard printers will print to some degree using a generic Hewlett Packard driver.
- Check the documentation and see what the printer **emulates**. Some printers can interpret data formulated for a different type of printer, if they are set to **emulate** or impersonate the other model.

The following sequence describes how to install a driver for a locally connected printer with a supplied Windows XP driver. Installing a network printer is a somewhat more complex task and will probably be automated or performed by a network technician.

To install a printer driver, do the following:

- Ensure the printer is connected to the computer. This could be via **parallel cable**, **USB**, **FireWire**, a **wireless connection**, etc.
- From the **Start** menu, open the **Printers and Faxes** window.
- Click **Add A Printer** in the task pane on the left.

Add a printer

The **New Printer** wizard will start.
- Click **Next**.

On the next page, the option to **Automatically detect and install my Plug and Play printer** will be preset.

Unless the printer is old and connected via a legacy connection, such as a parallel or serial cable, this setting should be left as it is.

Windows XP will search for newly connected printers and install the correct driver.

- Click **Next** until the last page of the wizard.
- Click **Finish**.

The new printer will be listed in the **Printer and Faxes** window.

4.4   Printing from an Application

When printing from an application, a **print job** is created and placed in the **print queue** for the printer. The queue enables many print jobs to be lined up, printed or deleted in an orderly fashion, so that the one printing job doesn't have to be completed before another can be sent.

The **print driver** is then used to translate the job into a form that the particular printer will understand, and finally it is sent to the printer itself. Reports come back from the printer about the progress of the job until it is complete, at which point it is removed from the queue.

4.4.1   Printing From WordPad (2.4.2.1)

Start **WordPad** from the **Accessories** menu (Open the Start menu, select All Programs, followed by Accessories and then Wordpad) and type in some text.

To print, do the following:

- Click the **Office Button** and select **Print** from the drop-down menu.

  The **Print** window opens, with the default printer already selected.

  A different printer can be selected from the list.

  The number of copies can be changed.

  The page(s), or range of pages to be printed can be changed.

Number of copies to be printed

Printer to be used

Pages to be printed

- When all the preferences have been set, click **Print**.

4.5   Viewing the Progress of Print Jobs (2.4.2.2)

It is possible to check the progress of a print job when it has been sent to the printer. This can be useful in estimating the time remaining for a large print job to complete.

To check the progress of a print job, do the following:

- Print from an application as normal.
- Open the **Printers and Faxes** window from the icon on the taskbar.
- Double-click the icon for the printer that the job was sent to.

    The printer queue contents will be shown in a window.

    The current status of any print jobs can be seen, along with the number of pages, the size and other information.

Printer icon

4.6   Managing Print Jobs (2.4.2.3)

It is also possible to manage a print job after it has been submitted. This is useful, for example, when a job needs to be cancelled.

To manage a print job, do the following:

- Print from an application as normal.
- Open the **Printers and Faxes** window from the icon on the taskbar.
- Double-click the icon for the printer that the job was sent to.

    The printer queue contents will be shown in a window.

- Right-click the job in the printer queue window.

Printer icon

- Select one of the options available from the drop-down menu.
  - o **Pause**: This pauses the selected job, which, for example, can be useful when more paper needs to be added to the printer. Select again to resume.
  - o **Restart**: This will restart a job from scratch, for example, in case there was a paper jam.
  - o **Cancel**: This will remove the job whether it is finished or not. Sometimes jobs get stuck in the queue and stop later jobs printing, this option can be useful in that situation to clear the traffic jam.

4.7   Printer Maintenance

Printer maintenance involves checking and replacing consumables, such as paper and toner cartridges, printing test pages and ensuring correct alignment of toner cartridges, dealing with paper jams and installing and updating printer driver files.

It is important to follow manufacturer's guidelines carefully when maintaining any electrical equipment. Ask advice from a skilled and experienced technician if in doubt. To find updates for your printer visit the manufacturer's website.

4.7.1 Printer Consumables (2.4.3.1)

Printer consumables are items that need to be replaced regularly such as paper and ink or toner cartridges.

The following indicates that printer consumables need replacing:
- Flashing lights on a printer can indicate the following:
  - a lack of paper;
  - a paper jam; and/or
  - that the printer toner cartridge needs refilling/replacing.

Before replacing printer consumables make the following checks.
- Check that there is power at the socket.
- Check the cabling and connectors. Is the cable securely connected to both computer and printer?
- Check that printer is on by looking for the green light. If an amber light is flashing, this could indicate that the printer has a paper jam, is out of paper, is offline or that the toner cartridge needs refilling/replacing.
- Check the paper tray to ensure that it contains sufficient paper.
- Check that there is not a paper jam. Be very careful when dealing with a paper jam (this will be indicated by a red exclamation mark). The printer rollers may be very hot and cause burns and fingers may become trapped in the machine parts. Cancel all print jobs first and turn off the printer for several minutes to enable it to cool down. Contact a technician if the paper is jammed between rollers – do not tear at the paper as this may leave bits of paper behind and make it harder to retrieve the remainder.
- Check the printer cartridge. Does it need refilling/replacing?

To replace printer consumables do the following:

Toner Cartridge

- Always use gloves to refill or remove a toner cartridge and be careful not to spill contents on bare skin.
- After handling toner, be careful not to touch eyes, nose or mouth before you have washed your hands.
- Check the manufacturer's guidelines for the type of toner cartridge required for your printer. Ensure that you know the make and model of your printer before going out to buy toner cartridges.
- Check the manufacturer's instructions for changing print cartridges – if you do not have these, go to the manufacturer's website.
- On some printers, the printer must be turned on before the cartridge can be removed. Ensure that it is turned off again before attempting to replace the cartridge.

Paper

- The paper tray may be at the bottom or paper may need to be fed at the top of the printer.
- Ensure that there are no print jobs being processed before opening the tray and replacing paper.

- Do not overfill the tray.
- Ensure that the paper is free from dirt and is not damp (also ensure that individual pieces of paper are not stuck together).
- Some paper may be too thick or too thin for your printer and cause a paper jam.
- Ensure that you are using the correct size of paper (e.g. A4).

4.7.2 Printer Tasks

To see available Printer Tasks, do the following:

- From the **Start** menu select the Control Panel.
- Click the **Printers and Faxes** icon.
- The **Printer and Faxes** window opens.
- Select a printer.
- The **Printer Tasks** pane becomes available.
- Click an options for instructions on the following:
  - Adding a printer.
  - Viewing the printer queue.
  - Selecting printer preferences.
  - Pausing printing.
  - Sharing the printer.
  - Renaming the printer.
  - Deleting the printer.
  - Setting printer properties.

Printer Tasks
Add a printer
See what's printing
Select printing preferences
Pause printing
Share this printer
Rename this printer
Delete this printer
Set printer properties

4.7.3 Visiting a Manufacturer's Website

To go to the manufacturer's website for advice, guidance or updates do the following:

- From the **Start** menu select the Control Panel.
- The **Control Panel** window opens.
- Select the **Printers and Faxes** icon.
- The **Printer and Faxes** window opens.
- Select a printer.
- Select the **Go to manufacturer's Web site** link.

See Also
Go to manufacturer's Web site

4.7.4 Printing a Test Page and Aligning Cartridges (2.4.3.2)

A test page is printed to test that all aspects of the printer are working correctly and to troubleshoot any printer issues. Toner cartridges need to be aligned correctly within the printer in order to work efficiently.

To print a test page, do the following:

- From the **Start** menu select the Control Panel.
- The **Control Panel** window opens.
- Select the **Printers and Faxes** icon.
- The **Printer and Faxes** window opens.
- Right-click the currently active printer and select **Properties**.
- The **Properties** window opens.
- Click the **Print Test Page** button.
- For further help in dealing with printer problems, cancel any open windows, deselect the printer and select the **Troubleshoot Printing** or **Get help with printing** links in the **Printer and Faxes** window.

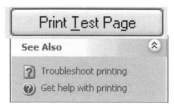

Toner cartridges should automatically align when replaced in the printer.

To align print cartridges, do the following:

- Right-click the printer and choose **Properties**.
  The **Properties** window opens.
- From the **Maintenance** tab choose the command to align the printer cartridges (this will differ depending on type of printer installed).

4.7.5 Dealing with Paper Jams (2.4.3.3)

If an amber light is flashing, this could indicate that the printer has a paper jam. Be very careful when dealing with a paper jam. The printer rollers may be very hot and cause burns and fingers may become trapped in the machine parts.

To clear a paper jam, do the following:

- Cancel all print jobs.
- Turn off the printer for several minutes to enable it to cool down.
- Open the printer (this may be at the front) and remove the paper (this may also involve removing the toner cartridge).

  Contact a technician if the paper is jammed between rollers – do not tear at the paper as this may leave bits of paper behind and make it harder to retrieve the remainder.

Section 5   Health and Safety

5.1   Ergonomics

5.1.1   Definition (2.5.1.1)
Ergonomics is the study of the interaction of workers with their environment, especially the equipment and machines they use. The main concern of ergonomics is that people can work with equipment safely and efficiently.

5.1.2   Lighting (2.5.1.2)
An important element of a worker's environment is the amount of light available and its direction to ensure that there is adequate visibility to undertake any work safely.

Areas to be aware of include:

- Ensuring that adequate lighting is available to reduce headaches and eye strain as well as mental fatigue and low morale.
- Installing appropriate lighting fixtures to reduce glare and ensure an even distribution of illumination that eliminates shadows.
- Using a desk lamp to provide local illumination where necessary.
- Positioning the monitor to avoid glare from lighting or from windows.
- Fitting windows with adjustable blinds to remove any reflection from the screen.

5.1.3   Desk Position and Posture (2.5.1.3)
The position of a desk, chair, foot or arm rests, and any computer hardware required to undertake the required work are of paramount consideration. The desk, chair and any rests necessary should ensure good posture and alleviate physical strain. The position of the keyboard, monitor, etc. should ensure that a worker is able to work in a comfortable environment.

Areas to be aware of include:

- Using an adjustable chair that conforms to current health standards.
- Using a chair with adjustable height and backrest facilities.
- Using a foot or arm rest if required.
- Ensuring the under-desk knee and thigh clearances are adequate for workers.
- Ensuring the elbow angle of workers is between 90° and 110°.
- Ensuring the worker is in a position to look down, not up, at the monitor.
- Placing the monitor on the desk rather than on top of the CPU box for the correct viewing level and to avoid neck strain.
- Setting the monitor back on the desk to avoid eye strain.
- Ensuring that the mouse and keyboard are positioned so that they do not cause discomfort.
- Having the keyboard and mouse at the correct level for the individual user.

The illustrations on page 90 are given as examples of a good arrangement for computer users. Please note that these recommendations are only general guidelines, manufacturer's guidelines and local health authority recommendations should always be consulted and followed.

Desktop Computers

Arms should be at an angle between 90° and 110°.

The top of the monitor should be at or slightly below eye level.

The back should be supported from the pelvis to the shoulder blades.

The angle of the knee should be greater than 90°.

Use footrest if required

Laptop Computers

The top of the monitor should be at eye level.

Arms should be at an angle between 90° and 110°.

The back should be supported from the pelvis to the shoulder blades.

The angle of the knee should be greater than 90°.

5.1.4   Other Precautions (2.5.1.4)

Stress-related illness can result from improper working conditions and practices. To avoid these and other problems and create a good working environment, simple precautions should be taken in the computer work environment.

2

- Areas to be aware of include:
- Ensuring the work area is comfortable and that an adequate temperature is maintained.
- Ensuring that there is adequate ventilation.
- Taking regular breaks to stretch and relax muscles in addition to using eye relaxation techniques, such as focusing on objects outside a window.
- Fitting a monitor filter to eliminate glare and eye strain.
- Use a document holder beside the screen and at the same level to minimise head and eye movements.
- Use the mouse on a mouse mat so that it will move smoothly.
- Complying with local fire and safety regulations.
- Examining plugs, sockets and leads for defects and have any necessary repairs carried out by qualified personnel.

5.2   Risks from Using IT (2.5.2.1)

Good health and safety guidelines should also include recognising hazards concerning hardware and to prevent accidents happening.

These include the following:
- Do not overload power sockets.
- Ensure all IT hardware and consumables are disposed of correctly (see Section 5.4).
- Ensure any cables are securely tied back to prevent a tripping hazard.
- Ensure walkways are free from obstruction, e.g. boxes, bags, etc.
- Ensure that electrical equipment is tested regularly.
- Always follow the correct procedure when lifting or moving hardware.
- Always turn off power before attempting any maintenance.

Guidelines on health and safety in the workplace can be found on the Health and Safety Authority website (www.hsa.ie). See also Section 5.1.

5.3   IT Guidelines and Procedures (2.5.2.2)

Guidelines and procedures for the correct and acceptable use of IT, should be provided by all employers and other organisations, such as colleges, to anyone authorised to use their computer systems.

These guidelines are an important because they:
- help to ensure a secure computing environment;
- prevent misuse and overuse of resources, e.g. printers and disk space;
- prevent intimidation and harassment by e-mail and other methods;
- protect the organisation in the event of its computing resources being used for illegal activities; and
- provide a legal mechanism for removing offending users from the organisation when necessary.

5.3.1 Learning and Adhering to Relevant Guidelines and Procedures

An organisation's procedures and guidelines, including its privacy policy, are normally provided to employees when they first join the organisation as part of the standard induction process, for example by the human resources department or college administration office. They may also be provided directly by the department or individual responsible for information technology within the organisation. Most organisations will also provide a copy of their guidelines on their website.

If necessary, employees should approach their immediate line manager for clarification of any part of the guidelines and procedures that are not clear. In an academic situation, the department or individual responsible for information technology should be contacted.

It is important that all stated guidelines and procedures are adhered to at all times, as failure could result in disciplinary proceedings up to and including expulsion from a particular organisation.

5.3.2 IT Security Checks
Guidelines and procedures will often detail checks for which users are responsible (see Section 6).

These include the following:
- Changing passwords regularly, taking into account rules for choosing strong passwords.
- Not sharing login details, as all activity that takes place under a particular login is the owner's responsibility.
- Maintenance of personal accounts to limit disk space usage.
- Encrypting confidential information.
- Performing anti-virus scans.
- Not participating in any activity that would potentially result in a malware incident.

5.3.3 Reporting Breaches of Guidelines and Procedures
Employees should report any breaches of the guidelines, either on the part of themselves or any another individual, that they become aware of. In the workplace, employees should contact their manager and, in universities, etc., the department or individual responsible for information technology should be contacted. If users do not know who to contact, they should report any breaches to an immediate line manager, college department head, etc.

5.4 Using and Disposing of Cleaning Materials (2.5.2.3)
Any materials used in the day-to-day cleaning of IT equipment and a user's working space should be disposed of in a safe and responsible manner.

The following guidelines should be adhered to.
- Always wear protective gloves when handling toxic fluids.
- Do not mix cleaning fluids as this may cause a chemical reaction.
- Ensure that cleaning fluids are kept in their original containers and that the labels to these containers, which provide information on the product or manufacturer, are not removed.
- Some materials should not be put in landfill, e.g. materials used in manufacture of hardware and consumables can be toxic when burned and can leak toxic chemicals into ground if left in landfill.
- Some types of hardware and consumables can be recycled or sent to third world countries or reconditioned for resale.
- The local council will be able to give advice on the best way to dispose of toxic materials and where to find the nearest hazardous waste site to which such materials can be taken.
- Look for product information or visit the manufacturer's website if you are unsure of the correct method of disposal.
- Do not pour cleaning fluids or other toxic fluids down the drain as they can harm aquatic life.

Section 6   Security

6.1   Authenticating User Identity

6.1.1   Usernames and Passwords (2.6.1.1)

When a person's data is entered into a computer system, it is the responsibility of the computer owner to ensure that the data is kept confidential. This confidentiality is covered by data protection legislation and is dealt with in more detail in Section 7.

Data in any organisation should be available only to those who have and need access rights to ensure the privacy of people whose details are kept in databases. These rights must be linked to a system of security clearance controlled by someone in authority. In order to control access rights, all computers or networks must be configured so that users are required to enter a username and password. The username is a special word or group of characters that uniquely identifies the user. A password, that is unique, should also be entered. A password is similar to an ATM PIN but is made up of characters and numbers.

This system of usernames and passwords protects data from being accessed by unauthorised people. As many computer systems are now accessible over the internet, the need for security is self-evident.

6.1.2   Good Password Policies (2.6.1.2)

Users are often lazy with passwords and use their surnames, or easily guessed words, such as 'password'. A determined intruder could gain access to a system with insecure passwords very easily. It is sensible to follow some basic guidelines for choosing passwords. On many systems, rules such as those below are actively enforced.

Points to be aware of:

- Do not share passwords with other users.
- Do not use words in the dictionary, or easily guessed passwords, such as 'password', 'letmein' or 'access'.
- Change passwords regularly.
- Use a password at least 8 characters in length.
- Use a mix of both upper and lower case letters and numbers and non-alphabetic characters.
- Use numbers in place of letters. For example, use 'B1@ckr0ck' instead of 'blackrock'.

6.2   Computer Security

6.2.1   Preventing Data Theft (2.6.2.3)

Physical Security

Computers can be physically secured against theft by using special cables and locks. All computers and laptops have a security slot designed to take one end of the cable. The other end can then be locked to an item of furniture or similarly heavy object.

Servers and other business-critical computers should be correctly mounted in racking units or cabinets and kept in a locked room.

Data Security

Security involves not only the physical security of the computer equipment, but also the security of the data contained on the hard disk and other storage media. After a computer malfunction or accident, hardware is easily replaced but data may be damaged and rendered completely useless. Companies can go out of business after a complete data loss.

It is essential that organisations and their employees are proactive in protecting important information. This is best achieved by introducing an information security policy.

An information security policy should include:

- A document covering company procedures for backing up data.
- Ensuring employees are aware of their responsibilities when working with sensitive data.
- Procedures for reporting and dealing with security incidents.
- Ensuring employees use passwords and user names (see Section 6.1).
- Ensuring BIOS passwords are used if available, so that the computer will not even start unless the correct password is supplied.

- Keeping sensitive data in an encrypted area of the hard drive, or password-protect document files containing this type of data.

- Using a security cable fastened to a desk or wall.

- The appointment of a person solely responsible for data security.

- Banning the use of all personal storage devices, including USB memory sticks and camera memory cards, from the workplace.

6.2.3   Risks with Online Activity (2.6.1.3)

Taking part in chat rooms and online discussions can be an engaging and rewarding experience where new friends can be made with people all over the world. Unfortunately, there is an element of risk involved in these types of online activities from cyber-bullies or online predators who seek to gain personal information to harass or cause other types of abuse.

Online harassment might seem rather unlikely because of the anonymous nature of the internet, but it is that anonymity that enables cyber-bullies and online predators to operate successfully. These criminals often masquerade as seemingly harmless people asking normal questions based on genuine interest. In other instances, cyber-bullies and online predators target a specific victim by gathering personal information from online profiles or websites that might contain contact details. Never provide your phone number, postal address or e-mail address on any public profile.

Following some simple rules and employing common sense will minimise risks with online activity.

- Use antivirus software and keep it up to date.

- Never reveal your entire name, full date of birth, contact details or other personal information to anyone whose identity you are not absolutely certain of.

- Ensure friends are happy for you to display photos, etc. on social networking sites, and do not alter photos in any way that is insulting or malicious.

- Use strong passwords and change them frequently.

- Use copy lists, e.g. cc: on an email, with discretion and do not 'reply to all' unless necessary. Respect the privacy of others, e.g. by using bcc: in e-mails, when appropriate.

- Do not use inappropriate language that may cause offence.

- Remember, typing in upper case is the equivalent of shouting.

- Ensure the operating system is kept up to date, especially with updates designed to fix security loopholes.

- Never open an unexpected e-mail attachment, even if it appears to be from a known sender.

- Learn to recognise phishing attempts.

- Where possible and appropriate, avoid entering real personal details, such as name, age or location, into forms on websites. It is necessary, to use correct personal information for banks or where credit card details are needed, but an invented online identity, called an **alias** or **handle** should be used for web forums, etc.

6.3   Backups (2.6.2.1)

Information on a computer is stored electronically. Because of this, there is always a possibility that it can be lost due to a malfunction in the system or through human error. To avoid total loss of data, it is important to have copies of all important files stored on disks or other removable media. These copies are called backups.

Frequent and comprehensive **backups** are vital in light of the many ways in which files can be lost or become corrupted.

In an office or academic situation, backups are usually the responsibility of the IT department and users must only ensure that their personal files are backed up to a stated location on a network drive. In the home, the responsibility for backups lies entirely with the users themselves. Backups can be made in several ways. At a basic level, taking a backup can be as simple as copying and pasting vital files to another location on the computer.

Taken a step further, the files can be simply copied to a variety of types of **storage media**.

- USB memory sticks are always increasing in storage capacity and decreasing in cost. They are easy to use because they appear as a new drive in the operating system.

- External hard drives can be used in the same way as USB memory sticks, however, they are larger and offer more storage space.

- Optical media, such as CD, DVD and Blu-Ray discs, provide a compact form of storage but have less capacity and must sometimes be written to or **burned** using special software.

- Businesses generally have much more vital data to protect than the home user, and often use expensive **tape backup** systems that require dedicated software to use.

> **NOTE**
> When simply copying files onto removable media the considerations already covered regarding encryption and data theft apply.

While data can simply be copied to a storage medium, it is better to use **backup software** for the task.

Some advantages of using backup software are:

- The backup can be scheduled to run automatically without the user having to remember to do it.

- The backup can be **incremental**, meaning that only the data that has changed since the last backup is copied, which reduces the space used and time taken.

- The backup file can be encrypted and protected with a password.

If backups are on a portable medium, such as a USB memory stick or DVD, it is a good idea to have several copies available and to keep at least one at a separate location to the rest, in case of fire, etc. Businesses commonly have a **disaster recovery** procedure involving multiple offsite backups which enable them to get back up and running as quickly as possible after files have been lost.

Online Backups

The continued growth and speed of broadband internet has meant that **online backup** has become increasingly used. In this scenario, the backup is stored in a remote location provided by a commercial online backup company. This storage is extremely secure and failure-tolerant, is often located in armoured underground locations and possibly replicated in several locations. The customer installs **client software** on their systems which can back them up over the internet to the secure storage location. This sort of facility is also offered to home users by companies, such as www.mozy.com.

Simple backup software can be readily downloaded for any operating system. The following images show some screens from an example of a free application.

6.4   Firewalls (2.6.2.2)

A computer connected to the internet is also connected to millions of other computers worldwide. This carries a huge risk of unauthorised access by malicious individuals or criminal organisations.

Firewalls act as a barrier between individual computers, or computer networks, and the wider internet, essentially making them invisible. Firewalls can exist in hardware, for example inside a broadband router, or in software. They can be configured to provide alerts if attempted intrusions occur.

Hackers often scan the internet looking for connected computers, and when one is found, it, in turn, is scanned for open **ports** which allow remote connection. A firewall hides the computer on the internet and also blocks most ports from being used.

6.5   Malware

6.5.1 Methods of Infection (2.6.3.1)

The term **malware** is used to describe a variety of unsolicited, and usually malicious, software programs. Malware is transferred between computers across networks and the internet using various methods (e.g. from malicious websites and in e-mail attachments) and they infect legitimate program files or exploit security weaknesses in operating systems.

Some types of malware actively destroy data, some steal passwords and private information, and some remain dormant until they are activated to use the computer they have infected as part of a huge attack on a corporate or government network. They are generally grouped into the headings of **viruses**, **worms**, **spyware**, **adware**, **Trojans** and **diallers**.

Viruses

These are small executable computer programs that can attach themselves secretly to other programs. When the infected program is run by a user, the virus hides in the computer's memory. Then, when other programs are run by the user, the virus infects them, thus spreading. Some modern viruses also change themselves constantly to avoid detection. They are called viruses because they behave in exactly the same as a biological virus. Some viruses are relatively harmless and simply exist to spread as widely as they can. Some can be actively malicious, for example they may delete the contents of disk drives.

Traditional viruses can be spread through variety of methods, for example running infected attachments in e-mail messages or pirate copies of software, whether on CD, DVD or downloaded from the internet. For this reason, pirate copies of software, even if they come from a friend or associate, should not be installed on a PC.

It should be assumed that all executable e-mail attachments are infected (i.e. all **.exe** files), even if sent or apparently sent by a known contact. In a business or educational situation where e-mail is received by a central mail server and then distributed to users, any infected attachments should be automatically removed by the server and a message sent to the user to his effect. It is in fact common for **all** executable attachments to be stripped out as a matter of network policy.

In a home situation, good anti-virus software should be able to trap infected e-mails as they come into the e-mail client (e.g. Outlook, Google Mail, etc.) and not allow them to be opened.

Trojan Horses (or Trojans)

These work in the same way as the horse in the classical story. It is an application that, when run, appears to do something useful but will also secretly perform some nefarious action. Modern Trojans usually create a **back door** enabling illegal remote access to the computer and its files if it is connected to the internet.

Trojans often rely on **social engineering** to spread rather than a virus-like infection. For example, a user may receive an attachment containing an executable file in an e-mail which seems to come from a trusted source.

Trojans are commonly used to give hackers access to a remote system over the internet without the owner's knowledge. The computer is then **compromised** and can be used to store illegal files or send junk e-mail. A **keylogger** may be installed, which can record what the user is typing and store it for later retrieval. A hacker can use this information to discover passwords, PINs and other private information.

Worms

These are similar in concept and effect to Trojans but can spread independently across computer networks by exploiting security problems in operating systems and network equipment, rather than requiring a user to do something, e.g. open an e-mail containing an executable file. If one computer on a network becomes compromised, the worm can then copy itself across network connections to uninfected computers without the users involved actively doing anything themselves to cause the infection.

Spyware and Adware

These are software that monitor user behaviour and collects personal information when the user browsing the internet. This information is then used to automatically redirect the user to a specific website or to produce a proliferation of 'pop-up' advertising windows which clutter the screen.

Spyware and adware can have other undesirable effects, such as slowing down the internet connection or a computer's performance in general. Most computers become infected with adware or spyware through techniques used on certain web pages that exploit security defects in internet browsers, such as Internet Explorer.

Rogue Diallers

These can use a modem connected to a computer to dial premium-rate telephone numbers, which generates revenue for the owner of the number. Some diallers appear to be genuine and to offer access to content, such as illegal downloads, others operate in secret without the user's knowledge. Because diallers use dial-up modems connected to telephone lines they will eventually disappear as all internet access gradually becomes via broadband.

6.5.2 Anti-Virus Software (2.6.3.2)

Anti-virus software is used to detect and remove all types of malware, not just viruses. The process of removing malware is called **disinfecting** or **cleaning**. To recognise problems, anti-virus applications use definition libraries, which are databases of all known malware.

Because malware can modify legitimate files, it may or may not be possible to remove the problem without damaging the original file. If it is not possible to remove the infection, and the files affected are a crucial part of the operating system, it could be necessary to reinstall the operating system.

Modern anti-virus applications usually have one or more of the following.

- A resident scanner that is loaded into the computer's memory when the computer starts up and monitors files as they are being read and written. If a file is infected, the user is notified and the file either deleted or moved to quarantine.

- Quarantine, a safe area where infected files are stored.

- An on-demand scanner. This will perform a scan of all vulnerable files on hard drives, and can usually be set to run automatically at a specified time.

- A mail scanner, which plugs into an e-mail client application, such as Outlook, and scans and disinfects e-mails as they arrive.

- A pop-up blocker.

- Anti-phishing technology. This will monitor each web page being visited and compare it against a database of known phishing websites, alerting the user if required.

- A firewall (see Section 6.4).

An example of the options available within a typical graphical anti-virus application on Windows XP is shown below.

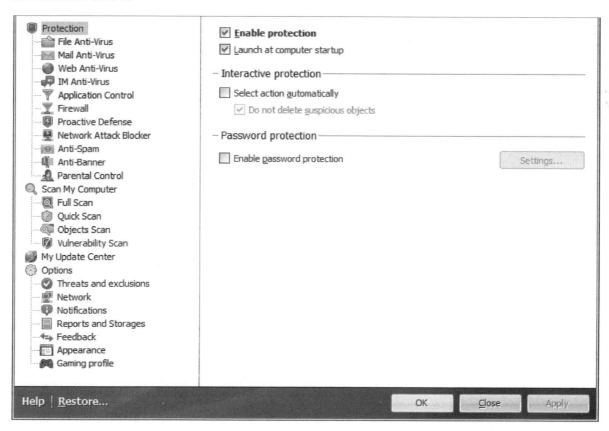

Scanning Files, Folders and Drives

Anti-virus software will scan files as they are accessed in the course of normal computer usage, and this activity is not visible to the user unless a threat is detected. In addition scheduled scans can examine the entire PC on a regular basis without any user intervention. It is also possible for a user to start an 'on-demand' scan to check a suspicious drive, file or folder at will. Most anti-virus software will enable this in two ways – via a menu option within the anti-virus software, or via a context menu within Windows Explorer.

Microsoft Security Essentials is a popular free anti-virus application for the Windows operating system. It can be made scan a specific drive or folder (but not individual file).

To scan a drive or folder, do the following:

- Open the **Microsoft Security Essentials** application, by double-clicking the icon in the system tray at the bottom right of the desktop.

  The **Microsoft Security Essentials** window opens.

- Select **Custom Scan**.

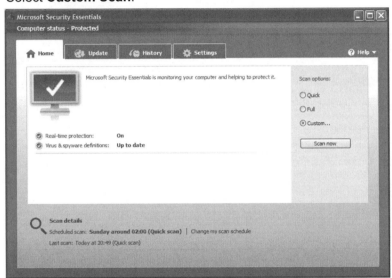

- Click **Scan Now**.

  A new window will open so that the drive or folder to be scanned can be selected.

- Select the item(s) to be scanned by placing a 'tick' in the box next to the item.

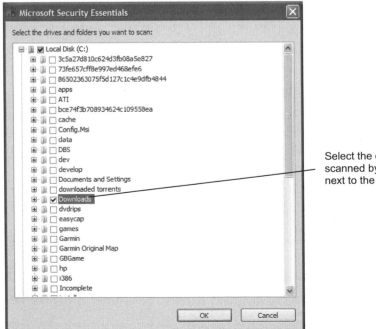

Select the drive or folder to be scanned by placing a tick in the box next to the item.

- Click **OK** to start the scan.

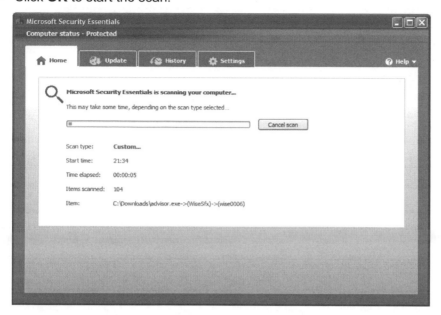

To scan an individual file or folder, do the following:

- Right-click the item.
- Select **Scan with Microsoft Security Essentials** from the pop-up menu.

  The **Microsoft Security Essentials** window opens.

- Select **Custom Scan**.

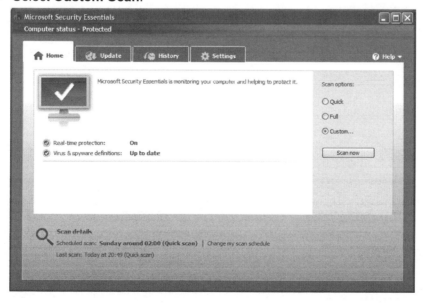

- Click **Scan Now**.

6.5.3 Updating Anti-Virus Software (2.6.3.3)

New viruses, Trojans and assorted other undesirable programs are created every day, so it is important to keep anti-virus software up to date. Companies that sell anti-virus software maintain central databases which are updated regularly, and modern software will keep itself updated automatically, via the internet, without the user having to do anything.

6.5.4 Recommended Practices for Preventing Malware Problems (2.6.3.3)

In addition to the use of e-mail filtering and anti-virus software, some basic rules can further reduce the chances of malware finding its way onto a computer.

- Never open attachments in unexpected e-mail messages, even if they appear to be from a trusted sender.
- Do not download illegal or pirated software from the internet.
- When installing software make sure to read the 'small print' and the EULA (End User Licence Agreement). Some software, for example, may offer a lot of free functionality but at the expense of a user agreeing, often unintentionally, to install adware and spyware alongside it.
- Be alert for any unusual problems with the computer, such as an unexplained slowing down of the computer or excessive disk activity.
- Never reply to junk e-mail messages, even if they provide a link which claims to provide an unsubscription service. Replying will only inform the sender that the e-mail address used was 'live'. The correct course of action is to mark the message as junk or delete it.

6.6   Spam

6.6.1 Definition

The widespread use of e-mail makes it a very attractive way for advertisers to reach large numbers of potential customers in a precisely targeted manner. This capability is used by legitimate marketing and advertising companies as well as businesses that are not so reputable.

Unwanted, unsolicited commercial e-mail is known as **spam** or **junk e-mail**. At the time of writing, it is estimated that 80 per cent of the 100 billion e-mails sent daily are spam.

6.6.2 Receiving Spam

Spam messages arrive in a user's e-mail inbox in the same way as normal messages. When the volume of these messages is low, it may not be regarded as much of a problem, however, large numbers can cause a serious inconvenience as the user may have to check each e-mail individually. In addition, the subject lines or content of these e-mails may be of an adult or otherwise offensive nature.

Large volumes of spam also have an impact on computer networks, as they take up storage space, take time to process and eliminate, and place an unnecessary amount of traffic on the internet.

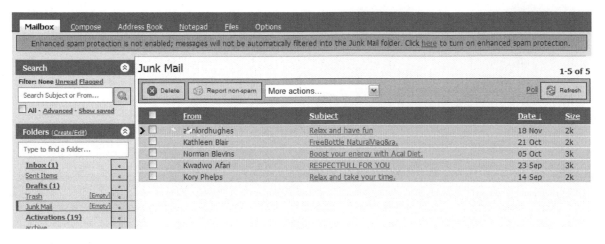

The image on page 101 shows a web-based e-mail client with received spam messages that have been moved into a **Junk Mail** folder.

6.6.3 Preventing Spam (2.6.3.4)

There a number of measures that can be taken to reduce or eliminate spam.

- Use a number of e-mail addresses, all of which can be received in the same e-mail inbox. One address might be used for business e-mail only and only given to those people with whom business is done. A second might be a main personal e-mail address used for friends and family. A third could be used when entering personal information on websites.

- Most modern e-mail systems offer sophisticated e-mail scanning and filtering, whether it is installed on a computer with an e-mail package, such as Outlook or Thunderbird, or a webmail service that is accessed via a web browser, such as Gmail or MSN Mail.

  Incoming e-mail is scanned using sophisticated rules and placed in a special junk mail folder. The user can then view the messages and empty the folder periodically. If unwanted messages remain in the Inbox most e-mail packages can be set up to identify spam messages and report them as being junk.

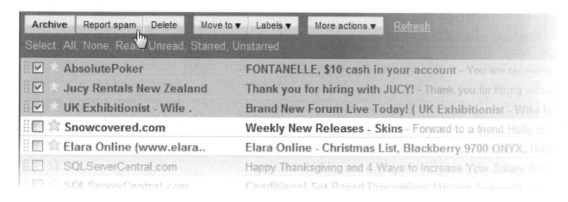

Section 7   Copyright and Legislation

7.1   Copyright (2.7.1.1)

Copyright is defined as a group of legal rights that protect creative works from being used, reproduced, performed or disseminated without permission from the creator of the work. Commercial software is covered by copyright similar to printed media, such as books. You are obliged to look after your software and not enable others to copy it. You should purchase and register your own software for your own use.

- Program or application disks should be copied only for the purposes of backing up and safekeeping as specified in the licence agreement. If the original disks are damaged or become corrupted, the backup copies can be used to reinstall the software.
- Sharing or lending program disks may be in breach of licensing agreements.
- Transferring or copying software over a network should only be carried out under the terms of the software license agreement. **Single user** or **stand-alone** copies of software should not be used on networks. **Site licences** are available for most network requirements.
- **Software piracy**, i.e. the illegal duplication, distribution, sale and use of software, is a criminal offence.
- Copyright legislation may also apply to shareware and freeware (see Section 7.4).

The internet enables access to a vast library of information in various formats. Material downloaded from the internet is the property of the person or organisation that put it there. Whether in paper or digital format, the majority of graphics, text, audio and video files on the internet are protected by copyright and the owner's permission must be sought if the material is to be used for any purpose other than that stated by them. Where websites reproduce other copyrighted materials – such as poems – copyright lies with the creator/author of the original work, e.g. the poet.

7.1.1 Disks and Copyright

Material stored on removable media, such as CDs and USB flash drives, must be checked for copyright before it is distributed. Commercial software produced on these media is likely to require your commitment to a licensing agreement.

7.2   Recognising Licensed Software (2.7.1.2)

Most commercial software is distributed with a **product ID number**. This unique number usually identifies the product item and distinguishes it from other versions of the same product that are licensed to users.

Some commercial software also requires an activation key. Where an activation key is used, it is normally entered as part of the installation process and the process will not continue without a valid key, the aim being to deter piracy. This key can sometimes be validated online.

When software has been installed, users can perform a registration process to inform the software supplier that a valid copy of the software has been installed and that it qualifies for updates. A valid Product ID will also often be requested if users access technical support for the software.

It is common practice amongst software developers to provide access to an application's product ID number.

To access the product ID number in Word 2007, do the following:

- Click the **Office Button**.
- Click **Word Options**.
  The **Word Options** window opens.
- Select the **Resources** tab.
- Click about Microsoft Office Word 2007 option by clicking the **About** button.

The **About Microsoft Office Word** window opens.

The Product ID is listed in this window.

Product ID number

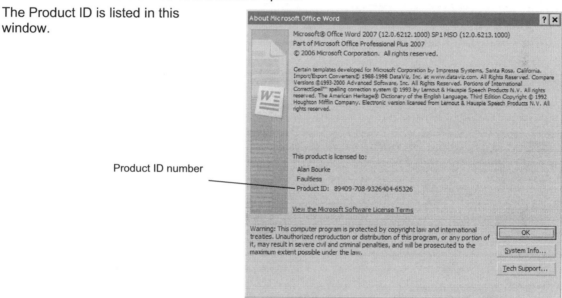

All software is supplied under a licence. Vendors such as Microsoft have their own licensing agreements which can also be viewed from the **About Microsoft Word** window.

7.3   End-User Agreements (2.7.1.3)

When a software package is purchased, you are not paying for ownership but for the right – a licence – to use the product. It is important to read the licensing agreement displayed on the packaging or in the accompanying documentation. It is also common practice among software companies to display the agreement on screen at some stage when the software is being installed on the computer. No matter where the licence agreement is displayed, you are legally obliged to adhere to it if you use the software.

Most copies of software are single-user copies. This means that the purchaser may only use the software on one computer. A site licence can be purchased if the software is to be installed on a number of computers. Only one copy of the software is supplied, but the site licence legally entitles the purchaser to install it on a specified number of computers. The cost of a site licence is generally much lower than the cost of buying individual copies of the software for each machine.

7.4   Shareware, Freeware, Public Domain Software and Open Source Software (2.7.1.4)

7.4.1 Shareware

Many computer programmers and hobbyists write software programs and allow them to be distributed freely as shareware. Distribution may be via the internet or on CDs distributed with magazines. Shareware is copyrighted software that enables you a try-it-out period before you make the purchase.

Payment for shareware is based on an honour system. If you wish to continue using the software after the trial period, you are required to send a payment, usually nominal, to the author. To encourage payment, many shareware programs will only function for a limited period or some functions may be disabled. Paid-up users may get additions and free updates.

The quality of shareware is variable, but some programs, such as early versions of the popular image-editing program Paint Shop Pro®, are of professional standard. Current versions of this program are no longer shareware.

7.4.2 Freeware

Freeware is similar to shareware. It is also distributed freely, but no payment is expected. Some authors may ask for feedback or for a reciprocal action ('Do something nice for someone' or 'Send me a postcard'). As with shareware, freeware comes in an 'as is' condition. Some developers freely distribute the first version of their product to benefit from users' reactions in the development of the program. Freeware authors often retain all the rights to their software under copyright legislation. Copying and distributing further copies of the material may not be allowed.

7.4.3 Public Domain Software

Public domain software is software which is not copyrighted. It is the property of whoever is using it, and can be copied and/or modified as if that user had created it themselves.

7.4.4 Open Source Software

Open source software is computer software which is, like public domain software, available for free and which can be shared, copied or modified by each user. Unlike public domain software, Open source software is licensed, generally under the GNU (General Public Licence) – GNU GPL or just GPL). Types of open source software include operating web browsers, databases and the Linux operating system.

7.5   Data Protection Legislation (2.7.2.1, 2.7.2.2 and 2.7.2.3)

Personal data is legitimately held by a number of institutions and agencies, for example people's detailed financial records may be held by a bank or financial lending institution with which they conduct business. Such records could include a person's monthly income, mortgage repayment details, schedules of loan repayments, overdraft requirements, credit rating, and savings and investments.

Local authorities may have details on services to which an individual is entitled that could include payment records of local taxes and charges, dog licences, applications for planning permission, planning objections and appeals. Some of this information may be stored for public access. Sensitive medical records will be held by various agencies, such as health boards, general hospitals, local area clinics and general practitioners.

In each of the above cases, it is important to govern access to the information and the use to which the information is put. Data protection legislation exists to ensure that appropriate levels of privacy are safeguarded and the information is used only in an appropriate manner.

In the United Kingdom, a Data Protection Act was passed on 16 July 1998 and came into force in early 1999. It was enacted to bring UK law into line with the 1995 European Directive requiring each member state to protect its citizens' fundamental rights and freedoms, especially their right to privacy in relation to the processing of personal data.

Similar legislation has been passed by other governments. You should contact the appropriate local authority regarding the legislation that applies in your own country.

Those who store or have access to data on individuals are under a legal obligation in most countries to protect this data. Below is an overview of the eight key principles (in the context of their definition in law) of information-handling practice outlined in the 1998 Data Protection Act.

1. Data may only be used for the specific purposes for which it was collected.
2. Data must not be disclosed to other parties without the consent of the individual whom it is about, unless there is legislation or other overriding legitimate reason to share the information (for example, the prevention or detection of crime). It is an offence for Other Parties to obtain this personal data without authorisation.
3. Individuals have a right of access to the information held about them, subject to certain exceptions (for example, information held for the prevention or detection of crime).
4. Personal information may be kept for no longer than is necessary and must be kept up to date.
5. Personal information may not be sent outside the European Economic Area unless the individual whom it is about has consented or adequate protection is in place, for example by the use of a prescribed form of contract to govern the transmission of the data.
6. Subject to some exceptions for organisations that only do very simple processing, and for domestic use, all entities that process personal information must register with the Information Commissioner's Office.
7. Entities holding personal information are required to have adequate security measures in place. Those include technical measures (such as firewalls) and organisational measures (such as staff training).
8. Subjects have the right to have factually incorrect information corrected (though this does not extend to matters of opinion).

In most countries, data protection legislation not only requires data controllers to take on specific responsibilities, but also outlines the rights of individuals whose data is being held. One of the most common of these rights is that of an individual to request a copy of his or her data from any data controller. Making such a request usually requires a written letter or e-mail along with the payment of a small fee to compensate the data controller for the time needed to process the request.

Another common right of the individual under data protection legislation is the right to seek compensation in court for any damage caused to the individual by the mishandling of their data. An example of this particular right may be if an individual's credit rating was not kept up to date by a financial institution and that person was subsequently denied a loan for a mortgage. In this case, the affected individual could take the financial institution that was responsible to court and sue for damages.

There may be other rights provided to individuals under various data protection legislation, depending on the country. This information is often widely available on the internet or by contacting the appropriate authority. It is important to be aware of such rights as they provide security against identity theft or other types of damage caused by the mishandling of personal data.

In many countries, data protection legislation deals with direct marketing organisations that send unsolicited mail and e-mail, or make unsolicited phone calls to an individual to obtain data. In these cases, individuals have the right to request that their information be deleted from the data collector to ensure that no further mail or phone calls are received. There are circumstances in which this right may be limited, for example, in a legal situation, a person who is standing trial for a crime will not be able to request certain data from the police.

Unit 3

Word Processing

3

Unit 3
Word Processing

3

Goals for Unit 3

Unit 3 Word Processing requires the candidate to demonstrate an ability to use a word processing application to create everyday letters and documents.

The candidate shall be able to:

- Work with documents and save them in different file formats.

- Choose built-in options such as the Help function to enhance productivity.

- Create and edit small-sized word processing documents that will be ready to share and distribute.

- Apply different formats to documents to enhance them before distribution and recognise good practice in choosing the appropriate formatting options.

- Insert tables, images and drawn objects in documents.

- Prepare documents for mail merge operations.

- Adjust document page settings and check and correct spelling before finally printing documents.

3

Introduction: What is Word Processing?

Word processing refers to the creation of documents using word processing software, such as Microsoft Word. There are various types of document that can be created using a word processing application, such as the following:

- Letters.

- Memos.

- Agenda.

- Minutes of meetings.

- Posters.

- Envelopes.

- Mailshots (standard document merged with addresses).

- Newsletters.

- Faxes.

- Reports.

- Flyers/adverts.

- Business cards.

> **Company Name**
> Address
> Tel No
>
> ---
>
> Date
>
> Customer Name
> Address
>
> Dear _____
> Main body of the letter can be indented or fully blocked to the left.
>
> Yours sincerely
>
> Name
> Status

Word processing software enables the user to insert automatic fields into headers and/or footers (such as dates or filename fields) and formatting can be performed to enhance the overall appearance of the document using the application's formatting tools. Editing is performed easily within a word processing document, using overtyping, inserting and deleting text. The layout of the document can be managed by changing margins, orientation and paper size.

Section 1   Using the Application

An **application** refers to the software package that is used to perform a task. The application that will be used for this training manual is Microsoft Office Word 2007. This is a comprehensive word processing package, capable of creating a variety of documents.

1.1   Working with Documents

A word processed document may be a letter, memo, report, fax, agenda, poster or a variety of other documents. Word processed files may be saved in a variety of formats, such as template format or text or rich text format. Documents can also be saved in different versions so that they can be accessed in previous software versions.

In this section, you will learn to do the following:

- Open and close a word processing application.
- Open and close documents.
- Create a new document based on a default template or other available template, such as a memo, fax or agenda.
- Save a document to a location on a drive.
- Save a document under another name to a location on a drive.
- Save a document as another file type, such as text file, Rich Text Format, template, or a software specific file extension and version number.

1.1.1   Opening a Word Processing Application (3.1.1.1)

Microsoft Word is a word processing package that comes as part of the Microsoft Office 2007 suite. This application will either be displayed as an icon on the desktop of your computer or found in the Start menu.

To open Word, do the following:

- Select the **Start** menu.
- Select **All Programs**.
- Select **Microsoft Office** and then select **Microsoft Office Word 2007**.

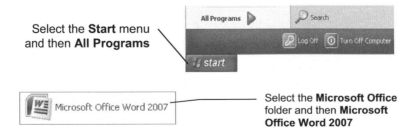

Select the **Start** menu and then **All Programs**

Select the **Microsoft Office** folder and then **Microsoft Office Word 2007**

Microsoft Word may be displayed as a shortcut icon on the desktop of your computer. If this is the case, double-click the shortcut to open it (or right-click the icon and select **Open** from the shortcut menu).

A **Microsoft Office Word 2007** window opens.

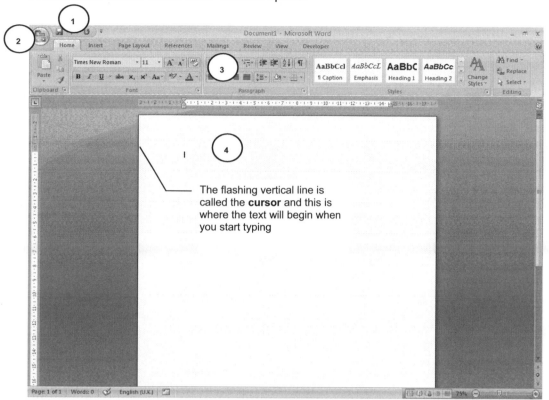

The screen layout will display the following:
①   The Quick Access Toolbar.
②   The Office Button.
③   The ribbon.
④   A new, blank document.

1.1.2 Closing a Word Processing Application (3.1.1.1)

To close Word, do the following:

- Select the **Office Button** from the top left of the screen.

- Select **Exit Word**.
  The **Word** program closes.

Office Button

Select **Exit Word**

Alternatively, Select the **Close X** button in the top right corner of the Title Bar.

Close X button

1.1.3 Opening a Document (3.1.1.1)

To open an existing document, do the following:

- Open **Word**.
- Select the **Office Button**.
- Select **Open**.

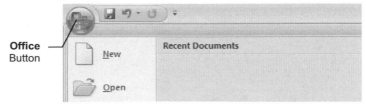

Office Button

The **Open** window opens.

- Select the location of the file to be opened by clicking the **Look in** arrow and choosing a drive and/or folder.
- Select the file.
- Click **Open**.

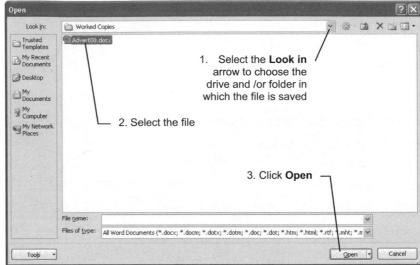

1. Select the **Look in** arrow to choose the drive and /or folder in which the file is saved

2. Select the file

3. Click **Open**

3

NOTE

To display the **Open** window using the keyboard, hold down the **CTRL** key on the keyboard and then click **O**.

Opening Recent Documents

Documents that have been opened recently can be accessed by selecting the **Office Button** and then selecting a file from the **Recent Documents** list.

Select a recently opened file from the **Recent Documents** list

To change the number of documents listed in Recent Documents, do the following:

- Select the **Office Button** followed by **Word Options**.
- Select the **Advanced** button and scroll down to the **Display** section.
- Enter the number of recent documents that should display in the Office Button menu.

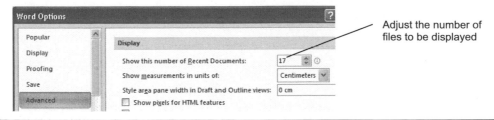

Adjust the number of files to be displayed

1.1.4 Closing a Document (3.1.1.1)

To close a document, do the following:

- Select the **Office Button**.
- Select **Close**.

NOTE

If changes have been made to the file, a message will appear asking if you want to save the file before closing.

- Click **Yes** to save the file.
- Click **No** to close the file without saving.
- Click **Cancel** to cancel the message and return to the document.

1.1.5 Creating a New Document (3.1.1.2)

A new document is based on the normal, default template. This template is created using default formatting and page layout settings. There are other templates available for use, such as memo, agenda, fax templates, among many other installed templates. A template is a document containing standard formatting/page layout that can be used repeatedly to create other documents.

To create a new document based on the normal, default template or on other available templates, do the following:

Default Template

- Select the **Office Button**.
- Select **New**.
  The **New Document** window opens.

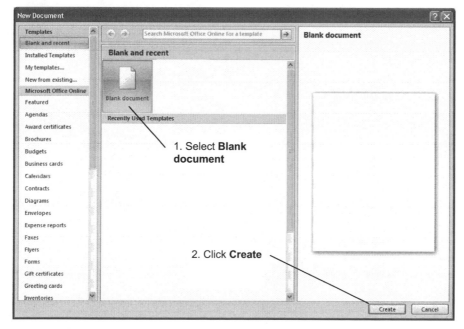

- Select **Blank and recent** from the **Templates** list.
- Select **Blank Document**.
- Select the **Create** button.
  A new blank document appears.

Title bar displays the name of the document

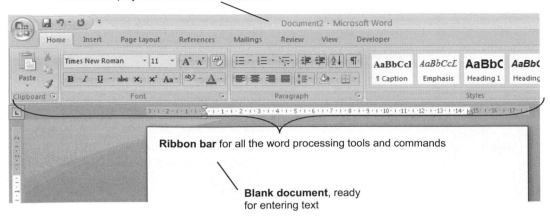

Ribbon bar for all the word processing tools and commands

Blank document, ready for entering text

Installed Templates

- Select the **Office Button**.

- Select **New**.
  The **New Document** window opens

- From the **Templates** list, select **Installed Templates**.

- Select a template, e.g. memo, fax or agenda.

- Select the **Document** option button to create a document based on the template (select the **Template** option button to create a template).

- Click **Create**.
  A document will open, based on the chosen template.

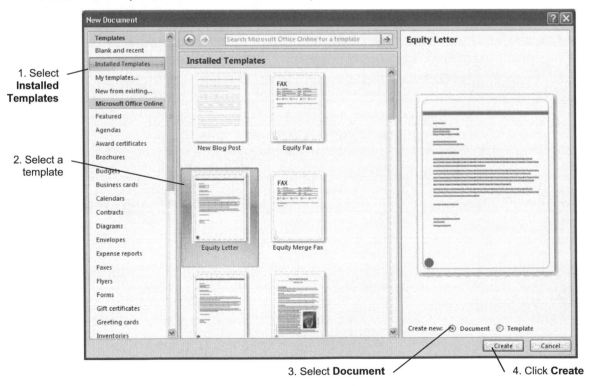

1. Select **Installed Templates**

2. Select a template

3. Select **Document**

4. Click **Create**

NOTE
You can also select a template from **Microsoft Office Online**.

Click one of the templates displayed in the Microsoft Office Online list of templates and then select the **Download** button. You may have to validate your copy of Microsoft Office 2007 software before continuing the download.

1.1.6 Saving a Document to a Location on a Drive (3.1.1.3)

To save a document for the first time, do the following:

- Select the **Office Button**.

- Select **Save**.

  The **Save As** window opens.

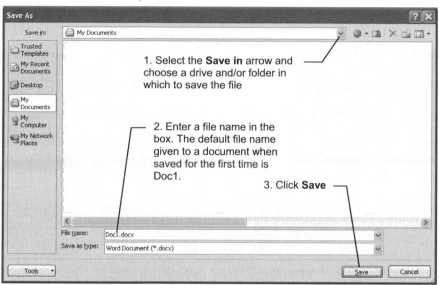

- Select the correct drive and/or folder from the **Save in** menu.

- Enter a name in the **Filename** box.

- Click **Save**.

NOTE
Click the **Save** button on the **Quick Access Toolbar** to save a file.
The keyboard combination to save is **CTRL + S**.

1.1.7 Saving a Document under Another Name (3.1.1.3)

To save an existing document with a different name, do the following:

- Select the **Office Button**.

- Move the mouse over the **Save As** menu option.

- From the **Save a copy of the document** sub-menu, select **Word Document**.

  The **Save As** window opens.

- Select the correct drive and/or folder from the **Save in** menu.

- Enter a different name in the **File name** box.

- Click **Save**.

Select the **Word Document** menu option to save the document in the default file format

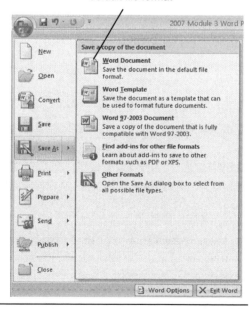

NOTE

When saving a document for the first time, clicking **Save** or **Save As** from the Office Button menu will result in the **Save As** window opening. Subsequent changes to a document can be saved by selecting the **Save** option from the **Office Button**. This will save the document with the same name and overwrite the original file.

1.1.8   Saving a Document as Another File Type (3.1.1.4)

A document can be saved in a variety of different formats. This is useful if the document is being opened in another version of Word or a different word processing program. The different formats available are listed below.

Word Format	
• Document (.docx)	• Template (.dotx)
• Text (*.txt)	• Version number (e.g. *.doc, Word 97-2003 Document)
• Rich Text Format (*.rtf)	• Software specific file extension (e.g. *.wps, Works 7.0)

To save a document in another file type, do the following:

Text Format (*.txt)

When a document is saved as a text file it loses all of its formatting features and graphics and saves in a format that enables it to be opened and viewed as text only.

- Click the **Office Button**.
- Move the mouse over the **Save As** menu option. The **Save a copy of the document** sub-menu opens.
- Select **Other Formats**.

Select **Other Formats**

The **Save As** windows opens.
- Select the **Save in** arrow and then select the correct drive and /or folder.
- Enter a file name into the **File name** box.
- Click the **Save as type** arrow.
- Select **Plain Text (*.txt)**.
- Click **Save**.

Click the **Save as type** arrow

Select **Plain Text (*.txt)**

Rich Text Format (*.rtf)

When a document is saved in Rich Text Format, it retains some of its formatting and enables the document to be opened in different applications, e.g. word processing or desktop publishing.

- Click the **Office Button**.
- Move the mouse over the **Save As** menu option. The **Save a copy of the document** sub-menu opens.
- Select **Other Formats**.

The **Save As** windows opens.

- Select the **Save in** arrow and then select the correct drive and/or folder.
- Enter a file name into the **File name** box and then click the **Save as type** arrow.
- Select **Rich Text Format (*.rtf)**.
- Click **Save**.

Select **Rich Text Format (*.rtf)**

Template

A template contains standard content that will appear on all pages in a document. A template can be used repeatedly to create other documents. This saves time and effort when creating a new document. Templates are saved with a **.dotx** file extension and, unless another location is specified, it saves in the following location: **C:/Documents and Settings/Computer Name/Application Data/Microsoft/Templates**.

To save a document as a template, do the following:

- Click the **Office Button**.
- Move the mouse over the **Save As** menu option.
  The **Save a copy of the document** sub-menu opens.
- Select **Word Template**.
  The **Save As** windows opens.

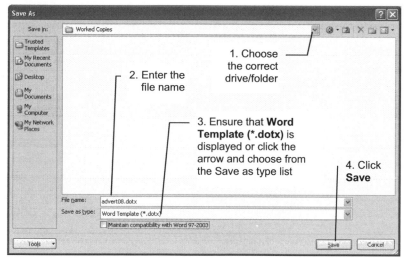

- Select the **Save in** arrow and then select the correct drive and/or folder.
- Enter a file name into the **File name** box and ensure that the **Save as type** box displays Word template (*.dotx).
- Click **Save**.

NOTE

To save a template in a previous version of Word, select Word 97-2003 Template (*dot).

You can by-pass the **Save a copy of the document** sub-menu by clicking the **Save As** menu command.

Version Number

Each version of Word has a different version number. If the document needs to be opened and viewed in a previous version of Word it can be saved with a different version number.

To check the version number of the software on your computer, do the following:

- Click the **Office Button**.
- Select **Word Options**.
- Click **Resources**.
- Click **About**.

The **About Microsoft Office Word** window opens.

This window provides information on the software version currently installed on your computer.

Information about currently installed software will be provided in this window

- Check the version number – it should be Microsoft Office Word **2007**.
- Click **OK** to close the current window.
- Click **OK** to close the Word Options window.

To save the document with a different version number, do the following:

- Click the **Office Button**.
- Move the mouse over the **Save As** menu command.
  The **Save a copy of the document** sub-menu opens.
- Select **Word 97-2003 Document** to save a copy of the document that is fully compatible with Word 97-2003.

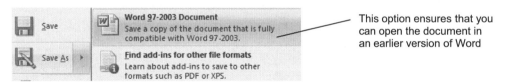

This option ensures that you can open the document in an earlier version of Word

The **Save As** windows opens.

- Select the **Save in** arrow and then select the correct drive and/or folder.
- Enter a file name into the **File name** box.
- Click the **Save as type** arrow.
  Note how the version is selected in the **Save As type** box.
  Alternatively, select the arrow and choose a version number.
- Click **Save**.

Word 97-2003 is an earlier version of the software

Software Specific File Extension

With Word 2007, the only option for converting documents to a software specific file extension is **.wps**. This relates to Microsoft Works files, which is a less expensive alternative to Microsoft Office suite, but has fewer features. It is now largely discontinued.

To save a document with a software specific file extension, do the following:

- Click the **Office Button.**
- Move the mouse over the **Save As** menu option. The **Save a copy of the document** sub-menu opens.
- Select **Other Formats**.

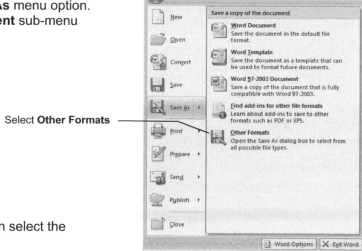

Select **Other Formats**

The **Save As** windows opens.

- Select the **Save in** arrow and then select the correct drive and /or folder.
- Enter a file name into the **File name** box.
- Click the **Save as type** arrow.
- Select **Works 6.0-9.0** or **Works 7.0 (*.wps)**.
- Click **Save**.

Click the **Save as type** arrow

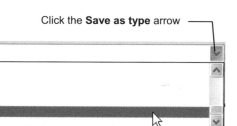

Select **Works 6.0-9.0** or **Works 7.0 (*.wps)**

1.1.9 Switching between Open Documents (3.1.1.5)

It is possible to have two or more documents open on your desktop. It is also possible to see two documents displayed together. Because they then both share the desktop, a much smaller part of each document is displayed. When you switch between open documents, you normally see them displayed full size on the desktop.

To switch between open documents, do the following:

- Select the **View** tab.
- In the **Windows** group, select the **Switch Windows** button.
  A tick will display beside the file name of the currently active document.
- Click another file name in the menu to make that the active document.

A tick beside the file name indicates that it is the active document, currently displayed on screen

---

NOTE

You can also switch between open documents or other programs by using the taskbar.

- Open more than one document.
  The documents will be displayed as tabs on the taskbar at the bottom of the screen.

- Click a tab to open a document.

To switch between open documents using the keyboard, hold down the **ALT** key and press **TAB**.

1.2   Enhancing Productivity

Productivity can be increased by setting user preferences, such as adding a user name and/or creating a default folder from which to open and in which to save all documents. Using the Help facility can also aid productivity by providing tips and advice on how to use the program effectively.

In this section you will do the following:

- Set basic options/preferences in the application: user name, default folder to open from, default folder to save documents to.

- Use available Help functions.

- Use magnification/zoom tools.

- Restore and minimise the ribbon.

1.2.1   Setting User Preferences (3.1.2.1)

User preferences refer to the user name and the default location of opened and saved files. These can be changed as necessary so that the user name is different or so that files can be opened or saved in another location.

To set user preferences, do the following:

User Name

- Click the **Office Button**.

- Select **Word Options**.
  The Word Options window opens.

- Select the **Popular** tab.

- In the **Personalize your copy of Microsoft Office** position the cursor in the User name box and delete the current user name.

- Enter the new user name.

- Click **OK**.

Enter or edit the **User name**

Default File Location to Open Files From and Save Files To

- Select the **Office Button**.

- Select **Word Options**.
  The **Word Options** window opens.

- Select the **Save** tab.

- In the **Default File Location** box, enter the required file location of opened and saved files (use the Browse… button to find the location if necessary).

- Click **OK**.

Enter the default
file location

1.2.2 Using the Help Function (3.1.2.2)

The Help function is available to give advice and help on aspects of the application you are using. This is useful when you are trying to perform an action and don't know how to proceed. Just ask the Help function a specific question and then select a relevant topic for the answer.

To use the Help function, do the following:

- Select the **Help** button or press the **F1** key.
  The **Word Help** window opens.

- Select a link to a relevant topic.

- A further set of links will appear that correspond with the selected topic.

- Select a relevant link to refine your search.

- Read the information on the chosen topic.

- Use the **Back** button to go back a step or the **Home** button to return to the first window of Word Help.

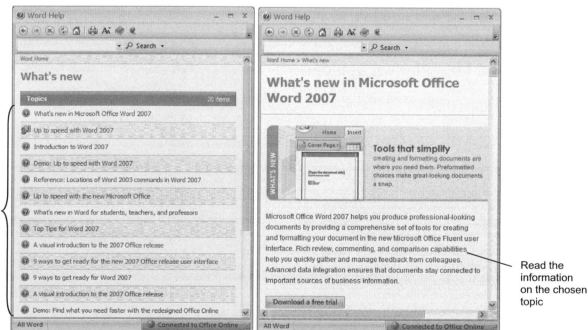

Select
a topic

Read the
information
on the chosen
topic

- Click **Print** to print a copy of the topic information.

You can also enter specific search criteria into the **Search** box to locate information on specific topics. To enter search criteria, do the following:

- Enter a question in the **Search** box.
- Click **Search**.
- A list of topic links relating to the search criteria will appear.
- Click a link to view the topic information.

Enter the search words here and click **Search**

A list of topics corresponding to the search criteria will be displayed

Click the **Close X** button to close the window when finished

Click the **Next** button to move through the pages or click the page numbers

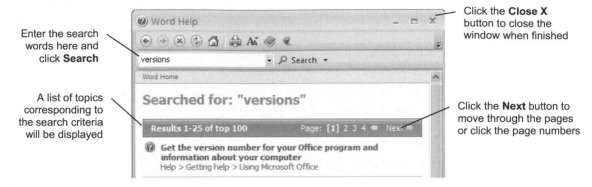

1.2.3 Using the Magnification (Zoom) Tools (3.1.2.3)

The magnification tools are used to zoom in and out in a document.

To use the magification tools, do the following:

- Select the **View** tab.

- From the **Zoom** group, select the following:
  - **Zoom** to open the **Zoom** window.
  - **100%** to zoom the window to full size.
  - **One Page** to see one page at a time (in reduced view).
  - **Two Pages** to see two pages at a time (side by side).
  - **Page Width** so that the width of the page matches the width of the window.

- In the **Zoom** group, click the **Zoom** button. The **Zoom** window opens.

- Select an option button to change the zoom percentage or change the amount or width of pages viewed or use the scroll wheels to increase or decrease the percentage in the **Percent** box.

- Click **OK**.

Select a **Zoom to** option button or select **Custom** and enter a percentage by which to increase or decrease the magnification

---

NOTE

You can also select the Zoom buttons on the Status Bar. Use the **Zoom Out** button to reduce the view. Select the **Zoom In** button to enlarge the view. *Alternatively*, drag the Slider towards the Zoom Out or Zoom In buttons to decrease/increase the view.

Zoom out   Zoom in

1.2.4 Minimising and Restoring the Ribbon (3.1.2.4)

The ribbon can be minimised and then restored if required.

To minimise and restore the ribbon, do the following;

Minimising the Ribbon

- Right-click the ribbon bar.
- Select **Minimize the Ribbon**. The ribbon is hidden.

Click **Minimize the Ribbon**

Restoring the Ribbon

- Right-click the bar containing the tabs.
- Click **Minimize the Ribbon** (note how a tick is displayed beside the menu command to indicate that it is active).

Click **Minimize the Ribbon** again to restore the ribbon

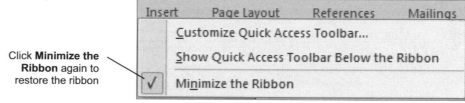

PRACTICE SEQUENCE

1   Open **Word** and create a new document.
2   Save this document as **sale** in the default document format in a default folder location that you specify.
3   Save another copy of the document in **Text** format with the filename **saleTXT**.
4   Reopen **sale** and practise switching between the two documents.
5   Zoom the **sale** document to **80%** and save.
6   Close both documents.
7   Use the **Help** function to find information on saving a document as a template.
8   Open the **sale** document and save in template format (ensure that it saves in the correct drive/folder).
9   Close the template file.
10 Open a new document and save with the name **version** in Word 97-2003 format.
11 Close all documents and exit Word.

Section 2   Document Creation

Text is entered into a new document by using the keyboard (or voice recognition software if required). The text appears in the cursor position as it is entered. Words should be separated by one space; performed by pressing the space bar after each word is entered onto the page. The text will display along a line (the line length depends on the margins and indentation) and then, when it reaches the end of that line, it will wrap around to the next line. The **Enter** key (or carriage return) is used to create a new paragraph. One or two spaces should be entered after a full stop, and one space after a comma, semi-colon or other punctuation mark. When the text fills the page, a new page is automatically created for text to continue. A document may contain multiple pages. Microsoft Word uses WYSIWYG (what you see is what you get), so what you see on the screen is how it will appear on the printed output when viewed in Print Layout view.

2.1   Entering Text

Text refers to characters, words or symbols entered into a document using a keyboard. The page can be viewed in different modes, such as draft for entering text or print layout to view how the page will appear when printed.

In the next section, you will learn about the following:

- Switch between page view modes.

- Enter text into a document.

- Insert symbols or special characters like: ©, ®, ™.

2.1.1   Page Views (3.2.1.1)

Page view refers to the way that the page is viewed on screen. The default page view is **Print Layout**. The page view buttons are displayed on the status bar and contain the following commands.

Print Layout	This enables you to see the page as it will look when it is printed.
Full Screen Reading	This enables you to see more than one page at a time (side by side) and increase text size for easier reading if required.
Web Layout	This enables you to see how the page will look when displayed as a web page.
Outline	This enables you to expand or collapse document titles and make changes to the document easily. This view also enables you to create sub-documents.
Draft	This was referred to as Normal View in previous versions of Word and enables you to see a draft of the document, along with page breaks. This view does not display images or page margins.

To change the page view, do the following:

- Select a page view command from the buttons displayed on the status bar.

  Alternatively, select the **View** tab and select a page view command from the **Document Views** group.

2.1.2 Entering Text in a Document (3.2.1.2)

Text is entered at the cursor position. The cursor is the black vertical flashing line on the page. The mouse icon is called the **insertion point**. The **click and type** option enables the user to click the insertion point in the left, centre or right of the page and start typing from that position.

To see whether the click and type option is selected, do the following:

- Click the **Office Button.**
- Select **Word Options**.
- Select the **Advanced** tab.
- In the **Editing** section of the window, select the **Enable click and type** checkbox (this enters a tick in the box).
- Click **OK**.

  Practise moving the insertion point to the middle of the page (double click to position the insertion point in the required location), the right of the page and the left of the page

To enter text, do the following:

- Use the keyboard to enter text on the page:
- Hold down the **Shift** key on the keyboard and then press a letter for an initial capital at the beginning of a sentence. Release the **Shift** key when the letter has been entered and then continue typing the remainder of the word/sentence.
- Press the **Caps Lock** key to type in upper case (this is a *toggle* key which turns on/off each time it is pressed – look for the green light at the top of the keyboard to indicate whether the Caps Lock key is active).
- Press the full stop key to end a sentence.
- Press the **Space bar** to create a space between words as you type (one space between words and one or two after a full stop).
- Type until the text to 'wraps around' to the next line.
- Press the **Enter** key to create a new paragraph.
- To use keyboard characters which are displayed **above** other characters on keys, hold down the **Shift** key and press the key.
- Enter numbers by pressing the number keys on the top row of the keyboard or use the number pad (you may need to press the **Num Lock** key to make the number pad active).

2.1.3 Inserting Symbols and Special Characters (3.2.1.3)

Symbols refer to the accented characters (e.g. é, ö, à, î) that are used in special characters. Special characters are the symbols (e.g. copyright or trademark symbols) or other characters (e.g. a telephone symbol before a telephone number).

To insert symbols and special characters, do the following.

Symbols

- From the **Insert** tab and the **Symbols** group, select the **Symbol** arrow.
- Choose a symbol from the menu or select **More Symbols**.

More symbols ————

The **Symbols** window opens with the **Symbol** tab the active tab.

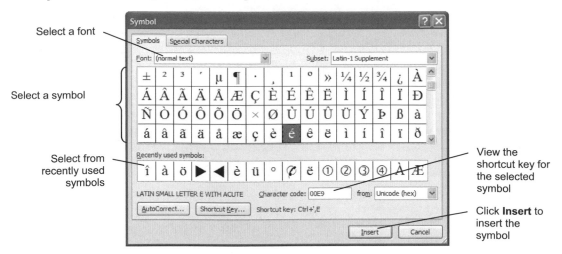

Select a font

Select a symbol

Select from recently used symbols

View the shortcut key for the selected symbol

Click **Insert** to insert the symbol

- Scroll through the list of symbols and select a symbol.
- Select **Insert**.
  Recently used symbols will display in the **Recently used symbols** section of the window.
  The shortcut key for the selected symbol will be displayed (e.g. **CTRL + '** and **e** for the **é** symbol).
- Click the **Font** arrow to see different fonts/symbols (**Wingdings** or **Webdings** are good fonts to use for pictorial symbols).
- Click **Close**.

Pictorial symbols can be selected from the **Wingdings** and **Webdings** font list. See examples below.

Wingdings	Webdings
☎ ☺ ✉ 💾 ☺ 📂 ✓ 🎞 ⇨	✂ ⓘ ? ⊘ 📡 🗇 ♫ 🔋 ℗

Special Characters

- From the **Insert** tab and the **Symbols** group, select the **Symbol** arrow.
- Select **More Symbols**.
  The **Symbol** window opens.
- Select the **Special Characters** tab.
- Select a special character, such as registered ®, copyright ©, trade mark™.
- Click **Insert**.
- Click **Close**.

Select the **Special Characters** tab

Select a special character

View the shortcut key for the selected symbol

Click **Insert**

2.1.4 Moving Text Around

In order to edit text, you need to be able to move the insertion point within text and position the cursor wherever you need to insert or delete characters/words.

To move the cursor around text, do the following:

Mouse

- Move the mouse and observe the Insertion Point (I).
- Position the insertion point in the required position and click the left mouse button. The cursor will appear in the selected position.

Keyboard

- Use the directional arrow keys on the keyboard to move around text.

→	Moves the cursor one character to the right or **CTRL + →** moves the cursor a **word** at a time.
←	Moves the cursor one character to the left or **CTRL + ←** moves the cursor a **word** at a time.
↑	Moves the cursor one line above or **CTRL + ↑** moves the cursor to the beginning of the paragraph before.
↓	Moves the cursor one line below or **CTRL + ↓** moves the cursor to the beginning of the next paragraph.
HOME/ END	Select **HOME** to move to the beginning of a line (use **CTRL + Home** to move to top of document). Select **END** to move to the end of a line (use **CTRL + End** to move to end of document).

PRACTICE SEQUENCE

1   Open **Word** and then open the **sales** document.
2   Switch to **Draft** view.
3   Enter the text as shown below, inserting symbols and special characters where required.
4   Switch to **Print Layout** view.
5   Save and close the **sales** document.

JUMBLE SALE

To be held at the Village Hall on Saturday, 16 August 2008, starting 12 noon

STALLS
Clothes · Toys · Bric a brac · Household goods · Shoes · Books

If you have any of the above items to donate, they will be gratefully received.

If you wish to volunteer to man one of the stalls, your help will be greatly appreciated. Please contact Mary on: ☎ 01234 567890

All profits to go to the Community Hall Refurbishment Fund

ⓘ Please note that we cannot use the CHRF logo on our flyers because the trade mark ™ is owned by another company. Please also note that when downloading images and text from the internet for advertising literature, that the original author owns the copyright ©.

2.2   Selecting and Editing Text

In this section, you will learn about the following:

- Displaying and hiding non-printing formatting marks, such as spaces, paragraph marks, manual line break marks and tab characters.

- Selecting a character, word, line, sentence, paragraph or the entire body text.

- Editing content by entering and removing characters and words within existing text, by overtyping to replace existing text.

- Using a simple search command for a specific word or phrase.

- Using a simple replace command for a specific word or phrase.

- Copying and moving text within a document and between open documents.

- Deleting text.

- Using the undo and redo commands.

2.2.1   Non-Printing Formatting Marks (3.2.2.1)

Non-printing formatting marks refer to marks such as spaces, paragraph marks, manual line breaks and tab characters. These marks do not display by default on screen, but they can be displayed if required. Displaying non-printing formatting marks can be useful to see where paragraphs have been made or tabs inserted.

To display and hide non-printing formatting marks, do the following:

- In the **Home** tab and **Paragraph** group, select the **Show/Hide** command (the keyboard shortcut is **CTRL + ***).

  The non-printing formatting marks will be displayed. This command is a *toggle* button which means that it is turned on/off each time it is selected.

- See the examples below of formatting marks within a document.

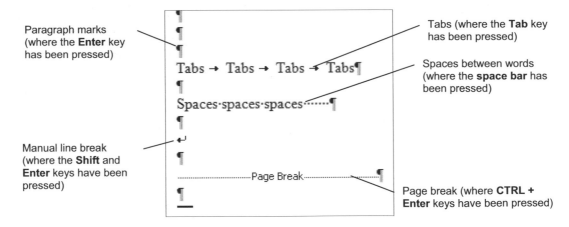

- o A **paragraph** mark is displayed when the Enter key has been pressed to create a new paragraph.
- o A **space** is displayed when the space bar is used.
- o A **manual line break** is used to create a new line, but not a new paragraph (this is when you may want another line that does not perform like a paragraph by starting a new line with an initial capital letter or with a number or bullet before the text). The keyboard shortcut is Shift + Enter.
- o A **tab** mark is displayed when the Tab key is pressed (tabs are used to create parallel columns of text).
- o A **page break** mark is displayed when a new page is created. The keyboard shortcut is **CTRL + Enter**.

2.2.2 Selecting (3.2.2.2)

Before text can be formatted or edited, it must first be selected. This can be done by using the mouse or by using the keyboard.

To select text, do the following:

Mouse

- Position the insertion point in front of the text to be selected.
- Hold down the left mouse button and drag over the text.
- Release the mouse button when you have selected all the required text.

To remove the selection, do the following:

- Click away from the selected area.

Other selection methods using the mouse are shown below	
A word	Position insertion point before, after or within word to be selected. Double-click the left mouse button.
A line	Move the cursor (which becomes an arrow) into the left margin so that the arrow tip is pointing at the line to be selected. Click the left mouse button.
A sentence	Move the cursor to the left of the first character in the sentence. Left-click the mouse button. Holding down the mouse button, drag to the right until the sentence is highlighted. *Alternatively*, place the cursor within the sentence, hold down the CTRL key and left-click the mouse button.
A paragraph	Move the cursor (arrow) into the left margin so that the arrow tip is pointing at the paragraph to be selected. Double-click the left mouse button.
Whole document	Move the cursor (arrow) into the left margin so that the arrow tip is pointing at the paragraphs to be selected. Treble-click the left mouse button.

Keyboard

- Position the insertion point in front of the character to be selected. Hold down the **Shift** key + press a directional arrow key to select the character. Hold down **CTRL, Shift** + directional arrow key to select a *word* at a time.

- To select the remainder of text in a document from a specific point in the document, position the cursor in front of the text to be selected, hold down the **Shift** + **CTRL** keys and press **End**.

- To select the whole document, press **CTRL + A**.

- To remove the selection, use a directional arrow key to move away from the selected area.

Ribbon Bar

- To select all of the text in the document, click the **Select** arrow from the **Home** tab/**Editing** group and then choose **Select All**.

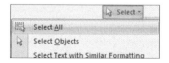

2.2.3 Editing Text (3.2.2.3 and 3.2.2.7)

Characters and words can inserted to or deleted from text or text can be overtyped.

To edit text, do the following:

Inserting Text

- Position the cursor where the text should appear (position the insertion point in the correct place and then click to position the cursor).
- Enter text (note how existing text moves to accommodate the newly inserted text).
- Ensure that there is one space between words and a full stop at the end of a sentence. There may be one or two spaces after a full stop.

Overtyping

- Press the **Insert** key on the keyboard.
- Position the cursor where the text should start and start typing.
  Existing text is overwritten with the newly inserted text.
- To turn Overtype off, press the Insert key again.

> **NOTE**
> If necessary, the Insert key control of the overtype mode can be activated by doing the following:
> - Click the **Office Button** followed by the **Word Options** button.
> - In the **Advanced** tab, tick **Use the Insert key to control overtype mode.**
>
>
> ☑ Use the Insert key to control overtype mode
> ☐ Use overtype mode

Deleting Text

- Position the insertion point in the correct place within the text and then click to position the cursor.
- Press the **Delete** key on the keyboard to delete characters to the right of the cursor position or press **Backspace** to delete characters to the left of the cursor position.
- Hold down the **CTRL** key and press **Delete/Backspace** to delete whole *words* instead of characters.
- To delete blocks of text, first select the text and then press the **Delete** key.

2.2.4 Searching Text (3.2.2.4)

Finding information in a document can be time consuming if it is a lengthy document containing lots of data. Using the Search command facilitates the process as it will find specific information throughout the document in one action.

To search for information, do the following:

- On the **Home** tab, click the **Find** command from the **Editing** group (or press **CTRL + F** to open the **Find** window).
  The **Find** window opens.
- Enter the search word or phrase into the **Find what:** box.

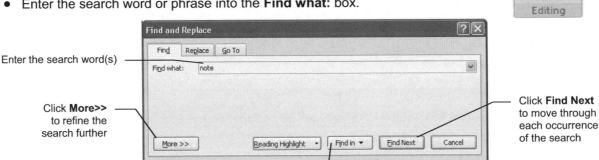

Enter the search word(s)

Click **More>>** to refine the search further

Click **Find In** to find occurrences of the search word in the main document, headers/footers or text boxes

Click **Find Next** to move through each occurrence of the search

- Select the **More>>** button to refine the search further.

- In this section of the **Find** window, you can do the following:
  - Match case (to ensure that the search word matches the case, e.g. upper/lower case, typed in the Find what box).
  - Find whole words only (to ensure that only whole words are found, e.g. the word **note** is found but not bank**note**, **note**worthy, end**note**, foot**note**, etc.).
  - Use wildcards (to stand in place of characters if you don't know the full word, e.g. **n??e** will find do**nate**, volu**ntee**r and **note**).
  - Sounds like (to find words that sound similar (e.g. **nite** will find **note, night** and **neat**).
  - Find all word forms.

- Press **Find Next** to find each occurrence of the search word(s) in the document.

Refine the search by matching the case or finding whole words only, etc.

- When the **Find** facility has finished searching for all occurrences of the search word, a confirmation window opens.
- Click **OK**.
- Click **Cancel** to close the **Find** window.

2.2.5 Replacing Text (3.2.2.5)

It can be time consuming to replace each occurrence of an existing word or phrase throughout a document with another word/phrase. If the word to be replaced appears many times, it is easier to use the Replace command to change the existing word throughout the document.

To replace words, do the following:

- On the **Home** tab, click the **Replace** command from the **Editing** group (or press **CTRL + H** to open the **Replace** window). The **Replace** window opens.
- Enter the search word or phrase into the **Find what** box.
- Enter the replacement word in the **Replace with** box.

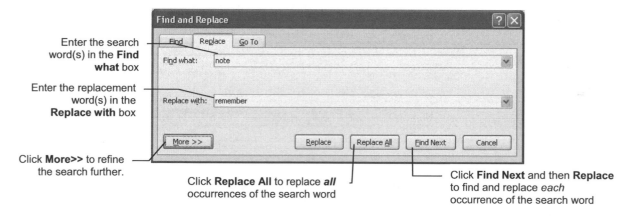

Enter the search word(s) in the **Find what** box

Enter the replacement word(s) in the **Replace with** box

Click **More>>** to refine the search further.

Click **Replace All** to replace *all* occurrences of the search word

Click **Find Next** and then **Replace** to find and replace *each* occurrence of the search word

- Select the **More>>** button to refine the search further.
- In this section of the **Find & Replace** window, you can do the following:
  - o Match case (to ensure that the search word matches the case, e.g. upper/lower case, typed in the **Find what:** box).
  - o Find whole words only (to ensure that only whole words are found, e.g. the word note is found but not bank*note*, *note*worthy, end*note*, foot**note**, etc.).
  - o Use wildcards (to stand in place of characters if you don't know the full word, e.g. **n??e** will find do**nate**, volu**ntee**r and **note**).
  - o Sounds like (to find words that sound similar (e.g. **nite** will find **note, night** and **neat**).
  - o Find all word forms.
- Press **Find Next** to find the first occurrence of the search word(s) and then press **Replace** or select **Replace All** to replace all occurrences of the search word(s) with the replacement word

Refine the search by matching the case or finding whole words only, etc.

- When **Replace All** is selected, a confirmation window opens informing you of the number of replacements that have been made.

- Click **OK**.
- Click **Cancel** to close the **Replace** window.

2.2.6 Copying and Moving Text (3.2.2.6)
Text can be moved within the same document or between open documents.

To copy and move text, do the following:

Within a Document
- To copy text within the same document, select the text and then, from the **Home** tab, select the **Copy** button from the **Clipboard** group (or press **CTRL + C**).
- Select a destination position within the document and then click the **Paste** button (or press **CTRL + V**).
The duplicated text will appear in the new position.
- To *move* text, follow the procedure above but click the **Cut** button (scissors) from the **Clipboard** group at Step 1 (or press **CTRL + X**).

Between Documents
- Open the required document files. Both files will be displayed as tabs on the taskbar at the bottom of the screen.
- Ensure that the document containing the text to be copied, is the active document.
- To **copy** text, select the text and then, from the **Home** tab, select the **Copy** button from the **Clipboard** group (or press **CTRL + C**).
- Click the other document on the taskbar or select the **View** tab and **Switch Windows**.
- Choose the other document from the list and ensure that the correct document is displayed.
- Position the mouse where you want the copied text to be placed.
- From the **Home** tab, in the **Clipboard** group, click the **Paste** button (or press **CTRL + V**).
The text will be duplicated in the selected position within the document.
- To **move** text to another document, repeat the above procedure but click the **Cut** button at Step 3 (or press **CTRL + X**).

> **NOTE**
> You can also copy, cut and paste text within and between documents by right clicking and selecting the **Cut**, **Copy**, **Paste** commands from the shortcut menu or by using the **Drag and Drop** method. The latter method uses the mouse to copy or move text to a different destination within the *same* document. To move text, select the text to be moved, hold down the mouse button and drag to the new destination (or hold down the **CTRL** key whilst dragging to **copy** the text to the new destination).

2.2.7 Undoing and Redoing (3.2.2.8)
If a mistake is made when entering, editing or deleting text, it can be corrected by using the undo button. To redo the action, the redo button is used.

To use undo and redo, do the following:
- To undo an action, click the **Undo** button from the **Quick Access Toolbar**.
Alternatively, press **CTRL + Z** to undo.

Undo ——— ——— Redo

——— Arrow

- To redo an action, click the **Redo** button from the **Quick Access Toolbar**.
  Alternatively, press **CTRL + Y** to redo.

- To see a list of actions, click the arrow between the buttons and select an action from the list.
  Any actions that exist before the selected action will also be undone.

The previous four
actions (highlighted)
will be undone from
this list

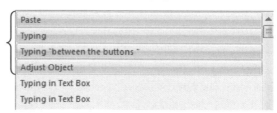

NOTE

The Redo button displays as a repeat button, until the Undo button is utilised. When the
Undo button is used, the Redo button becomes active.

Select the Undo arrow
to see a list of actions

The Redo button
displays as the **Repeat**
button until the Undo
command is used

PRACTICE SEQUENCE

1   Open Word and the document called **sale**.

2   Display the non-printing marks in the document (you should see where spaces and
    paragraphs have been created).

3   Hide the non-printing marks.

4   Select the word **Jumble.**

5   Remove the selection and select the final paragraph.

6   Remove the selection.

7   Select the whole document.

8   Remove the selection.

9   Edit the paragraph starting *If you wish to volunteer to man one of the stalls* so that it
    reads *If you wish to volunteer to help on one of the stalls*

10 Change the name **Mary** to **Deirdre**.

11 Using the search and replace facility, replace the word **note** with the word **remember**
    (there should be two replacements).

12 Move the text starting *If you have any of the above items to donate...* so that it displays
    after the telephone number (ensure there is a clear line space between the paragraphs).

13 Copy the text starting **Stalls** and ending **Books** into a new document.

14 Save this document as **stalls** and close.

15 Save and close the **sale** document.

Section 3   Formatting

Formatting refers to enhancing the appearance of text by changing fonts, sizes, colours and styles. Text can be further enhanced by changing the case to upper, lower or sentence case and by using hyphenation throughout the document to hyphenate long words at the end of a line of text. To ensure that a document is presented to a professional standard, text formatting should be consistent throughout a document and appropriate for the subject and content. For example, a legal document should appear professional, formal and consistent, without using colour, elaborate fonts or large font sizes throughout the document, whereas a poster should use all of these formatting features to grab attention.

3.1   Text

In this section, you will learn about the following:

- Changing text formatting: font sizes, font types.
- Applying text formatting: bold, italic, underline.
- Applying text formatting: subscript, superscript.
- Applying different colours to text.
- Applying case changes to text.
- Applying automatic hyphenation.

3.1.1 Text Formatting (3.3.1.1, 3.3.1.2 and 3.3.1.4)

Text can be formatted with a variety of different fonts, both serif and sans serif. Serifs are the 'tails' on characters; sans serif fonts don't have these 'tails'. See the examples below.

TIMES NEW ROMAN
COURIER NEW
CAMBRIA

These are serif fonts. Note the serifs ('tails') on the characters, such as on the **T** in Times.

ARIAL
MYRIAD PRO
ST HUNTINGTON

These are sans serif fonts. Note there are no serifs ('tails') on the characters. ST Huntington is an informal font, ideal for posters but not formal business documentation.

Font size can also be increased or decreased to enhance text. It is important to ensure that font size is consistent throughout the document (e.g. all headings share the same font size, as do the sub-headings and body text). Headings should be displayed in a larger font size than sub-headings, which should in turn be a larger font size than the main body text. See some examples below:

This is in font size 8.

This is in font size 12.

This is in font size 18.

To change the font type, size, style and colour of cell contents, do the following:

Font Types

Select the **Font** arrow

- Select the text to be formatted.
- From the **Home** tab and **Font** group, select the **Font** arrow.
- Select a font from the drop-down list.

Select a font from the list

Font Sizes

- Select the text to be formatted.
- From the **Home** tab and **Font** group, select the **Font Size** arrow.
- Select a size from the drop-down list.

  Alternatively, select the **Grow Font** or **Shrink Font** buttons to increase or decrease the font size (the font will grow/shrink by one point size each time the button is pressed).

Select the **Font Size** arrow

Select a **Font size**

Grow font —   — Shrink font

Font Colours

- Select the text to be formatted.
- From the **Home** tab and **Font** group, select the **Font Color** arrow.
- Select a colour from the drop-down list or select **More Colors** to see the **Colors** window for further colour options.
- Select a colour from the palette.
- Click **OK**.

Select the **Font Color** arrow

Select a font colour

Select **More Colors** to see the **Colors** window

The **Colors** window provides more colours

Font Styles

- A font style refers mainly to **bold**, *italic* and underline.
- Select the text to be formatted.
- From the **Home** tab and **Font** group, select the required font style.

Bold —

Italic —   — Underline

3.1.2 Subscript and Superscript (3.3.1.3)

Superscript refers to text that appears above the normal line of text, as in ^{TM}. A subscript refers to text that displays below the normal line of text, such as H_2O.

To apply superscript and subscript, do the following:

Superscript

- Select the text to be made superscript.
- From the **Home** tab and the **Font** group, select the **Superscript** command.
  Alternatively, select the command first and then type in the superscript text.

> **NOTE**
>
> Superscript can also be applied by pressing the keyboard combination of **CTRL + Shift + =**. Superscript can be removed by selecting the text and pressing **CTRL + space bar**.

Subscript

- Select the text to be made subscript.
- From the **Home** tab and the **Font** group, select the **Subscript** command.
  Alternatively, select the command first and then type in the subscript text.

> **NOTE**
>
> Subscript can also be applied by pressing the keyboard combination of **CTRL + =**. Subscript can be removed by selecting the text and pressing **CTRL + space bar**.

3.1.3 Change Case (3.3.1.5)

Case refers to UPPER CASE, lower case, Sentence case, tOGGLE cASE (the case of each character is reversed) and Title Case (each word is capitalised).

To change case, do the following:
- Select the text to be changed.
- From the **Home** tab and the **Font** group, select the **Change Case** command.
- Select a case from the menu.

  Alternatively, use the keyboard combination of **Shift + F3** to move through the different case options.

> **NOTE**
>
> All of the above formatting features are available in the Font window (select the Font window launcher icon).
>
>
>
> Click the **Font window** launcher icon to see the Font window
>
> From the **Font** tab select fonts, sizes, styles, font colours, underline styles and effects, such as All caps or superscript or subscript
>
>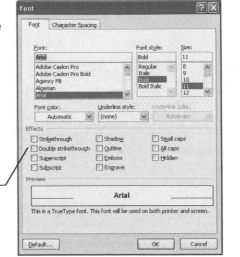

3.1.4 Automatic Hyphenation (3.3.1.6)

Hyphenation refers to using hyphens to break up a word when it is too long to fit at the end of a line. See the example below.

This text uses hyphena-
tion so that words that
are too long to fit at the
end of a line are broken
with a hyphen

Note how the text is hyphenated at the end of the first line in this example.

This text uses no
hyphenation so words
that are too long to fit at
the end of a line are
carried on to the next line
of text

In this example, there is no hyphenation and instead the word is wrapped around to the next line of text.

To apply automatic hyphenation, do the following:

- From the **Page Layout** tab and the **Page Setup** group, select the **Hyphenation** arrow

- Choose a hyphenation option from the drop-down menu, such as **Automatic** to use automatic hyphenation in the whole document.

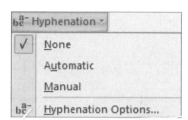

- Select **Hyphenation Options** to see further hyphenation features.
    - Select the **Automatically hyphenate document** checkbox (to enter a tick in the box) to use hyphenation in the whole document.
    - Select **Hyphenate words in CAPS** to use hyphenation on all upper case words in the document.
- Click **OK**.

PRACTICE SEQUENCE

1   Open the **sale** document.
2   Format the heading JUMBLE SALE with **Comic Sans MS** font, **24** font size, **dark blue** font colour, **bold** and underlined.
3   Format the text **STALLS** in **Comic Sans MS** font, **18** font size, **dark blue** font colour, **bold** and *italics*.
4   Change the case of the text STALLS to Sentence case.
5   Format the text **Village Hall** in *italics*.
6   Format the date and time of the jumble sale in **bold** and with a **red** font colour.
7   Format the telephone symbol as **bold** with a **red** font colour (do not format the telephone number).
8   The remainder of the text should display as Arial 12.
9   Apply automatic hyphenation to the document.
10   Apply superscript to the copyright © symbol.
11   Save the **sale** document and close.

3.2   Paragraphs

In this section, you will learn about the following:

- Creating and merging paragraphs.
- Inserting and removing a soft carriage return (manual line break).
- Recognising good practice in aligning text. Using align, indent and tab tools rather than inserting spaces. Aligning text to the left, centre, and right and justify text.
- Indenting paragraphs: left, right and first line.
- Setting, removing and using tabs: left, centre, right and decimal.
- Recognising good practice in paragraph spacing. Applying spacing between paragraphs rather than using the Enter key.
- Applying spacing above and below paragraphs. Applying single, 1.5 lines and double line spacing within paragraphs.
- Adding and removing bullets and numbers in a single level list. Switching between standard bullet and number styles in a single level list.
- Adding a box border and shading/background colour to a paragraph.

3.2.1   Creating and Merging Paragraphs (3.3.2.1)

A paragraph refers to one or more lines of text that are separated from previous or subsequent lines of text by a carriage return (press Enter).

To create and merge paragraphs, do the following:

Creating Paragraphs
- Position the cursor at the end of an existing paragraph or at the end of a sentence within a paragraph and then press the **Enter** key twice (to ensure that there is a clear line space between paragraphs).

Merging Paragraphs
- Position the cursor at the beginning of the second of the paragraphs to be merged and press the **Backspace** key twice to delete the line spaces between the paragraphs.
  Alternatively, position the cursor at the end of the first of the paragraphs to be merged and then press the **Delete** key twice.

3.2.2   Inserting and Removing Manual Line Breaks (3.3.2.2)

Manual line breaks are also referred to as *soft carriage returns*. A line break moves the cursor to the next line without creating a paragraph break. This is useful if you want to create a new line in a list without a bullet or number appearing automatically before the list item.

To insert a line break, do the following:
- Position the cursor on the page and then press the following key combination: **Shift + Enter**
- The cursor will move to the next line.
- Click the **Show/Hide** button (**Home** tab/**Paragraph** group) to see the line break mark.   ↵

To delete a line break, do the following:
- Click the **Show/Hide** button.
- Position the cursor in front of the line break mark (or double click to select the mark).
- Press **Delete**.

3.2.3 Aligning Text (3.3.2.3 and 3.3.2.4)

It is good practice to align text on a page by using the alignment tools, tabs or indents, rather than by entering spaces with the spacebar. This ensures that all text will line up accordingly and, when using indents and tabs, to a specific measurement on the page.

Text can be aligned horizontally to the left, right or centre of a page, or be displayed with fully justified alignment. See the examples below.

This text is left aligned with a ragged right margin and a justified left margin. This is the default alignment in Microsoft Word documents.	This text is right aligned with a justified right margin and ragged left margin.	This text is centred and neither of the margins are justified.	This text is justified with straight edges on both left and right margins. Justified text will stretch to reach the end of a line by creating spaces between words to ensure a straight edge on the right margin.

To align text, do the following:

- Select the text to be aligned.
- From the **Home** tab and **Alignment** group, select an alignment.

Left align text ——— · · · Right align text · · · ——— Justify text · Centre text ———

NOTE

The shortcut key combinations for alignment are:

CTRL + L = Left   **CTRL + R = Right**

CTRL + E = Centre   **CTRL + J = Justify**

3.2.4 Indenting Paragraphs (3.3.2.5)

Paragraphs can be indented from the left and/or the right margins by a specified measurement.

                        This is **indented** from the left by 9cm.

      This is a **first line indent** which will indent the first line of text by 1cm and then align the remainder of the paragraph to the left at 0cm. This type of indentation is used in some styles of letter writing and business documentation.

This is a 1cm **hanging indent** which will indent a paragraph from the left margin by 1cm, but leave the first line at 0cm, allowing text/number/symbol to be entered at the left margin before each paragraph.

To indent text, do the following:

- Select the paragraph(s) to be indented.
- From the **Home** tab and the **Paragraph** group select the **Increase Indent** command to indent the selected paragraph(s) by the default measurement of 1cm. Click again to increase the indent further.

- Notice the indent marker on the **ruler bar** indicating the indent measurement.

The ruler bar displays the indent markers and indicates the indent measurement

To decrease the indent, do the following:

- Select the **Decrease Indent** command.

Decrease indent ⟶ ⟵ Increase indent

The indent markers can be dragged to a specific measurement on the ruler bar to create different types of indent.

Drag the bottom indent to create a hanging indent ⟶ ⟵ Drag the top indent to create a first line indent

Drag the lower part of the indent marker to create a full indent

To enter a specific measurement for an indent, do the following:

- Select the **Paragraph** window launcher icon.
  The **Paragraph** window opens.
- In the **Indentation** section of the window, use the **Left** and/or **Right** scroll arrows to increase or decrease the current indent measurements (the upwards arrow increases the measurement and the downward arrow decreases the measurement).
- Select the **Special** arrow and choose an option, such as **Hanging** or **First Line**.
- Enter a measurement for the indent by selecting the **By** scroll arrow.

Use the scroll arrows to enter a measurement for the left and/or right indents ⟶ ⟵ Select the **Special** arrow and choose an option, then use the **By** scroll arrows to enter a measurement

- Click **OK**.

3.2.5 Using Tabs (3.3.2.6)

Tabs are used to position text in parallel columns to a specified position on the page. Tabs can be left, right, centre or decimal aligned. See the examples below:

Tab stops are displayed on the ruler bar

Dress	Blue	62	35.99
Blouse	White	110	25.50
Jeans	Denim	1114	55.00
Skirt	Yellow	2	13.75
Coat	Black	106	110.00

Left tab ⟶ Jeans

Decimal tab

Centre tab   Right tab

The dots between the tab stop positions are called **leaders**.

Tab alignment can be selected on the **ruler bar** by clicking the **Tab** button until the relevant tab alignment is displayed

To create tabs, do the following:

Ruler Bar

- Click the **Tab alignment** button on the **ruler bar** as shown above.
- Click the ruler bar to insert a **tab stop** in the specified position.
- Move a tab by dragging the tab stop along the ruler bar.
- Remove a tab by dragging the tab stop off the ruler bar.

Tabs Window

- Click the **Paragraph** window launcher icon.
  The **Paragraph** window opens.
- Select the **Tabs** button (at the bottom of the window).
  The **Tabs** window opens.
- The default tab stop position is displayed. This can be overridden by setting new tab stop positions.
- Enter a measurement for the first tab stop position.
- Select an alignment (use **Decimal** for numbers using decimal precision).
- Select a **Leader** if required.
- Select **Set**.
- Repeat this procedure to set further tabs.
- Click **OK**.

To remove a tab, do the following:

- Select the tab to be removed.
- Click **Clear** (or **Clear All** to clear all tab stops).
- Click **OK**.

3.2.6 Paragraph Spacing (3.3.2.7 and 3.3.2.8)

Paragraph spacing refers to the space above and below a paragraph. Line spacing refers to the space between lines of text within a paragraph. It is good practice to use paragraph spacing rather than using the Enter key to apply spaces between paragraphs. Pressing the Enter key to create spaces between lines of text in a paragraph affects justified alignment. When the Enter key is used to create paragraph spacing above and below paragraphs, the spacing may take on the font size of the previous paragraph and so appear bigger than other spaces in the document. To ensure consistency throughout the document it is recommended that you use both paragraph and line spacing.

To apply paragraph and line spacing, do the following:

Paragraph Spacing

- Select the paragraphs to which spacing is to be applied.
- From the **Home** tab, click the **Paragraph** window launcher icon.
- The **Paragraph** window opens.
- In the **Spacing** section use the **Before** and/or **After** scroll arrows to increase the spacing before and after paragraphs.
- Click **OK**.

Select the **Before** and/or **After** scroll arrows to increase the spacing before and after paragraphs

Line Spacing

- Select the paragraphs to which spacing is to be applied.
- From the **Home** tab, click the **Paragraph** window launcher icon. The **Paragraph** window opens
- In the **Spacing** section select the **Line Spacing** arrow and choose a line spacing option from the menu.
- After selecting **Multiple, Exactly** or **At Least** use the **At** scroll arrows to select a measurement.
- Click **OK**.

Alternatively

- Select the paragraphs to which spacing is to be applied.
- Click the **Line Spacing** command from the **Paragraph** group.
- Choose a line spacing option from the drop-down menu or select **Line Spacing options** to see the **Paragraph** window.

3.2.7 Bullets and Numbering (3.3.2.9)

Bullets and numbering are used to enhance the appearance and clarity of lists.

Bullets

- This is a bulleted list.
    - Bullets can be indented by a specific measurement from the left margin.
- The space between the bullet and the text can be altered.
- ❖ Bullets can be formatted to display with a different bullet symbol.
- Bullets can be formatted to display in a different font, size and colour.

Numbers

1. This is a numbered list.
    2. Numbered lists can be indented from the left margin.
3. The space between the number and the text can be altered.
A. Numbers can be formatted to display in a different format (a, b, c or i, ii, iii, etc.).
1. Numbers can be formatted to display in a different font, size and colour.

To apply bullets and numbering to lists, do the following:

- Select the text to which bullets or numbering are to be applied.
- From the **Home** tab and **Paragraph** group, click the **Bullets** or **Numbering** buttons to enter a standard bullet or number in front of text.
- Select the arrow to see the menu commands.

Bullets

Numbering

- Select a bullet or number from the Library options or select **Define New Bullet** or **Define New Number Format**
- From the **Define New Bullet** window, select the **Symbol** button and choose a symbol, or select **Picture** to select a saved image as a bullet. Select the **Font** button to change the font, size, style and colour. Click the Alignment arrow to select an alignment for the bullet. Click OK.
- From the **Define New Number Format** window, select the **Number Style** arrow and choose a number style from the list. Enter a **Number Format** into the box or retain the format provided for the chosen style and choose an alignment. Select the **Font** button to change the font, size, style and colour.
- Click **OK**.

3.2.8   Borders and Shading (3.3.2.10)

To apply borders and shading to a paragraph, do the following:

Borders

- Select the paragraph to which the border is to be applied.
- From the **Home** tab and **Paragraph** group, select the **Border** command.

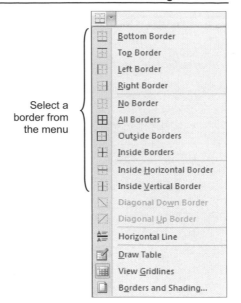

- Select a border from the menu.

Select a border from the menu

Alternatively, select **Borders and Shading** from the **Border** menu.

The **Borders and Shading** window opens.

- Ensure that the **Borders** tab is selected and choose a **Setting**, such as **Box or Shadow**.
- *Alternatively*, select the **Border** buttons to apply borders to specific parts of the paragraph (top, bottom, left or right).
- Select a **Style** for the border, such as a dashed style or solid border.
- Select the **Color** arrow and choose a colour for the border.
- Select the **Width** arrow and choose a line width.
- Ensure that **Paragraph** is displayed in the **Apply to:** box.
- Click **OK**.

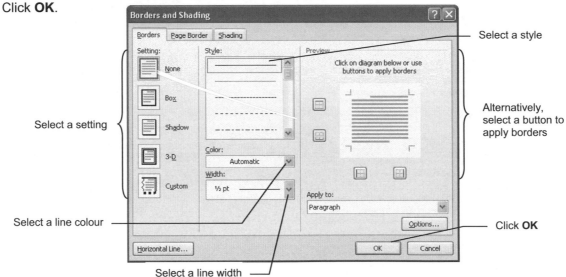

Select a style

Select a setting

Alternatively, select a button to apply borders

Select a line colour

Click **OK**

Select a line width

Shading

- Select the paragraph to which the shading is to be applied.
- From the **Home** tab and **Paragraph** group, select the **Shading** command.
- Select a shading colour from the menu.
- Select **More Colors** to see the colour palette.

Select a colour

Or choose **More Colors**

- Choose a colour.
- Click **OK**.

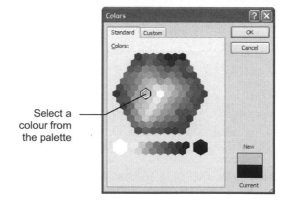

Select a
colour from
the palette

NOTE

Shading can also be applied from the **Borders and Shading** window. Select the **Borders** button from the **Paragraph** group and then select the **Borders and Shading** tab. Select the **Shading** tab and then click the **Fill** arrow. Choose a colour from the menu or select **More Colors** to see the **Colors** window. Choose a colour from the palette and click **OK**. Click **OK** to close the **Borders and Shading** window.

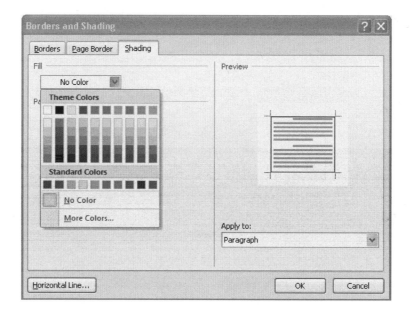

PRACTICE SEQUENCE

1   Open the **sale** document.

2   In the final paragraph, create a new paragraph for the sentence beginning **Please also remember that when downloading images...**.

3   Merge the paragraph beginning **All profits to go...** with the previous paragraph. Ensure that there is a full stop and at least one space separating the two sentences where the new paragraph merges.

4   Insert a line break beneath the final list item Books.

5   Align the heading **Jumble Sale** in the centre of the page. Align the telephone number to the right of the page.

6   Justify the final three paragraphs, all other paragraphs should remain left aligned.

7   Indent the paragraph starting **If you would like to volunteer...** from the left and right by **2cm**.

---

8   Format the paragraph beginning **If you have any of the above items…** with a **2cm** First Line Indent.

9   Apply **6pt** spacing before and after the final three paragraphs. Apply 1.5 line spacing to the final three paragraphs.

10   Add a black round bullet to the list of stalls. Ensure that the bullet is indented at 0cm and the bullet list is indented from the bullet symbol by 1cm.

11   Add a box border and pale grey shading to the final paragraph.

12   Delete the line break that you inserted at step 4.

13   Insert the following text one clear line space beneath the final paragraph: **Profits from last jumble sale:**

14   Insert the following tabs one clear line space beneath the newly entered text: 2cm left aligned tab, 5cm centre aligned tab, 8cm right aligned tab and a 10cm decimal aligned tab. Enter the tabulated text as shown below.

Mary	Sales	Toys	80.00
Joan	Sales	Clothes	98.65
Deirdre	Refreshments	Teas	99.60
John	Sales	Books	60.20
David	Sales	Household	77.45
Jackie	Sales	Shoes	45.50

15   Save and close the **sale** document.

3.3   Styles

In this section, you will learn about the following:

- Applying an existing character style to one or more paragraphs.
- Applying an existing paragraph style to one or more paragraphs.
- Using the copy format tool.

3.3.1 Applying Styles (3.3.3.1 and 3.3.3.2)

A style is a set of formatting features – such as fonts, sizes, colours, alignment, spacing, borders and shading – that can be applied to an entire document or selected areas of a document. Styles facilitate formatting by enabling more than one formatting characteristic, such as font, size and colour, to be applied in one action. Styles ensure consistency throughout a document.

A **Character style** contains formatting features (such as font, size, style, colour, borers and shading) that can be applied to text. Character styles do not contain formatting features that affect paragraphs, such as alignment or spacing.

A **Paragraph style** contains all of the formatting features of a character style, but also contains line spacing, alignments, indents and tabs.

NOTE

Applying a character style (a) will only alter the selected text.

Applying a paragraph style (p) will alter the entire paragraph.

To apply a style, do the following:

- Select the text to which the style is to be applied.
- From the Home tab, select the **Styles** window launcher icon.

Styles window launcher icon

The **Styles** task pane opens, displaying default and created styles.

- Select a style from the task pane to apply it to the selected text.
- Close the window by clicking the **Close X** button.

Alternatively

- Select the text to which the style is to be applied.
- From the Home tab, select the **More** button in the **Styles** group.
- Select **Apply Styles**.
  The **Apply Styles** window opens.
- Select a style from the **Style Name** menu to apply it to selected text.
- Close the window by clicking the **Close X** button.

Select the arrow and choose a style to apply to selected text

3.3.2 Format Painter (3.3.3.3)

Formatting can be copied by using the Format Painter tool. This tool enables you to copy formatting from selected text to another text item, line of text or paragraph.

To copy formatting, do the following:

- Select the text with the formatting that is to be copied.
- From the **Home** tab and **Clipboard** group, select the **Format Painter** button.
- Drag the mouse over the text which is to display the same formatting (note how the cursor changes to include a paintbrush icon).

> **NOTE**
> Double-click the **Format Painter** to keep it on whilst you copy formatting to more than one item of text or paragraph. Click the Format Painter button to turn it off.

PRACTICE SEQUENCE

1   Open the **sale** document.
2   Apply the **Heading 3** style to the telephone number (do not apply to the telephone symbol).
3   Apply the **Heading 2** style to text **Profits from last jumble sale**.
4   Copy the formatting of the telephone number to the paragraph beginning **Please also remember that when downloading...** (this paragraph should be formatted with a border and shading from the previous practice sequence).
5   Save and close the **sale** document.

Section 4   Objects

Objects refer to tables, images, pictures, diagrams, charts and drawn objects.

4.1   Table Creation

In this section, you will learn about the following:

- Creating a table ready for data insertion.
- Inserting and editing data in a table.
- Selecting rows, columns, cells and an entire table.

4.1.1   Creating a Table (3.4.1.1)

A table consists of rows and columns. The intersection between a row and a column is called a **cell**.

To create a table, do the following:

- From the **Insert** tab and the **Tables** group, select the **Table** arrow.
- There are two methods of creating a table:
  - o Drag the mouse over the number or rows and columns required for the table and then release the mouse.
  - o Select **Insert Table**.
- If method (b) is selected the **Insert Table** window will open.
- Use the scroll arrows to enter the number of columns and rows required to create the table.
- Click **OK**.

Use the scroll arrows to increase/decrease the number of rows and columns required

Click **OK**

4.1.2 Inserting and Editing Data in a Table (3.4.1.2)

To insert and edit data in a table, do the following:

- Position the cursor within the relevant cell of the table and enter data as required.
- Use the **Tab** key, or the directional arrow key to move to the next cell in the row (or click the mouse into the next cell).
- Use **Shift + Tab** to move back a cell at a time or use the mouse to click in the required cell.
- If the cell is not wide enough to show all the data that has been entered on one line the data will wrap around within the cell.
- To edit table data, position the cursor within the cell and then do the following:
  - Delete a character at a time by pressing the **Delete** key – this will delete characters to the right of the cursor position within the cell.
  - Delete a character at a time by pressing the **Backspace** key – this will delete characters to the left of the cursor position within the cell.
  - To delete a whole word at a time, hold down the **CTRL** key and then press either **Delete** or **Backspace**, depending on the position of the cursor.
  - To select cell contents, position mouse within a word and double-click to select the word. Treble-click to select more than one line of data within a cell (data that is not separated by a carriage return).
  - To remove a selection, click away from the selected cell.
  - To delete all the contents of a cell, select cell contents by positioning the mouse arrow to the left of the cell contents. The mouse arrow turns into a black arrow pointing at the cell. Left-click the mouse button. Press **Delete**.
  - Overtype data by pressing the **Insert** key on the keyboard and then entering data into the cell in front of existing data. The new data will overwrite the existing data. Press the **Insert** key to turn **Overtype** mode *off*.
  - Enter new data within existing data by positioning the cursor within the text and then start typing. The existing data will move to accommodate the new text (if **Overtype** mode is *off*).

4.1.3 Selecting Cells, Rows, Columns and an Entire Table (3.4.1.3)

Before the table, or individual rows/columns or cells, can be formatted or deleted, it must first be selected.

To select a cell, row, column or an entire table, do the following:

Cells

- Position the cursor near the cell you want to select.
- When a diagonal black arrow appears, left-click to select. *Alternatively,* make sure the cursor is in the cell to be selected.
- From the **Layout** tab, click **Select**, and then **Cell**.
- To select text in a cell, click within the cell and select the text using one of the usual text selection methods.

Rows

- Move the cursor to the left of the row to be selected.
- Left-click the mouse to select.

Columns

- Move the cursor above the column to be selected.
- The insertion point turns into a black arrow.
- Left-click the mouse to select.

Table

- Move the cursor over the table to see a table tag.
- Left-click the tag to select.

> **NOTE**
> This tag also enables you to move a table.

> **NOTE**
> Tables, rows, columns and individual cells can be selected by using the **Select** command.
>
> Click the mouse into a cell within the table, row or column to be selected and then, from the **Table Tools/Layout** tab and the **Table** group, select the **Select** command. Choose **Select Cell**, **Select Row**, **Select Column** or **Select Table**.

Select an option from the menu

4.1.4 Inserting and Deleting Rows and Columns (3.4.1.4)

To insert rows and columns, do the following:

Inserting

- Position the cursor within the table and then, from the **Table Tools/Layout** tab and the **Rows & Columns** group, select an **Insert** command.
- Select an option to insert a row above or below the selected row or to insert a column to the left or right of the selected column.

Select an option from the menu: insert above/below for rows and insert left/right for columns

> **NOTE**
> If you select multiple rows or columns before inserting further rows/columns, then the same number of rows/columns will be inserted.

Deleting

- Select the row or column to be deleted.
- From the **Table Tools/Layout** tab and the **Rows & Columns** group, select a **Delete** option.

Select an option from the menu

PRACTICE SEQUENCE

1   Open the **sale** document.

2   At the end of the document, beneath the tabulated data, enter the following title: **Helpers** and format with the **Heading 3** style.

3   Beneath the title, enter a 2 column and 3 row table.

4   Enter the data as shown on the right.

Mary Roberts	Teas
Bill Smith	Stalls
Deirdre Connor	Raffle

5   Edit the first cell in the table to read **Marie Robertson**.

6   Edit the cell in row 1, column 2 to read **Refreshments**.

7   Insert a new row above **Deirdre Connor** and insert the following data: **Neil Brennan, Sales**.

8   Delete the row for **Bill Smith**.

9   Save **sale** and close.

4.2   Table Formatting

In this section, you will learn about the following:

*   Modifying column width and row height.
*   Modifying cell border line style, width and colour.
*   Adding shading/background colour to cells.

4.2.1   Modifying Column Width and Row Height (3.4.2.1)

Rows and columns can be adjusted by increasing or decreasing the row height and/or column width. A command on the ribbon bar enables both row, and columns to be adjusted to fit the contents of the cells, to fit the window or to display a specific measurement.

To adjust column widths and row heights, do the following:

Column Width

*   Select the column or columns to be adjusted.

*   From the **Table Tools/Layout** tab and the **Cell Size** group, select the **Table Column Width** scroll arrows to increase/decrease the current width measurement.

*   *Alternatively*, select the **Cell Size** window launcher icon to see the **Table Properties** window.

*   Select the **Column** tab and then, from the **Size** section of the window, select the **Measure in** drop down menu to select a measurement type (percentage or centimetres).

*   Use the **Preferred width** scroll arrows to increase or decrease the current column width measurement.

*   Click **OK**.

Row Height

- Select the row or rows to be adjusted.
- From the **Table Tools/Layout** tab and the **Cell Size** group, select the **Table Row Height** scroll arrows to increase/decrease the current height measurement.
  Alternatively, select the **Cell Size** window launcher icon to see the **Table Properties** window.
- Select the **Row** tab and then, from the **Size** section of the window, select the **Specify height** checkbox (to enter a tick in the box). Use the scroll arrows to increase the row height measurement.
- Select the **Row height is** arrow and choose an option, such as **At least** or **Exactly**.
- From the **Options** section of the window, select whether to allow rows to break across pages by entering a tick in the box and/or select the **repeat as header row at the top of each page** (if the table will span more than one page it is useful to see the table headings at the top of the table on each page).
- Select **Previous Row** to adjust the previous row in the table or select **Next Row** to adjust the next row in the table.
- Click **OK**.

Select the **Specify height** tick box and enter a measurement

Select a row height option (Exactly or At least)

4.2.2 Border Line Styles (3.4.2.2)

The default setting is for tables to display an outside and grid border. The existing border can be removed or formatted to display a different line style and line width and colour. To format cells within a table with borders and lines, do the following:

No Border

- Select the table or individual cells, rows or columns.
- From the **Table Tools/Design** tab and **Table Styles** group, select the **Border** arrow.
- Select **No Border**.

Select **No Border**

Gridlines

A table with no borders will display *gridlines*. Gridlines do not appear on a printout but are useful to display on screen to make it easier to enter data and edit and format a table.

To turn on/off gridlines, do the following:
- From the **Table Tools/Layout** tab and the **Table** group, select the **View Gridlines** command (this is a *toggle* button, which means that it is turned on/off each time it is selected).

Table displaying gridlines but no borders

Table displaying borders

Applying Borders

- Select the cell, row, column or table to be formatted.
- From the **Table Tools/Design** tab and **Table Styles** group, select the **Borders** arrow.
- Select a border from the menu or select **Borders and Shading** at the bottom of the menu.

  The **Borders and Shading** window opens, with the **Borders** tab selected.
- From the **Settings** section of the window, select a border setting, such as **Box**.
- From the **Style** section, scroll down the list of line styles and select a line style.
- Select the **Color** arrow and choose a line colour (the default line colour is black).
- Select the **Width** arrow and choose a line width (the default line width is ½ pt).
- Click the **Apply to** arrow and choose a page element to which to apply the border/lines (such as table or cell).

  From the **Preview** section refine the border(s) by selecting top, bottom, left, right, middle or diagonal border buttons (these are *toggle* buttons which are turned on/off each time they are selected) to apply or remove a border.
- Click **OK**.

4.2.3 Shading (3.4.2.3)

To format the background of a cell with colour, do the following:

- Select the cell, row, column or table to be formatted.
- From the **Table Tools/Design** tab and **Table Styles** group, select the **Shading** arrow.
- Choose a colour from the available **Theme Colors** or from **Standard Colors**.
- To see further colour choices, select **More Colors**.

Select **No Color** if you don't want cell shading

Select a colour

Select **More Colors** for further colour options

The **Colors** window opens.

- Select a colour.
- Click **OK**.

The **Colors** window provides more colours

Colors

Standard | Custom

Colors:

Choose a colour

New

Current

OK

Cancel

NOTE

You can also apply shading through the **Borders and Shading** window. Select the **Borders** arrow and then select **Borders and Shading**. Select the **Shading** tab. Select a colour and click OK.

4.3 Graphical Objects

A graphical object refers to a picture (from a stored location on a drive or in the Clip Art gallery), image, chart or drawn object.

In this section, you will learn about the following:
- Inserting an object (picture, chart, drawn object) to a specified location in a document.
- Selecting an object.
- Copying, moving an object within a document and between open documents.
- Resizing and deleting an object.

4.3.1 Inserting an Object (3.4.3.1)

Objects, such as pictures, images, shapes (drawn objects) and charts, can all be inserted from the **Insert** tab/**Illustrations** group. They are placed at the position of the cursor within a document.

Select **Clip Art** to insert a picture from the Clip Art gallery

Select **Chart** to insert a chart

Select **Picture** to insert a picture from file

Select **Shapes** to insert a drawn object

To insert an object, do the following:

Picture
- Position the cursor where the picture is to be inserted.
- From the **Insert** tab and the **Illustrations** group select the **Picture** command.

The **Insert Picture** window opens.

- Select the **Look in** arrow to select the correct drive and/or folder in which the picture is stored.
- Select the picture file.
- Click **Insert**.

The picture will be inserted into the cursor position in the document.

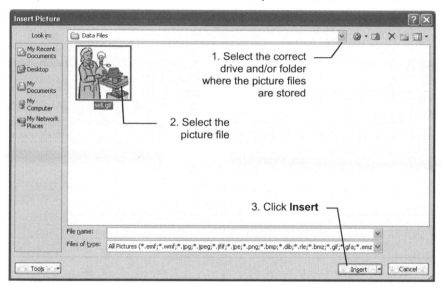

ClipArt Image

- Position the cursor where the image is to be inserted.
- From the **Insert** tab and the **Illustrations** group select the **ClipArt** command.

  The **ClipArt** task pane opens.

- Select the **Search in** arrow and choose whether to search **Everywhere**
  or to look only in a specific collection for the images.

- Select the **Results should be** arrow and choose an option, such as **All media types** (to find images from the internet as well as from ClipArt collections), or **ClipArt, Photographs**, **Movies** or **Sounds**.

- Position the cursor in the **Search for** box and enter a search word (the name of the picture you wish to find, e.g. **computer** will find a variety of computer images).

- Click **Go**.
- A gallery of clip art images will display within the task pane.
- Move the mouse over an image to see a menu arrow.

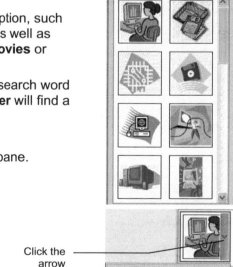

- Click the arrow.
- Click **Insert**.

  Alternatively, just click an image to insert it in the cursor position).

- The picture will be inserted in the cursor position within the document.

Drawn Object

Drawn objects refer to **shapes**.

- From the **Insert** tab and the **Illustrations** group select the **Shapes** command.

- Select a shape from the menu.

- Move the cursor onto the page where the shape is to be inserted.

  The cursor turns into a black crosshair.

- Hold down the left mouse button and drag the mouse to create the shape.

NOTE

Hold down the **Shift** key whilst drawing a shape, such as rectangle or oval, to create a perfect square or circle. Holding down the **Shift** key whilst using the line tool, will result in a straight line.

Chart

A chart is created from data existing in a datasheet. There are a variety of chart types, such as a bar/column chart, a pie chart or a line chart, examples of which are given below.

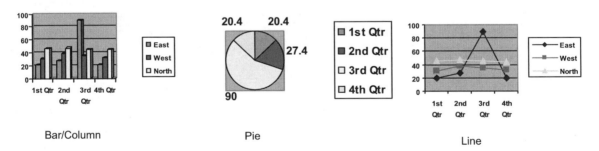

Bar/Column   Pie   Line

- From the **Insert** tab and the **Illustrations** group select the **Chart** command.

- A default column chart with a data sheet containing sample data will be displayed.

- Change the data in the sample datasheet.

- Click away from the datasheet to see the results in the chart.

Sample data is displayed in the datasheet

A column chart is displayed created from the sample data

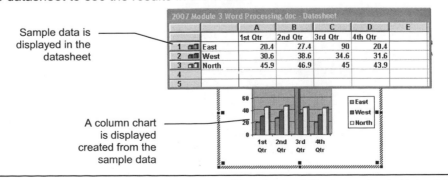

4.3.2 Selecting an Object (3.4.3.2)

Before an object can be edited, formatted or manipulated, it must first be selected.

To select an object, do the following:

- Click an object (picture, chart or shape).
- The object will display with small blue squares (called handles) surrounding it.

Handles

> **NOTE**
>
> Charts are selected with one click, but they cannot be edited or formatted unless the **Chart Tools** are active. To do this, double-click the chart. The **Chart Tools** and the **Chart** menu become active. From the **Chart** menu, you can change the chart type and select chart options, such as axis labels and titles.

4.3.3 Copying and Moving Objects (3.4.3.3)

Objects can be copied or moved within a document or between open documents. The Clipboard group contains the copy, cut and paste tools.

To copy or move an object, do the following:

Within a Document

- To **copy** an object, select the object and then, from the **Home** tab and the **Clipboard** group, select the **Copy** button (or use the keyboard shortcut **CTRL + C**).
- Move the cursor to the new location within the document.
- Select the **Paste** button (or press the keyboard shortcut **CTRL + V**).
- Objects can be **moved** by using the same procedure as above, but select the **Cut** button at step 1 (or the key combination **CTRL + X**).

Between Open Documents

- To **copy** an object between open documents, select the object and then, from the **Home** tab and the **Clipboard** group, select the **Copy** button (or use the keyboard shortcut **CTRL + C**).
- Open documents display on the taskbar at the bottom of the screen.
- Switch to the other document by clicking the tab on the taskbar (or select the **View** tab and then, from the **Window** group, select the **Switch Windows** command, then select the document by clicking the document name in the **Switch Windows** menu).
- Move the cursor to the new location where the object is to be copied within the second document.
- Select the **Paste** button (or press the keyboard shortcut **CTRL + V**).
- Objects can be **moved** by using the same procedure as above, but select the **Cut** button at step 1 (or the key combination **CTRL + X**).

> **NOTE**
> You can also copy, cut and paste objects within and between documents by right-clicking and selecting the Cut, Copy, Paste commands from the shortcut menu or by using the Drag and Drop method. The latter method uses the mouse to copy or move objects to a different destination within the **same** document.
>
> To move an object, select the object to be moved, hold down the mouse button wond drag to the new destination (or hold down the **CTRL** key whilst dragging to **copy** an object to the new destination).

4.3.4 Resizing Objects (3.4.3.4)

It is important that the original proportions of an object are retained when it is resized, otherwise it may appear distorted.

To resize an object, do the following:

Picture Tools

- Select the object and then, from the **Picture Tools/Format** tab and the **Size** group, use the **Height/Width** scroll arrows to increase or decrease the height and/or width of the object.

- Ensure that the object retains its original proportions by changing only the **Height** or the **Width**.

Format Picture Window

- Select the object and then, from the **Picture Tools/Format** tab, select the **Size** window launcher.

  The **Format Picture** window opens.

- Select the **Absolute** scroll arrows to increase or decrease the **Height** and/or **Width** measurements.

- To maintain the original proportions of the object, ensure that the **Lock Aspect Ratio** checkbox displays a tick and only change the height *or* the width (when the height is changed the width will alter proportionally).

- Click **OK**.

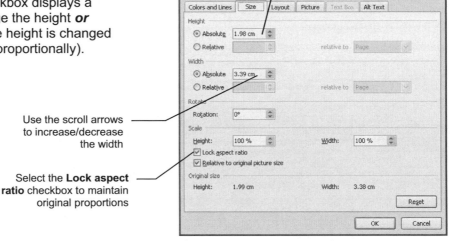

Use the scroll arrows to increase/decrease the height

Use the scroll arrows to increase/decrease the width

Select the **Lock aspect ratio** checkbox to maintain original proportions

Mouse

- Select the object and then position the cursor over a corner handle (resizing from a corner handle maintains original proportions and prevents distortion).

- The cursor turns into a black, double headed arrow when positioned over a handle. Hold down the left mouse button and drag inwards to reduce the size or outwards to increase the size.

- Release the mouse when the object is the required size.

The mouse arrow turns into a black double headed arrow when positioned over a handle

4.3.5 Deleting Objects (3.4.3.4)

To delete an object, do the following:

- Select the object and then press the **Delete** key on the keyboard.

PRACTICE SEQUENCE

1   Open the **sale** document.

2   Position the cursor beneath the title **Jumble Sale** and insert the picture called **sell.gif** so that it displays beneath the title with centre alignment.

3   Resize the **height** of the image to **2cm**.

4   Using Clip Art, find a suitable image relating to one of the following: clothes, shoes, household goods, books or toys. Insert an appropriate image above the **Stalls** title.

5   Resize the image if necessary, ensuring that the original proportions are maintained. Move the Clip Art image so that it is positioned on the right side of the **sell** image beneath the title **Jumble Sale**.

6   Copy the **sell** image to a new document.

7   Resize the height of the copied image to **4cm**.

8   Save the new document as **Advert08** and close.

9   Delete the Clip Art image (retain the **sell** picture in its current position).

10   Create an arrow shape beside the bulleted list with the tip of the arrow towards the bulleted items.

11   Resize the object with a height of 1.5cm and a width of 5.2cm.

12   Save and close the **sale** document.

Section 5   Mail Merge

The mail merge procedure facilitates the process of sending standard documents to customers by storing a data file of information (e.g. addresses), which can then be merged easily with any document, such as a mailshot document. (A mailshot is a document, such as a letter or flyer that is sent out to hundreds or thousands of addresses.)

To facilitate this procedure, a mail merge is performed by merging the names and addresses of existing or potential customers with the standard document. The individual items of data that are merged with the document are called **fields** (e.g Title, First Name and Last Name are all fields). Other fields may also be merged within the main body of the document.

\<Title\> \<First Name\> \<Last Name\> **\<Address1\>** **\<City\>** **\<County\>** **\<Postcode\>** Dear **\<Title\> \<Last Name\>** Please be advised that you have been chosen to receive **\<prize\>** in our monthly draw. All you need to do is contact **\<contact name\>** on **\<contact no\>** to release the prize. We look forward to hearing from you! Regards Sally Jones Manager

This letter displays the merge fields

Miss Louise Connor **The House** **City on the Walls** **Chessington** **CS2 5TH** Dear **Miss Connor** Please be advised that you have been chosen to receive **£40,000** in our monthly draw. All you need to do is contact **John** on **01234 567890** to release the prize. We look forward to hearing from you! Regards Sally Jones Manager

This letter displays the merged data

A mail merge procedure can also be used to create mailing labels.

5.1   Preparation

In this section, you will learn about the following:

- Opening and preparing a document as a main document for a mail merge.
- Selecting a mailing list or other data file for use in a mail merge.
- Inserting data fields in a mail merge main document (letter, address labels).

5.1.1 Main Document (3.5.1.1)

A main document is a standard document, such as a mailing letter, that is merged with a data file.

To create a main document, do the following:

- Create a new document.
- Select the **Mailings** tab and then, from the **Start Mail Merge** group, select the **Start Mail Merge** command.
- Select a document type from the menu, such as **Letters**.
- Enter the standard information into the document.
- Save the main document.

5.1.2 Mailing List (3.5.1.2)

A mailing list is also referred to as a **data file**. The mailing list contains merge fields that can be merged with any main document, such as letter, labels, memo, agenda, minutes, flyer. A mailing list may be created in Word as a table or in another application, such as Microsoft Access or Excel.

To select a mailing list for use in a mail merge, do the following:

- Open the main document.
- From the **Mailings** tab and the **Start Mail Merge** group, select the **Select Recipients** command.
- From the menu, select **Use Existing List**.
- Select the correct drive and/or folder from the **Look in** menu.
- Select the data file.
- Click **Open**.

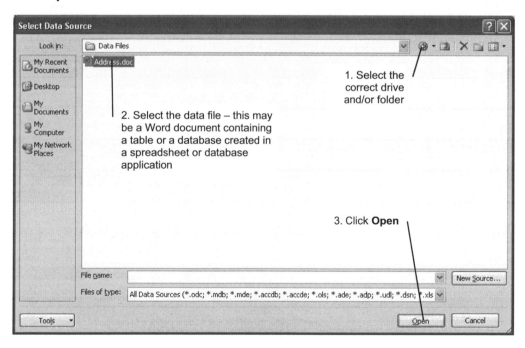

- Save the main document.

5.1.3 Inserting Fields (3.5.1.3)

Once the data source is attached to the main document, you can insert the mail merge fields.

To insert merge fields, do the following:

- Open the main document and esnure that the cursor is in the correct position for inserting the merge fields.

- From the **Mailings** tab and the **Write & Insert Fields** group, select the **Insert Merge Field** command.

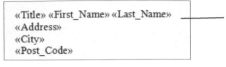

- From the menu select the first merge field.

- Press the space bar to create a space between fields appearing on the same line, or press **Enter** to create a new paragraph for fields appearing on a separate line.

- Select the **Insert Merge Field** command and select the second merge field. Repeat this procedure to enter the remaining merge fields. (See the example below.)

«Title» «First_Name» «Last_Name»
«Address»
«City»
«Post_Code»

Ensure that there is a space between fields that appear on the same line or press Enter to insert fields on a separate line

- Save the main document.

> **NOTE**
>
> When opening a document that contains merge fields, a message may appear informing you that opening the document will run an SQL command and asking if you wish to continue. Click Yes.
>
>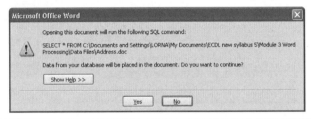

5.1.4 Labels (3.5.2.1 and 3.5.1.3)

In the previous section you learned how to perform a mail merge procedure to create a form letter. In addition to letters, mail merge can also be performed to create labels.

To create labels do the following:

- Open a new document.

- From the **Mailings** tab and the **Start Mail Merge** group, select the **Start Mail Merge** command.

- Select **Labels** from the menu.
  The **Label options** window opens.

- Select the **Label vendors** arrow and choose a name from the list, such as Microsoft or Avery.

- Select a **Product Number** and check the product information for the labels you have chosen.

- Click **OK**.

- Select the **Select Recipients** command and choose **Use Existing List**.

- Locate the mailing list (data source).

- Click **Open**.

- Insert merge fields into the first label and then click the **Update Labels** command (each of the labels will display the merge fields).

- Save the labels and close.

5.1.5 Previewing Results and Finding Recipients

When merge fields have been inserted within a main document, they are displayed as fields and not actual data. For example, <<**First Name**>> will display rather than the data **Mary**. The merge fields can be previewed to see how they will look on printed output.

To preview the results of a mail merge procedure, do the following:

- From the **Mailings** tab and the **Preview Results** group, select the **Preview Results** command.

  The merge fields will be replaced by the data.

- Enter a number in the **Go To Record** box to go to a specific record or select the arrow to scroll through each record in the mailing list.

- Select the **Find Recipient** button.

  The **Find in Field** window opens.

Find Recipient button

- Enter the search word in the **Find What** box.
- Click the **In field** arrow and choose the field.
- Click **Find First**.
- Click **Close** to close the **Find in Field** window.

5.1.6 Using the Step-by-Step Mail Merge Wizard

The above steps can all be performed through the Mail Merge Wizard.

To use the Mail Merge wizard, do the following:

- Create a new document.
- Select the **Mailings** tab and then, from the **Start Mail Merge** group, select the **Step-by Step Mail Merge Wizard** command.
- Select a document type from the task pane, such as **Letters**.
- Click **Next: Starting document**.
- Select **Use the current document**.
- Click **Next: Select recipients**.
- Select **Use an existing list** and then click **Browse**.
- Locate the data file/mailing list from the correct drive/folder, select the file.
- Click **Open**.

  The **Mail Merge Recipients** window opens, displaying the records within the mailing list.

- Click **OK** to close the window and return to the main document.
- Select **Next: Write your letter.** Enter the standard information into the document.
- Position the cursor where the merge fields should appear in the document and then, from the **Mail Merge** task pane, select **More items**.

  The **Insert Merge Fields** window opens.

- Select the first field and click **Insert**.
- Click **Close**.
- Insert a space with the space bar if the next field should appear on the same line or press **Enter** if the next field is to appear on a separate line. Reselect **More items** and choose another field – repeat the above procedure to insert each of the fields into the main document.
- Select **Next: Preview your letters**. Use the **Go to** arrows >> and << to scroll through the records in the mailing list or use the **Find a recipient** button to find a specific record (from this step of the Wizard, you can edit the recipient list or exclude specific records from the mail merge procedure).

- Select **Next: Complete the merge**.
- Select **Edit individual letters** to merge to a new document (alternatively, select **Print** to merge to printer without completing the mail merge procedure).
- Click **All**.
- Click **OK**.
- Save the document.
- Print the merged document, if you didn't perform this action at Step 6 of 6.
- Close the document.

PRACTICE SEQUENCE

1   Open the **activities** letter that is provided for this practice sequence.

2   Prepare the **activities** letter as a main document for a mail merge.

3   Select the **Address** mailing list for use in the mail merge.

4   Insert the merge fields in the letter where indicated (delete the existing text, e.g. <title> – these are not fields but are included as a guide only).

5   Preview the results and scroll through each record in the mailing list.

6   Save and close the **activities** document.

7   Create mailing labels, using the **Address** mailing list, with 30 Microsoft labels per page (use the second option in the **Product Number** list).

8   Update all of the labels to display the merge fields.

9   Preview the results and then save as **Labels**.

10 Close all open documents.

5.2   Outputs

Output refers to an onscreen or printed copy of a document.

In this section, you will learn about the following:
- Merging a mailing list with a letter or label document as a new file or printed output.
- Printing mail merge outputs: letters and labels.

5.2.1 Merge (3.5.2.1)

The mail merge document will comprise an individual letter until the mail merge procedure is finalised. The merge procedure is not complete until the **Finish & Merge** command is used. This will merge each of the records in the mailing list with the main document. The resulting document will comprise many pages, subject to the amount of records that are merged with the main document. For example, if the original main document comprises one page and it is merged with a mailing list containing 5 addresses, the resulting merged document will comprise 5 pages.

To complete the mail merge procedure, do the following:
- Open the main document containing the merge fields.
- From the **Mailings** tab and the **Finish** group, select the **Finish & Merge** command.
- Select **Edit Individual Documents** to finalise the merge or select **Print Documents** to print the documents without completing the merge process.

  The **Merge to New Document** window opens (or the **Merge to Printer**, depending on the menu option selected).

- Select the **All** option button to merge all records with the main document.
- Click **OK**.

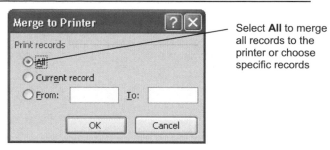

Select **All** to merge all records to the printer or choose specific records

---

NOTE

The number of pages will change on the status bar, when the **Merge to New Document** menu option is selected, to display a document for each of the records in the mailing list.

- If the **Merge to Document** menu option is selected, save the merged document with a different name to the main document (the main document can be used again with the same or different mailing list at a future date).
- If the **Merge to Printer** menu option is selected, without completing the mail merge procedure, save the document with the same name.

5.2.2 Printing a Mail Merge Document (3.5.2.2)

To print a merged document (e.g. letter or labels), do the following:

- Open the merged letter or merged labels.
- From the **Office Button**, select the **Print** command.
- Select **Print** from the **Preview and print the document** sub-menu (or press the keyboard combination of **CTRL + P**).
  The **Print** window opens.
- Click **OK** to print the mail merge outputs (letters and/or labels).

NOTE

To print a mail merged document quickly without using the Print window, select the **Quick Print** option from the **Office Button**.

PRACTICE SEQUENCE

1   Open the **activities** document.
2   Complete the mail merge process by merging the letter with all of the records in the mailing list to a new document.
3   Save the merged document as **Activmerge.doc**.
4   Print the merged **Activmerge** document and close.
5   Open the **Labels** document and complete the mail merge process by merging to a new document.
6   Save the merged labels as **Merged Labels**.
7   Print the merged **Merged Labels** document.
8   Close the document.

Section 6   Preparing Outputs

6.1   Setup

Output refers to the way that a document is viewed, either on-screen or as printed hard copy. Both types of output require preparation by choosing an appropriate output format, such as changing orientation and margins or printing to a specific number of pages. It is good practice to check document text and correct any errors to ensure the finished document is presented to a professional standard.

In this section, you will learn about the following:

- Changing a document's orientation: portrait and landscape.
- Changing paper size of a document.
- Changing the margins of an entire document: top, bottom, left and right.
- Recognising good practice in adding new pages: inserting a page break rather than using the Enter key.
- Inserting and deleting a page break in a document.
- Adding and editing text in headers and footers.
- Add fields in headers and footers: date, page number information and file name.
- Apply automatic page numbering to a document.

6.1.1   Orientation (3.6.1.1)

Orientation refers to the shape of the paper being used. It can be either Portrait or Landscape. The default orientation in Word is Portrait. Portrait orientation is taller than it is wide. Landscape orientation is wider than it is tall. You may need to change the orientation so that text and objects fit on the page. Changing the orientation of the document not only enhances the presentation of the printed output, it can also save paper. See the examples below.

This is displayed in portrait

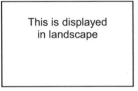
This is displayed in landscape

To change orientation, do the following:

- From the **Page Layout** tab and the **Page Setup** group, select the **Orientation** command.
- Select the required orientation – Portrait or Landscape.

6.1.2   Paper Size (3.6.1.1)

The default paper size is A4 (21cm x 29.7cm in portrait orientation). The paper size can be altered to another of your choice, such as A5, B3 or a variety of other sizes suitable for the intended printed output.

To change the paper size, do the following:

- From the **Page Layout** tab and the **Page Setup** group, select the **Size** command.

  A drop-down menu opens, displaying a variety of paper sizes.

- The default paper size is A4. Select the required paper size.

- To see further size options, select the **More Paper sizes** command at the bottom of the menu.

  The **Page Setup** window opens with the **Paper** tab the active tab.

- Select the **Paper size** arrow and choose a paper size from the list.

- Click **OK**.

6.1.3 Margins (3.6.1.2)

Margins are the space between the edge of the paper and the document text. To enhance the layout of the printed document the top, bottom, left and right margins can all be increased or decreased if required.

To change margins, do the following:

- From the **Page Layout** tab and the **Page Setup** group, select the **Margins** command.

  A drop-down menu opens.

- From this menu, you can select normal default margin settings, or select from the list of settings.

- To see further margin options, select **Custom Margins**.

- The **Page Setup** window opens with the **Margins** tab the active tab.

Use the scroll arrows to increase or decrease the current margin setting

- Use the scroll arrows to increase or decrease the current margin measurements for the Top, Bottom, Left and Right margins.

- Click **OK**.

6.1.4 Good Practice when Adding New Pages (3.6.1.3)

It is good practice to use page breaks to create new pages within a document rather than using carriage returns (the Enter key). When the Enter key is pressed it creates a paragraph mark which can be formatted in the same way as text. If the paragraph marks are deleted then text beneath the paragraph marks will move up the page. If a page break is inserted, text and objects can be inserted, edited and formatted without affecting previous or subsequent pages in the document. A page break can be deleted if no longer required.

6.1.5 Inserting and Deleting Page Breaks (3.6.1.4)

To insert and delete page breaks, do the following:

Inserting

- Position the cursor where the page break should be inserted.
- Select the **Insert** tab from the ribbon.
- Select **Page Break** from the **Pages** section.

Page break

A page break will inserted and the cursor will appear at the top of the new page.
Alternatively Position the cursor where the page break should be inserted and then hold down the **CTRL** key and press **Enter**.

Deleting

- Select the **Show/Hide** command from the **Home** tab/**Paragraph** group so that you can see the page breaks in the document.

- Position the cursor in front of the page break and press the **Delete** key.
- The page break is deleted.

6.1.6 Headers and Footers (3.6.1.5)

Headers appear at the top of the page and footers appear at the bottom of the page. A header or footer can display information that you type in, such as your name or copyright information, or display page numbers or dates.

To create a header and a footer, do the following:

- From the **Insert** tab and the **Header & Footer** group, select the **Header** or **Footer** command.
- Select a built-in header/footer style or select **Edit Header** or **Edit Footer** to start entering the header or footer information.

  The **Header** or **Footer** area opens above your document, ready for you to enter the header/footer information.

- Press the **TAB** key once to align the cursor to the centre or twice to align the cursor to the right.
- Enter the required header text.

  The **Header & Footer Tools** contextual tab becomes active and displays the **Design** tab commands. From this ribbon bar, you can choose to insert page numbers, number of pages, date, time, file path (location) and file name.

- To switch between the header and footer area, select **Go to Footer** or **Go to Header**.

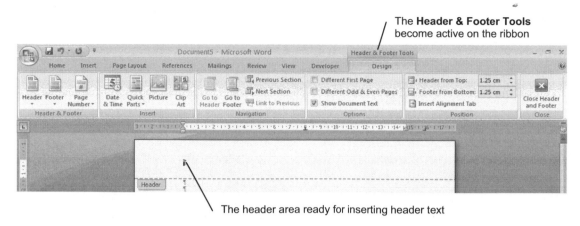

The **Header & Footer Tools** become active on the ribbon

The header area ready for inserting header text

- To close the Header and Footer area, click away from the header/footer area into the main document.

Editing and Deleting a Header or Footer

To edit part of a header or footer, do the following:

- From the **Insert** tab and the **Header & Footer** group select the **Header** or the **Footer** command.
- Select **Edit Header** (or **Edit Footer**).
- Position the cursor within the header/footer text and make changes as required (header/footer text can be edited in the same way as ordinary document text).

To delete part of a header or footer, do the following:

- Select the header/footer text to be deleted.
- Press the **Delete** key on the keyboard.

To remove a header or footer, do the following:

- From the **Insert** tab and the **Header & Footer** group, select the **Header** or the **Footer** command.
- Select **Remove Header** or **Remove Footer**.
  This command removes the entire header or footer.
- To close the header and footer area, click away from the header/footer area into the main document.

6.1.7 Inserting Fields (3.6.1.6)

Fields are items of header or footer data, such as dates and filename fields that update automatically.

To insert fields, do the following:

- From the **Insert** tab and the **Header & Footer** group select the **Header** or the **Footer** command.
- Select **Edit Header** (or **Edit Footer**).
  The **Header/Footer** area opens, ready for you to insert the field or fields.
- Press the **TAB** key once to align the cursor to the centre of the page or twice to align the cursor on the right of the page.
  The **Header & Footer Tools** contextual tab becomes active and displays the **Design** tab commands. From this ribbon bar, you can choose to insert page numbers and the date and time. From the Quick Parts menu, you can insert fields, such as, number of pages, date, time, file path (location) and file name.

- From the **Insert** group, select **Quick Parts**.

Select **Page Number** to insert page numbering information

Select **Date & Time** to insert the current date/time

Select **Quick Parts** to insert fields

- Select **Field**....

Select **Field**...

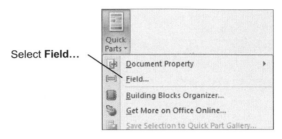

The **Field** window opens.

- Select a category from the **Categories** drop down menu (e.g. **Document Information** or **Date and Time**).
- Select a field name from the list of **Field names** (e.g. from the **Document Information** category, select **FileName** or **NumPages**, or from the **Date and Time** category, select **CreateDate**).
- Format the field if required in the **Field properties** section.
- Click **OK**.

File Name or Number of Pages

Select a category

Select a field name, such as **FileName**

Select **NumPages** to insert the number of pages in the document

Add path (file location)

Change properties

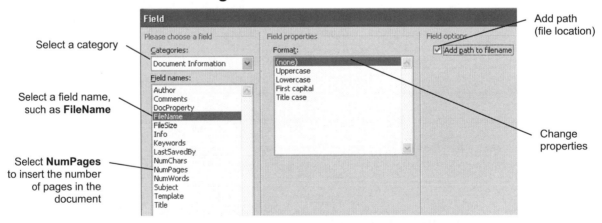

Date or Time

Select a category

Select a Field name

Select a date and/or time format

Example

Lorna Bointon   sale.docx   Monday, 18 August 2008

Header text   Automatic file name   Date

Alternatively, to insert a date and/or time, select the **Date & Time** command.
The **Date and Time** window opens.

- Select a date format and a language.
- Ensure that the **Update automatically** checkbox is selected (there is a tick in the box).
- Click **OK**.

Select a date/time format

Select a language

Ensure that the checkbox is ticked

To switch between the header and footer area, do the following:

- Select **Go to Footer** or **Go to Header**.

To close the header/footer, do the following:
- Click away from the header/footer area into the main document.

6.1.8 Inserting Automatic Page Numbers (3.6.1.7)

To insert automatic page numbers, do the following:

- From the **Insert** tab and the **Header & Footer** group, select **Page Number**.
- From the menu, select a page number option, such as **Top of Page**, **Bottom of Page** or **Current Position**.

  Each of these menu options will open a further sub-menu with page number formats displayed, such as simple number formats or **X of Y** (e.g. Page 1 of 3).
- Select a number format.
- Select **Format Page Numbers.**
  The **Page Number Format** window opens.
- Select the **Number Format** arrow and select a number format from the menu.
- In the **Page Numbering** section of the window, select the **Continue from previous section** option button to apply automatic numbering to each page in the document (alternatively, select the **Start at** option button if you want to start page numbering from a specific page).

Select a number format

Select an option button

- Click **OK**.

PRACTICE SEQUENCE

1   Open the **sale** document.

2   Change the top and bottom margins to 2cm and the left and right margins to 1.5cm.

3   Check that the paper size is A4.

4   Ensure that the orientation is Portrait.

5   Create a new page after the final paragraph of shaded and bordered text (so that the heading **Profits from last jumble sale** and the tabulated text and the **Helpers** title and table appear on the second page).

6   Enter a left aligned header with your name.

7   Enter a centre aligned header with an automatically updating filename field (do not include the path).

8   Enter a right aligned header with an automatically updating date field.

9   Enter a centre aligned footer with a number of pages field.

10 Edit the header by removing the date field.

11 Edit the footer by inserting a left aligned date field and deleting the number of pages field.

12 Apply centre aligned automatic page numbers.

13 Save and close the **sale** document.

6.2   Checking and Printing

In this section you will learn about the following:

- Spell checking a document and make changes: correcting spelling errors and deleting repeated words.

- Adding words to a built-in custom dictionary using a spell-checker.

- Previewing a document.

- Printing a document from an installed printer using output options: entire document, specific pages and number of copies.

6.2.1 Checking (3.6.2.1)

It is important to check text within a document. Incorrect text appears unprofessional and affects the overall presentation of the document. It can also affect the understanding and assimilation of the subject matter if the text contains errors.

Therefore, you should do the following:

- Proofread the document text carefully for errors.

- Correct errors where necessary.

- Use the spell check facility to check spelling and grammar.

Checking Spelling

* From the **Review Tab** and the **Proofing** group, select the **Spelling & Grammar** command.

  The **Spelling and Grammar** window opens.

* Unrecognised words (words that are not in the Spelling dictionary) will be displayed and suggestions provided.

* Select a suggestion and then click **Change** if you want to change the spelling of a word to the suggested spelling.

* Select **Change All** to change all occurrences of the word throughout the document.

* Select **Ignore Once** if you know that the spelling is correct (such as proper names) or **Ignore All** if you want to ignore all occurrences of the word through the document.

* Repeated words are picked up within the document and displayed in the **Repeated word** box.

* Select **Delete** to delete repeated words (or click **Ignore Once** if you wish to keep the repeated word).

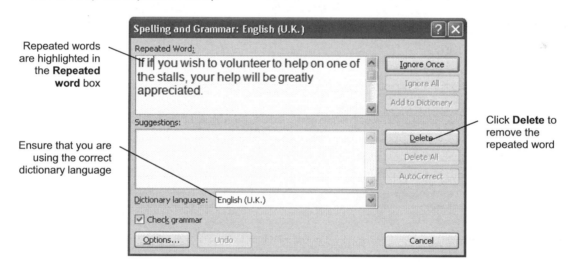

Repeated words are highlighted in the **Repeated word** box

Ensure that you are using the correct dictionary language

Click **Delete** to remove the repeated word

* When the **Spelling** tool has completed the spell check, a window will open.

* Click **OK**.

6.2.2 Adding Words to a Dictionary (3.6.2.2)

The Spelling tool uses a built-in dictionary against which it matches words and provides suggestions. If the Spelling tool does not recognise the spelling of the word, it may provide unsuitable suggestions. Words can be added to the dictionary if required. This is useful if you use unfamiliar words, such as medical, technical or scientific terms within a document.

Words can be added to the dictionary through the **Spelling and Grammar** window or through the **Office Button** and **Word Options**.

Using Word Options

If the spelling check is complete, you will be unable to reopen the **Spelling and Grammar** window and so will have to open **Word Options** from the **Office Button**.

To add words to a dictionary using Word Options, do the following:

- From the **Spelling and Grammar** window, select the **Options** button (the **Proofing** tab is selected).

  Alternatively, from the **Office Button** select **Word Options**. In the **Word Options** window, select the **Proofing** tab.

- Select **Custom Dictionaries**.

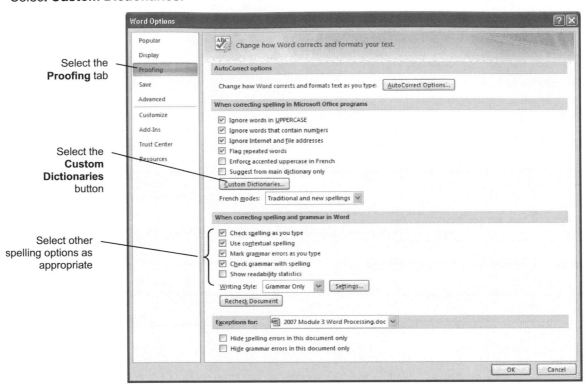

The **Custom Dictionaries** window opens.

- Click **Edit Word List**.

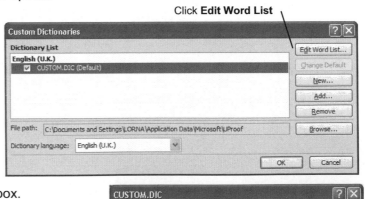

- Enter the word into the **Word(s)** box.
- Click **Add**.

- Click **OK** (three times to exit Word Options).

Using the Spelling and Grammar Window

When completing a spell check, it is possible to add words to the dictionary as you come across them.

To add words to the dictionary using the Spelling and Grammar window, do the following:

- From the **Review Tab** and the **Proofing** group, select the **Spelling & Grammar** command.

   The **Spelling and Grammar** window opens.

   Unrecognised words (words that are not in the Spelling dictionary) will be highlighted in the normal way.

   For words that are not recognised, the Suggestions area will either offer alternative suggestions or read (**No Spelling Suggestions**).

- Click the **Add to Dictionary** button to add the unrecognised word.

   The word will automatically be added to the dictionary and will not be queried during future spell checks.

6.2.3 Previewing a Document (3.6.2.3)

It is good practice to check the layout of a document before printing it.

To preview a document, do the following:

- From the **Office Button**, select **Print** and then **Print Preview**.

   The **Print Preview** window opens, displaying the document.

   Page setup options, such as margins, orientation and size can all be performed from Print Preview. The page(s) can also be printed from this window.

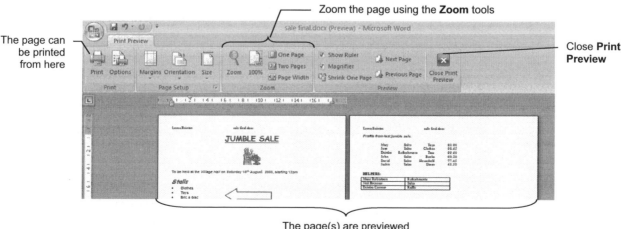

The page(s) are previewed

- Select **Next Page** or **Previous Page** to view each page of the document.

- To zoom in and out, select the **Magnifier** checkbox (ensure there is a tick in the box). Click the magnifying glass icon on the page to zoom in/out (the magnifying glass displays a cross to zoom in and a minus sign to zoom out).

- Select the **Zoom** command to change the way that the page(s) are viewed. Select a **Zoom to** option button or select the **Percent** scroll arrows to enter a zoom percentage.

Many Pages

- If the document contains more than one page, click the **Many Pages** option button in the Zoom window and then select the drop down arrow. Drag the mouse over the number of pages that you want to view.

- Click **OK**.

Drag the mouse over the number of pages that you want to view

- Close Print Preview by selecting the **Close Print Preview** command.

6.2.4 Printing (3.6.2.4)

There are various options that you can choose when printing. For example, you can print the entire document (which may contain multiple pages) or print specific pages and/or a specific number of copies. The default setting is for printing one copy.

To print, do the following:
- From the **Office Button**, select **Print**.
- From the print sub-menu, select **Quick Print** to print a document without changing settings.
- Select **Print** to see the **Print** window (or press the keyboard shortcut **CTRL + P**).

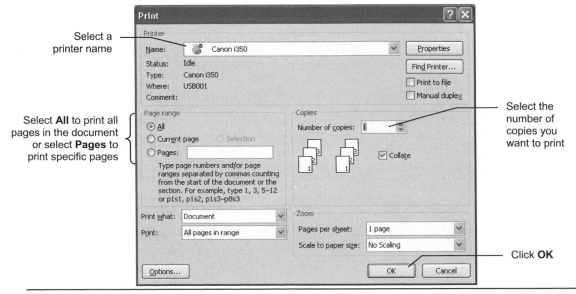

Select a printer name

Select **All** to print all pages in the document or select **Pages** to print specific pages

Select the number of copies you want to print

Click **OK**

Entire Document
- Select the **All** option button in the **Page** range section of the **Print** window.
- Click **OK**.

Specific Pages
- From the **Print** window, select the **Pages** option button.
- Enter the page numbers, separated by a comma if you want non-adjacent pages or separate with a hyphen if you want to print a page range (for example, **1, 4, 6** will print pages 1, 4 and 6 only and exclude pages 2, 3 and 5. However, if **1-6** is entered, pages **1 to 6** will be printed, including pages 2, 3 and 5).
- Click **OK**.

Number of Copies
- From the **Print** window, use the scroll arrows on the **Number of Copies** list box to increase/decrease the required number of printed copies.
- Click **OK**.

PRACTICE SEQUENCE
1   Open the **sale** document.
2   Check the spelling of text within the document and correct any errors.
3   Add the word **Blackrock** to the custom dictionary.
4   Preview the document.
5   Print two copies of page 1 of the document.
6   Save and close the **sale** document.

Unit 4

Spreadsheets

4

Unit 4
Spreadsheets

4

Goals for Unit 4

Unit 4 Spreadsheets requires the candidate to understand the concept of spreadsheets and to demonstrate an ability to use a spreadsheet to produce accurate work outputs.

The candidate shall be able to:
- Work with spreadsheets and save them in different file formats.
- Choose built-in options such as the Help function within the application to enhance productivity.
- Enter data into cells and use good practice in creating lists. Select, sort and copy, move and delete data.
- Edit rows and columns in a worksheet. Copy, move, delete and appropriately rename worksheets.
- Create mathematical and logical formulas using standard spreadsheet functions. Use good practice in formula creation and recognise error values in formulas.
- Format numbers and text content in a spreadsheet.
- Choose, create and format charts to communicate information meaningfully.
- Adjust spreadsheet page settings and check and correct spreadsheet content before finally printing spreadsheet.

What is a Spreadsheet?

A spreadsheet is used for mathematical calculations and analysis, such as to plot figures to find profits and losses based on income and expenditure, and for communicating information through charts and graphs. A spreadsheet consists of a grid containing rows and columns. Rows are numbered (e.g. **1**) and columns are lettered (e.g. **A**). The intersection between a row and a column is called a **cell**. Cells are named with the column letter and row number (e.g. **A1**). Cell names are referred to as **cell references**. A range of cell references (e.g. A1:A10) is called a **cell range**.

Spreadsheets use cell references in formulas and functions, rather than figures, which makes it easier to modify and update data in a spreadsheet. For example, =A1+B1 will total the contents of cells A1 and B1. When data is modified, or rows/columns deleted or inserted, formulas and functions will automatically update to reflect the modifications. Formulas can be copied (referred to as **replicating**) across or down over subsequent cells and the cell reference will change to match the cell to which the formula is replicated. A normal cell reference is called a **relative cell reference**, because it is relative to the cell to which the formula is being copied. Sometimes, an **absolute cell reference** may be required in a formula if the cell reference should not change during replication, but should remain constant. An example of this is in a spreadsheet which uses a cell, such as VAT which will remain constant. A formula using absolute cell references looks like this: =A1+$B$1. The relative cell reference A1 will change when copied downwards to cells A2 and A3, but the absolute cell will remain constant and refer to cell B1.

Spreadsheets should have relevant and appropriate row and column headings to identify data.

Section 1   Using the Application

An **application** refers to the software package that is used to perform a task. The application that will be used for this training manual is Microsoft Office Excel 2007. This is a comprehensive spreadsheets package, capable of creating complex spreadsheets consisting of formulas, functions, charts and graphs.

1.1   Working with Spreadsheets

A spreadsheet is a grid consisting of rows and columns. Each spreadsheet file (also referred to as a **workbook**) can contain many worksheets. Spreadsheet files may be saved in a variety of formats, for use in different applications.

In this section, you will learn about the following.
- Opening and closing a spreadsheet application.
- Closing a spreadsheet.
- Creating a new spreadsheet.
- Switching between open spreadsheets.
- Saving a spreadsheet to a location on a drive and with a different name.
- Saving a spreadsheet in another format, such as template, text file, software specific file extension and version number.

1.1.1   Opening a Spreadsheet Application (4.1.1.1)

Excel is a spreadsheet package that comes as part of the Microsoft Office 2007 suite. This application will either be displayed as an icon on the Desktop of your computer or found in the Start menu.

To open Excel, do the following:
- Select the **Start** menu.
- Select **All Programs**.
- Select **Microsoft Office** and then select **Microsoft Office Excel 2007**.

All Programs

Start menu

Select the Microsoft Office folder and then Microsoft Office Excel 2007

NOTE
To keep the taskbar visible, point and right-click on the taskbar and, from the pop-up menu, click Properties. The Taskbar and Start Menu Properties window opens. Click the box to the left of 'Auto-hide the taskbar' to uncheck this option

---

Microsoft Office Excel 2007 opens.

The screen layout will display the following:

① The Quick Access Toolbar.

② The Office Button.

③ The ribbon.

④ A new, blank spreadsheet.

1.1.2 Closing a Spreadsheet Application (4.1.1.1)

To close Excel, do the following:

* Select the **Office Button**.
* Select **Exit Excel**.

  The Excel program will close.

Exit Excel

Alternatively, select the **Close X** button in the top right corner of the title bar.

1.1.3 Opening a Spreadsheet (4.1.1.1)

To open an existing spreadsheet, do the following:

- Open **Excel**.
- Select the **Office Button**.
- Select **Open**.

Office Button

The **Open** window opens.

- Select the location of the file by clicking the **Look in** arrow and choosing a drive and/or folder.
- Select the file.
- Click **Open**.

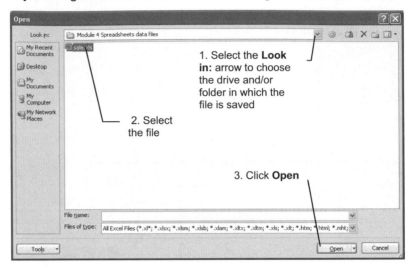

1. Select the **Look in:** arrow to choose the drive and/or folder in which the file is saved

2. Select the file

3. Click **Open**

NOTE

To display the **Open** window using the keyboard, hold down the **CTRL + O**.

Opening Recent Documents

Documents that have been opened recently can be accessed by selecting the **Office Button** and then selecting a file from the Recent Documents list.

Select a recently opened file from the **Recent Documents** list

To change the number of documents listed in **Recent Documents**, select the **Office Button** and then **Excel Options**. Select the **Advanced** button and, in the **Display** section, enter the number of documents that you want to display.

Enter the number of recent documents that should display

1.1.4 Closing a Spreadsheet (4.1.1.1)

To close a spreadsheet, do the following:

- Select the **Office Button**.
- Select **Close**.

NOTE

If changes have been made to the file, a message will appear asking if you want to save the file before closing.

- Click **Yes** to save the file.
- Click **No** to close the file without saving.
- Click **Cancel** to cancel the message and return to the spreadsheet.

1.1.5 Creating a New Spreadsheet (4.1.1.2)

To create a new spreadsheet, do the following:

- Select the **Office Button**.
- Select **New**.
  The **New Spreadsheet** window opens.
- Select **Blank and recent** from the **Templates** list.
- Select **Blank Workbook**.
- Click **Create**.

Select **Blank Workbook**

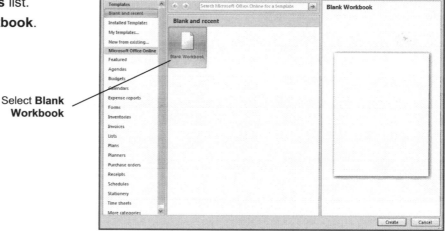

A new blank spreadsheet opens.

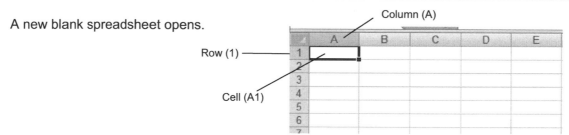

1.1.6 Saving a Spreadsheet to a Location on a Drive (4.1.1.3)

To save a spreadsheet for the first time, do the following:

- Select the **Office Button**.
- Select **Save**.
  The **Save As** window opens.
- Select the correct drive and/or folder from the **Save in** menu.
- Enter a name in the **File name** box.
- Click **Save**.

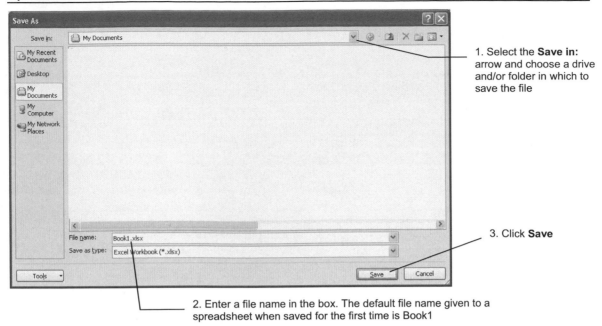

1. Select the **Save in:** arrow and choose a drive and/or folder in which to save the file

3. Click **Save**

2. Enter a file name in the box. The default file name given to a spreadsheet when saved for the first time is Book1

NOTE

Click the **Save** button on the **Quick Access Toolbar** to save a file.

The keyboard combination to save is **CTRL + S**.

1.1.7 Saving a Spreadsheet with Another Name (4.1.1.3)

To save an existing spreadsheet with a different name, do the following:

- Select the **Office Button**.
- Move the mouse over the **Save As** menu option.
- The **Save a copy of the document** sub-menu opens.
- Select **Excel Workbook**.

Select the **Excel Workbook** menu option to save the file in the default file format

The **Save As** window opens.

- Select the correct drive and/or folder from the **Save in** menu.
- Enter a name in the **File name** box.
- Click **Save**.

NOTE

When saving a spreadsheet for the first time, clicking **Save** or **Save As** from the **Office Button** menu will result in the **Save As** window opening. Subsequent changes to a spreadsheet can be saved by selecting the **Save** option from the **Office Button**. This will save the spreadsheet with the same name and overwrite the original file.

1.1.8 Saving a Spreadsheet as Another File Type (4.1.1.4)

A spreadsheet can be saved in a variety of different formats. This is useful if the spreadsheet is being opened in another version of Excel or a different spreadsheet program. Some of the common formats are listed below.

Excel Format	
Spreadsheet (.xlsx)	Version number (Excel 95-2003 Workbook)
Text (*.txt)	Software specific file extension (e.g. *.xls or xlsx)
Template (.xltx)	

To save the spreadsheet in another file type, do the following:

Text Format (Tab Delimited)

When a spreadsheet is saved as a text file, it loses all of its formatting features and saves in a format that enables it to be opened and viewed as text and values only. Columns of data are separated by tabs and each row ends in a carriage return (Enter).

To save a file in text format, do the following:

- Select the **Office Button**.
- Move the mouse over the **Save As** menu option.
  The **Save a copy of the document** sub-menu opens.
- Select **Other Formats**.
  The **Save As** windows opens.
- Select the **Save in** arrow.
- Select the correct drive and/or folder.
- Enter a file name into the **File name** box.
- Click the **Save as type** arrow.
- Select **Text (Tab Delimited) (*.txt)**.
- Click **Save**.

Click **Other Formats**

Click the **Save as type:** arrow

Select **Text (Tab Delimited) (*.txt)**

> **NOTE**
> Other text formats include **Formatted Text (Space Delimited)** which loses all formatting and in which columns are separated by commas and end with carriage returns; **Text (Unicode)** which can be read in Windows NT Notepad; and **Comma Separated Value** (.csv) which displays text and values as they appear in the active worksheet and converts cells containing formula to text values. Columns of data are separated by commas and rows end in a carriage return. Again, with this format, all formatting is lost but it is a useful format for importing data between applications.

Template

A template contains standard content/formulas that will appear on all sheets in a spreadsheet. A template can be used repeatedly with other spreadsheets. This saves time and effort when creating a new spreadsheet. Templates are saved with a **.xltx** file extension and, unless another location is specified, will automatically save in the following location: **C:/Documents and Settings/ Computer Name/Application Data/Microsoft/Templates**.

To save a spreadsheet as a template, do the following:
- Select the **Office Button**.
- Move the mouse over the **Save As** menu option.

  The **Save a copy of the document** sub-menu opens.
- Select **Other Formats**.

  The **Save As** windows opens.

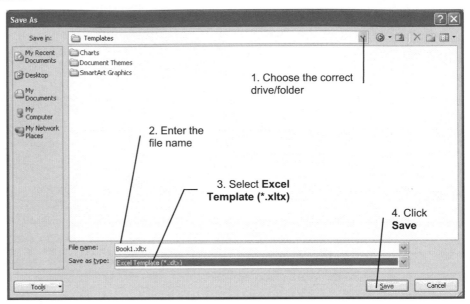

- Select the **Save in** arrow and then select the correct drive and/or folder.
- Enter a file name into the **File name** box.
- Click the **Save as type** arrow.
- Select **Excel Template (.xltx)**.
- Click **Save**.

NOTE

To save a template in a previous version of Excel, select Excel 97-2003 template (*xlt).

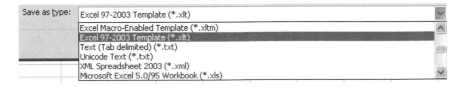

You can by-pass the **Save a copy of the document** sub-menu by clicking the **Save As** menu command.

Version Number

Each version of Excel has a different version number. If the spreadsheet needs to be opened and viewed in a previous version of Excel it can be saved with a different version number.

To check the version number of the software on your computer, do the following:

- Select the **Office Button** and select **Excel Options**.
- Select the **Resources** button.
- Select the **About** button.

| about Microsoft Office Excel 2007 | About |

The **About Microsoft Office Excel** window opens. This window provides information on the software version currently installed on your computer.

Information about currently installed software will be provided in this window.

- Check the version number – it should be **Microsoft Office Excel® 2007**.
- Click **OK** to close the current window.
- Click **OK** to close the Excel Options window.

To save the spreadsheet with a different version number, do the following:

- Select the **Office Button**.
- Move the mouse over the **Save As** menu command.
  The **Save a copy of the document** sub-menu opens.
- Select **Excel 97-2003 Spreadsheet** to save a copy of the spreadsheet that is fully compatible with Excel 97-2003.

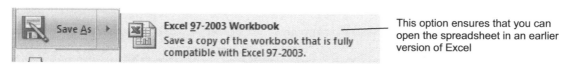

This option ensures that you can open the spreadsheet in an earlier version of Excel

The **Save As** windows opens.
- Select the **Save in** arrow and then select the correct drive and /or folder.
- Enter a file name into the **File name** box.
- Click the **Save as type** arrow.
  Note how the version is selected in the **Save As** type box.
  Alternatively, select the arrow and choose a version number.
- Click **Save**.

Excel 97-2003 is an earlier version of the software

NOTE

To save to a software specific extension, such as **XML Data (.xml)**, **DIF (.dif)** or **CSV (.csv)**, choose the extension from the drop-down list in the **Save as type** field.

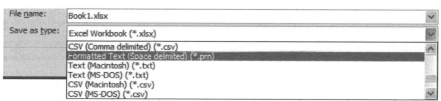

You can by-pass the **Save a copy of the document** sub-menu by clicking the **Save As** menu command.

1.1.9 Switching between Open Spreadsheets (4.1.1.5)

Open spreadsheets will be displayed as tabs on the task bar.

To switch between open spreadsheets, do the following:

- To switch between different spreadsheets within Excel, select the **View** tab.
- In the **Windows** group, select the **Switch Windows** button.

  A tick will display beside the file name of the currently active spreadsheet.
- Click another file name in the menu to make that the active spreadsheet.

A tick beside the file name indicates that it is the active spreadsheet, currently displayed on screen

---

NOTE

You can also switch between open worksheets or other programs by using the taskbar.

- Open more than one spreadsheet.
- The spreadsheets will be displayed as tabs on the taskbar at the bottom of the screen.
- Click a tab to open that spreadsheet.

To switch between open spreadsheets using the keyboard hold down the **ALT** key and press **TAB**.

1.2 Enhancing Productivity

Productivity can be increased by setting user preferences, such as adding a user name and/or creating a default folder from which to open and in which to save all spreadsheets. Using the Help facility can also aid productivity by providing tips and advice on how to use the program effectively.

In this section, you will learn about the following:

- Setting user preferences.
- Using available Help functions.
- Using magnification/zoom tools.
- Restoring and minimising the ribbon.

1.2.1 Setting User Preferences (4.1.2.1)

User preferences refer to the user name and the default location from where opened files are saved to. These can be changed as appropriate so that the user name is different or so that files can be opened or saved in another location.

To set user preferences, do the following:

User Name

- Select the **Office Button**.
- Select **Excel Options**.
- Select the **Popular** tab.
- In the **Personalize your copy of Microsoft Office**, position the cursor in the User name box and delete the current user name.

- Enter the new user name.
- Click **OK**.

Enter or edit the **User name**

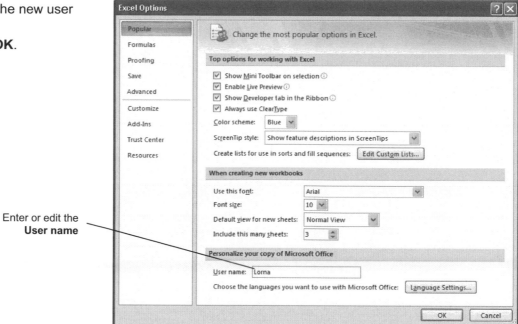

Default File Location

- Select the **Office Button**.
- Select **Excel Options**.
- Select the **Save** tab.
- In the **Default File Location** box, enter the required file location from where files will be opened from and saved to.
- Click **OK**.

Enter the file location

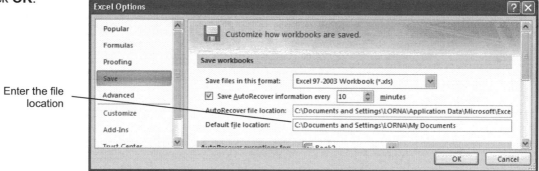

1.2.2 Using the Help Function (4.1.2.2)

The Help function is available to give advice and help on aspects of the software that you are using. This is useful when you are trying to perform an action and don't know how to proceed further. Just ask the Help function a specific question and then select a relevant topic for the answer.

To use the Help function, do the following:

- Select the **Help** button or press the **F1** key.
  The **Excel Help** window opens.
- Select a link to a relevant topic.
  A further set of links will appear that correspond with the selected topic.
- Select a relevant link to refine your search.
- Read the information on the chosen topic.
- Use the **Back** button to go back a step or the **Home** button to return to the first
  window of Excel Help.

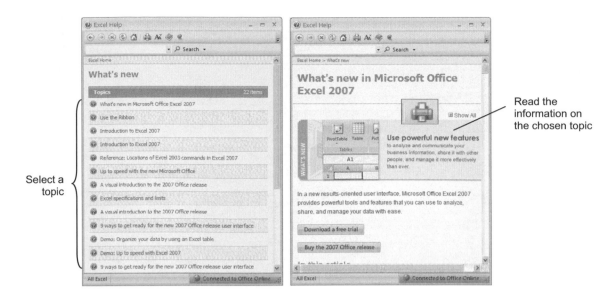

• Select **Print** to print a copy of the topic information.

You can also enter specific search criteria into the **Search** box to locate information on specific topics.

To enter search criteria, do the following:
• Enter a question in the **Search** box.
• Click **Search**.
    A list of topic links relating to the search criteria will appear.
• Click a link to view the topic information.

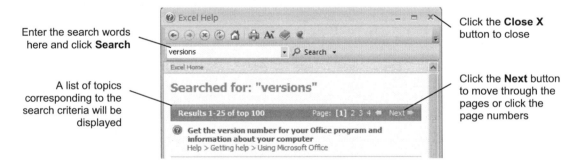

1.2.3 Using Magnification (Zoom) (4.1.2.3)

The magnification tools are used to zoom in and out in a spreadsheet.

To use the magification tools, do the following:
• Select the **View** tab.
• In the **Zoom** group, click the **Zoom** button.
    The **Zoom** window opens.
• Select **Fit** to ensure that the selected are of the spreadsheet will fit the window.
• Select an option button to change the view percentage or use the scroll wheels to increase or decrease the percentage in the **Percent** box.
• Click **OK**.

Select a **Zoom to** option button or select **Custom** and enter a percentage by which to increase or decrease the magnification

NOTE

You can also select the Zoom buttons on the status bar. Use the **Zoom Out** button to reduce the view. Select the **Zoom In** button to enlarge the view. Alternatively, drag the **slider** towards the Zoom Out or Zoom In buttons to decrease/increase the view.

Zoom In

Zoom Out

1.2.4 Minimising and Restoring the Ribbon (4.1.2.4)
The ribbon bar can be minimised and then restored if required.

To minimise and restore the ribbon, do the following;

Minimising the Ribbon

*   Right-click the ribbon bar.
*   Select **Minimize the Ribbon**.
    The ribbon is hidden.

Click **Minimize the Ribbon**

Restoring the Ribbon

*   Right-click the bar containing the tabs.
*   Click **Minimize the Ribbon** (note how a tick is displayed beside the menu command to indicate that it is active).

    The ribbon is restored and is visible again.

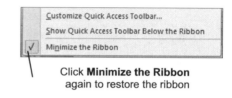

Click **Minimize the Ribbon** again to restore the ribbon

4

PRACTICE SEQUENCE

1   Open Excel and create a new spreadsheet.
2   Save this spreadsheet as **sale** in the default spreadsheet format in a default folder location that you specify.
3   Save another copy of the spreadsheet in **Text** format with the filename **saleTXT**.
4   Reopen **Sale** and practise switching between the two spreadsheets.
5   Zoom the **Sale** spreadsheet to **80%** and save.
6   Close both spreadsheets.
7   Use the **Help** function to find information on saving a spreadsheet as a template.
8   Open the **Sale** spreadsheet and save in template format (ensure that it saves in the correct drive/folder).
9   Close the template file.
10 Open a new spreadsheet and save with the name **version** in **Excel 97-2003** format.
11 Close all spreadsheets and exit Excel.

Section 2   Cells

A spreadsheet is a grid comprising rows and columns. The intersection between a row and a column is called a **cell**. Cells are named with the grid reference referring to its location; this is called a **cell reference**. For example, the cell named A1 refers to the cell positioned in column A and row 1. Multiple cells are referred to as a **cell range**. An example of a cell range is A1:A12 (a cell range is separated by a colon).

2.1   Inserting and Selecting Data

Data refers to text, dates and numerical figures. Each of these data items can be entered into a cell and then selected so that editing or formatting can be performed.

In this section, you will learn about the following:

- Understanding that a cell in a worksheet should contain only one element of data (for example, first name detail in one cell, surname detail in adjacent cell).

- Recognising good practice in creating lists: avoiding blank rows and columns in the main body of the list, inserting a blank row before the Total row and ensuring cells bordering list are blank.

- Entering a number, date or text in a cell.

- Selecting a cell, range of adjacent cells, range of non-adjacent cells or an entire worksheet.

2.1.1   Good Practice (4.2.1.1 and 4.2.1.2)

A cell should only contain one element of data, such as a first name in one cell and a last name in an adjacent cell. This enables the user to edit or format cell elements individually, e.g. with different fonts, sizes and styles, or sort columns in a specified order.

	A	B
1	**First Name**	**Last Name**
2	Anne	Jones
3	Bill	Smith

When creating numerical lists, it is good practice to avoid creating blank rows and columns in the main body of the list. This is because a blank row or column can affect formula results. However, to enhance clarity, it is good practice to insert a blank row before a Total row to separate the main list from the formula result. Any cells bordering a numerical list used in a calculation should remain blank. This ensures that the data and the results are clearly defined and can be easily identified and understood.

JUMBLE SALE	
ITEM	**PRICE**
Dress	£2.99
Vase	£1.50
Decanter set	£3.45
TOTAL	**£7.94**

2.1.2   Entering Data (4.2.1.3)

The default position for text within a cell is left aligned. The default position for numbers and dates is right aligned. Numbers will not display decimal precision unless formatted to a specific number of places. For example, when you enter 1.50, it will display as 1.5.

To enter text, numbers or dates into a cell, do the following:

- Click a cell to select it and then enter text or a number directly into the cell.

- Press **Enter** to complete the entry.

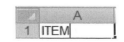

   Alternatively, position the cursor in the **Formula bar** and enter the data.

   Press **Enter** to complete the entry.

2.1.3 Selecting Cells (4.2.1.4)

A cell must be selected before data can be entered, edited or formatted. This may entail selecting a single cell or a range of adjacent or non-adjacent cells.

To select a cell or cells, do the following:

Single Cell

- Click a cell to select it. A dark border displays around a selected cell.

Adjacent Cell Range

- Select the first cell and then, holding down the left mouse button, drag over the cells to be selected and release. The first cell in the selected range appears to be unselected.

ITEM	PRICE	
Dress	£2.99	
Vase	£1.50	
Decanter Set	£3.45	

Non-Adjacent Cell Range

- Select the first cell or range of cells and, holding down the **CTRL** key, click the cell or drag over the cells to be selected and release.

	A	B	C
1	ITEM	PRICE	DONATED BY:
2	Dress	£2.99	Mrs Jones
3	Vase	£1.50	Mr Brown
4	Decanter Set	£3.45	Miss Smith

Entire Worksheet

- Select the button on the top left of the spreadsheet (above row number 1 and to the left of column A). All cells in the worksheet will be selected.
  Alternatively, press **CTRL + A**.

	A
1	ITEM

Click away from a cell range to remove the selection.

PRACTICE SEQUENCE

A spreadsheet containing the data shown below is also provided on CD for your use. Note that the spreadsheet refers to profits from Jumble Sales.

1   Open Excel and then open the **sales** spreadsheet.

2   Enter the data in the correct columns and rows as shown below (don't worry if the data overlaps; you will adjust column widths later).

	A	B
1	PROFITS 1ST QTR 2008	
2	EXPENDITURE	
3	Transport costs	15
4	Venue hire	50
5	Refreshment Costs	20
6	Other expenses	50
7	Total Expenditure	
8	SALES	
9	Entrance Fees	50
10	Sales of goods	650
11	Refreshment Sales	60
12	Total Sales	

3   Select cells A1 and cell B3.

4   Select the cell range A1:B12.

5   Remove the selection.

6   Close the **sales** spreadsheet.

2.2   Editing and Sorting

In this section, you will learn about the following:

- Editing cell content and modify existing cell content.
- Using the undo and redo commands.
- Using the search command for specific content in a worksheet.
- Using the replace command for specific content in a worksheet.
- Sorting a cell range by one criterion in ascending or descending numeric order and ascending or descending alphabetic order.

2.2.1 Editing Cells (4.2.2.1)

Cell content can be edited or modified by positioning the cursor within a cell and making modifications, such as entering characters or deleting characters, or by selecting a cell and editing the contents in the Formula Bar.

To edit or modify cell content, do the following:

- Double-click a cell to position the cursor within the cell (the cursor will appear wherever the insertion point is positioned when you double-click).

    Alternatively, select a cell and then position the cursor on the Formula Bar either in front, in the middle or behind the cell contents.

- Delete characters by positioning the cursor in front of a character and pressing **Delete** (the **Delete** key deletes characters to the right of the current cursor position) or by positioning the cursor behind a character and pressing **Backspace** (the **Backspace** key deletes characters to the left of the current cursor position).

- Enter characters by positioning the cursor in the correct position and then typing.

- To replace the whole contents of a cell, select the cell and type over existing contents.

2.2.2 Using the Undo and Redo Commands (4.2.2.2)

If a mistake is made when entering, editing or deleting data, it can be corrected by using the undo button. To redo the action, the redo button can be used.

To use undo and redo, do the following:

- To undo an action, click the **Undo** button from the **Quick Access Toolbar** (or press **CTRL + Z**).

- To see a list of actions, click the arrow and select an action from the list. Any actions that exist before the selected action will also be undone.

The **Redo** button displays as the **Repeat** button until the Undo command is used

Select the Undo arrow to see a list of actions

- To redo an action, click the **Redo** button from the **Quick Access Toolbar** (or press **CTRL + Y**).

> **NOTE**
> The Redo button displays as a repeat button, until the Undo button is utilised. When the Undo button is used, the Redo button becomes active.
>
> Undo Redo

2.2.3 Searching (4.2.2.3)

Finding information in a spreadsheet can be time consuming if it is a lengthy spreadsheet containing lots of data. Using the Search command facilitates the process as it will find specific information throughout the spreadsheet in one action.

To search for information, do the following:

- On the **Home** tab, click the **Find & Select** command from the **Editing** group (or press **CTRL + F** to open the **Find** window).
- Select **Find** from the menu.
  The **Find** window opens.
- Enter the search word or phrase into the **Find what** box.

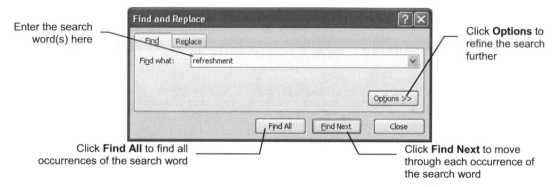

Enter the search word(s) here

Click **Options** to refine the search further

Click **Find All** to find all occurrences of the search word

Click **Find Next** to move through each occurrence of the search word

- Select the **Options>>** button to refine the search further.
  - In this section of the **Find** window, you can do the following:
  - Search within a sheet or a workbook (if the workbook contains many sheets).
  - Search by rows or columns.
  - Look in formulas, values or comments.
  - Match the case of search word (upper/lower case)
  - Match entire cell contents or only part of a cell (e.g. if you select this checkbox and enter **Refreshment** as the search word it will find cells containing the word **Refreshment** but will not find **Refreshment Costs** or **Refreshment Sales**).

Refine the search by looking within a sheet or a workbook. Search by rows or columns. Look in Formulas, values or comments

Choose to match case or match entire cell contents or part of a cell

Click to close the **Options** section

- Press **Find Next** to find the first occurrence of the search word(s) or **Find All** to find all occurrences of the search word(s).

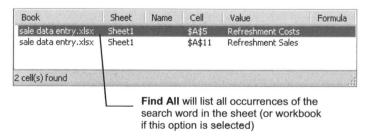

Find All will list all occurrences of the search word in the sheet (or workbook if this option is selected)

- Click **Close** to close the **Find** window.

2.2.4 Replacing (4.2.2.4)

It can be time consuming to replace the contents of multiple cells with another value if the spreadsheet is lengthy and contains many rows and columns of data. If the search word appears many times, it is easier to use the Replace command to replace the contents of the cell with a specified value throughout the spreadsheet.

To replace the contents of cells, do the following:

- On the **Home** tab, click the **Find & Select** command from the **Editing** group (or press **CTRL + H** to open the **Replace** window).
- Select **Replace** from the menu.
  The **Replace** window opens.

Enter the search word(s) here

Enter the replacement word(s) here

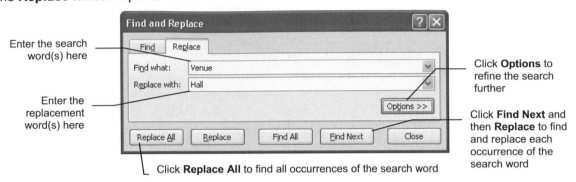

Click **Options** to refine the search further

Click **Find Next** and then **Replace** to find and replace each occurrence of the search word

Click **Replace All** to find all occurrences of the search word

- Enter the search word or phrase into the **Find what** box.
- Enter the replacement word in the **Replace with** box.
- Select the **Options>>** button to refine the search further.
- In this section of the **Find** window, you can do the following:
  - o Search within a sheet or a workbook (if the workbook contains many sheets).
  - o Search by rows or columns.
  - o Look in formulas, values or comments.
  - o Match the case of the entered replacement word (upper/lower case).
  - o Match entire cell contents or only part of a cell (e.g. if you select this checkbox and enter **Refreshment** as the search word it will find and replace cells containing only the word **Refreshment** but will not find and replace the cells containing **Refreshment Costs** or **Refreshment Sales**).

Replace within a sheet or a workbook. Find and replace by rows or columns. Look in Formulas, values or comments

Choose to match case or match entire cell contents or part of a cell

Click to close the **Options** section

- Press **Find Next** to find the first occurrence of the search word(s) and then press **Replace** or select **Replace All** to replace all occurrences of the search word(s) with the replacement word.

  When **Replace All** is selected, a message window opens informing you of the number of replacements that have been made.

- Click **OK**.
- Click **Close** to close the **Replace** window.

2.2.5 Sorting (4.2.2.5)

Data can be sorted to display in ascending or descending order in either numerical or alphabetical order. See the examples below.

Alphabetical (Ascending, A–Z)

Clothes
Ornaments
Shoes
Toys

Alphabetical (Descending, Z–A)

Toys
Ornaments
Shoes
Clothes

Numerical (Ascending, smallest–largest)

£1.99
£2.50
£2.99
£3.00
£3.50

Numerical (Descending, largest–smallest)

£3.50
£3.00
£2.99
£2.50
£1.99

To sort data, do the following:

Numerical Order

- Select the numerical data to be sorted (you must also include adjacent cells in the selection if these cells are to be sorted alongside the numerical data).
- From the **Home** tab. click **Sort & Filter** from the **Editing** group.
- Select **Sort Smallest to Largest** for ascending order or **Sort Largest to Smallest** for descending order.

Alphabetical Order

- Select the text to be sorted (you must also include adjacent cells in the selection if these cells are to be sorted alongside the text).
- From the **Home** tab, click **Sort & Filter** from the **Editing** group.
- Select **Sort A to Z** for ascending order or **Sort Z to A** for descending order.

> **NOTE**
>
> The **Sort** option is also available through the **Data** tab. The text/numerical data should be selected, then click either the **Sort A-Z** or **Sort Z-A** buttons to sort. Clicking the **Sort** button provides further options by which to sort.

PRACTICE SEQUENCE

1   Open Excel and the spreadsheet called **sale**.

2   Edit the title in cell A1 so that it reads **PROFIT 1st QTR JAN – MAR 2008**.

3   Modify cell A8 to read **INCOME**.

4   Using the Search and Replace command, find all occurrences of the word **Venue** and replace with the word **Hall**. Ensure that the case is matched.

5   Select the cell range A3:B6 (start the selection from B6 and drag backwards up to A3 so that the Sort command identifies that it is the numerical data that should be sorted).

6   Sort this cell range in descending order (largest–smallest).

7   Select the cell range A9:B11 (start the selection from cell A9 so that the Sort command identifies that the sort should be performed on the text).

8   Sort this cell range in ascending order (A–Z).

9   Save and close the **sale** spreadsheet.

2.3 Copying, Moving and Deleting

The contents of a single cell or a range of cells can be duplicated or moved within a worksheet or between open worksheets. Values in cells can be copied to other cells or, if sequential numbers or months, days or dates, are required these can be incremented by using the AutoFill tool (for example, if you type in Monday and then copy this across or down other cells, the data entry will be incremented to display as Tuesday, Wednesday, etc). Cells containing formula, that use cell references, can be replicated across other cells. Spreadsheet data can be updated by deleting outdated cell contents.

In this section, you will learn about the following:

- Copying the content of a cell and a cell range within a worksheet, between worksheets and between open spreadsheets.

- Using the AutoFill tool/copy handle tool to copy and increment data entries.

- Moving the contents of a cell and a cell range within a worksheet, between worksheets and between open spreadsheets.

- Deleting cell contents.

2.3.1 Copying and Moving Cell Contents (4.2.3.1 and 4.2.3.3)

To copy or move cell contents within or between worksheets, do the following:

Within a Worksheet

- To **copy** the contents of a cell, select the cell (or range of cells) and then, from the **Home** tab, click **Copy** from the **Clipboard** group (or press **CTRL + C**).

- Select the destination cell within the worksheet and click **Paste** (or press **CTRL + V**).

  The duplicated cell contents will appear in the new position.

- To *move* cell contents, follow the procedure above but click **Cut** (scissors) from the **Clipboard** group at Step 1 (or press **CTRL + X**).

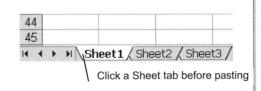

NOTE

Cell contents can be copied or moved **between** worksheets by following the procedure above, but open a new worksheet by clicking a **Sheet tab**, before pasting the contents in the new destination.

Click a Sheet tab before pasting

Between Spreadsheets

- Open the required spreadsheet files. Both files will be displayed as tabs on the taskbar at the bottom of the screen.

- Ensure that the spreadsheet containing the cell contents to be copied, is the active spreadsheet.

- To **copy** cell contents, select the cell or cell range and then, from the **Home** tab, click **Copy** from the **Clipboard** group.

- Click the other spreadsheet on the taskbar or select the **View** tab and **Switch Windows**.

- Choose the other spreadsheet from the list and ensure that the correct worksheet is displayed.

- Click the mouse in the destination cell.
- From the **Home** tab, in the **Clipboard** group, click **Paste**.
  The cell contents will be duplicated in the selected position within the spreadsheet.
- To *move* cell contents to another spreadsheet, repeat the above procedure but click Cut (scissors) at Step 3.

NOTE

You can also copy, cut and paste cell contents within and between spreadsheets by right-clicking and selecting a command from the shortcut menu or by using the Drag and Drop method. The latter method uses the mouse to copy or move cell contents to a different destination within the *same* worksheet. Point at the border of a cell or cell range containing the contents to be copied or moved, hold down the mouse button and drag to the destination cell to move the contents or hold down the **CTRL** key whilst dragging to copy the cell contents.

2.3.2 Using the AutoFill Tool (4.2.3.2)

The AutoFill tool or Copy Handle replicates formulas, or increments data entries over other cells within the spreadsheet.

To use the AutoFill tool, do the following:
- Position the mouse over the **fill handle** (this is the small black square in the lower right corner of a cell) and then hold down the left mouse button.
  The cursor becomes a black cross. +
- With the mouse button depressed, drag over subsequent cells to increment entries.

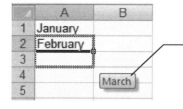

When months are copied using the Fill handle, a tag appears displaying the incremented month before it appears in the cell

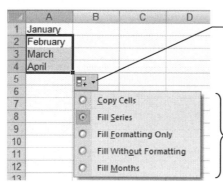

When the mouse button is released, the AutoFill Options command appears. Click the arrow to see the AutoFill menu

Copy Cells will copy the cell but not increment **Fill series** will increment each entry (as with dates). You have the option of copying cell contents without also copying the cell formatting. **Fill Months** will also increment with each subsequent month

Alternatively, enter the first number or date and then select the cells into which you want the incremented numbers/dates/months to appear.
- From the **Home** tab and the **Editing** group, select the **Fill** arrow.

- Select a **Fill** option from the drop down menu – select **Down**, **Right**, **Left** or **Up** to copy a value without incrementing the value.

- Select **Series** for further incremental options, such as AutoFill for months or Linear for numbers.
- Click **OK**.

2.3.3 Deleting Cell Contents (4.2.3.4)

To delete cell contents, do the following:

- Select the cell or cell range containing the content to be deleted.
- Press the **Delete** key on the keyboard or select the **Delete** button from the Home tab/**Cells** group.

  Alternatively, from the **Home** tab and the **Editing** group, select the **Clear** arrow and then choose the **Clear All** or **Clear Contents** commands from the drop down menu.

Selecting **Clear All** deletes the contents of the selected cell, along with the formatting and any comments. To only delete the cell contents, select **Clear Contents**

PRACTICE SEQUENCE

1   Open the **sale** spreadsheet.

2   Copy the contents of cell A2 to cell A1 in Sheet2.

3   Ensure that you are on Sheet1. Move the title in cell A1 to cell F1.

4   Move the title from cell F1 back to its original position in cell A1.

5   Copy the cell range A1:B12 to a new worksheet.

6   Edit the title to read **PROFITS 2ND QTR APR – JUN 2008**.

7   Delete the contents of the cell range **B3:B11**.

8   Save the spreadsheet with the name **sales 2nd Qtr 2008** and close.

9   Create a new spreadsheet and enter **January** into cell A1.

10   Copy this down over cells **A2:A12** so that the data entries increment with each month (you should end up with 12 months Jan–Dec).

11   In cell **B1** enter the number **1**.

12   Highlight the cell range **B1:B10** and then select the **Fill** command (from the **Home** tab/**Editing** group). Ensure that the numbers will increment in a linear series from 1-10.

13   In cell **C1** enter **=B1+2**.

14   Copy this formula down over the cell range **B2:12**.

15   In cell **D1** enter **Monday**. Highlight the cell range **D1:D7** and then use the AutoFill command to increment the days (Monday–Sunday).

16   In cell **E1** enter **Monday** and fill down the cell range E2:E7 without incrementing.

17   Save the spreadsheet as **AutoFill** and close.

Section 3   Managing Worksheets

A spreadsheet is also referred to as a **workbook**. In the same way that a book has many pages, a workbook can have many **worksheets**. A new spreadsheet or workbook contains three default worksheets. The worksheet name is displayed on a sheet tab at the bottom of the screen, such as Sheet1, Sheet2, Sheet3. Worksheets contain many rows and columns that can be deleted, or modified with a different column width/row height or frozen to make it easier to scroll through multiple rows/columns of data without losing sight of the spreadsheet titles. In addition to inserting new rows/columns, you can also insert new worksheets and rename and rearrange the order of worksheet tabs. Worksheets can also be copied or moved within a spreadsheet.

3.1   Rows and Columns

Rows and columns can be selected, whether adjacent or non-adjacent, so that editing and formatting can be performed. It is useful to freeze spreadsheet titles so that they remain in the same position when you scroll through the remainder of the spreadsheet. Sometimes row height or column widths need to be modified to accommodate cell contents; this can be achieved through dragging the row/column to the required height/width or by entering a specific measurement for the row/column.

In this section, you will learn about the following:

- Selecting a row, range of adjacent rows and range of non-adjacent rows.
- Selecting a column, range of adjacent columns and range of non-adjacent columns.
- Inserting and deleting rows and columns.
- Modifying column widths and row heights to a specified value and to the optimal width or height.
- Freezing and unfreezing row and/or column titles.

3.1.1   Selecting Rows (4.3.1.1)

To select a single row, a range of adjacent rows or a range of non-adjacent rows do the following:

Single Row

- Position the mouse icon on the row selector for the row that you want to select.
  The mouse icon displays as a black arrow.
- Click the left mouse button to select the row.

The mouse icon turns into a black arrow when positioned over a row selector

Range of Adjacent Rows

- Position the mouse icon on the row selector for the first row that you want to select.
  The mouse icon displays as a black arrow.
- Click the left mouse button to select the row.
- Hold down the left mouse button and drag the mouse over the required rows. Note the tag that appears as you drag the mouse. This will indicate the number of rows that have been selected.

The tag indicates the number of rows that have been selected

Range of Non-Adjacent Rows

- Position the mouse icon on the row selector for the first row that you want to select.
  The mouse icon displays as a black arrow.
- Click the left mouse button to select the row.
- Hold down the **CTRL** key on the keyboard and then select more rows as required (by clicking the row selector).
- Release the **CTRL** key when you have finished selecting the rows.

3.1.2 Selecting Columns (4.3.1.2)

To select a single column, a range of adjacent columns or a range of non-adjacent columns, do the following:

Single Column

- Position the mouse icon on the column selector for the column that you want to select
  The mouse icon displays as a black arrow.
- Click the left mouse button to select the column.

	A	B	C
1	PROFITS 1ST QTR JAN - MAR 2008		
2	EXPENDITURE		
3	Hall hire	50	
4	Other expenses	50	
5	Refreshment Costs	20	
6	Transport costs	15	
7	Total Expenditure		
8	INCOME		
9	Entrance Fees	50	
10	Refreshment Sales	60	
11	Sales of goods	650	
12	Total Sales		

Range of Adjacent Columns

- Position the mouse icon on the column selector for the column that you want to select.
  The mouse icon displays as a black arrow.
- Click the left mouse button to select the column.
- Hold down the left mouse button and drag over adjacent columns to select them.
- Release the mouse when all columns have been selected. Note the tag indicating the number of columns that have been selected as you drag.

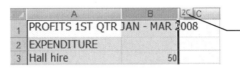

	A	B	2C C
1	PROFITS 1ST QTR JAN - MAR 2008		
2	EXPENDITURE		
3	Hall hire	50	

Note the tag indicating the number of columns that have been selected

Range of Non-Adjacent Columns

- Position the mouse icon on the column selector for the first column that you want to select.
  The mouse icon displays as a black arrow.
- Click the left mouse button to select the column.
- Hold down the **CTRL** key on the keyboard and then select more columns as required (by clicking the column selectors).
- Release the **CTRL** key when you have finished selecting the columns.

3.1.3 Inserting and Deleting Rows and Columns (4.3.1.3)

Rows and columns can be inserted in a specified position within a worksheet.

To insert and delete rows and columns, do the following:

Inserting Rows

- Select the row below where the new row is to be inserted (the row will be inserted above the selected row).

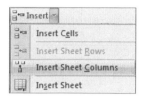

- From the **Home** tab and the **Cells** group, select the **Insert** arrow and then select **Insert Sheet Rows**.

  A new row will be inserted *above* the currently selected row.

Inserting Columns

- Select the column to the *right* of where the new column is to be inserted (the column will be inserted to the *left* of the selected column).

- From the **Home** tab and the **Cells** group, select the **Insert** arrow and then select **Insert Sheet Columns**.

  A new column will be inserted to the *left* of the currently selected column.

Deleting Rows and Columns

- Select the row(s) or column(s) to be deleted.

- From the **Home** tab and the **Cells** group, select the **Delete** arrow and then select **Delete Sheet Rows** or **Delete Sheet Columns**.

  This will delete the whole row or column and all of the data within the row/column.

3.1.4 Modifying Column Widths and Row Heights (4.3.1.4)

Column widths and row heights can be modified to accommodate cell contents by increasing or decreasing their size.

To modify row height or column width, do the following:

Column Width

- Select the column to be modified.
- From the **Home** tab and the **Cells** group, select the **Format** button.
- Select **Column Width**.

  The **Column Width** window opens.

- Enter a new measurement into the box.

- Click **OK**.

Enter a new column width measurement

Row Height

- Select the row to be modified.
- From the **Home** tab and the **Cells** group, select the **Format** button.
- Select **Row Height**.

  The **Row Height** window opens.

- Enter a new measurement into the box.

Enter a new row height measurement

- Click **OK**.

NOTE

Column widths and row heights can also be modified by dragging a row/column to increase or reduce size. Position the cursor over the column or row border and the mouse icon turns into a black cross. Hold down the mouse button and drag to the right to widen a column or drag down to resize a row. Note the column width and row height indicators as you drag. This provides the current measurement as you resize the row or column.

The mouse icon turns into a black cross when positioned over a column border

---

Cells in a worksheet can be automatically adjusted to a size that best fits the data.

To use adjust cells to an optimal size, do the following:

- Click the **Select All** button to select the cells.
  *Alternatively, s*elect individual columns or rows.
- From the Home tab, click the **Format** button in the **Cells** group.
- Select **AutoFit Column Width** from the drop-down menu.
- Select **AutoFit Row Height** from the drop-down menu.
  The row height and column width of the selected cells adjusts to the optimal size for the data within them.

Select **AutoFit Row Height** and **AutoFit Column Width**

NOTE

The optimal row height and column width for data can also be set by double-clicking the row or column border on the worksheet.

For the optimal column width, do the following:

- Position the cursor on the border to the right of the column to be resized.
- Double-click.

For the optimal row height, do the following:

- Position the cursor on the border to the bottom of the row to be resized.
- Double-click.

3.1.5 Freezing and Unfreezing Row and/or Column Titles (4.3.1.5)

To ensure that spreadsheet titles can be viewed whilst scrolling through a spreadsheet, the row and/or column titles should be frozen.

To freeze and unfreeze rows and columns, do the following:

Freezing

- Select the cell, row or column to freeze (for example, select cell B2 to freeze both column A and row 1).
- From the **View** tab and the **Window** group, select **Freeze Panes**.
- From the menu, select a command:

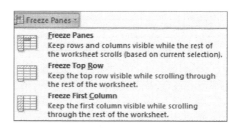

- o Select **Freeze Panes** if you want to freeze panes based on your current selection.
- o Select **Freeze Top Row** to keep the top row visible whilst you scroll through the remainder of the spreadsheet.
- o Select **Freeze First Column** to keep the first column visible whilst you scroll through the remainder of the spreadsheet.

Unfreezing

- Select the cell, row or column to unfreeze.
- From the **View** tab and the **Window** group, select **Freeze Panes**.
- From the menu, select **Unfreeze Panes**.

PRACTICE SEQUENCE

1   Open the **sale** spreadsheet and practise selecting rows and columns:
- Select Row 1.
- Select Row 1 and Row 3.
- Select Rows 1 to 5.
- Select Column A.
- Select Column A and Column C.

2   Insert a new column between Columns A and B.

3   In the **Expenditure** section of the spreadsheet, insert a row before the **Total Expenditure** row (to become Row 8).

4   Insert a row after the title **Profits 1ST QTR JAN - MAR 2008**.

5   In the **Income** section of the spreadsheet, insert a row before the **Total Sales** row (to become Row 15).

6   Insert a row above the **INCOME** row (to become Row 10).

7   Delete Column B.

8   Modify Column A to display with a column width of **25**.

9   Modify Row 1 to display with a row height of **22**.

10   Freeze Column A and Row 1 (select B2), to keep this column and row visible when scrolling down or across the remainder of the spreadsheet.

11   Scroll down and across the spreadsheet to test that the panes are frozen as specified.

12   Unfreeze panes in the spreadsheet.

13   Save the **sale** spreadsheet and close.

3.2   Worksheets

In the previous section you practised editing a worksheet by inserting, deleting and freezing rows and columns within a worksheet. In addition to working with rows and columns, you can also edit the worksheet by renaming it, inserting a new worksheet or deleting worksheets.

In this section, you will learn about the following:

- Switching between worksheets.
- Inserting a new worksheet and delete a worksheet.
- Recognising good practice in naming worksheets: using meaningful worksheet names rather than accepting default names.
- Copying, moving and renaming a worksheet within a spreadsheet.

3.2.1 Switching between Worksheets (4.3.2.1)

The default number of worksheets in a workbook is three. You may wish to work on more than one worksheet within a workbook. To do this you need to switch between sheets.

To switch between worksheets, do the following:

- The example below displays the currently active worksheet tab as Sheet1.
- Select a different sheet tab to make it the active worksheet.

Active worksheet _____   Insert **New Sheet**

3.2.2 Inserting a New Worksheet (4.3.2.2)

You can add more worksheets to a workbook if required. It will be inserted to the left of a selected sheet. Therefore, select a sheet tab to the right of where you want to insert the new worksheet.

To insert a new worksheet, do the following:

- Select a sheet tab to the right of where the new worksheet is to be inserted.
- From the **Home** tab and the **Cells** group, select the **Insert** arrow.
- From the menu select **Insert Sheet**.
  Alternatively, select the **Insert New Sheet** button on the tab bar.

NOTE

Press **Shift** and **F11** to insert a new worksheet or right-click a sheet tab and choose **Insert**. Select **Worksheet** and click **OK**.

3.2.3 Deleting a Worksheet (4.3.2.2)

A worksheet can be deleted if required, but please note that all data is lost in a deleted worksheet, so be careful to delete the correct worksheet.

To delete a worksheet, do the following:

- Select the sheet tab to be deleted.
- From the **Home** tab and the **Cells** group, select the **Delete** arrow.
- From the menu select **Delete Sheet**.

If the worksheet contains data, the following message will appear.

*   Click **Delete** to complete deletion of the worksheet.

3.2.4 Naming Worksheets – Good Practice (4.3.2.3)

Worksheets should be renamed with meaningful names, appropriate to the worksheet subject, such as **sales2008** or **QTR1sales**, etc. It is good practice to use appropriate names that are easily identifiable. Using **Sheet1** and **Sheet2**, etc., makes it harder to differentiate between different worksheets and more meaningful names should be used to facilitate locating and identifying relevant worksheets within a workbook.

3.2.5 Renaming Worksheets (4.3.2.4)

To rename a worksheet, do the following:

*   Select the worksheet tab to be renamed.
*   From the **Home** tab and **Cells** group, select the **Format** arrow.
*   Select **Rename Sheet**.

    The tab name will be selected, ready for you to type over the existing tab name.
*   Enter a meaningful name for the worksheet.
*   Press **Enter**.

Example of a renamed worksheet

> **NOTE**
> Worksheets can also be renamed by double-clicking the tab to select the default name, e.g. Sheet1, and then typing a meaningful name to replace it.
>
>

3.2.6 Copying and Moving Worksheets (4.3.2.4)

To copy a worksheet, do the following:

*   Select the worksheet tab to be copied.
*   Holding down the left mouse button and the **CTRL** key, drag the worksheet tab to the required position.

    The mouse icon changes to a white arrow with a cross at its tip.

    The copied worksheet will display with (2) after the worksheet name e.g. **Qtr1 (2)**

To move a worksheet, do the following:

*   Select the worksheet tab to be moved.

- Holding down the left mouse button, drag the worksheet tab to the required position.

  The mouse icon changes to a white arrow with a blank sheet of paper at its tip. Watch for the downwards facing black arrow that moves with the mouse and indicates where the worksheet will be positioned when the mouse is released.

Alternatively, do the following:

- Select the worksheet to be copied or moved, and then, from the **Home** tab and **Cells** group, select the **Format** command.
- Select **Move or Copy Sheet** from the menu.

  The **Move or Copy** window opens.
- Ensure that the correct workbook is selected from the **To book** menu.
- Choose the location of the moved or copied worksheet from the **Before sheet** list of sheets or **Move to end**.
- Select the **Create a copy** checkbox if you want to copy the worksheet rather than move it.
- Click **OK**.

NOTE

An alternative method to insert, delete, rename, move or copy a worksheet, is to right-click the worksheet tab and then select the relevant menu command.

4

PRACTICE SEQUENCE

1   Open the **sale** spreadsheet.

2   Insert a new worksheet before **Sheet1**.

3   Rename the new worksheet as **practise**.

4   Move the **practise** worksheet so that it is at the end of the other worksheets within the spreadsheet.

5   Rename Sheet1 as **Qtr1**.

6   Delete the **Practise** worksheet.

7   Save and close the **sale** spreadsheet.

Section 4   Formulas and Functions

Formulas and functions are used to create calculations and find results. Arithmetic formulas use arithmetic operators, such as + (addition), - (subtraction), * (multiplication) and / (division).

Functions are used to find totals, averages, minimum and maximum figures, to count numbers and text entries and to round figures up or down. A logical function is used to find a result if a value corresponds with specified criteria. For example, **if** a salesman makes over £10,000, he will get a bonus, if the amount earned is below £10,000 he will not get the bonus. Logical functions use comparison operators, such as = (equals), < (less than) and > (greater than).

It is good practice in creating formulas and functions to use cell references rather than inputting numbers into the formula. This makes it easier to update the formula/function when the worksheet is edited or new data is added.

4.1   Arithmetic Formulas

Arithmetic formulas use arithmetic operators:

+ (addition) **-** (subtraction) ***** (multiplication) **/** (division)

It is important to understand and remember the principles of BODMAS when using arithmetic operators. BODMAS stands for:

(B)rackets

(O)rder

(D)ivision

(M)ultiplication

(A)ddition

(S)ubtraction

When creating a formula, you need to be aware that numbers will be divided before multiplication, addition or subtraction takes place, which can alter the results of a formula. See the example below.

=30+3*10/2	This formula should yield 165 as the answer, but will actually yield 45. This is because the formula divides 30 by 2 and then multiplies 3 by 10.
=(30+3)*(10/2)	This formula yields 165 due to the brackets used in the formula. The brackets force the first part of the formula to be performed first, regardless of the BODMAS principle.

In this section, you will learn about the following:

* Recognising good practice in formula creation: referring to cell references rather than type numbers into formulas.

* Creating formulas using cell references and arithmetic operators (addition, subtraction, multiplication and division).

* Identifying and understanding standard error values associated with using formulas: #NAME?, #DIV/0! and #REF!.

* Understanding and using relative and absolute cell referencing in formulas.

4.1.1 Formula Creation – Good Practice (4.4.1.1)

When creating formulas, always use cell references rather than numbers.

Both of the examples above will yield the same result (70). However, in the above good practice example, the formula result will change if data is edited in either cell A1 or B1. In the bad practice example, if the figures are changed in cells A1 or B1, the formula result will remain the same.

Using cell references also means that you can copy (replicate) a formula to other cells and insert/ delete cells, rows and columns and the formula result will update accordingly.

4.1.2 Arithmetic Operators (4.4.1.2)

To create a formula using arithmetic operators, do the following:

To **add** the contents of cells together:
- Enter the following formula (changing the cell references as appropriate): **=A1+B1**.

To **subtract** the content of one cell from another cell:
- Enter the following formula (changing the cell references as appropriate): **=A1-B1**.

To **divide** the contents of one cell by the contents of another cell:
- Enter the following formula (changing the cell references as appropriate): **=A1/B1**.

To **multiply** the contents of one cell by the contents of another cell:
- Enter the following formula (changing the cell references as appropriate): **=A1*B1**.

> **NOTE**
> Remember BODMAS principles when using arithmetic operators and use brackets if you want an arithmetic operator to perform in a certain order (Tip: the BODMAS order is Divide, Multiply, Add and Subtract.)

4.1.3 Error Values (4.4.1.3)

Error values sometimes occur when you are creating formulas in a spreadsheet. To identify error values associated with using formulas, see the table below.

Error Value	Error	Solution
######	Column is too narrow to display data.	Widen the column to accommodate all of the data.
#NAME?	Excel does not recognise text in a formula.	Check that you have typed the function name correctly.
#DIV/0	Division by 0 or a cell with no value.	Ensure that the cell reference is correct and does not contain a null value or 0.
#REF!	Cell reference is not valid.	Check the cell references used in the formula.

When an error occurs in a formula, a green triangle appears in the top left of the cell containing the error. When this is clicked, the **Error Checking** button appears.

Click the arrow to see the menu options.

Select **Help on this error** if you need help in resolving the error

Select **Error Checking Options** to see further options in resolving formula errors

---

NOTE

If you don't see the green triangle error indicator, select the **Office Button** and then **Excel Options**. Select the **Formulas** tab and then select the **Enable background error checking** checkbox. Click **OK**.

To change the colour of the error indicator, do the following:

- Select the **Office Button** and then **Excel Options**.
- Select the **Formula** tab.
- From the **Error Checking** section of the window, select **Indicate errors using this color:**.
- Select a colour from the palette.
- Click **OK**.

4.1.4   Cell Referencing (4.4.1.4)

Spreadsheets use cell references in formulas and functions, rather than figures, which makes it easier to modify and update data in a spreadsheet. For example, =A1+B1 will total the contents of cells A1 and B1.

When data is modified, or rows/columns deleted or inserted, formulas and functions will automatically update to reflect the modifications. Formulas can be copied (referred to as **replicating**) across or down over subsequent cells and the cell reference will change to match the cell to which the formula is copied.

A normal cell reference is called a **relative cell reference**, because it is relative to the cell to which the formula is being copied. Sometimes an **absolute cell reference** may be required in a formula if the cell reference should not change during replication, but should remain constant. An example of this is in a spreadsheet which uses a cell, such as VAT which will remain constant.

A formula using absolute cell references looks like this: =A1+$B$1. The relative cell reference A1 will change when copied downwards to cells A2 and A3 (i.e. =A2+$B$1, =A3+$B$1) but the absolute cell will remain constant and refer to cell B1.

Relative Cell References

- Select the cell that is to contain the formula.
- Enter the cell reference, e.g. A1 or B3 , or click the cell containing the contents to be used in the calculation.

Absolute Cell References

- Select the cell which is to contain the formula.
- Enter the cell reference, e.g. $A$1 or $B$3 using the dollar sign before the column and before the row.

   Alternatively, enter the cell reference e.g. A1 or B3, or click the cell, and then press **F4** to make the cell reference absolute.

PRACTICE SEQUENCE

1   Open the **sale** spreadsheet.

2   In cell B9 enter a formula to find the total expenditure for the **1st Qtr Jan–Mar 2008**. (Tip: use cell references and the arithmetic operator **+**.)

3   In cell B9 find the total sales by entering a formula that uses cell references and arithmetic operators.

4   In cell A18 enter the title **PROFITS**.

5   In cell A19 enter a formula that will find the profits for the **1st QTR Jan–Mar 2008**. (Tip: subtract total expenditure from the total sales.)

6   In cell A20 enter **PROJECTED PROFIT 2008**.

7   In cell A21 enter a formula to find the profit for the whole year, based on the profits for the 1st QTR (tip: multiply the Profits for the 1st QTR by 4 to get a projected profit for the whole year).

8   In cell A22 enter **AVERAGE SALES**.

9   In cell A23 enter a formula to find the monthly profit. (Tip: divide the profit for the 1st QTR by 3).

10   Save the spreadsheet as **Arithmetic** and close.

11   Create a new spreadsheet and, starting in cell A1, enter the following data:

	A	B	C
1	COURSES 2008/2009		
2			
3	*Sept Increase*	1.02	
4			
5	COURSE NAME	PRICE	PRICE INCREASE
6	Word Processing	45	
7	Databases	52	
8	Spreadsheets	50	
9	Presentations	42	
10	Internet and Email	40	
11	File Management	35	

12   In cell C6 multiply the price for Word Processing by the Sept Increase figure (in cell B3). You will need to use an absolute cell reference for the Sept Increase.

13   Copy (replicate) this formula over the cell range C7:C11.

14   Save the spreadsheet as **absolute** and close.

4.2   Functions

In this section, you will learn about the following:

- Using SUM, AVERAGE, MINIMUM, MAXIMUM, COUNT, COUNTA, COUNTBLANK and ROUND functions.
- Using the logical function IF (yielding one of two specific values) with comparison operator: =, > and <.

4.2.1 Using Functions (4.4.2.1)

- The **SUM** function is used to find the total of a specified cell range.
- The **AVERAGE** function is used to find the average value in a specified cell range.
- The **MINIMUM** and **MAXIMUM** functions are used to find smallest and largest values in a specified cell range.
- The **COUNT**, **COUNTA** and **COUNTBLANK** functions are used to count the number of entries in a specified cell range.
- The **ROUND** function is used to round figures up or down (towards or away from zero).

To create a function, do the following:

Sum

- All formulas and functions begin with the equals sign (**=**).
- After the equals sign, enter the function **SUM**.
- As you enter the function name, a menu appears with alternative SUM function options. Double-click the SUM option or do the following:

  o Enter an open round bracket (**(**.
  o Enter the cell range, e.g. **=SUM(A1:A12**.
  o Close the bracket, e.g. **=SUM(A1:A12)**.

Alternatively, after the open bracket, drag the mouse over the cell range to select it and press Enter. This will find the total of the specified cell range.

Average

- All formulas and functions begin with the equals sign (**=**).
- After the equals sign, enter the function **AVERAGE**.
- As you enter the function name a menu appears with alternative AVERAGE function options. Double-click the AVERAGE option or do the following:

  o Enter an open round bracket (**(**.
  o Enter the cell range, e.g. **=AVERAGE(A1:A12**.
  o Close the bracket, e.g. **=AVERAGE(A1:A12)**.

Alternatively, after the open bracket, drag the mouse over the cell range to select it and press Enter. This will find the average of the specified cell range.

Minimum

- All formulas and functions begin with the equals sign (**=**).
- After the equals sign, enter the function **MIN**.
- As you enter the function name a menu appears with alternative MIN function options. Double-click the MIN option or do the following:

  o Enter an open round bracket (**(**.
  o Enter the cell range, e.g. **=MIN(A1:A12**.
  o Close the bracket, e.g. **=MIN(A1:A12)**.

Alternatively, after the open bracket, drag the mouse over the cell range to select it and press Enter. This will find the smallest number or minimum value in the specified cell range.

Maximum

- All formulas and functions begin with the equals sign (=)
- After the equals sign, enter the function **MAX**.
- As you enter the function name a menu appears with alternative MAX function options. Double-click the MAX option or do the following:
  - o Enter an open round bracket (.
  - o Enter the cell range, e.g. **=MAX(A1:A12**.
  - o Close the bracket, e.g. **=MAX(A1:A12)**.

Alternatively, after the open bracket, drag the mouse over the cell range to select it and press Enter. This will find the largest number or maximum value in the specified cell range.

COUNT

The COUNT function counts the number of cells in a range of cells that contain numbers.
- All formulas and functions begin with the equals sign (**=**).
- After the equals sign, enter the function **COUNT**.
- As you enter the function name a menu appears with alternative COUNT function options. Double-click the COUNT option or do the following:
  - o Enter an open round bracket (.
  - o Enter the cell range, e.g. **=COUNT(A1:A12**.
  - o Close the bracket, e.g. **=COUNT(A1:A12)**.

Alternatively, after the open bracket, drag the mouse over the cell range to select it and press Enter. This will count the number of cells containing numbers in the specified cell range.

COUNT A

The COUNTA function counts the number of cells in a range that are not empty (will count cells containing numbers and text).
- All formulas and functions begin with the equals sign (=).
- After the equals sign, enter the function **COUNTA**.
- As you enter the function name a menu appears. Double-click the COUNTA option or do the following:
  - o Enter an open round bracket (.
  - o Enter the cell range, e.g. **=COUNTA(A1:A12**.
  - o Close the bracket, e.g. **=COUNTA(A1:A12)**.

Alternatively, after the open bracket, drag the mouse over the cell range to select it and press Enter. This will find the number of cells in the specified cell range that are not blank.

COUNTBLANK

The COUNTBLANK function counts the number of cells in a range that are empty (will count cells containing no numbers or text).
- All formulas and functions begin with the equals sign (=).
- After the equals sign, enter the function **COUNTBLANK**.
- As you enter the function name a menu appears. Double-click the COUNTBLANK option or do the following:
  - o Enter an open round bracket (.
  - o Enter the cell range, e.g. **=COUNTBLANK(A1:A12**.
  - o Close the bracket, e.g. **=COUNTBLANK(A1:A12)**.

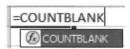

Alternatively, after the open bracket, drag the mouse over the cell range to select it and press Enter. This will find the number of cells in the specified cell range that are blank.

ROUND

The ROUND function rounds figures up or down to a specified number of digits. Rounddown rounds figures down to zero (0). Roundup rounds figures up away from zero (0).

- All formulas and functions begin with the equals sign (=).
- After the equals sign, enter the function **ROUND** to round figures to a specified number of digits, **ROUNDDOWN** to round a figure down towards zero or **ROUNDUP** to round a figure up away from zero.
- As you enter the function name a menu appears. Double-click an option or do the following:
  - Enter an open round bracket **(**.
  - Enter the cell, e.g. **=ROUND(A1**.
  - Enter a comma followed by the number of digits by which you want to round down or up. Close the bracket, e.g. **=ROUND(A1,0)**.

Alternatively, after the open bracket, drag the mouse over the cell range to select it and press Enter.

For example typing =ROUND(B4,2) will round the number in cell B4 rounded to 2 decimal places.

NOTE
Numbers in a range of cells can also be rounded. For example, typing =ROUND(A1:C5,3) will round the numbers in the range A1 to C5 to 3 decimal places.

When rounding numbers in a range of cells hold down **CTRL** before pressing **Enter**. This ensures that all the numbers in the range are rounded and not just the first one.

4.2.2 Using Logical Functions (4.4.2.2)

The **IF** function is called a **logical function** and it checks whether or not a condition has been met, returning one value if **TRUE** and another value if **FALSE**. The IF function uses comparison operators to find values equal to, greater than or less than a specified amount.

=	equal to
>	greater than
<	less than
>=	greater than and equal to
<=	less than and equal to

- All formulas and functions begin with the equals sign (=).
- After the equals sign, enter the function **IF**.
- As you enter the function name a menu appears.
- Double-click the IF function or do the following:
  - Enter an open round bracket **(**.
  - Enter the condition e.g. **=IF(A1>10000**.
  - This means: **If the figure in cell A1 is greater than 10000…**
  - Enter a comma to separate the condition from the values that should be returned subject to the condition being met, e.g. **=IF(A1>10000,**.
  - Enter the TRUE value that should appear when the condition is met, e.g. **=IF(A1>10000, "Yes"**.

Text values that will be returned subject to condition being met should be enclosed in quotation marks. You can use cell references as TRUE or FALSE values so that a specific cell is referenced if the condition is met or not.

o   Enter a comma to separate the TRUE value from the FALSE value.

o   Enter the value that should be returned if the condition is not met, e.g. **=IF(A1>10000, "Yes", "No".**

o   Close the bracket e.g. **=IF(A1>10000, "Yes", "No").**

If the condition is met (the contents of cell A1 is greater than 10000), then the value **Yes** will be returned; if the condition is not met (the contents of cell A1 is 10000 or below), then the value **No** will be returned.

NOTE

You can also insert functions by doing one of three methods shown below.

1.   From the **Home** tab and **Editing** group, select the **Sum** arrow and then choose a function from the list or click **More Functions** to see the **Insert Function** window.

2.   Select the **fx** function button on the Formula Bar to see the **Insert Function** window.

The **Functions Argument** window opens. This window enables you to add values and/or conditions.

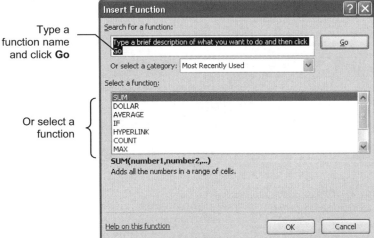

3.   From the **Formulas** tab, select functions from the **Function Library** group.

PRACTICE SEQUENCE

1   Open the **sale** spreadsheet.

2   In cell B9 use the SUM function to find the total expenditure.

3   In cell B16 use the SUM function to find the total sales.

4   In cell A18 enter **PROFITS**. In cell B18 enter a formula to find the profits (subtract B9 from B16).

5   In cell A19 enter **AVG EXPENSE**. In cell B19 enter a function to find the average expenditure cost

6   In cell A20 enter **MIN EXPENSE**. In cell B20 enter a function to find the minimum expenditure cost.

7   In cell A21 enter **MAX EXPENSE**. In cell B21 enter a function to find the maximum expenditure cost.

8   In cell A22 enter **AVG ROUND DOWN**. In cell B22 enter a function to round down the Average result in B19 to 0 digits.

9   In cell A23 enter REFRESHMENTS VIABLE?.

10   In cell B23 enter a logical function to test whether or not it is viable to sell refreshments at the jumble sales. If the Refreshment Costs are less than the Refreshment Sales, then the cell should display **Yes**, otherwise **No**.

11   In cell A24 enter **COUNT OF EXPENDITURE**. In cell B24 enter a function to count the number of Expenditure items (you may use **COUNTA** to count the Labels, or **COUNT** to count the numeric cells).

12   Save and close the **sale** spreadsheet.

4

Section 5   Formatting

Formatting can be applied to text, dates and numbers.

- Text can be formatted to display with different fonts, sizes, styles, colours and alignment.
- Dates can be formatted to display in different formats: 10/10/2008, 10-Oct-08, 10 October 2008.
- Numbers can be formatted to display as percentages or with or without currency symbols or decimal places. Numbers can also be formatted to display with a thousand separator, e.g. **10000** can be formatted to display as **10,000**.
- Cell contents can be aligned to display on the left, right or centre of a cell and also vertically aligned or orientated by an amount of specified degrees.
- Titles can be merged across cells and centred.
- Border effects and shading further enhances cell appearance.

5.1   Numbers and Dates

In this section, you will learn about the following:

- Formatting cells to display numbers to a specific number of decimal places and to display numbers with or without a separator to indicate thousands.
- Formatting cells to display a date style and to display a currency symbol.
- Formatting cells to display numbers as percentages.

5.1.1 Format Numbers (4.5.1.1, 4.5.1.2 and 4.5.1.3)

When numbers are first entered into a new, unformatted worksheet, they display without decimal precision or currency symbols, e.g. 1.50 will display as 1.5 and 1.00 will display as 1.

To format numbers, do the following:

Decimal Places

- Select the cell or cell range containing the numerical data to be formatted.
- From the **Home** tab and the **Cells** group, select the **Format** arrow.
- Select **Format Cells**.
- In the **Format Cells** window and the **Number** tab, select **Number** from the list of categories.
- Use the **Decimal Places** scroll arrows to increase or decrease the number of decimal places. A preview of the selected format is provided in the Sample box.
- Click **OK**.

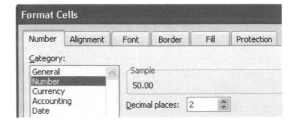

Percentages

- Select the cell or cell range containing the numerical data to be formatted.
- From the **Home** tab and the **Cells** group, select the **Format** arrow.
- Select **Format Cells**.
  The **Format Cells** window opens.

- In the **Number** tab, select **Percentage** from the list of categories.

- Use the **Decimal Places** scroll arrows to increase or decrease the number of decimal places. A preview of the selected format is provided in the Sample box.

- Click **OK**.

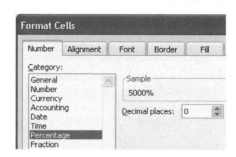

Currency

- Select the cell or cell range containing the numerical data to be formatted.

- From the **Home** tab and the **Cells** group, select the **Format** arrow.

- Select **Format Cells**.

- In the **Format Cells** window and the **Number** tab, select **Currency** from the list of categories.

- Use the **Decimal Places** scroll arrows to increase or decrease the number of decimal places.

- Select the **Symbol** arrow to select a currency symbol. A preview of the selected format is provided in the Sample box.

- Click **OK**.

Thousand Operator

- Select the cell or cell range containing the numerical data to be formatted.

- From the **Home** tab and the **Cells** group, select the **Format** arrow.

- Select **Format Cells**.

- In the **Format Cells** window and the **Number** tab, select **Number** from the list of categories.

- Use the **Decimal Places** scroll arrows to increase or decrease the number of decimal places.

- Select the **Use 1000 Separator** (,) checkbox (place a tick in the box). A preview of the selected format is provided in the Sample box.

- Click **OK**.

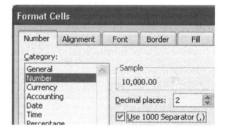

5.1.2 Format Dates (4.5.1.2)

Dates can be formatted to display in different styles, e.g. long date, short date or medium date format.

To format a date, do the following:
- Select the cell or cell range containing the date(s).

- From the **Home** tab and the **Cells** group, select the **Format** arrow.

- Select **Format Cells**.

- In the **Format Cells** window and the **Number** tab, select **Date** from the list of categories.

- Select a date type from the **Type** list.

- Select the **Locale (Location)** arrow to choose a location (this may affect the date style, e.g. US dates display the month before the day).

- Click **OK**.

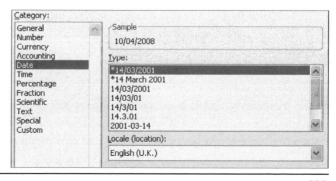

> **NOTE**
>
> You can also format numbers and dates by selecting the **Number Format** arrow (from the **Home/Number**) and choosing a format from the menu. *Alternatively*, select the **Number** group window launcher icon to see the **Format Cells** window.
>
>

PRACTICE SEQUENCE

1   Open the **sale** spreadsheet.

2   Format the cell range B4:B16 to display with a currency symbol and 2 decimal places.

3   Format the cell B18 to display with 2 decimal places but no currency symbol.

4   Enter today's date in cell C2.

5   Format the date in long date format (e.g. 07 August 2008).

6   In cell D2 enter **Our current target for the year is:**.

7   In cell D3 enter **2500**.

8   Format the number in cell D3 to display with 2 decimal places and a thousand separator.

9   In cell D4 enter **The increase for next year is:**.

10   In cell D5 enter **0.05**.

11   Format this number to display as a percentage with 1 decimal place.

12   Save and close the **sale** spreadsheet.

5.2   Cell Content

The appearance of cell content can be enhanced by formatting, such as changing fonts, sizes, styles, colours, alignment, orientation, shading and borders.

In this section, you will cover the following:

- Changing cell content appearance: font size and font type.
- Applying formatting to cell contents: bold, italic, underline or double underline.
- Applying different colours to cell content and cell background.
- Copying the formatting from a cell, cell range to another cell or a cell range.

5.2.1 Fonts (4.5.2.1, 4.5.2.2 and 4.5.2.3)

To change the font type, size, style and colour of cell contents and background, do the following:

Font Types

- Select the cell or cell range to be formatted.
- From the **Home** tab and **Font** group, select the **Font** arrow.
- Select a font from the drop-down list.

Select the
Font arrow

Select a
font

Font Sizes

- Select the cell or cell range to be formatted and then, from the **Home** tab and **Font** group, select the **Font Size** arrow.
- Select a size from the drop-down list.
  Alternatively, select the **Increase** or **Decrease Font Size** buttons.

Increase font size Decrease font size

Select the
Font size
arrow

Select a
font size

Font Colours

- Select the cell or cell range to be formatted and then, from the **Home** tab and **Font** group, select the **Font Color** arrow.
- Select a colour from the drop down list or select **More Colors** to see further colour options.
- Select a colour from the palette.
- Click **OK**.

Select the **Font Color** arrow

Select a
font colour

Select **More Colors** to
see the palette

The **Colors**
window provides
more colours

Chose a colour
and click **OK**

Font Styles

- Font style refers to **bold**, *italic* and <u>underline</u>.
- Select the cell or cell range to be formatted and then, from the **Home** tab and **Font** group, select the required font style.

Bold   Underline

Italic

Double Underline

- Select the cell or range of cells to be formatted.
- From the **Home** tab and **Font** group, select the **Borders** button.
- Select **Bottom Double Border** to apply a double underline at the bottom of selected cells.
- Select **Top and Double Bottom Border** to apply a double underline to the top and bottom of selected cells.

Select **Bottom Double Border** to apply a double underline effect to the bottom of the selected cell(s)

Format Cell Background

- Select the cell or range of cells to be formatted.
- From the **Home** tab and **Font** group, select the **Shading** arrow.
- Choose a colour from the available **Theme Colors** or from **Standard Colors**.
- To see further colour choices, select **More Colors**. The **Colors** window opens.
- Select a colour.
- Click **OK**.

Select the **Shading** arrow

Select a colour

Select **No Fill** if you don't want cell shading

The **Colors** window provides more colours

Select **More Colors** for further colour options

Choose a colour and click OK

NOTE

You can open the **Font** window by selecting the **Font** window launcher icon. The **Font** tab contains all of the formatting options listed above.

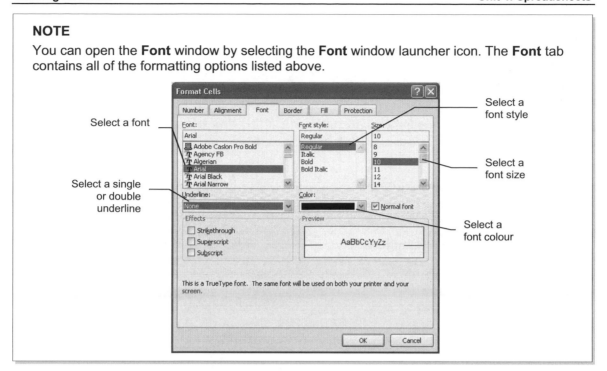

5.2.2 Copy Formatting (4.5.2.4)

Formatting can be copied by using the Format Painter. This tool enables you to copy formatting from one cell or range of cells to another cell or range of cells.

To copy formatting, do the following:

- Select the formatted cell or range of cells to be copied.
- From the **Home** tab and **Clipboard** group, select the **Format Painter** button.
- Drag the mouse over the cell or range of cells which are to display the same formatting (note how the cursor changes to include a paintbrush icon).

NOTE

Double-click the **Format Painter** to keep it on whilst you copy formatting to more than one cell/range of cells. Click the Format Painter button to turn it off.

PRACTICE SEQUENCE

1   Open the **sale** spreadsheet.

2   Format the title in cell A1 with **Comic Sans MS** font type, **Dark Blue** font colour, **Bold, Italic** font style and font size **14**.

3   Format cell A1 with a pale blue background.

4   Format the cell A3 (Expenditure) with **Comic Sans MS** font type, **Dark Blue** font colour, **Italic** font style and font size **12**.

5   Copy this formatting to cells A9 (Total Expenditure), A11 (Income) and A16 (Total Sales).

6   Format cell B9 with a double underline.

7   Copy this formatting to cell B16.

8   Format the cell range A18:B24 as **Times New Roman**, **12**, **Red**.

9   Format the date as dark blue and bold.

10   Format cell D2 as **Times New Roman**, **14**, **Red**.

11   Copy this formatting to cell D4.

12   Format the cell range D2:D5 in italics.

13   Save and close the **sale** spreadsheet.

5.3 Alignment and Border Effects

In this section, you will cover the following:

- Applying text wrapping to contents within a cell and a cell range.
- Aligning cell contents both horizontally and vertically. Adjusting cell content orientation.
- Merging cells and centre a title in a merged cell.
- Adding border effects to a cell and a cell range, including lines and colours.

5.3.1 Text Wrapping (4.5.3.1)

To wrap text within a cell, do the following:

- Select the cell or cell range to be formatted.
- From the **Home** tab and **Alignment** group, select the **Wrap Text** button.
- Adjust the column width and row height if necessary.

5.3.2 Alignment (4.5.3.2)

Cell contents can be aligned horizontally and/or vertically.

To align cell contents, do the following:

Horizontally

- Select the cell or cell range to be aligned.
- From the **Home** tab and **Alignment** group, select an alignment:

Vertically

- Select the cell or cell range to be aligned.
- From the **Home** tab and **Alignment** group, select an alignment:

5.3.3 Adjusting Cell Orientation (4.5.3.2)

To change the orientation of a cell's contents, do the following:

- Select the cell or cell range to be formatted.
- From the **Home** tab and **Alignment** group, select the **Orientation** arrow.

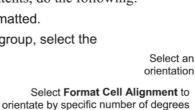

- Select an orientation or select **Format Cell Alignment**.
- The **Format Cells** window opens with the **Alignment** tab the active tab.
- Select an orientation by dragging the **Text** orientation slider in the required direction or use the **Degrees** scroll arrows to select a specific number of degrees.

- Choose the direction of the orientation by selecting the **Text Direction** arrow and then choosing a direction.

Select the **Text direction** arrow and choose a direction for the orientation

5.3.4 Merge Cells (4.5.3.3)

To merge cells, do the following:

Select the **Merge** arrow

- Select the cell range to be merged.
- From the **Home** tab and **Alignment** group, select the **Merge Cells** arrow.
- Choose a merge option from the menu.

Select an option from the menu

Select **Unmerge Cells** to undo the merge (the relevant cells should be selected first)

Alternatively, select the **Alignment** group window launcher icon to open the **Format Cells** window and ensure that the **Alignment** tab is the active tab.

- Under **Text Control**, select the **Merge Cells** checkbox (click to enter a tick in the box).
- Click **OK**.

5.3.5 Adding and a Title (4.5.3.3)

Often a worksheet has a title that you wish to centre across a number of columns, not just within a single cell.

To centre a title across a range of cells, do the following:
- Type the title and press **Enter**.
- Select the cell containing the heading and the adjacent cells across which the title is to be centred.
- From the **Home** tab and **Alignment group**, select the **Merge Cells** arrow.
- Choose **Merge & Center** from the drop-down menu.

Select **Merge & Center**

5.3.6 Border Effects (4.5.3.4)

To format cells with borders and lines, do the following:
- Select the cell or cell range to be formatted.
- From the **Home** tab and **Font** group, select the **Border** arrow.
- Select a border from the menu or select **More Borders** at the bottom of the menu.
- The **Format Cells** window opens with the **Borders** tab selected.
- From the **Line** section of the window, select a line **Style** and/or a line **Colour**.
- From the **Presets** section, select the type of border you require.

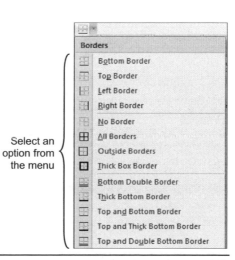

Select an option from the menu

- From the **Border** section refine the border by selecting top, bottom, left, right, middle or diagonal border buttons (these are *toggle* buttons which are turned on/off each time they are selected) to apply or remove a border.
- Click **OK**.

Select a
preset border

Select
a line
style

Turn specific
borders on/off

Select a
line colour

Click **OK**

PRACTICE SEQUENCE

1   Open the **sale** spreadsheet.

2   Merge and centre the title in cell A1 across the cell range A1:D1.

3   Format cell A3 to be vertically aligned with **Middle Alignment**.

4   Copy this formatting to cells A9, A11 and A16.

5   Right align the contents of cells A9 and A16.

6   Centre the date in cell C2.

7   Wrap the contents in cells A23 and A24 (Refreshments Viable? and Count of Expenditure) so that the content in each of the cells display on two lines (you may need to adjust column width/row height).

8   Format cells A9 and A16 to be orientated by -10^0 degrees (Text Direction - Context).

9   Apply a thick black outline border to cells A1:D1.

10 Apply a 2pt dark blue, dashed border to cells A3 and cell A11.

11 Apply an inside and outline black border to the cell range A4:A7.

12 Repeat this formatting for cell range A12:B14.

13 Apply a double, dark blue, outline border to the cell range D2:D5.

14 Repeat this formatting for the cell range A18:A24.

15 Save and close **sale**.

Section 6   Charts

Charts are visual graphical representations of numerical data, making it easier to see results 'at a glance'. Charts can be displayed in different formats, such as pie, bar/column and line, and can be formatted with colour and fonts, size and styles.

To use charts you need to input data in a spreadsheet. This data is then displayed in chart format in the chart type that you specify. The chart can be modified if required to display a different chart type. Chart titles can also be added or removed as required. The chart data is described by the data labels that are applied. For example, the following chart is meaningless without the data labels, but makes sense once data labels are applied:

This chart does not contain data labels and so is meaningless

This chart contains category and percentage data labels which describe the segments

6.1   Creating Charts

In this section, you will learn about the following:

* Creating different types of charts from spreadsheet data: column chart, bar chart, line chart and pie chart.
* Selecting a chart.
* Changing the chart type.
* Moving, resizing and deleting a chart.

6.1.1   Chart Types (4.6.1.1)

Charts can be displayed in a variety of types, such as a bar chart, column chart, line chart or pie chart. The type of chart that you choose should be suitable for the data being represented.

Column chart:
Values are displayed on the vertical Y axis and labels are displayed on the horizontal X axis

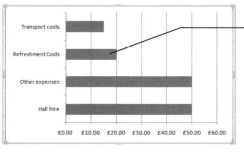

Bar chart:
Values are displayed on the horizontal axis and labels are displayed on the vertical axis

Line chart:
Values are displayed on the vertical Y axis and labels are displayed on the horizontal X axis

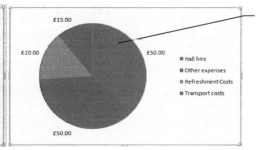

Pie chart:
Values are displayed around the chart and a legend displays the category labels (labels can also be displayed with the values)

6.1.2 Creating a Chart (4.6.1.1)

To create a chart, do the following:

Column Chart

- Select the spreadsheet data.
- From the **Insert** tab and **Charts** group, select the **Column** command.

  A list opens, displaying different column chart sub-types.
- Select a sub-type from the list or select **All Chart Types**.

  The **Insert Chart** window opens.
- Select a column sub-type or select a different chart type if required.
- Click **OK**.

Select a column sub-type if required

NOTE

Bar charts are created in exactly the same way – just select the **Bar** command from the **Charts** group.

Line Chart

- Select the spreadsheet data.
- From the **Insert** tab and **Charts** group, select the **Line** command.

  A list opens, displaying different Line chart sub-types.
- Select a sub-type from the list or select **All Chart Types**.

  The **Insert Chart** window opens.
- Select a Line sub-type or select a different chart type if required.
- Click **OK**.

Pie Chart

- Select the spreadsheet data.
- From the **Insert** tab and **Charts** group, select the **Pie** command.

  A list opens, displaying different Pie chart sub-types.
- Select a sub-type from the list or select **All Chart Types**.

  The **Insert Chart** window opens.
- Select a Pie sub-type or select a different chart type if required.
- Click **OK**.

6.1.3 Selecting a Chart (4.6.1.2)

Before a chart can be edited, resized, moved, deleted or formatted it first needs to be selected.

To select a chart, do the following:
- Click the chart to select it.

  A border appears around the chart with small dots in the middle and corners of the surrounding border.

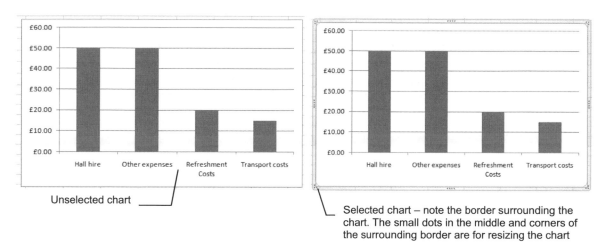

Unselected chart

Selected chart – note the border surrounding the chart. The small dots in the middle and corners of the surrounding border are for resizing the chart

Alternatively, do the following:

- From the **Home** tab and **Editing** group, select the **Find & Select** command.
- Select the **Selection Pane** command from the menu.
- Select objects from the task pane that opens (click the 'eye' icon to hide/unhide objects on the worksheet).

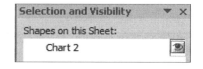

6.1.4 Changing the Chart Type (4.6.1.3)

The chart can be altered, if required, to another type.

To change the chart type of a selected chart, do the following:
- Select the chart.
- From the **Chart Tools/Design** tab and the **Type** group, select **Change Chart Type**.

  The **Change Chart Type** window opens.
- Select a different chart type and a chart sub-type.
- Click **OK**.

6.1.5 Moving, Resizing and Deleting a Chart (4.6.1.4)

A chart can be moved to a different position on the same worksheet or moved to another worksheet or spreadsheet. If a chart overlaps or obscures spreadsheet data, it should be moved to a new position. A chart can also be resized to make it bigger or smaller. When a chart is no longer required it can be deleted.

To move, resize and delete a chart, do the following:

Moving a Chart (Within a Worksheet)

- Select the chart and then, holding down the left mouse button, drag to the new location within the worksheet (note how the mouse arrow changes to the black cross icon when moving the chart).

  Alternatively, select the chart and then, from the **Home** tab and **Clipboard** group, select the **Cut** button. Select the cell where the chart is to be positioned within the worksheet, and select the **Paste** button.

NOTE

The keyboard shortcuts are: **CTRL + C** (copy), **CTRL + X** (cut) and **CTRL + V** (paste).

Moving a Chart (Between Worksheets)

- Select the chart.
- From the **Home** tab and **Clipboard** group, click **Cut**.
- Select a new sheet tab.
- Select the cell where the chart is to be positioned within the worksheet.
- Click **Paste**.

  Alternatively, from the **Chart Tools/Format** tab and **Location** group, select **Move Chart.**

  The **Move Chart** window opens.

- Select the **New sheet** button if you want the chart to be moved to a new sheet.

- Enter a new name for the sheet if required.

- Select **Object in** if you want the chart to be positioned as an object in an existing sheet.

- Choose the sheet from the **Object in:** menu.

- Click **OK**.

Resizing a Chart (Using the Mouse)

- Select the chart.
- Point the cursor at a corner of the chart (containing small dots).
- The cursor turns into a double-headed black arrow when positioned over the resizing handles.
- Hold down the left mouse button and drag in the required direction to increase/decrease the size (note how the double-headed black arrow turns into a black crosshair whilst resizing).
- Release the mouse button when the chart is the required size.

NOTE

When using the mouse to resize a chart, always drag from a corner resizing handle to maintain the original chart proportions.

Resizing a Chart (Using Chart Tools)

- Select the chart.
- From the **Chart Tools/Format** tab and the **Size** group, select a specific size for the height and/or width of the chart by selecting the **Shape Height** and/or **Shape Width** scroll arrows.

  Alternatively, select the **Size** window launcher icon to see the **Size and Properties** window.

- Change the size of the chart by increasing/ decreasing the measurements in the **Height** and/or **Width** boxes.
- Select the **Lock aspect ratio** option button before selecting a height to ensure that the width alters proportionally to the height (or vice versa).

Select **Lock aspect ratio** to maintain proportions

Select a **Height** or **Width** measurement

Deleting a Chart

- Select the chart.
- Press **Delete** on the keyboard or right-click the chart and select **Delete** from the shortcut menu.

PRACTICE SEQUENCE

1   Open the **sale** spreadsheet.
2   Copy the cell range A4:B7 to Sheet2 and position in cell A3 (beneath the EXPENDITURE title that you copied in an earlier task.
3   Rename Sheet2 as Expenditure.
4   In the Expenditure sheet, create a bar chart from the cell range A3:B6.
5   Move the chart so that it is positioned beneath the spreadsheet data, starting in cell A12 (approximately).
6   Resize the chart to have a height of 8cm and a width of 14cm.
7   Using the same cell range, create a pie chart.
8   Position this chart on the right hand side of the spreadsheet data in cell D1 (approx).
9   Resize the pie chart as Height: 5.5 and Width 9.5.
10 Using the same cell range, create a line chart
11 Position this chart beneath the pie chart (to the right of the bar chart).
12 Resize the line chart to Height: 6.5 and width 11.
13 Change the chart type of the bar chart to a column chart.
14 Delete the line chart.
15 Save and close the **sale** spreadsheet.

6.2   Editing Charts

In this section, you will learn about the following:

- Adding, removing and editing a chart title.
- Adding data labels to a chart: values/numbers and percentages.
- Changing chart area background colour and legend fill colour.
- Changing the column, bar, line or pie slice colours in a chart.
- Changing the font size and colour of chart title, chart axes and chart legend text.

6.2.1 Adding, Removing and Editing a Chart Title (4.6.2.1)

To add, remove or edit a chart title, do the following:

Adding a Chart Title

- From the **Chart Tools/Layout** tab and the **Labels** group, select the **Chart Title** command.
- From the **Chart Title** list, select a position, such as **Above Chart**. A **Chart Title** box appears on the chart in the selected position.
- Position the cursor within this box and delete the existing text.
- Enter the chart title.

Select a position for the title

Editing a Chart Title

- Position the cursor within the chart title box and delete or enter text as required.

Deleting a Chart Title

- Select the chart title box and press **Delete** on the keyboard.
  Alternatively, select the **Chart Tools/Layout** tab.
- Select the **Chart Title** command.
- Select **None**.

NOTE

Other chart elements can also be deleted by selecting the chart element and pressing **Delete**. To select different parts of a chart, do one of the following:

- Click the chart element to select it or, from the **Chart Tools/Format** tab and the **Current Selection** group, select the **Chart Elements** arrow.
- Select a chart element from the menu.

6.2.2 Adding Data Labels (4.6.2.2)

Data labels help to identify the X and Y axes data in the chart.

To add data labels, do the following:
- Select the chart.
- From the **Chart Tools/Layout** tab and the **Labels** group, select the **Data Labels** command.

- Select a position for the data labels.
  Alternatively, select **More Data Label options** to open the **Format Data Labels** window.

Select a position for the data labels

Select **More Data Label Options...**

- Select a label type such as **Value**.

- Select a label position, such as **Outside End**.

- Select **Include legend key in label** if you want the category labels to display as a legend.

- Click **Close**.

The options shown in this illustration are for **bar**, **column** and **line** charts

---

NOTE

When using **pie charts**, the options for data labels are different. Pie charts have the option of displaying the data as percentages.

The options shown in this illustration are for **pie** charts and include **Percentage**

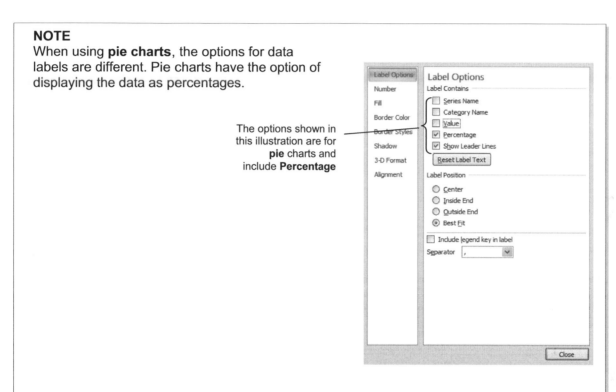

6.2.3 Changing the Chart Area and Legend Background (4.6.2.3)

The background of the chart and the background of the legend can be formatted to display with a solid fill colour.

To change the chart area and legend background, do the following:

- Select the chart element to be formatted (**Chart Area** or **Legend**) by clicking the chart element to select it.

  Alternatively, select the **Chart Element** arrow from the **Chart Tools/Format** tab and the **Current Selection** group, and select the chart element from the list.

- From the **Chart Tools/Format** tab and the **Shape Styles** group, select the **Shape Fill** command.

- Select a colour from the menu or choose **More Fill Colors** to see the colour palette.

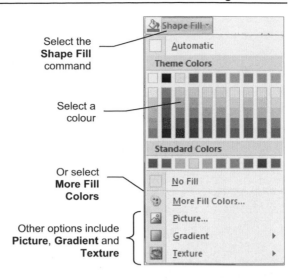

Select the **Shape Fill** command

Select a colour

Or select **More Fill Colors**

Other options include **Picture**, **Gradient** and **Texture**

- Choose a colour from the palette.
- Click **OK**.

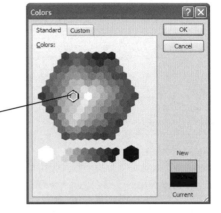

Select a colour from the palette

6.2.4 Changing Column, Bar, Line or Pie Slice Colours (4.6.2.4)

The lines, bars, columns or pie slices of a chart can be formatted with a different colour if required.

To change the colour of a bar, column, line or pie slice, do the following:

- Select the column/bar/line/pie slice for the series to be formatted (by double-clicking to select or by selecting the **Chart Element** arrow from the **Chart Tools/Format** tab and the **Current Selection** group, and selecting the chart element from the list, such as Series1 or Series2).

- From the **Chart Tools/Format** tab and the **Shape Styles** group, select the **Shape Fill** command.

Select the **Shape Fill** command

Select a colour

Or select **More Fill Colors...**

Other options include **Picture**, **Gradient** and **Texture**

Select a colour from the palette

6.2.5 Formatting a Chart (4.6.2.5)

The font type, size and colour of the chart title, legend or axis labels can all be changed if required.

To format a chart element, do the following:

- Click the chart element (chart title, legend or axis labels).

    Alternatively, select the **Chart Element** arrow from the **Chart Tools/Format** tab and the **Current Selection** group, and select the chart element from the list.

- From the **Home** tab and the **Font** group, select a font type, font size or font colour.

Select a font, size and colour

Alternatively, select the **Font** window launcher icon to see the **Font** window. Select font type, font size and font colour as required. Click **OK**.

Select a font type, font size, font style and font colour

PRACTICE SEQUENCE

1   Open the **sale** spreadsheet and the Expenditure sheet.

2   Add a chart title to the pie chart as follows: **1st QTR 2008**.

3   Edit the chart title to read **1st QTR Expenditure 2008**.

4   Add a chart title to the column chart as follows: **Expenditure 2008**.

5   Add data labels to the pie chart as percentages (ensure that the pie chart displays a legend).

6   Change the pie chart area background to a pale blue colour.

7   Change the pie chart legend colour to a darker blue (darker than the background colour of the chart area).

8   Format the pie slice colours as follows: Refreshment costs=yellow; Transport Costs=Red; Hall Hire=green; Other Expenses=orange.

9   Format the chart title on the pie chart to be **Comic Sans Serif**, **14** and **dark blue**.

10 Delete the chart title from the column chart.

11 Move the column chart to a new sheet called **Column**.

12 Save and close the **sale** spreadsheet.

Section 7   Preparing Outputs

Output refers to the way that the spreadsheet is viewed, either on screen or as printed hard copy. Both types of output require preparation by choosing an appropriate output format, such as displaying gridlines, row and column headings, or printing to a specific number of pages. It is good practice to check spreadsheet calculations and text and correct any errors to ensure the finished spreadsheet is presented to a professional standard. The layout of a spreadsheet can be altered so that it displays in a different orientation and paper size.

7.1   Setup
In this section, you will learn about the following:

- Changing worksheet margins: top, bottom, left and right.
- Changing worksheet orientation: portrait, landscape.
- Changing the paper size.
- Adjusting page setup to fit worksheet contents on a specified number of pages.
- Adding, editing and deleting text in headers and footers in a worksheet.
- Inserting and deleting fields: page numbering information, date, time, file name and worksheet name into headers and footers.

7.1.1   Margins (4.7.1.1)
Margins are the space between the edge of the paper and the spreadsheet data. To enhance the layout of the printed spreadsheet the top, bottom, left and right margins can all be increased or decreased if required.

To change margins, do the following:

- From the **Page Layout** tab and the **Page Setup** group, select the **Margins** command.
- From the drop-down menu, select the last custom margin setting used, select normal default margin settings or select wide or narrow settings.
- To see further margin options, select **Custom Margins**.
  The **Page Setup** window opens with **Margins** tab active.
- Use the scroll arrows to increase or decrease the current margin measurements for the **Top**, **Bottom**, **Left** and **Right** margins.
- Click **OK**.

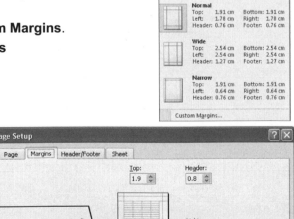

Use the scroll arrows to increase or decrease the current margin measurement for each margin

The spreadsheet can be centred on the page, horizontally and/or vertically

|

7.1.2 Orientation (4.7.1.2)

Orientation refers to Portrait and Landscape. The default orientation in Excel is Portrait.

You may need to change the orientation so that the data fits on the page. For example, a spreadsheet containing many columns but few rows (a wide spreadsheet), may display better in landscape orientation. Likewise, a spreadsheet with many rows and few columns (a long, narrow spreadsheet) may display better in portrait orientation. Changing the orientation of the spreadsheet not only enhances the presentation of the printed output, it can also save paper usage.

To change orientation, do the following:

- From the **Page Layout** tab and the **Page Setup** group, select the **Orientation** command.
- Select the required orientation – Portrait or Landscape.

7.1.3 Paper Size (4.7.1.2)

The default paper size is A4 (210mm x 297mm for portrait orientation). The paper size can be altered to another of your choice, such as A5, B3 or a variety of other sizes suitable for the intended printed output.

To change the paper size, do the following:

- From the **Page Layout** tab and the **Page Setup** group, select the **Size** arrow.
  A drop-down menu opens, displaying a variety of paper sizes.
  The default paper size is A4.
- Select the required paper size.
- To see further size options, select the **More Paper sizes** command at the bottom of the menu.
  The **Page Setup** window opens with **Page** the active tab.
- Select the **Paper size** arrow and choose a paper size from the list.
- Select a **Print quality**.
- Select **OK**.

7.1.4 Fitting to a Specified Number of Pages (4.7.1.3)

You may want to fit the spreadsheet to a certain number of pages; for example, to reduce paper wastage or to enhance clarity of the spreadsheet by ensuring that data fits on one sheet.

The default scale of an Excel spreadsheet is 100%. This scale alters depending upon which **Width** (to shrink the width of printed output to fit a maximum number of pages) or **Height** (to shrink the height of printed output to fit a maximum number of pages) option is selected.

To ensure that the spreadsheet fits to a specified number of pages, do the following:

- From the **Page Layout** tab and the **Scale to Fit** group, select the **Width** or **Height** arrow.
- From the drop-down menu, choose how many pages to which to fit the spreadsheet.
- To see further page options, select **More Pages**.
  The **Page Setup** window opens.
- Select the **Fit** option button and then use the scroll arrows to choose the number of pages to which to fit the spreadsheet.
- Click **OK**.

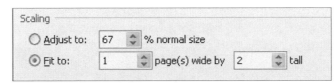

7.1.5 Headers and Footers (4.7.1.4)

Headers appear at the top of the page and footers appear at the bottom of the page. A header or footer can display information that you type in, such as your name or copyright information, or display page numbers or dates.

Creating a Header or Footer

To create a header or a footer, do the following:

- From the **Insert** tab and the **Text** group, select **Header & Footer**.
  The **Header** area opens above your spreadsheet, ready for you to enter the header information.
- Use the **Tab** key to align the cursor to the right or **Shift + Tab** to move the cursor back a step to the left.
  The **Header & Footer Tools** contextual tab becomes active and displays the **Design** tab commands. From this ribbon bar, you can choose to insert a preset header or footer by selecting the **Header** or the **Footer** arrow. Further header or footer elements include: page numbers, number of pages, date, time, file path (location), file name and sheet name.
- To switch between the header and footer area, select **Go to Footer**.

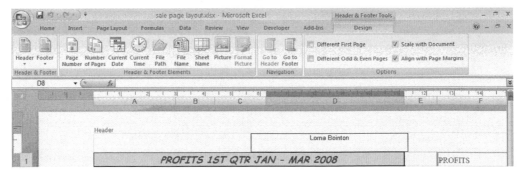

- To close the header and footer area, click away from the header/footer area into the main spreadsheet.

NOTE

All of the above commands can also be accessed through the **Page Setup** window. To open this window, click the **Page Setup** group window launcher icon. Select the relevant tab.

Editing a Header

To edit a header, do the following:

- From the **Insert** tab and the **Text** group, select **Header & Footer**.
- The **Header & Footer Tools** tab becomes active.
- Click in the header and select the text to be edited.
- Click the **Home** tab and apply the desired formatting.
- Click away from the **Header** to view the changes.

NOTE

Footers are edited in the same way as Headers. Click inside the Footer to select the text before formatting.

Deleting a Header or Footer

- Click the header or footer area and then click the header/footer to be deleted.
- Press **Delete**.

7.1.6 Inserting Fields (4.7.1.5)

Fields are items of header or footer data, such as dates, time, worksheet name and filename fields that update automatically.

To insert fields, do the following:

- From the **Insert** tab and the **Text** group, select **Header & Footer**.
  The **Header** area opens above your spreadsheet, ready for you to insert the field or fields.
- Use the **Tab** key to align the cursor to the right or **Shift + Tab** to move the cursor back a step to the left.
- The **Header & Footer Tools** contextual tab becomes active and displays the **Design** tab commands. From this ribbon bar, you can choose to insert page numbers, number of pages, date, time, file path (location), file name and sheet name.

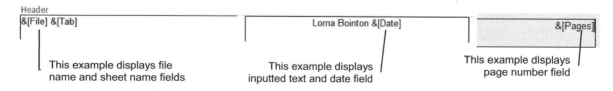

- To switch between the header and footer area, select **Go to Footer**.
- To close the header/footer, click away from the header/footer area into the main spreadsheet.

7.1.7 Deleting Fields (4.7.1.5)

- Click the header or footer area.
- Select the field to be deleted.
- Press **Delete**.

PRACTICE SEQUENCE

1   Open the **sale** spreadsheet and the **QTR1** sheet.
2   Change the top and bottom margins to 1.5 cm and the left and right margins to 2cm.
3   Check that the paper size is A4.
4   Ensure that the orientation is portrait.
5   Move the cell range A18:B24 to start in cell F2.
6   Adjust page setup so that the page fits to 1 page wide by 1 page tall.
7   Enter a centre aligned header with your name and a date field.
8   Enter a left aligned header with a file path field.
9   Enter a right aligned header with a page number field.
10   Enter a centred footer with a number of pages field.
11   Edit the header by removing the file path field and replacing with a filename and sheet name field.
12   Edit the footer by deleting the number of pages field and inserting a left aligned time field.
13   Open the **Expenditure** sheet and change the orientation to landscape.
14   Save and close the **sale** spreadsheet.

7.2 Checking and Printing

In this section, you will learn about the following:

- Checking and correcting spreadsheet calculations and text.
- Turning on and off the display of gridlines and the display of row and column headings for printing purposes.
- Applying automatic title row(s) printing on every page of a printed worksheet.
- Previewing a worksheet.
- Printing a selected cell range from a worksheet, an entire worksheet, a number of copies of a worksheet, the entire spreadsheet and a selected chart.

7.2.1 Checking (4.7.2.1)

It is important to check both the text and the calculations within a spreadsheet. Incorrect text appears unprofessional and affects the overall presentation of the spreadsheet. It can also affect the understanding and assimilation of numerical data if the row/column headings are incorrect. If numerical data is incorrect, this could affect calculations and charts based on that data, and may also affect linked calculations on different sheets. Incorrect data and calculations appear unprofessional and may make a spreadsheet unworkable. Therefore, you should do the following.

- Proofread the spreadsheet data carefully for errors (numerical and textual).
- Correct errors where necessary.
- Check calculations – comparison/arithmetic operators, functions, cell references and brackets.

Checking Spelling

- From the **Review Tab** and the **Proofing** group, select the **Spelling** command. The **Spelling** window opens.

- Unrecognised words (words that are not in the Spelling dictionary) will be displayed and suggestions to correct them provided.

- Select a suggestion and then click **Change** if you want to change the spelling of a word to the suggested spelling.

- Select **Change All** to change all occurrences of the word throughout the spreadsheet.

- Select **Ignore Once** if you know that the spelling is correct (such as proper names).

- Select **Ignore All** if you want to ignore all occurrences of the word through the spreadsheet.

  When the **Spelling** tool has completed the spell check, a confirmation window opens.

- Click **OK**.

Checking Calculations

- From the **Formulas Tab** and the **Formula Auditing** group, select the **Error Checking** command.

  If errors have been made in the calculations the **Error Checking** window opens..

In this example, there is an error in cell D9 – the contents of cell B9 have been divided by 0, which is incorrect

To resolve errors, select **Help on this error** or **Show Calculation Steps** so that you can work it out yourself.

Click **Ignore Error** if you know that the calculation is correct

Select **Edit in Formula Bar** to modify the calculation

Select **Previous** or **Next** to see previous or further errors

- When error checking is complete, a confirmation window opens.
- Click **OK**.

7.2.2 Gridlines (4.7.2.2)

Printed spreadsheets can be displayed with or without gridlines. The default setting is to **view** the gridlines on screen, but to **print** without gridlines.

To display gridlines on printed output, do the following:
- From the **Page Layout** tab and the **Sheet Options** group, in the **Gridlines section**, select the **Print** checkbox (to enter a tick in the box).

- Select the **Sheet Options** window launcher to see the **Page Setup** window.

  The **Sheet** tab should be the active tab in the **Page Setup** window.

- In the **Print** section, ensure that the **Gridlines** tick box is selected.

- Click **OK**.

7.2.3 Row and Column Headings (4.7.2.2)

Spreadsheets can be printed with or without the row and column headings displayed. The default setting is to print without row and column headings. The row and column headings refer to the row numbers and the column letters. Viewing row and column headings on printed output can help a reader to locate data on the spreadsheet by supplying visual grid references.

To display row and column headings on printed output, do the following:
- From the **Page Layout** tab and the **Sheet Options** group, select the **Print** checkbox (enter a tick in the box) in the **Headings** section.

Alternatively, select the **Sheets Options** window launcher icon and, in the **Print** section, select the **Row and Column Headings** checkbox (enter a tick in the box).
- Click **OK**.

7.2.4 Automatic Title Rows (4.7.2.3)

Automatic row titles can be set to print on every page of a printed spreadsheet.

To apply automatic row titles, do the following:
- From the **Page Layout** tab and the **Page Setup** group, select the **Print Titles** command.

    The **Page Setup** window opens with the **Sheet** tab the active tab.
- In the **Print Titles** section of the window, select the **Rows to repeat at top** button.

Click here

- Select the row titles on the spreadsheet and then click the **Rows to repeat at top** button.

Click here

- Check the row reference is correct.
- Click **OK**.

7.2.5 Previewing a Worksheet (4.7.2.4)

It is good practice to check the layout of a spreadsheet before printing. To preview a spreadsheet, do the following (there are two methods shown below):

Method 1
- From the **Office Button**, select **Print** and then **Print Preview**.

Method 2
- From the **Page Layout** tab and the **Page Setup** group, select the **Page Setup** window launcher icon.

    The **Page Setup** window opens.

- Select **Print Preview**.

  The **Print Preview** window opens, displaying the spreadsheet.

- To zoom in and out, use the **Zoom** command.

- Close **Print Preview** by selecting the **Close Print Preview** command.

Print Preview

Close **Print Preview**

Select **Page Setup** or **Print**

Zoom the page

The page is previewed

7.2.6 Printing (4.7.2.5)

There are various options that you can choose when printing. For example, you can print the entire worksheet or the entire spreadsheet (which may contain multiple worksheets), a selected area of a spreadsheet, a chart and also a specific number of copies. The default setting is for printing active worksheets.

To print, do the following:

- From the **Office Button**, select **Print**.

- From the print sub-menu, select **Quick Print** to print a worksheet without changing settings.

- Select **Print** to see the **Print** window (or press the keyboard combination of **CTRL + P**).

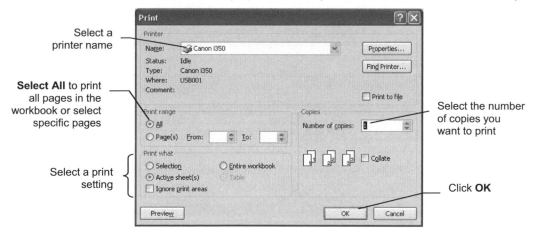

Select a printer name

Select All to print all pages in the workbook or select specific pages

Select the number of copies you want to print

Select a print setting

Click **OK**

Entire Spreadsheet

- Select the **Entire Workbook** option button.

- Click **OK**.

Entire Worksheet

- Select the **Active Sheet(s)** option button.

- Click **OK**.

Selected Range

- Select the cell range to be printed on the worksheet.
- From the **Print** window, select the **Selection** option button.
- Click **OK**.

    Alternatively:

    o Select the cell range to be printed on the worksheet.

    o From the **Page Layout** tab and the **Page Setup** group, select the **Print Area** command.

    o Select **Set Print Area** from the **Print** window.

    o Click **OK**.

- To remove the print area, select **Clear Print Area**.

Chart

- Click the chart to select it (if displayed as an object within a worksheet).
- From the **Print** window, select the **Select Chart** option button.
- Click **OK**.

Number of Copies

- From the **Print** window, use the scroll arrows on the **Number of Copies** list box to increase/decrease the required number of printed copies.
- Click **OK**.

PRACTICE SEQUENCE

1 Open the **sale** spreadsheet and the **QTR1** sheet.

2 Check the spelling of text within the spreadsheet and correct any errors.

3 Check the calculations in the spreadsheet and correct any errors.

4 Turn on gridlines and row and column headings for printing.

5 Preview the worksheet.

6 Print one copy of the cell range **A3:B7**.

7 Print one copy of the entire **QTR1** worksheet.

8 On the **Expenditure** sheet, print the pie chart.

9 Save and close the **sale** spreadsheet.

10 Open **Skills.xls** and apply automatic row titles that will print on every page of the **Profit** worksheet (Row 5).

11 Save and close the **Skills** spreadsheet.

Unit 5

Databases

5

Unit 5

Databases

5

Goals for Unit 5

Unit 5 Databases requires the candidate to understand the concept of a database and demonstrate
competence in using a database.

The candidate shall be able to:
- Understand what a database is and how it is organised and operated.
- Create a simple database and view the database content in various modes.
- Create a table, definite and modify fields and their properties; enter and edit data in a table.
- Sort and filter a table or form; create, modify and run queries to retrieve specific information from a database.
- Understand what a form is and create a form to enter, modify and delete records and data in records.
- Create routine reports and prepare outputs ready for distribution.

5

Section 1   Database Theory

1.1   What is a Database? (5.1.1.1)

A database, like a word processing document or spreadsheet, is a file containing information that is kept on some form of electronic storage medium. Database files differ from other files, such as word processing documents, in that information in a database is added and retrieved in a controlled way and is stored in a structured manner.

Databases speed up many processes, particularly the retrieval of information. For example a car tax database used by a government would enable details on individual vehicles to be retrieved quickly, and would enable the automation of certain processes such as the mailing of renewal notices.

The accounts for a small business could be kept in a series of spreadsheet files, for example. But entering information into spreadsheets in an uncontrolled manner would be error-prone. It would be difficult to prepare a balance sheet, next to impossible to produce any level of reporting and difficult to search for information. In contrast, a software application designed for small business accounting would use a database to store the accounts data. Users would enter invoices and so on via on-screen forms, governed by certain rules. Reports could be designed and run, using database queries to retrieve the required information. All the data could be searched quickly with the use of indexes.

1.2   Common Uses of Databases (5.1.1.4)

It might not be immediately apparent, but most people use databases of one sort or another every day, either directly or indirectly.

Some examples are:
- The Apple iTunes music library.
- Airline booking system.
- Accounts and payroll application software used by businesses.
- The contacts list on a mobile phone.
- A list of an electorate and other government records.
- Bank account records.
- Hospital patient records.

These can be compact databases that can be used on portable devices or databases housed in secure facilities and managed by mainframe computers.

1.3   Data and Information (5.1.1.2)

The terms **data** and **information** are often used interchangeably but actually have different meanings.

Data is the raw low-level binary information that a computer can store on a disk or in memory, down to the level where a tiny magnetised area on a disk represents a '1' and a non-magnetised area a '0'. The letter 'A', for example, can be stored as the binary number '01000001' using this approach . That binary number equates to 65 in the normal decimal system, and character number 65 in the standard ASCII character set is the letter 'A'.

Computers and computer software know how to take this raw data and turn it into **information** that is understandable to a user. In the case of a database application, the files that comprise the database consist of nothing but binary '1' and '0', yet the computer operating system and the database software can represent all this as **human-readable** information. Database users should only come in contact with the information that the data in the file represents, not the underlying data itself.

1.4   Microsoft Access

This unit will use **Microsoft Office Access 2007**, a straightforward **desktop database application.** Since it is included in the Microsoft Office suite it is very popular and is commonly used. Microsoft Access has database design, reporting and query tools that are closely integrated with its **JET database engine**, all under the umbrella of a single application. As such, it is a good learning tool.

It is useful for creating small databases that can be simultaneously accessed by a small number of users, but it does not scale to many users accessing large databases using a network and is slow when used in this way. In these situations, **professional databases** such as MySQL, PostgreSQL and SQL Server are used. While they are much more powerful, they also require more professional expertise to design and maintain them. The letters **SQL** in these names stand for **Structured Query Language**, a standard language used for retrieving data from and adding data to databases. Microsoft Access can also use this language.

1.5   Database Design and Administration (5.1.4.1, 5.1.4.2, 5.1.4.3 and 5.1.4.4)

Professional, large-scale database systems are designed and created by groups of people with specialised skills. The structure of the database might be designed by one group of specialists, the data entry forms and reports designed by programmers and the maintenance of the database performed by a **database administrator (DBA)**. However, over time, these distinctions have often become blurred. Database design and report creation tools have become easier to use, and it often now falls to programmers to implement all aspects of the creation and design of a database through to the **user interface (UI)** that database users see on their screens. Database users enter data into the database, change and update existing data, and retrieve information from the database. The users of a professional database are often the general employees of a company and might not necessarily be aware of how a database actually works. The role of the database administrator is still essentially to ensure that the database is available to users at all times.

The typical duties of a DBA include:
* Choosing the physical hardware and operating systems used for hosting the database.
* Overseeing security, for example determining the levels of access that individual users have to parts of the database.
* Optimising performance by analysing the design of the database and the capacity of the hardware.
* Implementing a database backup strategy and recovering databases after system crashes or other catastrophic failures.

1.6   Database Overview

1.6.1 The Components of a Database (5.1.1.3, 5.1.2.1 and 5.1.2.2)

Microsoft Access is a **relational database management system (RDBMS)**. It enables the creation of **databases** that contains **tables**, each of which, in turn, stores information on a particular topic. **Relationships** can then be defined to bring all the information together. Data relating to unique subjects is stored in **tables**.

In a database created to manage a club, there might be individual tables as follows:
* **Members**: Name and address details for club members.
* **Fees**: Details of fees paid and due.
* **Competitions**: Competition results for members.

Note that each table is concerned only with one distinct subject – there is no **Fees And Competitions** table, for example.

A table is the 'primary structure' in a database that stores fields and records.

- A **field** is a single item of data, like a person's first name.
- A **record** is a collection of fields, such as a person's first name, surname, address and phone number.

Fields and records make up other database objects, such as forms, reports and queries.

In a database, it is possible to store many different types of data, but care must be taken when the database is being organised. A field should contain only one element of data. For example, a field might contain a person's first name. That same field should not contain any other elements of data, such as the person's surname or title.

In Access, there are different types of fields, depending on what type of data they hold. The most common types of field are text fields and number fields.

- **Text fields** contain letters, such as a name, or combinations of letters and numbers, such as an address.
- **Number fields** contain data used in mathematical calculations.

The other types of field include: **Yes/No** fields, **Memo** fields, used for long entries of text, **Currency** fields, used for numbers that represent money, and **Date/Time** fields, used for numbers that represent a date or time.

1.6.2 A Note on Terminology

The terms **field** and **column**, **record** and **row** can be seen throughout Microsoft Access. The terms **column** and **row** are used when referring to the visual representation of a table in grid form within DataSheet View. When discussing the structure of the data, **record** is used instead of **row**, and **field** instead of **column**.

In the illustration, the table called **Members** has fields called **Forename**, **Surname** and **Age**.

The table must naturally be able to store information on more than one member. Each unique member in the **Members** table would be stored as a **record** or **row**. The illustration shows the table with four records, each containing data describing a different member.

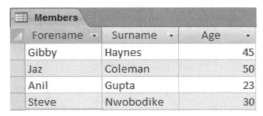

Note that the fields are repeated in each record. This means that each individual item of data can be changed or retrieved if the record number is known. The value of the **Surname** field in record 3 is 'Gupta', for example.

Records and fields can be thought of as being organised in the same way as rows and columns in a spreadsheet. Microsoft Access uses the terms 'rows' and 'columns', 'records and 'fields' interchangeably.

1.6.3 Field Types (5.1.2.3)

When a table is created each field in that table is given a name and a data type, which determines the type of data it can hold.

The types available in Microsoft Access 2007 are, in alphabetical order, as follows.

Type	Used For	Notes
Attachment	Attaching any type of file	The Attachment type is used to attach many types of file to a record. For example, an image file containing a photograph and a word processing document containing employment details could be attached to each employee's record in a personnel database. In the example below, the first record has two attachments. | ID	Date Of Birth	Gross Pay	Homepage	
1	09/07/1967	€120,229.23	www.bec.ie	(2)
2	16/07/1972	€32,323.00	www.rte.ie	(0)
3	15/12/1970	€45,000.00	www.metafilter.com	(0)	 Double-clicking the field will open an Attachments window, from where attachments can be opened, added and deleted. **Attachments** Attachments (Double-click to open) Secret Base Plans.doc Team List.doc Add... Remove Open Save As... Save All... OK Cancel
AutoNumber	Unique identifiers	A type used primarily for **primary key** indexes. When a new record is added to a table, Access will automatically enter a numeric value which is one greater than the previous record, making every record uniquely numbered. In the example here, the ID field is an AutoNumber field. If a new record were added, Access would automatically place the number 4 in the ID field for that new record. Users cannot overwrite the value in an AutoNumber field. 	ID	Date Of Birth	Gross Pay	Homepage
1	09/07/1967	€120,229.23	www.bec.ie
2	16/07/1972	€32,323.00	www.rte.ie
3	15/12/1970	€45,000.00	www.metafilter.com	
Currency	Currency values	Stores numeric data to 4 decimal places, and Access will include a currency symbol and commas when the data is displayed on a form or report, as appropriate for the regional settings of the database. Gross Pay: €120,229.23
Date/Time	Dates and times	Using this type of field for dates and times means that when a date is inputted it can be easily validated to be in a particular format, such as American or British, incorrect dates can be rejected. Access will also provide a **date picker** beside the field when it is displayed on a form. Date Of Birth: 09/07/2008 July 2008 M T W T F S S 30 1 2 3 4 5 6 7 8 9 10 11 12 13 14 15 16 17 18 19 20 21 22 23 24 25 26 27 28 29 30 31 1 2 3 4 5 6 7 8 9 10 Today
Hyperlink	Web hyperlinks	This stores a **hyperlink** to a web location, which is displayed as such on forms and can be clicked to launch a web browser. Homepage: www.bec.ie http://www.bec.ie
Lookup	Predefined lists	A Lookup field displays a list of items to choose from. The items in the list can be fixed or can come from another table in the database. Member 100100 John Smith 212980 Dave McGee 982882 Tanya Donnelly

Number	Numeric data	This field is used to store numbers of varying types. The most common are: **Long Integer**, which can store numbers with no decimal place from 2,147,483,648 to 2,147,483,647 **Double**, which can store decimal numbers from 4.94×10^{-324} to $1.79769313486231 \times 10^{308}$
OLE Object	Embedding documents from other applications	Microsoft Word documents, graphics, sounds and many other types of file can be stored inside the Access database using this type of field. It has been superseded in Access 2007 by the **Attachment** type, but remains so that databases created by earlier versions of Access can still be used.
Text	Text data	One of the most common field types, used for names, etc. Can also include a combination of letters and numbers, as in an address.
Yes/No	'True or false' values or similar	By default, fields of this type are displayed as **checkboxes** when data is being entered.

1.6.4 Field Properties (5.1.2.4)

In addition to defining the **type** of a field, various other **properties** can also be set, and these are determined by their type.

The properties of a Text-type field are shown in the illustration below.

Some important properties are:
- **Field size**: This is the maximum number of letters and/or numbers that can be entered into this field.
- **Required**: This means that this field cannot be left empty when a new record has been created and data is being entered.
- **Indexed**: Whether or not an index is present for this field.
- **Format**: Format relates to how data in a field is displayed, e.g. a format might specific the Times New Roman font, size 10 pt.

General	Lookup
Field Size	255
Format	
Input Mask	
Caption	
Default Value	
Validation Rule	
Validation Text	
Required	No
Allow Zero Length	Yes
Indexed	No
Unicode Compression	Yes
IME Mode	No Control
IME Sentence Mode	None
Smart Tags	

The properties of a number-type field look like the illustration below (note that some properties are the same as text-type fields):

Some important properties are:
- **Field size**: The most common sizes for number fields are Long Integer if no decimals are required, and Double if decimals are required. Other types such as byte and decimal can be also specified.
- **Decimal places**: When the Field Size is set to one of the decimalised types, then decimal places can be changed as required.
- **Format**: Format relates to how data in a field is displayed, e.g. a format might specific the Times New Roman font, size 10 pt.

General	Lookup
Field Size	Long Integer
Format	
Decimal Places	Auto
Input Mask	
Caption	
Default Value	
Validation Rule	
Validation Text	
Required	No
Indexed	No
Smart Tags	
Text Align	General

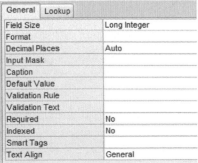

Field properties should be set appropriately with sizes defined so that they are large enough to hold any data that is likely to be entered, but not so large that most of the capacity is wasted. A record in a table takes up an amount of storage on disk that is determined by the field properties as shown on the previous page. If all the text-type fields in a table are of Field Size = 255 when this capacity is not needed, then disk space will be wasted. As tables grow larger, this, in turn, has an impact on the speed of searches.

1.6.5 Setting a Default Value (5.1.2.4)

Default Value is another field property. If it is defined for a field, then the field will automatically be set to this value when a new record is created. The value can then be changed or removed if required. This saves time in data entry, and also to help ensure data integrity. Default Values can be applied to Text, Memo, Number, Date/Time, Currency, Yes/No and Hyperlink fields.

Setting a **Yes/No** field to the default value of **Yes** will ensure it always displays a ticked checkbox when a new record is created.

Entering a number in the Default Value for a Currency field will display that value when a new record is created.

The effect of these settings on a new record can be seen in the following illustration.

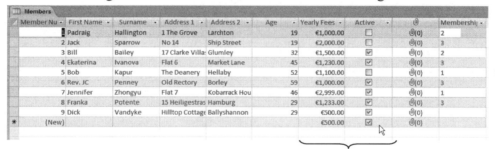

Default values

1.6.6 Changing Field Dimensions and Properties (5.3.2.4)

Field sizes and properties can be changed when there is data in the table. However, reducing the size or changing the type of a field may result in the loss of data in some records.

For example, changing a Number field of type Double to type Integer would cause a number like 45.12 to be rounded to 45. If the field type were to be changed back to Double at a later stage, the table would contain 45.00, not the original value of 45.12. Similarly, reducing the field size of a Text field might truncate the text in some records. The removed data cannot be retrieved.

Access will display a warning before allowing these changes to happen.

1.6.7 Indexes (5.1.2.6)

There are two ways to find a number in a phone book. One is to start at the beginning and read every entry until the number is found. This is obviously a hugely inefficient approach. A far more efficient approach is to utilise the fact that the phone numbers are **indexed** using the surnames of their owners. It is then possible to locate the required number very quickly by searching using the surname.

A similar approach is used within database tables. As part of the design process, fields that will be used to search frequently should have indexes defined for them.

An index can involve one or more fields. For example, in a table containing orders for a company's products, an index could be created on the order number and product code.

1.6.8 Primary Key Indexes (5.1.2.5)

A primary key is a field or fields used for uniquely identifying each row in a table, e.g. a member number in a table containing information about club members. A field such as member number is a good choice for a primary key because it is unique to each member, it should never be empty and the values in it will never change. Fields of the AutoNumber type (see Section 1.6.3) are also a good choice. A name or address field is a bad choice because the information in these may change over time.

A primary key should be created for every table, and an index defined for it. If there are no likely candidates, create an autonumber-type field called 'ID' and specify this as the primary key. Otherwise, there will be no easy way of uniquely identifying each record.

When a table is created in Microsoft Access 2007 datasheet view, a primary key field called **ID** and associated index are created automatically.

In the illustration on the right, the Member Number field is a primary key as indicated by the key icon beside it.

Primary Key icon

1.6.9 What should Fields Hold? (5.1.2.2)

Each field in a table should contain a single item of data.

It would be possible but incorrect to define a table like the one illustrated below.

Combining information in one field is bad practice. Each field should contain only one piece of data

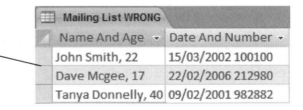

In this example, Names and Ages are contained in one field called **Name And Age**, and Date Joined and Member Number in another called **Date And Number**. This design would make searching and reporting on the data extremely difficult and is bad design practice.

The correct approach would be as follows.

Each field should contain only one piece of data

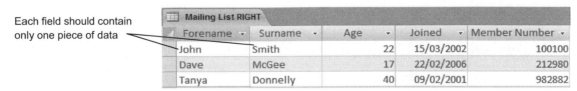

It is now possible to search easily for data based on surname, name, age, for example, or any combination of these fields.

1.6.10   What should Tables Hold? (5.1.2.1)

At the table level, good database design dictates that each subject has its own table.

It would be possible to store information about fees due and fees paid in the same table as the member names and addresses. However, since each member will have many sets of fees applied to them over a period of time, this would cause repetition of data.

Databases should
avoid needless
repetition of data

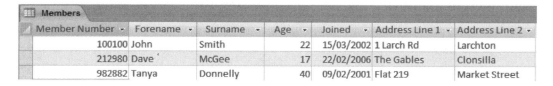

The **Fee Payment History** table in the illustration above has been created to store information about fees due to be paid by club members.

A new record has been created in the table each time yearly fees are due for members. Since the fees information has been stored in the same table as the member details, the member name, surname, age and so on are needlessly repeated.

For example, taking the two records where Forename is **John**, and Surname is **Smith**, it is evident from examining the **Fee Due** and **Fee Paid** fields in those records that the fees due on 01/01/2009 are not paid, and the fees that were due on 01/01/2008 have been paid. If this table should only store information about fees, then the rest of the fields, those that contain name and address data, should not be present and also are storing needlessly repeated information.

1.6.11   Relationships (5.1.3.1 and 5.1.3.2)

As discussed, the example in Section 1.6.10 is poor database design. Member name and address information has been mixed together in one table with fees information, whereas each of these individual subjects should have their own table.

In other words, there should be a table containing just information about members, such as their name, address and member number.

Member Number	Forename	Surname	Age	Joined	Address Line 1	Address Line 2
100100	John	Smith	22	15/03/2002	1 Larch Rd	Larchton
212980	Dave	McGee	17	22/02/2006	The Gables	Clonsilla
982882	Tanya	Donnelly	40	09/02/2001	Flat 219	Market Street

There should be a separate table containing dates on which fees are due from each member.

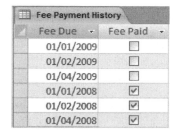

However, although good practice, separating data in this way creates a problem. The Fee Payment History table contains the dates on which fees are due, and an indication of whether they have been paid, but no way of **relating** this information to which member each record belongs to.

To get around this problem, a **relationship** must be established between the two tables. Relationships are based on a field or fields that are common between the two tables.

In the current example, the member number is the ideal candidate, as it is the primary key in the Member Numbers table. The Fee Payment History table does not contain a member number field, so it must be added, and it must be of the same type and size as the member number field in the Members table.

A field should be added that is common to both tables – this creates a relationship between them and gives context to the data

The common field should be the same type and size in both tables

With this in place, a relationship can now be defined between the Members and Fee Payment History tables, and is indicated by the arrow in the diagram on the right. Details of how to create and define a relationship are covered in Section 2.7.

This is a **one-to-many** relationship. Member numbers are unique, so for every individual record in the Members table on the left there may be no fee payment records on the right, or one fee payment record, or many fee payment records.

The diagram below shows this relationship using the current example data:

The tables are related on the Member Number field, which is common to each. Member 100100 in the Members table has two related records in the Fee Payment History table, indicating the two separate dates on which fees for this member were due and whether or not the fees have been paid.

This relationship would be useful when designing queries, reports and forms, as fields from both tables can be used easily without having to worry about defining how the tables relate to each other at the time of designing the report or query.

1.6.12 Maintaining Integrity (5.1.3.3)

The main use of relationships is to maintain **referential integrity** between tables. In the example in Section 1.2.10, if the relationship was not in place and a member was deleted from the Members table, this would result in **orphaned records** in the Fee Payment History table. These records would have a member number that matched them to a member who no longer existed.

A rule can be created against the relationship to ensure that if a member is deleted from the Members table, then any records belonging to that member in the Fee Payment History table are **automatically** deleted. This maintains integrity and ensures that there are no orphaned records.

1.7   Queries (5.4.2.1)

Queries are requests for data to be returned from a database, based on certain rules. The results of a query can be used as a source of data for reports or forms. They can also be used in the opposite direction – to send data into a database.

Microsoft Access, and most other databases, use a special language for performing queries called **Structured Query Language (SQL)**.

An example of an SQL query is to return the First Name, Surname and Member Number field for all members whose age is greater than 18 from the Members table.

```
SELECT Members. [First Name], Members.[Surname], Members.[Age],
Members.[Member Number]
FROM Members
WHERE (((Members.[Age])>18));
```

In Access, queries can be created by entering the SQL directly, or by using a point-and-click Wizard. See Section 2.5 for more information and practice with Queries.

1.8   Forms

1.8.1 Definition (5.5.1.1)

A **form** uses some or all of the data contained in an existing table and displays it in a user-friendly layout. You can use a form to easily display records in a database. For example, the **Golf Club** database table contains all the data about members of the golf club, including a complete list of names, addresses and membership numbers. If certain information is required from this table, such as a list of membership numbers, but not addresses, a form is used to filter this information from the table.

Using a form, it is also possible to maintain records, to enter new records and change existing records in a database.

> **NOTE**
> Any changes made to data in a form will be updated in the table.

5

1.8.2 Using Forms for Data Entry

Almost all applications that use databases only allow users to enter data via a **form**. Even something as simple as a contact list on a mobile phone will have a simple **user interface layer** providing a form for controlled data entry.

Data can be entered into any table in **Datasheet View**.

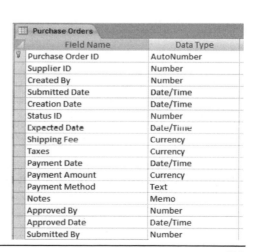

Purchase Orders	
Field Name	Data Type
Purchase Order ID	AutoNumber
Supplier ID	Number
Created By	Number
Submitted Date	Date/Time
Creation Date	Date/Time
Status ID	Number
Expected Date	Date/Time
Shipping Fee	Currency
Taxes	Currency
Payment Date	Date/Time
Payment Amount	Currency
Payment Method	Text
Notes	Memo
Approved By	Number
Approved Date	Date/Time
Submitted By	Number

The table can also be displayed in **DataSheet View**, which presents the data in a tabular format and allows data entry and navigation.

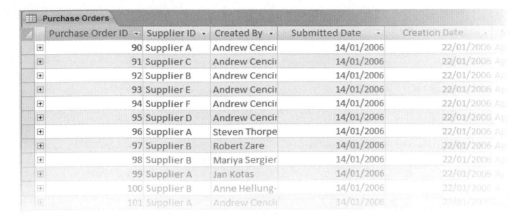

It is possible to enter data directly into the tables that make up the database using **DataSheet View** in Microsoft Access.

However, this is rarely allowed for anything other than direct manipulation of the tables by an administrator, for three main reasons.
- The interface is not particularly user-friendly.
- There are fewer opportunities to control and limit what users are entering.
- A form may ultimately update a variety of tables almost simultaneously, and this would be difficult to achieve by entering data directly.

Microsoft Access has a sample database application called Northwind Traders. It contains a form specially designed for entering Purchase Orders, and this is the interface that end users of the database see.

1.9   Reports (5.6.1.1)

There is not much point in having data in a database if it cannot be extracted and used when needed. Reports are a vital part of almost all applications that use databases and are used to print selected information from a table or query.

A payroll application that uses a database to store employee and pay information would have a range of reports available, such as:
- Employee lists.
- Tax records.
- The payslips that are sent out to employees.

Microsoft Access contains a built-in report writing tool, and the options for outputting reports include being previewed to screen, printed and exported to Microsoft Excel. See Section 2.9 for more information and practice with reports.

1.10 Switching Between View Modes (5.2.2.2)

Database objects such as tables, forms, queries and reports all have different view options. Each view option enables you to carry out a variety of functions. The most common views are listed below.

- **Tables** have a DataSheet View, where the data is displayed and can be manipulated in a variety of ways, and a Design View.
- **Forms** have Form View, Layout View and Design View.
- **Queries** have DataSheet View and Design View.
- **Reports** have Report View, Layout View, Design View and a Print Preview.

To change between views, do the following:
- Open the table, form or report.
- Select the **Home** tab on the ribbon.
- In the **Views** section, click the **View** button.
- Select the required view (these will be different, as listed above, depending on what is open).

Click **View**

Select the required view

Alternatively
- Right-click the table, form or report name in the **Navigation Pane** at the left of the Access window. Select **Open** from the menu to open the table in **Datasheet View**.
  Alternatively, double-click the table name to open it in **Datasheet View**.
- Select **Design View** from the menu to open the table in **Design View**.

NOTE

The View options for tables, forms, queries and reports are covered in detail in later sections.

Section 2   Practice

Because of the integrated nature of databases, the remainder of this unit will look at the creation and manipulation of a database called **Golf Club.accdb**, using a single set of data in Microsoft Access 2007.

2.1   Basic Operations

2.1.1   Opening and Closing a Database Application (5.2.1.1)

Opening

There are several ways to open Microsoft Access, the database application being used in this unit. Depending on the particular PC setup, the icon to start Microsoft Access 2007 may be present in one or more locations.

- If the Access icon is visible on the desktop or within a folder, double-clicking it will start the application.

- The icon may also be visible in the favourites area of the **Start menu**.

Access 2007 icon

- Access can be opened using the Start menu.
  - Click the **Start** button.
  - Select **All Programs**.
  - Select **Microsoft Office**.
  - Select **Microsoft Office Access 2007** from the sub-menu that appears.

- Double-clicking any **Microsoft Access database file** in Windows will open the file within the application.

Closing

Microsoft Access can be closed in the same way as any other application.

To close Access, do the following:
- Click the **Close X** button at the top right of its window.

    Alternatively
    o Click the **Office Button** at the top left of the window.
    o Click **Exit Access** on the menu that appears.

2.1.2 Opening and Closing a Database (5.2.1.2)

Opening

A database can be opened easily by double-clicking its icon from within Windows, as mentioned in Section 2.1.1. Doing this will automatically start Microsoft Access and open the database.

To open an existing database from within Microsoft Access, do the following:
- Click the **Office Button**.
- Click **Open** in the drop-down menu that appears.

The **Open** window opens.
- Locate the database.
- Select it by clicking it.
- Click **Open**.

    Alternatively, click the database name in the **Recent Documents** list on the right of the **Access** window.

Closing

To close a database, do the following:

- Click the **Office Button**.
- Select **Close Database** from the drop-down menu.

Close Database

2.1.3 Using Help (5.2.1.5)

As with any Windows application, Help is readily available by pressing the F1 key, or clicking on the Help icon at the top right of the Access window.

See Section 7 in the BYB for more information on Help.

2.1.4 The Ribbon

The ribbon made its debut in Office 2007 and acts as the main application menu in all the Office applications, including Access. It is displayed at the top of the Access window and contains buttons and menus for all the most commonly performed tasks, grouped into tabs.

Clicking the title text of a tab will change the ribbon to display that group of commands, as in the two examples below.

Home tab

Create tab

In addition there is a **Quick Access Toolbar**. By default, this is shown at the top of the window, beside the Office button.

Clicking the arrow icon at the right of the toolbar will display a customisation menu.

Click arrow to display
the **Quick Access
Toolbar** menu

Ticking items on this menu will add that command to the **Quick Access Toolbar**. In the illustration on the right, the **Quick Print** and **Print Preview** commands have been added.

2.1.5   Minimising and Restoring the Ribbon (5.2.1.4)

The ribbon can also be minimised or hidden. When minimised, only the titles of the various ribbon tabs (Home, Create, etc.) are visible. Clicking any of these will cause the ribbon to pop up and display that tab.

Minimising the Ribbon

To minimise the ribbon, do the following:
- Right-click anywhere on the ribbon.
  A drop-down menu is displayed.
- Select **Minimize the Ribbon**.

Click **Minimize
the Ribbon**

The ribbon will now be displayed as in the illustration below.

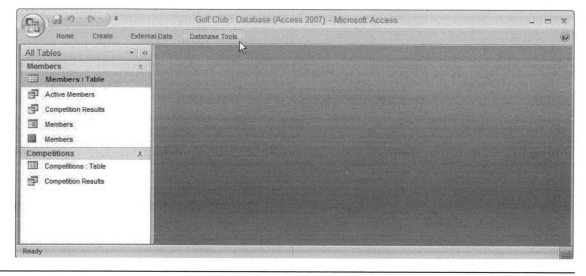

- Clicking a tab heading, such as **Database Tools**, will expand the ribbon enabling an option from that tab to be selected.

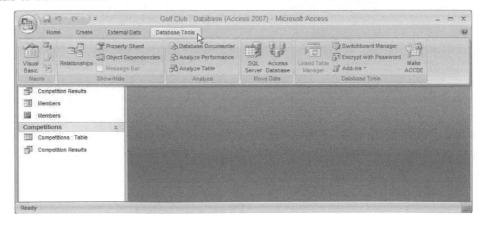

- Selecting an option will hide the ribbon again.

Restoring the Ribbon

To restore the ribbon, do the following:

- Right-click the bar containing the tabs.
- Click **Minimize the Ribbon**.

  Note how a tick is displayed beside the menu command to indicate that it is active.

- Select the option again to restore the ribbon to its normal appearance.

Click **Minimize the Ribbon** again to restore the ribbon

2.2   First Steps with Databases

From this point onwards the text will take the form of the step-by-step creation of a new database, with an associated data entry form and report.

Follow each step and complete the Practice Sequences.

2.2.1 Creating and Saving a New Database (5.2.1.3)

Creating a New Database

To create a new database, do the following:

- Start **Microsoft Access** using any of the methods detailed in Section 2.1.1.

  Initially, the **Getting Started with Microsoft Access** page is displayed.

Office Button

- Click the **Office Button**.
- Select **New** from the drop-down menu that appears.

New

A **New Database** pane appears to the right, and a default name, normally **Database1.accdb** will be already present in the **File Name** textbox.
- Change the file name to **Golf Club.accdb**.
- Click **Create**.

NOTE
Microsoft Access is unusual in that its databases comprise of a single **.accdb** file. All the tables, indexes, queries, reports, etc. that are created within a database reside within the file. This has the advantage of making it very easy to move an entire database to a different location if needed.

Saving a New Database

The default location in which the **.accdb** database file will be saved is displayed below the File Name textbox.

Location to which the file is automatically saved

Browser button

To save a database to a different location, do the following:
- Add a new database, and give it a name for it as described above.
- **Do not** click Create.
- Click the browser icon to the right of the **File Name** textbox.
  A **File New Database** window opens.
- Navigate to the desired location.
- Click **OK** to save the file.

2.3   Tables

2.3.1   Creating a Table (5.3.2.1)

When a new database has been created, a new table called **Table1** will be created automatically and presented in **Datasheet View**. An AutoNumber field called **ID** has also been created automatically and marked as the primary key, to provide a unique identifier for each record.

- This table will be used to hold personal details and a unique membership number for each member.

  These personal details are contained in fields (represented by columns in the table (and different types of data – e.g. text, number, date/time or yes/no – are kept in separate fields. See Section 2.3.4 for more on creating fields.

NOTE
See Section 1.6.3 for a full list of field types.

- Right-click the ID field and choose **Rename Column** from the pop-up menu.

The cursor will move to the field heading.
- Overtype the word **ID** with the words **Member Numbers**.
- Press **Enter** to accept the change.

At this stage, the table should be saved.

2.3.2   Saving a Table (5.2.2.1)

To save the table, do the following:

- Click the **Save** icon beside the Office button at the top left of the Access window.

  If this is the first time the table has been saved, a window will open prompting for a name.
- Enter a name for the table.
- Click **OK** to save.

2.3.3 Other Actions with Tables (5.2.2.1 and 5.2.2.3)

Opening a Table

The standard way to open a table is as follows:
- Start **Microsoft Access**.
- Open the required database (see Section 2.1.2).
  The objects comprising the database are listed in the **Navigation Pane**.
  Tables are displayed with **: Table** after their name, e.g. **Members : Table** and **Competitions : Table** in the illustration on the right.
- Double-click the desired table to open it in DataSheet View.

Alternatively, right-click the table name and select **Design View** to open it in that mode.

Closing a Table

To close a table, do the following:
- Click the **Close X** button at the right of the Access window.

Close X button

Reopening a Table

To reopen a table or other Access object (e.g. form, query, etc.), do the following:

- Double-click it in the Navigation Pane.
  The table will open in a tab in the middle part of the Access window.
  Multiple tables and other Access objects can be open simultaneously on different tabs.

Deleting a Table

To delete a table or other Access object (e.g. form, query, report), do the following:

- Ensure it is not open.
- Right-click the name of the table (or form, query or report) in the **Navigation Pane**.
- Select **Delete** from the pop-up menu that appears.
  A confirmation window opens.
- Click **Yes** to delete.
- Click **Cancel** to keep the table.

2.3.4 Creating Fields and Applying Field Properties (5.3.2.1 and 5.3.2.2)

To define new fields, it is more convenient to use **Design View**. This mode is specifically intended for this purpose.

To switch to Design view, do the following:

- Right-click the title tab of the table.
- Select **Design View** from the pop-up menu that appears.

Design View lists the table fields and their types at the top of the window, and the properties associated with the currently highlighted field at the bottom.

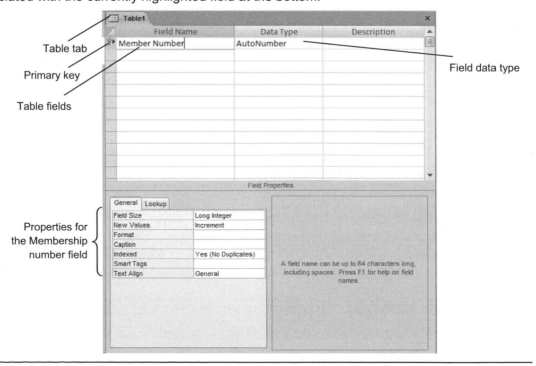

In Design View, the Data Type of a field can be changed as follows:
- Click in the **Data Type** column in the list of fields.
- Select the required **Data Type** from the drop-down list.

Select the data type from the drop-down list

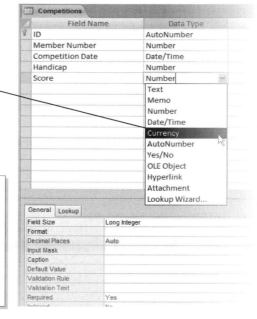

Properties of a Text Field

After Membership Number, the next field that is required is for the members' first names.
- Click in the **Field Name** column, in the row below the existing **Member Number** row.
- Enter **First Name** as the field name.
- Press the Enter key.
  The default **Data Type** of **Text** is correct and so doesn't need to be changed.

The maximum length of the **First Name** field should be specified.
- Ensure the **First Name** row is highlighted in the top of the screen.
- In the **Field Properties** section, click in the cell to the right of the **Field Size** property.
- Enter the value 30.

Field size

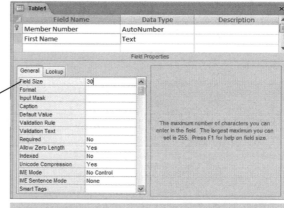

The First Name field is a required field – it should not be possible for a new record to be saved with no First Name entered.

To set the Required field property, do the following:
- Move the mouse cursor over the **Required** field property.
- Click the arrow.
- Select **Yes** from the drop-down list.

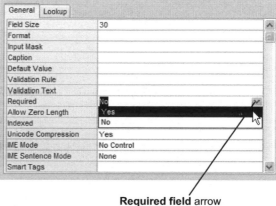

Required field arrow

Properties of a Number Field

The properties available for a number field are shown in the illustration below.

- **Field Size**: determines the type of numbers that will be stored. The two most common types are **Long Integer**, where decimals are not needed and **Double** where decimals are needed. There are various other types such as **byte**. For potentially large databases careful consideration should be given to the type, as some types take more storage space and result in slower processing.
- **Decimal Places**: controls the number of decimal places if extra precision is needed.
- **Format**: Format relates to how data in a field is displayed, e.g. a format might specific the Times New Roman font, size 10 pt.

Properties of a Date/Time Field

The properties available for a Date/Time field are shown in the illustration on the right.

- **Format**: Format determines whether a Date and Time, or Date or Time are stored and how they are displayed.

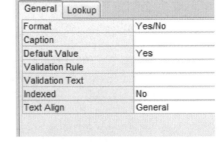

Properties of a Yes/No Field

The properties available for a Yes/No field are shown in the illustration on the right.

- **Default Value**: Setting the Default Value to Yes will ensure it always displays a tick checkbox when a new record is created. See Section 1.6.5 for more on Default Values.

- **Format**: Format controls what is actually displayed for the field. This can be one of the three options on the right. The field will contain a **0** for **False/No/Off** and a **1** for **True/Yes/On**.

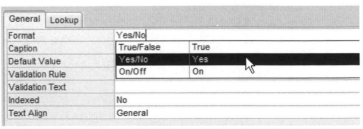

PRACTICE SEQUENCE

1   Create a table called **Members** with the following fields and listed properties.

Field Name	Data Type	Field Size	Properties
Member Number	[created automatically]	[created automatically]	[created automatically]
First Name	Text	30	Required: **Yes**
Surname	Text	50	Required: **Yes**
Address 1	Text	50	Required: **Yes**
Address 2	Text	50	
Age	Number	Long Integer	Required: **Yes**
Yearly Fees	Number	Currency	Default Value: **500.00** Required: **Yes**
Date Joined	Date/Time	Short Date	Required: **Yes**
Active	Yes/No	[not applicable]	Default Value: **Yes**
Photo	Attachment	[not applicable]	

2.3.5 Creating a New Table (5.3.2.1)

Another table is needed to hold details of competitions that the member has played in.

To add a new table, do the following:
- Click the **Create** tab on the ribbon.
- Click **Table** in the list of commands.

A new table, also called **Table1**, will be created.
- Change the view to Design View.
- Name the table **Competitions** and save it.
- Add the fields shown in the list below.

Field Name	Data Type	Properties
ID [created automatically]	AutoNumber	Set automatically
Member Number	Number	Field size: **Long Integer** Required: **Yes**
Competition Date	Date/Time	Format: **Short Date** Required: **Yes**
Handicap	Number	Field Size: **Long Integer** Required: **Yes**
Score	Number	Field Size: **Long Integer** Required: **Yes**

> **NOTE**
> A Primary Key field called ID is automatically created. The ID field will provide a unique identifier for each row in the Competitions table.

Lookup Wizard

The last field to be added is a **Lookup Wizard** field. In this database, it is used to indicate whether or not the member is a Gold, Silver or Bronze member.

This field will be a Text-type field, but the values will come from a predefined list. This is set up as follows:
- Add a new field with the name **Membership Level**.

- Set the data type to **Text** in the normal way.
- Open the **Data Type** list for the field again, but this time select **Lookup Wizard**.
- Select the second option **I will type in the values that I want**.
- Click **Next**.

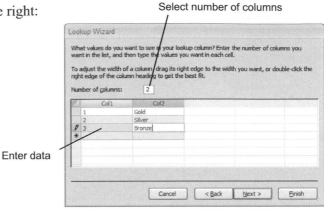

Select
second option

Select number of columns

In the next window, like the example on the right:
- Change the number of columns to 2.
- Click in the table list.
- Enter data as follows:
  1. Gold
  2. Silver
  3. Bronze
- Click **Finish**.

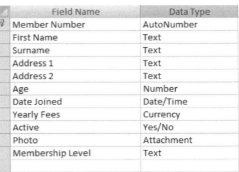

Enter data

The finished list of fields should look like the example on the right.

Field Name	Data Type
Member Number	AutoNumber
First Name	Text
Surname	Text
Address 1	Text
Address 2	Text
Age	Number
Date Joined	Date/Time
Yearly Fees	Currency
Active	Yes/No
Photo	Attachment
Membership Level	Text

2.3.6 Validation Rules (5.3.2.3)

In addition to the properties already set, such as Required and Default Value, additional **Validation Rules** can be applied to fields to further control what can be entered. In our Golf Club, club rules state that members must be at least 18. It is also unlikely that any will join past the age of 100. Therefore, a rule can be applied to limit the ages entered to this range.

Number Fields

To set limits – validation rules – on what data can be entered in a number field, do the following:
- In **Design View**, click on the **Age** field in the field list at the top of the screen.
- The Validation Rule and Validation Text is one of the field properties at the bottom of the screen.
- Enter the following text next to **Validation Rule**:
  - **>=18 And <=100**

Enter the following text next to **Validation Text**:
  - **Age must be between 18 and 100.**

Validation Rule	>=18 And <=100
Validation Text	Age must be between 18 and 100.

- If a value less than 18 or greater than 100 is entered into the field (in DataSheet View or via a form, or any other method), then an error message using the Validation Text will occur. This rule will be applied when adding a new record, or editing an existing record and modifying the value in the **Age** field.

Text Fields

Validation rules can be applied to Text-type fields in a similar way.

To prevent the use of the surname **Ahern**, do the following:

- Open the Members table in Design View.
- Select the **Surname** field in the field list.
- Enter the following text against **Validation Rule** in the properties list: **<>"Ahern"**.

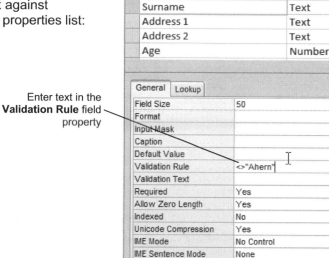

Enter text in the **Validation Rule** field property

- When the table is saved a prompt will appear to confirm the change.

Currency Fields

To configure the Yearly Fees field to only accept values between 100 and 3000, do the following:

- Open the **Members** table in **Design View**.
- Select the **Yearly Fees** field in the field list.
- Enter the following text against **Validation Rule** in the properties list: **>100 and <3000**.
- Enter **Fees must be between 100 and 300** against the **Validation Text** property.
- When the table is saved a prompt will appear to confirm the change.

Enter text in the **Validation Rule** field property and **Validation Text** field property

Date/Time Fields

The Golf Club was founded on 13 April 1960. It is therefore impossible that any member participated in a competition before this date.

To add a rule to the **Competitions** table preventing dates before the founding date being used, do the following:

- Open the **Competitions** table in Design View.
- Highlight the **Competition Date** field in the field list.
- Enter the following text against the **Validation Rule** property: **>= #13/04/1960#**
- Enter **Date must be on or after April 13th 1960** against the **Validation Text** property.

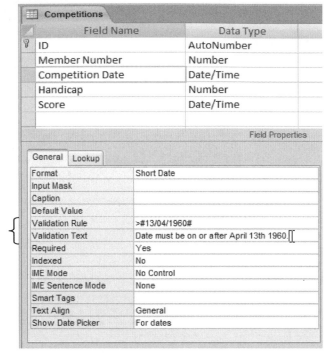

Enter text in the **Validation Rule** field property and **Validation Text** field property

- When the table is saved a prompt will appear to confirm the change.

NOTE
A date can be entered into the validation rule in the following format: #January 23, 1982#. It will then be converted to a short date format appropriate for the region.

2.3.7 Setting a Field as a Primary Key (5.3.2.5)

A **primary key** is a field or fields used for uniquely identifying each row in a table, for example a member number in a table containing information about club members. A primary key should be created for every table, and an index defined for it.

To set a field as a primary key, do the following:

- Open the **Members** table in **Design View**.
- In the field list, highlight the **Member Number** field.
- Right-click in the area to the left of the field name.
- Select **Primary Key** from the menu.

NOTE
The key icon is displayed beside the field name.

2.3.8   Creating an Index (5.3.2.6)
Fields that will be used to search should have indexes defined for them. An index can involve one or more fields. For example, in a table containing orders for a company's products, an index could be created on the order number and product code.

To create an index, perform the following steps:
- Open the **Members** table in **Design View**.
- Select the **Age** field in the field list.
- Click the **Indexed** property in the Field Properties list.
- As there can be multiple members with the same age, therefore, select **Yes (Duplicates OK)** from the menu that is displayed.

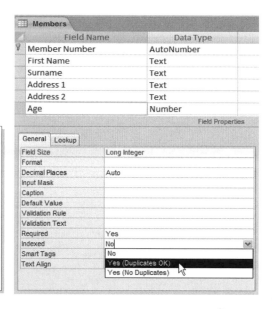

> **NOTE**
> Click **Yes (Duplicates OK)** if more than one record can have the same data in this field, e.g. there may be several members with the same last name.
>
> Click **Yes (No Duplicates)** to ensure that no two records are the same, e.g. giving stock items a unique name.

In the **Members** table it would be useful to be able to search on the Member's full name, but the name is stored in two fields – **First Name** and **Surname**.

It is possible to create an index involving multiple fields, as follows:
- Open the **Members** table in **Design View**.
- On the ribbon, click the **Indexes** option.

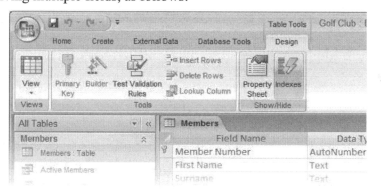

The **Indexes** window opens.
- In the **Index Name** column, define a new index name by entering **Full Name** in the first empty cell.

- Click the **Field Name** cell to the right and select **First Name** from the drop-down menu.

- Add the **Surname** field below the **First Name** field in the same way.

- Close the **Indexes** window with the **Close X** button at the top right to save the changes.

PRACTICE SEQUENCE

1　Add a validation rule to the **Yearly Fees** field, to check that the fees are between 1000 and 3000.

2　Add appropriate **Validation Text**.

3　Change the Primary Key (right-click the existing key and select **Primary Key** from the menu that appears).

4　Ensure the **Primary Key** stays as the **Member Number** field.

5　An index must be added to the **Surname** field because users will often search on this field.

6　Still in **Design View**, click the **Surname** field in the field list at the top to display the properties at the bottom of the screen.

7　Click the **Indexed** property to display a menu with the following options.

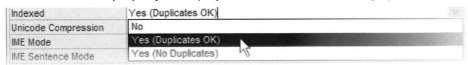

- **No**: No index is present on this field.
- **Yes (Duplicates OK)**: No checking for duplicates will be done as records are added.
- **Yes (No Duplicates)**: When a record is added, all existing records will be checked to see if any have the same value in this field. If one already exists, the addition of the record will be disallowed and a message displayed.

In this case, there could be many members with the same surname, therefore, duplicates should be allowed.

8　Click **Yes (Duplicates OK)**.

2.3.9   Adding, Deleting and Modifying Data in a Record (5.3.1.2)

It may be necessary to add, change or delete data, such as a change of address or telephone number. This is most easily done in DataSheet View.

- To add data, select the required field and type in the new data.
- To change or update data, select the required field and type in the new data.
- To delete data, select the data and use the Delete command in the Edit menu.

When you change or delete data, Access automatically saves the updates.

2.3.10   Changing the Width of Columns in a Table (5.3.2.8)

The basic structure of a datasheet is columns and rows. When you enter information, you may find that the data is obscured because the column is not wide enough.

In order to widen the columns, do the following:
- Right-click the column to be widened.
- A **Column Width** menu will be shown, enabling a precise width to be specified.
- Click the **Best Fit** button to automatically size the column to the size of the widest entry in the field (or field title).

Alternatively, the width can also be altered interactively by clicking and dragging with the mouse.
- o In datasheet view, position the mouse cursor at the right edge of the field title.
- o The arrow cursor will change to a resize cursor.
- o Click and hold down the left mouse button.
- o Move the mouse left or right to resize the column.

Resize cursor

2.3.11   Navigating Records in a Table (5.2.2.4)

Records can be selected by clicking on any field within the record. The currently highlighted record is then displayed with a darker background.

In addition a navigation toolbar is displayed at the bottom of the screen.

2.3.12 Adding a Field to an Existing Table (5.3.2.7)

New fields can be added to existing tables in exactly the same way as they are added to a new table.

To add a new Yes/No field called **Deceased** to the Members table, do the following:

- Open the **Members** table in Design View.
- In the field list, enter **Deceased** in the first empty cell in the **Field Name** column.
- Change the Data Type to **Yes/No**.
- Save the table.

2.3.13 Adding Records to a Table (5.3.1.1)

To create a new record, do the following:

- Click the **New Record** button on the **Navigation** toolbar.
  Alternatively, click the record marked with the asterisk.

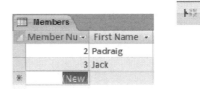

- Enter, delete or modify data in the normal way as necessary to include all the necessary data for the record.
  Fields of some data types, such as Yes/No, will have checkboxes or other types of **control** as appropriate.
  The contents of the **Member Number** field are filled automatically and cannot be changed.
  The **Membership Type** can be selected from a drop-down list, as it is a **Lookup Wizard** field.

When all the data has been entered into the record, it should be saved.

To save a record, do the following:

- Navigate to another record.
  Alternatively, close the table.

> **NOTE**
> To abandon changes to a field, do the following:
> - Press the **Escape** key.
>
> This will restore the original value of the field, prior to any changes.

2.3.14 Deleting Records in a Table (5.3.1.1)

To delete a record, do the following:

- Select the record to be deleted by clicking the row header to the left of the record to the left of the record.

Select row header

- Right-click to show a pop-up menu.
- Select **Delete Record** from the menu.
  A confirmation box opens.
- Click **Yes** to delete the record.
- Click **No** to return to the table.

NOTE

To delete all records in a table, right-click the Select All button and select Delete Record from the pop-up menu that appears.

Select All button

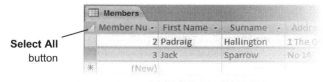

PRACTICE SEQUENCE

1   Open the **Members** and **Competitions** tables.

2   Using the information in sections 2.3.6–2.3.10, add a few records similar to those in the illustrations and experiment with resizing columns and deleting rows.

2.3.15 Applying a Filter to and Removing a Filter from a Table (5.4.1.2 and 5.4.1.3)

Data can also be **filtered** in DataSheet View. This can be useful for limiting the number of records that a user has to view or deal with, or that field searches have to cover. Filters can be applied to more than one field at the same time.

To filter the Members table so that only Members with an age greater than 30 are included, do the following:

- In **DataSheet View** or **Form View**, click in the **Age** field of any record.
- Select the **Filter** command in the **Sort & Filter** section of the ribbon.

- In the menu that opens, click the **Number Filters** option.
- Select **Greater Than** from the sub-menu that opens.

- In the **Custom Filter** window, enter the value **30**.
- Click **OK**.
  Only records where the Age field is greater than 30 are now available. This applies both to DataSheet View and Form View.

The **Navigation Bar** changes to indicate that the table is filtered.

To remove the filter, do the following:
- Click in the **Age** field.
- Click the **Filter** icon.
- Select **Clear Filter From Age**.
  The filter is removed and all records are, once again, available to view.

2.4   Forms

As discussed in Section 1.5, almost all user data entry into databases is done via **forms**.

These provide a clear and controlled interface for data maintenance across one or more tables, and are more appropriate for end users than DataSheet view. Microsoft Access can create forms automatically based on the fields in a table.

2.4.1 Creating a Form (5.5.1.2)

To create a data entry form for the Members table, do the following:
- In the **Navigation Pane**, ensure the **Members** table is highlighted by clicking it.
- On the ribbon, click the **Create** tab.
- In the **Forms** section, click the **Form** button.

A new form is created, and the first record in the table is displayed.

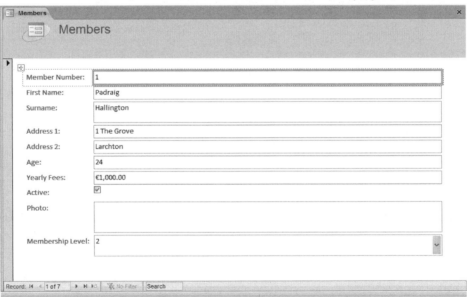

- The form is in **Layout View**, which is intended for defining the placement of elements.
- Data can be viewed but not added or modified in **Layout View**, enabling elements to be positioned and resized by clicking them and dragging with the mouse.
- The layout consists of **labels**, which display the name of each field, and **controls** which are used for data entry.
- A label/control pair is generated automatically for each field in the Members table.
- The type of control is dictated by the type of the underlying field. So the name and address fields use **TextBox** controls. The Active field uses a **CheckBox** control and the Membership Level uses a **ComboBox**.
- Data can be viewed but not added or altered in **Design View**.
- In a real-world application, the form might act as a **front end** for more than one table, and may or may not have controls for all available fields, as dictated by the person who designed it.

> **NOTE**
> The same navigation toolbar that was seen in table **DataSheet View** is again present
> at the bottom of the screen and can be used to move between the records in the underlying
> table.

2.4.2 Form Design View (5.2.2.2)

The contents of a form are actually defined using Design View.

To change to this view, do the following:
- Right-click the form in the **Navigation Pane**.
- Select **Design View**.

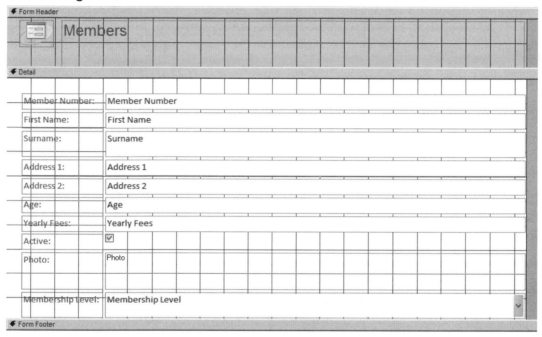

The process of automatically creating a form as described above generates a view similar to that in
the above illustration. Using this view, controls for field labels and fields can be added and edited.

2.4.3 Naming and Saving a Form (5.2.2.1 and 5.5.1.2)

To save a form, do the following:
- Click the **Save** icon, beside the Office button, at the
  top left of the Access window.

  If this is the first time the Form has been saved,
  a window will open prompting for a name.
- Enter a relevant name.
- Click **OK** to save.

2.4.4 Opening and Closing a Form (5.2.2.1)

Opening a Form

To open a form, do the following:

- Start **Microsoft Access**.
- Open the required database (see Section 2.1.1).
- The objects comprising the database are listed in the **Navigation Pane**.

> **NOTE**
> Each database object has a different icon.
> Forms are displayed like this:
>
> :▣ Members

- Double-click the desired Form to open it in **Form View.**

  Alternatively, right-click the Form name and select **Design View** or **Layout View** to open in in that mode.

Closing a Form

To close a form do the following:

- Click the **Close X** button at the right of the Access window.

Close X button

2.4.5 Navigating Records in Form View (5.2.2.4)

When viewing a form in **Form View**, the standard navigation toolbar is displayed at the bottom of the screen. Clicking on the different sections of the toolbar will change the form to display another record.

Previous record   Current record   Next record

Record: I◄ ◄ 2 of 2 ► ►I ►⁕   New record

First record   Last record

2.4.6 Headers and Footers in a Form (5.5.1.6)

New items, such as the date and time, can be added to the form header or footer.

To add new items, do the following:
* Open the form in **Design View**.
* In the **Controls** section on the ribbon, click the **Date and Time** button.

Date and Time button

* Choose the page position for the new controls and click OK.
  New controls for the **Date and Time** are added to the form header area.
* Position the cursor at the bottom edge of the **Form Footer** bar.
  The cursor changes to a resize cursor.
* Click and drag the footer edge downwards to resize the footer area to two grid boxes.
* In the **Controls** section of the ribbon, click the page **Numbers** button.
* Choose the page position for the new controls and click OK.
* Click the **Label** button on the ribbon.

  The cursor changes to a label cursor.

^+A

* Click anywhere in the **Form Footer**.
* Type some text into the new label control.
* Save and close the form, then reopen it in Form View.
  Note the date and time in the header and the text in the footer.

2.4.7 Inserting New Records Using a Form (5.5.1.3)

To use the form for data entry and to insert new records, do the following:
* Double-click the form in the **Navigation Pane**.
  This activates **Form View**.
* To add a new record, click the **New Record** button on the navigation toolbar.

New Record button

Alternatively, click the Home tab on the ribbon, and then click the **New** command from the **Records** section.

A blank record will be added, and the form will reflect this by displaying empty fields.

- When data entry is complete, click the **Save** button in the **Records** section of the ribbon to save the new record.
- Notice that the record count on the Navigation Toolbar is increased by one.

2.4.8 Deleting Records in Form View (5.5.1.4)

To delete a record, do the following:
- Navigate to the record using the **Navigation Toolbar**.
- Click the **Home** tab on the ribbon.
- In the **Records** section of the ribbon, click the arrow at the right of the **Delete** button.
- Select the **Delete Record** option.

Click **Delete** arrow

A confirmation window opens to check you want to delete the record.
- Click **Yes** to delete the record.

2.4.9 Using the Search Command (5.4.1.1)

To search for a specific word, number or date, enter the search term in the search section of the Navigation toolbar. The contents of each field will be searched as text is entered, and any matches will be highlighted.

> **NOTE**
> This search is across all records. If a match is found in a record different to the one selected in DataSheet View or Form View, then the focus will change to the record with the matching text.

Searching for a Word

In this examle, the word **Grove** has been entered in the Search field and the first match is highlighted.

Search text

Searching for a Number

In this example, the number 19 has been entered in the search field, and the first match in **DataSheet View** is highlighted.

Searching for a Date

In this example, the date 17 May 2007 has been entered and is highlighted in **DataSheet View**.

Using Find and Replace

The search function above is useful for quick searches, but sometimes a more thorough search is needed and the **Find and Replace** facility should be used. This can be accessed using the **Find** icon in the **Home** tab of the ribbon.

To search the Members table for the name **Sparrow**, do the following:
- Open the **Golf Club** database.
- Open the **Members** table.
- Double-click the **Members** table to open it in **DataSheet View**.
- Click the **Find** icon on the ribbon.
  The **Find and Replace** window opens.

- Enter **sparrow** into the **Find What** textbox.
- Use the drop-down list arrow to select **Members** in the **Look In** list, if it is not already selected.
- Click the **Find Next** button.
- When the record has been found, click **Cancel** to close the **Find and Replace** window.

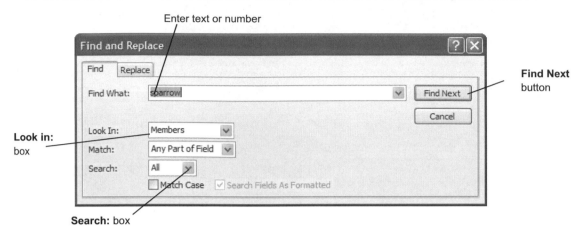

The following table explains the different options displayed in the Find window.

Option	Choice	Action
Look In	Table Specific Field	Searches the complete table. Searches the specific field.
Match	Any Part of Field Whole Field Start of Field	Don will find **Don**caster or Lon**don**. **London** finds London, not Londonontario. **Caster** finds Casterbridge, not Doncaster.
Search	All Up Down	Searches all of the table. Searches towards the first record. Searches from the first record.
Match Case	If selected If deselected	Will only look for the case arrangement as it is specified in the Find what box. Will not be case sensitive.
Search Fields As Formatted	If selected If deselected	Data found will be in the same format as that in the Find what box. For example, a date stored as 1/3/9 but searched for in the format 01-Mar-91 will not be found. When deselected, the accepted formats can be matched across one another.

The **Find and Replace** option may be used to narrow down or widen out the search. For example, to search for the number 11 in the address 11 River Road, there are two options to locate the number.

First you may select **Any Part of Field** in the **Match:** box. Should the number 11 appear anywhere in a field, it will be located no matter what other text is there.

Selecting **Start of Field** will locate the number 11 only where it occurs at the very beginning of a field. Should the number be preceded by a currency label, it won't be recognised.

Choosing **Whole Field** will locate the number 11 only where the number itself is the entire field entry. Numbers with currency symbols will not be recognised with this option.

If you select the **Find Next** button, the computer will continue to search until the last instance of the criteria specified has been found, then an information window will display. Clicking **OK**, terminates the search.

2.4.10   Applying and Removing a Filter to a Form (5.4.1.2)

A filter can be applied when viewing in **Form View** in the same way as for a table in DataSheet View. See Section 2.3.14.

2.4.11   Sorting Data (5.2.2.5)

It is useful to be able to sort data in a table or form. For example, it might make sense to view the data in the Members database in surname order, even though this is not the order that data will have been entered.

Data in a table, a form or a query can be sorted into numeric or alphabetical order. The A–Z button sorts selected text from A to Z and selected numbers from 1 to 10. The Z–A button sorts selected text from Z to A and selected numbers from 10 to 1.

To sort data, do the following:

Sort by Number

To sort on a number, e.g. members' age, do the following:
*   Open the **Members** table in **DataSheet View**.
*   Right-click the **Age** field.
*   Select **Sort Smallest To Largest** from the menu that is displayed.
*   The order of the records will change in **DataSheet View**, with the youngest members listed first.

Sort by Date

To sort on a date, e.g. a competition date, do the following:
*   Open the **Competitions** table in DataSheet view.
*   Right-click on the **Competition Date** field.
*   Select **Sort Newest To Oldest** from the menu that is displayed.
    The order of the records will change to place the most recent competition dates first.

Sort by Text

To sort on text, e.g. members' surnames, do the following:

- Open the Members table in **DataSheet View**.
- Right-click in the **Surname** field.
- Select **Sort A to Z** from the pop-up menu that appears to sort by surname in ascending order.
  The order of the records will change.
- This is most obvious in **DataSheet View**.
- Navigating through the records will confirm that they are in surname order.

> **NOTE**
> The Member Numbers are no longer in sequence.
> This does not matter as long as they are unique.

Multiple Filters

Multiple filters can be active at the same time.

In the Competitions table, if a filter were applied to the Competition Date field first, then the Score field, the sorting would be by date first, and then score within that.

Most types of field can be sorted:

- Number, Currency, AutoNumber.
- Text, Memo, Hyperlink.
- Yes/No.
- Date/Time.

The wording of the **Sort** menu will change depending on the field type. For example, sorting on the Age field will give the menu on the right. The sorting is saved when the table is closed and reapplied when it is reopened.

To clear all sorting that is active on a table, do the following:

- Click the **Clear All Sorts** command button in the **Sort & Filter** section of the ribbon.

2.4.12 Using Forms to Add, Modify and Delete Data in a Record (5.5.1.5)

It is possible to add, change or delete data, such as a change of address, when the data is being displayed in a form.

- Open the form and select the record whose data is to be modified or deleted or to which text is to be added.
- Select the field to be changed.
- Make the necessary changes, as follows:
  - o Select the text and type to replace text.
  - o Press **Delete** to delete the text.
  - o Position the cursor where text is to be added and type.

  As soon as the changes have been made and the cursor is clicked outside the field, the changes are accepted and saved.

PRACTICE SEQUENCE

1   Using the form that has been created for the Members table, add and amend records as necessary to produce the following list of members.

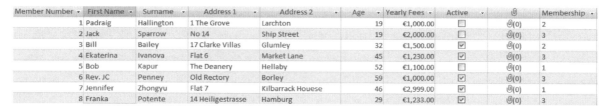

Member Number	First Name	Surname	Address 1	Address 2	Age	Yearly Fees	Active	🖉	Membership
1	Padraig	Hallington	1 The Grove	Larchton	19	€1,000.00	☐	(0)	2
2	Jack	Sparrow	No 14	Ship Street	19	€2,000.00	☐	(0)	3
3	Bill	Bailey	17 Clarke Villas	Glumley	32	€1,500.00	☑	(0)	2
4	Ekaterina	Ivanova	Flat 6	Market Lane	45	€1,230.00	☑	(0)	3
5	Bob	Kapur	The Deanery	Hellaby	52	€1,100.00	☐	(0)	1
6	Rev. JC	Penney	Old Rectory	Borley	59	€1,000.00	☑	(0)	3
7	Jennifer	Zhongyu	Flat 7	Kilbarrack Houese	46	€2,999.00	☑	(0)	1
8	Franka	Potente	14 Heiligestrasse	Hamburg	29	€1,233.00	☑	(0)	3

Deleting Records

If there is already data in the Members table, it may be necessary to delete the existing records.

* Open the table in DataSheet View.
* Click the **Select All** button at the top left of the grid of records. This will select all the records in the table.

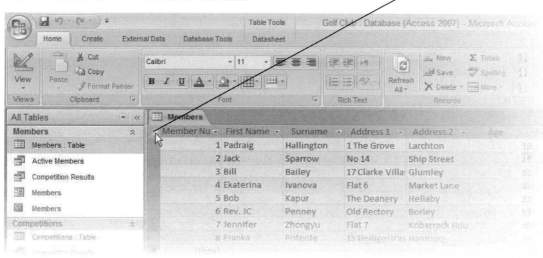

Select All button

* Press **Delete**.
  A confirmation window opens.
* Click **Yes** to delete the records.

Resetting the AutoNumber Field

The act of deleting all the existing entries in the Members table does not restart the numbering of the Member Number field. Therefore, it is necessary to open the Members **table** and use **Design View** to delete the Member Number field and then re-add it as an AutoNumber field and set it as the Primary Key. This will have the effect of restarting the Member Numbers from 1.

To reset the AutoNumber field, do the following:
* Open the **Members** table in **Design View**.
* Right-click the **Member Number** field in the field list.
* Select **Delete Rows** from the menu.

5

A confirmation window opens.
- Click **Yes**.

As the **Member Number** field is a **Primary Key**, a second confirmation window opens.
- Click **Yes**.

- The **First Name** field should now be the first in the list.
- Click in the **First Name** field to select it.
- Click the **Insert Rows** button on the ribbon to add a new field.
  A new entry is created in the field list, with the cursor in the **Field Name**.

- Enter **Member Number** as the field name.
- Select **AutoNumber** from the **Data Type** list.
- Close **Design** View.
- Save the table when prompted.

2.4.13 Adding Attachments to Records

Attachments can be added to attachment-type fields. This is useful for storing a graphic file, e.g. a member's photograph, with the member's record.

- Opens the **Members** table in Design View. A field name **Photo** and field type **Attachment** should have been added earlier. If not add it here.

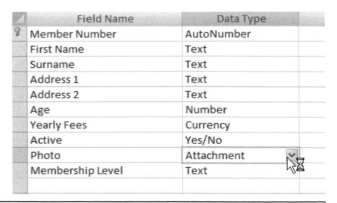

To attach a file to a record, do the following:
- Ensure that the Members table is open in **DataSheet View**.
- Double-click the **Photo** field of the record to which the photograph is to be attached.

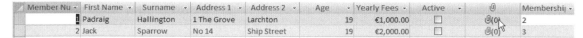

The **Attachments** window opens.
- Click **Add**.

The **Choose File** window opens.
- Browse to locate the required photograph.
- Click **Open**.
  The selected graphics file will appear in the **Attachments** window.

- Click **OK** to attach the file to the record.

2.5   Queries

Queries are the cornerstone of database work. They are requests for data to be returned from a database, based on certain rules. The results of a query can be used as a source of data for reports or forms.

2.5.1 Opening, Closing and Saving a Query (5.2.2.1)

Opening a Query

To open a query, do the following:
- Start **Microsoft Access**.
- Open the required database file.
  The objects comprising the database are listed in the **Navigation Pane**.

NOTE
Each database object has a different icon. Queries are displayed like this:

5

- Double-click the desired query to open it in **DataSheet View**.
  Alternatively, right-click the query name and select **Design View** to open it in that mode.

Saving a Query

To save a query, do the following:
- Click the **Save** icon beside the Office Button.

If this is the first time the query has been saved, a window will be displayed prompting for a name.
- Enter the name.
- Click **OK** to save.

The query is then added to the Navigation Pane alongside the Members table and form.

Closing a Query

To close a query, do the following:
- Click the **Close X** button at the right of the Access window.

Close X button

2.5.2 Creating a Simple Query (5.4.2.2)

To create a query, which will return all active members from the Members table, do the following:
- Select the **Create** tab on the ribbon.
- In the **Other** section, click the **Query Design** command button.

A new query, called **Query1**, is created and is displayed, with a **Show Table** window in the foreground.

- Select the **Members** table.
- Click **Add**.
- Click **Close**.

The table (and its fields) is added to the table list at the top of the query designer.

Below the table list is a grid. This is used to define which fields are to be included in the query and to sort criteria for inclusion.

Within each column, a field name can be chosen from the **Field:** drop-down list.

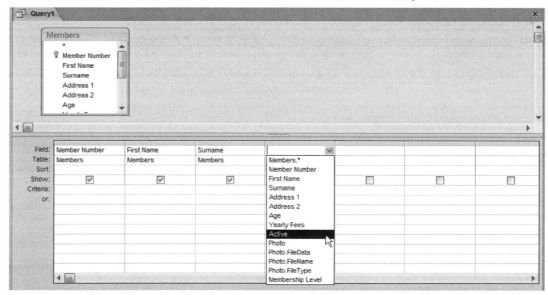

- Add the Member Number, First Name, Surname and Active fields as shown above.
- Ensure that the **Show:** checkbox is ticked for each.
- Save the table.

As only active members should be returned by this query, a criterion must be added to select only relevant records.

2.5.3 Adding Criteria to a Query (5.4.2.4 and 5.4.2.5)

It is possible to specify precisely the information that a query needs to return by adding **criteria**.
In adding criteria to queries, you can more precisely specify the information you require.
Operators such as **less than**, **greater than** or a combination of these are commonly used to define
criteria. Specific mathematical symbols are used to express these criteria.

>	Greater than	<	Less than
>=	Greater than and equal to	<=	Less than and equal to
=	Equal to	<>	Not equal to

In addition, the logical operators **And**, **Or** and **Not** can be used to refine searches in queries.

And	Returns records matching all criteria listed (can involve two or more criteria).
Or	Returns records matching any listed criterion (can involve two or more criteria)
Not	Returns records not matching listed criteria.

To add a criterion to the query for the Members table, do the following:
- In the column for the **Active** field, enter **=true** in the **Criteria**: cell.

Criteria: row

To test the query, do the following:
- Click the **View** command button in the **Results** section of the ribbon.

The **Competition Results** query needs to be amended and criteria added to only return records
where the score is between 75 and 85.

To add criteria to a query, do the following:
- Right-click the query entry in the Navigation Pane.
- Select **Design View** from the menu.
  The criteria to be added apply to the score field.
- Click in the Criteria cell in the Score column.
- Enter the criteria **>=75 AND <=85**.
- Save and run the query.
- Verify that the scores returned are in the correct range.

2.5.4 Running a Query (5.4.2.9)

To run the query, do the following:
- Click the **Run** button.

A **DataSheet View** of the query results
will be shown.

Member Number ▾	First Name ▾	Surname ▾	Active ▾
3	Bill	Bailey	☑
4	Ekaterina	Ivanova	☑
6	Rev. JC	Penney	☑
7	Jennifer	Zhongyu	☑
8	Franka	Potente	☑

> **NOTE**
> Only the fields listed in the query (see Section 2.5.2) are included in the results. The results
> only contain active members.

2.5.5 Creating a Two-Tabled Query (5.4.2.3)

It is also possible to create a query to return data from more than one table, where the results are **joined** into a single result table. In our example, competition details will be returned. The Competitions table does not hold the names of members. It does, however, contain the member number for each individual competition result, and this field will be used to link to the Members table.

To create a two-tabled query, do the following:

- Select the **Create** tab on the ribbon.
- In the **Other** section, click the **Query Design** command button.
  A new query, called **Query1**, is created and is displayed,
  with a **Show Table** window in the foreground.
- In the **Show Table** window, highlight the **Competitions** table.
- Click **Add**.
- Highlight the **Members** table.
- Click **Add**.
- Click **Close**.

The table list area in the query designer should look like the illustration on the right.

Fields can be added to the query in the same manner as outlined in Section 2.5.2.

The drop-down list on the Field row contains the fields from both tables.

As both tables contain fields with the same name, a method of specifying which table to take the field from is needed. This is done by using the notation **tablename.fieldname**, etc.

NOTE

The tables are **joined** using the Member Number fields. Since both tables contain this field and it is of the same data type in both tables, Access has created the join automatically. It can also be created manually.

NOTE

The Table row also contains a drop-down list when the line is highlighted. This list contains the tables that are being used to create the query. Changing the table will change the list of fields available in the drop-down list in the Field row. The fields available will be those in the selected table.

NOTE

Fields can also be added to the query by dragging them from the top section of the query designer to the Field row. Highlight the field to be dragged (note a ghost image of the field appears) and, holding down the mouse button, drag the ghost image to the Field row.

5

- Add the following fields to the query:
  - Competitions.Member Number
  - Members.First Name
  - Members.Surname
  - Competitions.Competition Date
  - Competitions.Score

Field:	Member Number	First Name	Surname	Competition Date	Score
Table:	Competitions	Members	Members	Competitions	Competitions
Sort:					
Show:	☑	☑	☑	☑	☑
Criteria:					
or:					

To test the query, do the following:

- Click the **View** button in the **Results** section of the ribbon.
  The results are presented as if they are a single table. They can be used in this way in forms and reports. The results can be navigated using the **Navigation Toolbar** in the same way as tables and forms.

Query1

Member Nu ▾	First Name ▾	Surname ▾	Competitioi ▾	Score ▾
1	Padraig	Hallington	03/05/2007	85
1	Padraig	Hallington	10/05/2007	81
1	Padraig	Hallington	17/05/2007	83
2	Jack	Sparrow	03/05/2007	86
2	Jack	Sparrow	10/05/2007	81
2	Jack	Sparrow	17/05/2007	80
5	Bob	Kapur	10/05/2007	88
5	Bob	Kapur	17/05/2007	90
7	Jennifer	Zhongyu	03/05/2007	78
7	Jennifer	Zhongyu	10/05/2007	77

- Save the query, calling it
  Competition Results.

2.5.6 Navigating Records in Queries (5.2.2.4)

A query produces a set of results in a similar way to a table, but they should be regarded as being read-only and not changed. When a query is executed the results are normally shown in DataSheet View.

When viewing query results, the standard navigation toolbar is displayed at the bottom of the screen. Clicking the different sections of the toolbar, as shown below, will change the DataSheet View to move to another record and highlight it onscreen.

PRACTICE SEQUENCE

1   Open the **Competitions Results** query in **Design View**.

2   Modify the criterion to include scores between **75** and **80**.

3   Retest the results.

4   Modify the query again, and remove the criterion by deleting the text.

5   Retest to verify that all records are once again returned.

2.5.7   Editing a Query by Adding, Editing or Removing Criteria (5.4.2.7)
The criteria for the query can be added to, changed to alter or further refine the results.

To amend the query that has just been created to include scores between 75 and 90, do as follows:
- Open the Query in **Design View.**
- Click in the criterion cell for the **Score** field.
- Change **>=75 And <=85** to **>=75 And <=90**
- Press **Enter** to register the change.
- Save the query.
- Rerun the query to test it.

To remove criteria, do the following:
- Open the query in Design View.
- Click anywhere in the **Criteria row** and in the **Query Setup** section of the ribbon select **Delete Rows**.

> **NOTE**
> To delete one part of multiple criteria, place your cursor in the Criteria row beneath the field and delete it manually.

2.5.8   Editing a Query by Fields (5.4.2.8)
It is possible to alter the fields in a query to further refine results.

Adding a Field
To add a field to a query, do the following:
- Open the query in **Design View**.
- In the column after **Score**, select **Competitions.Handicap** from the **Field** drop-down list.

Moving a Field
A field can be moved within a query to control where it is placed in the results.

To move the **Handicap** field so it appears after the **Score** field in the query that has been created, do the following:

- Open the query in **Design View**.
- Move the cursor over the narrow bar just above the **Score** field in the list of fields, until the cursor changes to a downward-pointing arrow.
- Click to select the column, as in the illustration on the right.

Cursor changes to an arrow

Cursor changes to a move cursor

- With the column selected, left-click again in the same place and hold it down.
  The cursor changes to a move cursor.
- With the mouse button held down, drag the mouse to the right-hand side of the **Handicap** column, then release the button. The **Score** column will drop into place to the right of the **Handicap** column.
- Save and run the query and verify that the order of the fields has changed.

Deleting a Field

To delete a field in a query, do the following:
- Click inside the field name textbox of the field to be deleted and delete the text.
- Press **Enter**.
  Alternatively, select the field's column and press the **Delete** key on the keyboard.

Hiding a Field

It may be necessary to include fields in a query, perhaps to add criteria to them, but stop them actually being included in the result.

The **Show:** checkbox

To hide a field in a query, do the following:
- Open the query in **Design View**.
- Untick the **Show:** checkbox for the field that is to be hidden.

Unhiding a Field

To unhide a field in a query, do the following:
- Open the query in **Design View**.
- Tick the **Show:** checkbox for the field that is to be unhidden.

2.5.9 Wildcards (5.4.2.6)

Wildcards can be employed in query criteria to perform partial comparisons, e.g. to perform a query on a specific section of the table.

In our example, we will return details about active members whose surname begins with **P**.

To add a wildcard, do the following:
- Open the **Active Members** query in **Design View**.
- Add **P*** as a new criterion to the **Surname** field. Access will change the entered text to **LIKE "P*"**.
- **Save** the query.
- **Run** the query.
  Only those active members whose surnames begin with P are returned.

The asterisk means 'match any number of characters'. The criterion **LIKE "Sm*"** would return surnames such as "Smith", "Smedley", "Smyth" and "Smallwood". This wildcard character can appear either as the first or last character in the criterion, so **LIKE "*ley"** would match "Woodley", "Smedley" and "Godley".

- Another common wildcard character is the question mark (?).
  This is used to represent any single character. For example specifying **LIKE "B?rley"** as the Surname criterion would return "Barley" and "Borley".

2.6 Reports

Storing data in a database is a pointless exercise unless it can be extracted and presented in some human-readable way. Most often, this takes the form of **reports**, which can be printed to paper, PDF and other formats, or emailed, or exported to Excel and other formats.

> **NOTE**
> If Excel is not given as an option on the Export tab when working with reports, the Office 2007 Suite Service Pack 2 should be installed. See http://support.microsoft.com/kb/934833.

2.6.1 Opening, Closing and Saving a Report (5.2.2.1)

Opening a Report

To open a report, do the following:
- Start **Microsoft Access**.
- Open the desired database file as detailed above.
- The objects comprising the database are listed in the **Navigation Pane**.

> **NOTE**
> Each database object has a different icon.
> Reports are displayed like this:
>
> Members

- Double-click the required report to open it in **Report View**.

Alternatively, right-click the report name and select **Design View** or **Layout View** to open in in that mode.

Right-click to open the report
in **Layout** or **Design** view

Closing a Report

To close a report, do the following:

- Click the **Close X** button at the right of the Access window.

Close X
button

Saving a Report

To save a report, do the following:

- Click the **Save** icon beside the **Office Button**.

If this is the first time the report has been saved, a window will be displayed prompting for a name.

- Enter a name.
- Click **OK** to save.

2.6.2 Creating a Report (5.6.1.2)

Reports are based on any **data source**. In Access terms, this means **tables** and **queries**. Creating a basic report is very similar to creating a form.

To create a report based on the Members table, do the following:

- In the **Navigation Pane**, click the **Members** table to select it.
- Click the **Create** tab on the ribbon.
- Click **Report** button in the **Reports** section.

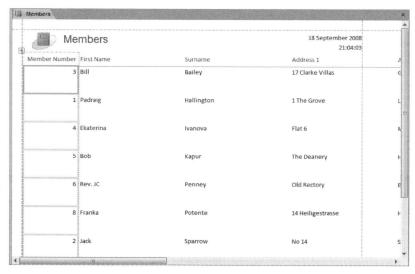

A new report will be generated from the table, given the same name as the table, and displayed in **Layout View**.

The table has an active sort on the **Surname** field, hence the ordering.

2.6.3 Changing the Arrangement of Data Fields (5.6.1.3)

As with a form, the elements of the report can be positioned in Layout View by dragging them with the mouse.

The **First Name** and **Surname** fields on the report need to be switched. This can be done in Layout View, as follows:

- Change the view to **Layout View**.
- Click the heading text **First Name** and hold down the mouse button. The cursor changes to a cross.

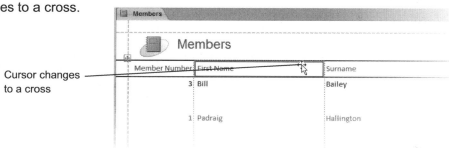

Cursor changes to a cross

- With the mouse button held down, drag the cursor to the right-hand side of the **Surname** column heading.
- Release the mouse button. The order of the columns will change.

2.6.4 Adding, Modifying and Rearranging Text in Headers and Footers (5.6.1.5)

Headers and footers can help identify a report by giving it an appropriate label.

In our example, the heading of the Members report needs to be amended to read **Members Report**.

Modifying Text in a Header

To modify the text in the header, do the following:

- Right-click the report in the **Navigation Pane**.
- Select **Design View** from the menu.

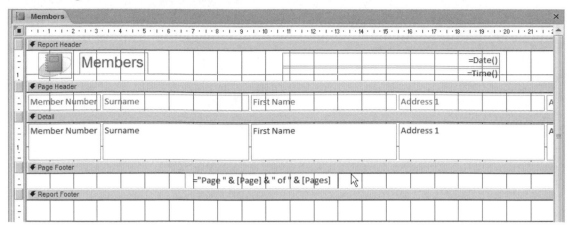

The **Members** heading text is displayed using a **Label** control.

- Select this control by double-clicking its box.

A **properties** list is visible on the right side of the Access window, listing the properties of the selected control.

- In the properties list, click to the right of the **Caption** property.
- Change the text to read **Members Report**.
- Press **Enter**.
  The report will change to reflect the new caption.

However, the label is too narrow to display all the text.
To widen the label, do the following:

- Left-click the border on the right side of the label on the report design.
- Hold down the mouse button.
- The cursor changes to a resize cursor.

Resize cursor

- Drag the mouse to the right to resize the label.

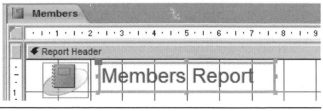

Adding Text to a Footer

The footer area of the report should display a copyright notice.

To add this text, do the following:
*   Click the **Label** button in the **Controls** section of the ribbon.

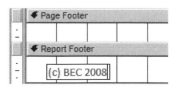

*   The cursor changes to a crosshair.
*   Click in footer area of the report.
*   Enter © **BEC 2008**.

Rearranging Text in a Footer

The position of the text that has been added to the footer, or of any other item on the report layout, can be altered by dragging and dropping the item with the mouse.

To alter the position of the copyright text label that has just been added, do the following:
*   Ensure the report is open in **Design View**.
*   Click the label item to select it.
    A selection border will be shown enclosing it.

*   Move the cursor over the top border line, until it changes to a move cursor.
*   Click the mouse button, hold it down and drag the label to another position in the footer.
*   Release the button to complete the move.
*   Save the report and run it to verify the new position.

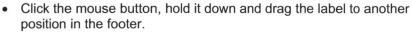

Move cursor

2.6.5 Grouping Records (5.6.1.4)

In addition to simply displaying data, reports can employ **grouping**. Records can be displayed together based on the contents of a field or fields.

To group records, do the following:
*   Open the **Members** report in **Layout View**.
*   Scroll across to view the columns.
*   Right-click the **Active** column and select **Group On Active** from the pop-up menu that appears.

    The order of the records, and the layout, will change.

Click **Group On Active**

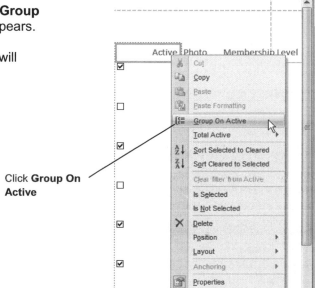

All records with **Active ticked** will be displayed together.
All records with **Active unticked** will be displayed together.

Grouping can also be defined using the **Group & Sort** button in the **Grouping & Totals** section of the ribbon.

Clicking this button displays a new **Group, Sort & Total** pane at the bottom of the screen. Initially, this pane displays two buttons for adding a group and adding a sort respectively.

Clicking the Add Group Button displays a menu from which a field can be chosen.

When a field has been selected, it is displayed as a menu bar in the **Group, Sort and Total** pane. Further options can be selected using the drop-down menus on the menu bar.

New **Add a group** and **Add a sort** buttons appear below the most recently added bar. Using these buttons, multiple levels of grouping and sorting can be defined.

The order of precedence of each bar can be changed using the up and down arrows at the right of the bar. The bar can be removed using the **Close X** button.

Totalling Options

When you present specific fields in a grouped report, you may avail of a number of options that summarise numeric information. These numeric fields will be located in the **Summary Options** section.

You can display numeric information by total (**sum**), mean (**avg**), maximum (**max**) or minimum (**min**).

- In **Layout View**, right-click the **Yearly Fees** column.
- Select the **Total Yearly Fees** menu option.
  The totalling options are listed on a sub-menu.
- Select **Sum**.

A total will be placed in the **Yearly Fees** column at each group break, and an overall total at the end of the report (circled below).

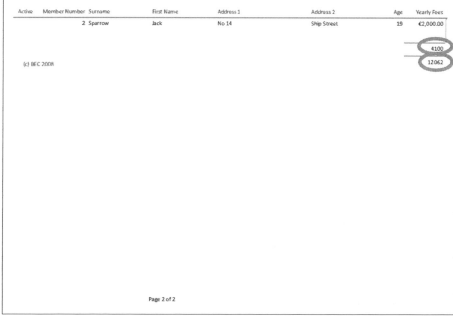

Further Examples of Totalling Options

- Consider the following simple table, called **Rep Sales**.
- It holds information about orders won by sales reps.

ID	Rep Name	Month Num	Month Nam	Orders Won
1	Bill	1	January	€12,000.34
2	Dave	1	January	€13,400.62
3	Mike	1	January	€9,000.27
4	Bill	2	February	€8,000.00
5	Dave	2	February	€9,484.00
6	Mike	2	February	€12,928.00
7	Bill	3	March	€22,342.30
8	Dave	3	March	€30,998.02
9	Mike	3	March	€29,827.00
10	Bill	4	April	€34,242.89
11	Dave	4	April	€13,949.00
12	Mike	4	April	€45,998.87
13	John	1	January	€18,772.98
14	John	4	April	€23,992.34

- A basic report can be created using this table, grouped by **Month Number**.

Rep Sales   21 September 2008
                                                                  21:36:01

Month Number	ID	Rep Name	Month Name	Orders Won
1				
	13	John	January	€18,772.98
	3	Mike	January	€9,000.27
	2	Dave	January	€13,400.62
	1	Bill	January	€12,000.34
2				
	6	Mike	February	€12,928.00
	5	Dave	February	€9,484.00
	4	Bill	February	€8,000.00
3				
	9	Mike	March	€29,827.00
	8	Dave	March	€30,998.02
	7	Bill	March	€22,342.30
4				
	14	John	April	€23,992.34
	12	Mike	April	€45,998.87
	11	Dave	April	€13,949.00
	10	Bill	April	€34,242.89
				284936.63

Page 1 of 1

- Totalling the Orders Won column by **Sum** in the **Rep Sales** will produce a report, with sum totals for each group.

Rep Sales   21 September 2008
                                                                  21:39:16

Month Number	ID	Rep Name	Month Name	Orders Won
1				
	13	John	January	€18,772.98
	3	Mike	January	€9,000.27
	2	Dave	January	€13,400.62
	1	Bill	January	€12,000.34
				53174.21
2				
	6	Mike	February	€12,928.00
	5	Dave	February	€9,484.00
	4	Bill	February	€8,000.00
				30412
3				
	9	Mike	March	€29,827.00
	8	Dave	March	€30,998.02
	7	Bill	March	€22,342.30
				83167.32
4				
	14	John	April	€23,992.34
	12	Mike	April	€45,998.87
	11	Dave	April	€13,949.00
	10	Bill	April	€34,242.89
				118183.1
				284936.63

Page 1 of 1

- Selecting **Average** will give the average order value for the month.

Rep Sales — 21 September 2008 — 21:46:00

Month Number	ID	Rep Name	Month Name	Orders Won
1				
	13	John	January	€18,772.98
	3	Mike	January	€9,000.27
	2	Dave	January	€13,400.62
	1	Bill	January	€12,000.34
				13293.5525
2				
	6	Mike	February	€12,928.00
	5	Dave	February	€9,484.00
	4	Bill	February	€8,000.00
				10137.3333
3				
	9	Mike	March	€29,827.00
	8	Dave	March	€30,998.02
	7	Bill	March	€22,342.30
				27722.44
4				
	14	John	April	€23,992.34
	12	Mike	April	€45,998.87
	11	Dave	April	€13,949.00
	10	Bill	April	€34,242.89
				29545.775
				20352.6164

Page 1 of 1

- Choosing **Count Records** will yield the number of records in each group.

Rep Sales — 21 September 2008 — 21:47:24

Month Number	ID	Rep Name	Month Name	Orders Won
1				
	13	John	January	€18,772.98
	3	Mike	January	€9,000.27
	2	Dave	January	€13,400.62
	1	Bill	January	€12,000.34
				4
2				
	6	Mike	February	€12,928.00
	5	Dave	February	€9,484.00
	4	Bill	February	€8,000.00
				3
3				
	9	Mike	March	€29,827.00
	8	Dave	March	€30,998.02
	7	Bill	March	€22,342.30
				3
4				
	14	John	April	€23,992.34
	12	Mike	April	€45,998.87
	11	Dave	April	€13,949.00
	10	Bill	April	€34,242.89
				4
				14

Page 1 of 1

- Selecting **Max** will show the highest value in the group, as shown on the right.
- Selecting **Min** will show the lowest value.

Rep Sales — 21 September 2008 — 21:49:42

Month Number	ID	Rep Name	Month Name	Orders Won
1				
	13	John	January	€18,772.98
	3	Mike	January	€9,000.27
	2	Dave	January	€13,400.62
	1	Bill	January	€12,000.34
				18772.98
2				
	6	Mike	February	€12,928.00
	5	Dave	February	€9,484.00
	4	Bill	February	€8,000.00
				12928
3				
	9	Mike	March	€29,827.00
	8	Dave	March	€30,998.02
	7	Bill	March	€22,342.30
				30998.02
4				
	14	John	April	€23,992.34
	12	Mike	April	€45,998.87
	11	Dave	April	€13,949.00
	10	Bill	April	€34,242.89
				45998.87
				45998.87

Page 1 of 1

2.6.6 Viewing a Report

Apart from the Layout and Design Views, it is possible to view the records in Report View. Report View displays the report exactly as it will be output to a printer, screen or other output destination.

To view records in Report View, do the following:
*   Double-click the report in the **Navigation Pane**.
    This will open it in **Report View**.

2.7   Defining a Relationship

Relationships are based on a field or fields that are common between two tables in a database and provide a method for linking the tables (see Section 1.6.11).

To create a relationship, do the following:
*   Open the **Golf Club** database.
*   Ensure that **no** tables, reports or other items are open.
*   On the ribbon, select the **Database Tools** tab.
*   In the **Show/Hide** group, click the **Relationships** option.

If this is the first time that a relationship has been defined in the database, a **Show Table** window will be displayed.
If the **Show Table** is not displayed automatically, click the **Show Table** option in the **Relationships** section of the ribbon.

*   In the **Show Table** window, click the **Members** option in the list of tables to highlight it.
*   Click **Add**.

*   In the Show Table window, click the **Competition** option in the list of tables to highlight it.
*   Click **Add**.
*   Click **Close** to close the **Show Table** window.
    The tables should now be visible in the **Relationship Designer**.

The **Relationship Designer** is the main part of the window

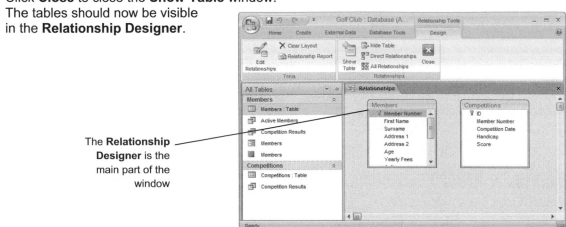

As there can be many competition results for each individual member, a one-to-many relationship is needed. The tables have a Member Number field in common, so this can be used to define the relationship.

To create a one-to-many relationship, do the following.
* In the **Relationship Designer**, move the cursor over the **Member Number** field name in the **Members** table.
* Click and hold the mouse button.
* With the mouse button held down, drag the cursor to the **Member** number field in the **Competitions** table.
  The cursor changes to a pointer with a plus sign.

* Release the mouse button.
  The **Edit Relationships** window opens.
* The **Relationship Type** will be set automatically to **One-To-Many**.

The **One-To-Many** type is set automatically

* Click the **Enforce Referential Integrity** option.
* Click the **Create** button.
* The relationship will be created and the **Relationship Designer** window updated to reflect this. A line will be shown linking the fields.

The relationship is shown by a line linking the fields

> **NOTE**
> The line has a '1' on the Members side and the symbol for infinity on the Competitions side. This represents the one-to-many nature of the relationship.

* Save the relationship by clicking the **Save** icon next to the **Office Button**.

One advantage of defining a relationship is that this automatically informs queries about how tables are linked.

To demonstrate this, do the following:
* Create a new query (see Section 2.5.4).
* In the **Show Table** window, add the **Members table** first, then the **Competitions table**.
* Close the **Show Tables** window.

The tables are automatically joined using the relationship that was defined. Without defined relationships tables in queries, tables would have to be joined manually within the query every time they were used.

* Save or discard the query as required.

To demonstrate how enabling the **Referential Integrity** (see Section 1.6.12) option on the Relationship enforces data integrity, do the following:

- Open the Members table in Datasheet View.
- Highlight the record with the **Member Number '1'**.
- Press the **Delete** key.
  A message window opens indicating that the record will not be deleted or changed because the **Competitions** table includes related records. Deleting the record in the **Members** table would leave orphaned records in the **Competitions** table – records in the **Competitions** table with a **Member** number no longer existing in the members table.

Datasheet View is also enhanced by a defined relationship. To see this, do the following:

- Open the **Members** table in **Datasheet View**.
  Each record now has an expansion box to the left of the **Member Number** field.
- Click this box to expand the grid to display the records related to that member that exist in the **Competitions** table.

Clicking the expansion box shows records from the **Competitions** table

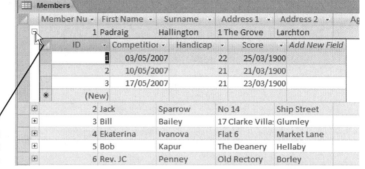

To delete a relationship, do the following.
- Open the **Relationship Designer**.
- Click the line joining the tables to select it.
- Press **Delete**.
  A confirmation window opens.
- Click **Yes**.
- Save the relationship.

2.8   Printing

2.8.1   Previewing a Report, Form or Table

It is important to always view your table, form or report before you print it. This option is known as **preview**.

To use the preview option, do the following:
- Click the **Office Button**.
- Select **Print** from the drop-down menu.
  A sub-menu with three options is displayed.
- Select **Print Preview**.

Print preview

This will present the data in different ways depending on whether a report, form, table or query is involved.

A report will be exactly as it appears in **Report View**.

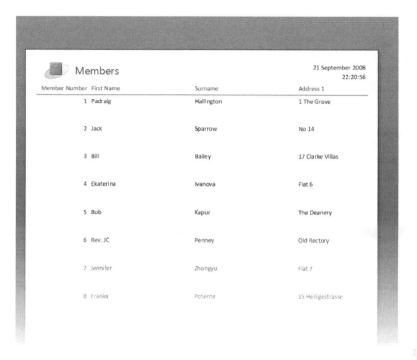

Previewing a table or query displays information in the way presented in the illustration below.

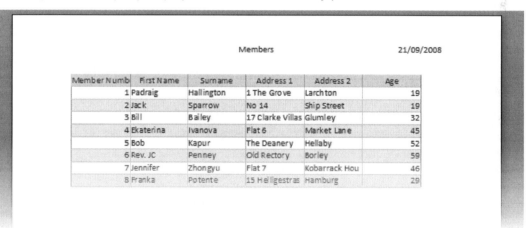

Previewing a form displays information in the way presented in the illustration on the right.

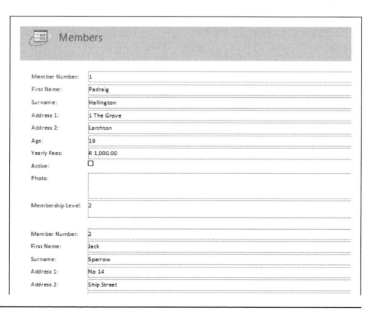

When in **Print Preview** mode, the ribbon changes to display a range of printing options.

To print from **Print Preview** mode, do the following:
- Click **Print** at the left of the ribbon.

2.8.2 Changing Orientation (5.6.2.1)
There are two types of page orientation, **Portrait** and **Landscape**. Portrait is a vertical orientation. Landscape is a horizontal orientation.

This is landscape orientation

This is portrait orientation

To change the page orientation, do the following:
- In **Print Preview** mode, the ribbon has a **Page Layout** section.

  The orientation of the output can be changed between Portrait and Landscape using the appropriate command button.

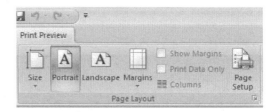

2.8.3 Printing a Report, Form, Query or Table (5.6.2.2, 5.6.2.3, 5.6.2.4 and 5.6.2.5)
To print a report, form, table or query, do the following:
- Open the report, form, query or table from the **Navigation Pane**.
- Click the **Office Button**.
- Select **Print** from the drop-down menu.
  A sub-menu with three options is displayed.
- Select **Print**.

The **Print** window opens.
Use this window to select a printer, the number of copies required and pages to be printed.

- Choosing the **All** option in the **Print Range** box means that all the contents of the table would be printed.

- Choosing the **Pages From** option means that you can choose which pages you want to print, i.e. if you type in 1 in the **From** box and type in 5 in the **To** box, pages 1, 2, 3, 4 and 5 would be printed.

NOTE
Quick Print will send the output to the default printer, using the default print options.

Any filters or ordering that has been imposed on tables, queries or forms will be maintained in the printed output.
- When all the printing options have been set, click **OK**.

NOTE
When a query has been run, the results are presented as a table and can be printed in the same way as a table.

2.8.4 Printing Selected Output from a Table (5.6.2.2)

Sometimes, it is only necessary to print a selection of the data in a table.

To print a range of records, do the following:
- In **DataSheet View**, click one record to select it.
- Hold down the **Shift** key.
- Click a second record.
- Both the records, and any in between, will be selected.

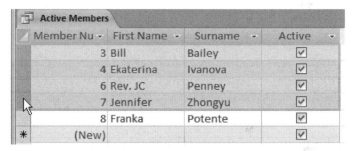

When the records have been selected, open the **Print** window by selecting **Print** from the drop-down menu in the **Office Button**.
- In the Print window, click the **Selected Record(s)** option in the **Print Range** area.

Selected Record(s) checkbox

NOTE
It is not possible to select separated records for printing, only ranges from one record to another.

PRACTICE SEQUENCE

1   Experiment with previewing and printing a report, form, query.

2.9 Exporting

In addition to printing, Access 2007 provides a range of options to **export** data to various formats. Exporting in different formats is useful if the information needs to be displayed in another application, such as Excel or Word.

> **NOTE**
> Note that changes to the files produced by exporting are not reflected in the Access database itself.

To export, do the following:
- Open the table or query from the **Navigation Pane**.
- Click the **External Data** tab on the ribbon.
  A **Data** section will appear.

The most commonly used options have their own buttons.

Excel – will create a .XLS file that can be used in Excel 2007.

	A	B	C	D	E
1	**Member Number**	**First Name**	**Surname**	**Active**	
2	3	Bill	Bailey	TRUE	
3	4	Ekaterina	Ivanova	TRUE	
4	6	Rev. JC	Penney	TRUE	
5	7	Jennifer	Zhongyu	TRUE	
6	8	Franka	Potente	TRUE	
7					

Word – creates a .RTF (Rich Text Format) file that can be used in Word 2007 or WordPad.

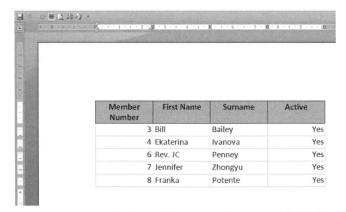

Member Number	First Name	Surname	Active
3	Bill	Bailey	Yes
4	Ekaterina	Ivanova	Yes
6	Rev. JC	Penney	Yes
7	Jennifer	Zhongyu	Yes
8	Franka	Potente	Yes

This illustration shows the results of exporting to text without formatting. This is called a **CSV** (Comma Separated Value) file, as the fields are separated by commas.

```
3,"Bill","Bailey",1
4,"Ekaterina","Ivanova",1
6,"Rev. JC","Penney",1
7,"Jennifer","Zhongyu",1
8,"Franka","Potente",1
```

Text – can create a text file with formatting, as in the illustration on the right.

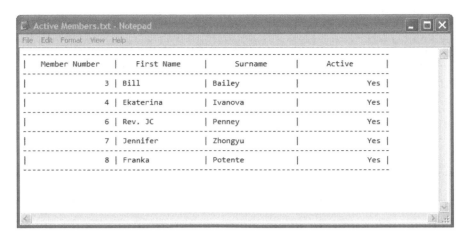

Clicking the **More** menu in the Data section displays additional options.

XML File – produces an .XML (Extensible Markup Language) file, a commonly understood format for exchanging data between applications over the internet.

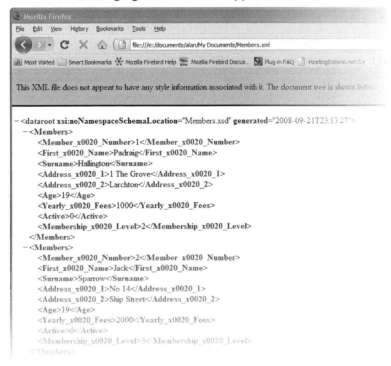

When an export is performed, an **Export Options** wizard is displayed.

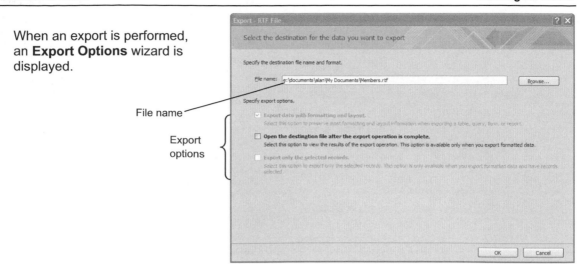

File name

Export options

- The **File Name** section is where the name and location of the export file are specified. Below this are options.
- One or more of these may be unavailable depending on the type of export.
- Clicking **OK** may present further options, before actually producing the output file.

2.9.1 Exporting to a Location on a Drive (5.6.1.6)

To export the Members table in Excel format to a specified location on a drive, do the following:
- Open the **Members** table in **DataSheet View**.
- Click the **External Data** tab on the ribbon.
- Click the **Excel** button in the **Export** section displayed on the ribbon.
- On the first Wizard page, click the **Browse** button beside the **File Name** textbox.

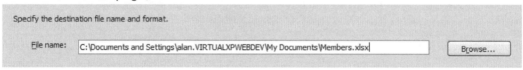

A **File Save** window opens.
- Navigate to the required folder and change the **file name** if necessary.

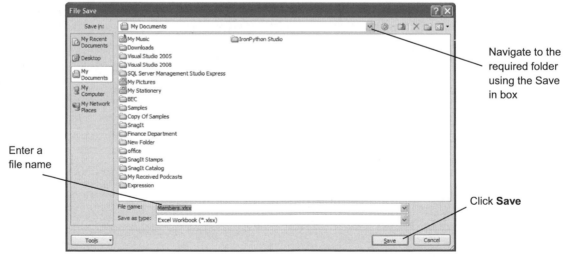

Enter a file name

Navigate to the required folder using the Save in box

Click **Save**

- Click **Save** to save the file.

PRACTICE SEQUENCE

1   Experiment with exporting a table and query to text with and without formatting (the **Export Data With Formatting And Layout** option on the wizard).

2   Experiment with exporting a table and query to XML, then opening the .XML file in a web browser.

Unit 6

Presentations

Unit 6

Presentations

6

Goals for Unit 6

Unit 6 Presentations requires the candidate to demonstrate competence in using presentation software.

The candidate shall be able to:

- Work with presentations and save them in different file formats
- Choose built-in options such as the Help function within the application to enhance productivity
- Understand different presentation views and when to use them, choose different slide layouts and designs
- Enter, edit and format text in presentations. Recognize good practice in applying unique titles to slides
- Choose, create and format charts to communicate information meaningfully
- Insert and edit pictures, images and drawn objects
- Apply animation and transition effects to presentations and check and correct presentation content before finally printing and giving presentations.

What is a Presentation?

A presentation is a set of slides that display on screen in sequence and present information to an audience. The subject matter can be aimed at a specific group, i.e. age and range of knowledge, or be aimed at the widest audience available. Presentations are created using an application such as **Microsoft PowerPoint** or similar software package. A slide show can be presented by a speaker or set to loop continuously. When presented by a speaker, the presentation can be projected onto a whiteboard so that it is visible to a large audience. A presentation needs to be presented with slides structured in a logical sequence.

❶

A guide to PowerPoint

❷

- What is PowerPoint?
- What is a presentation?
- Creating a slide show

❸

Audience
and
Assimilation

6

Section 1   Using the Application

An **application** refers to the software package that is used to perform a task. The application that will be used for this training manual is Microsoft Office PowerPoint 2007. This is a comprehensive presentations package, capable of creating slide shows with multiple slides containing a variety of media, such as images, animations and effects.

1.1   Working with Presentations

A presentation consists of a set of slides in an ordered sequence that are all related to a specific subject.

In this section, you will learn about the following:

- Opening an existing presentation.
- Closing a presentation.
- Creating a new presentation.
- Switching between open presentations.
- Saving a presentation to a location on a drive and with a different name.
- Saving a presentation in another format, such as rich text format, template, show, image file format and version number.

1.1.1   Opening a Presentation Application (6.1.1.1)

PowerPoint, the presentation application used in this unit, will either be displayed as an icon on the desktop of your computer or found in the **Start** menu.

To open PowerPoint, do the following:

- Select the **Start** menu.
- Select **All Programs**.
- Select **Microsoft Office**.
- Select **Microsoft Office PowerPoint 2007**.

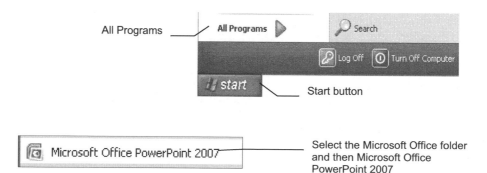

All Programs

Start button

Microsoft Office PowerPoint 2007 ───── Select the Microsoft Office folder and then Microsoft Office PowerPoint 2007

Alternatively, Microsoft PowerPoint may be displayed as a shortcut icon on the desktop of your computer.

- Right-click the icon and select **Open** from the shortcut menu (or double-click to open).

Microsoft Office PowerPoint 2007

Microsoft Office PowerPoint 2007 opens.

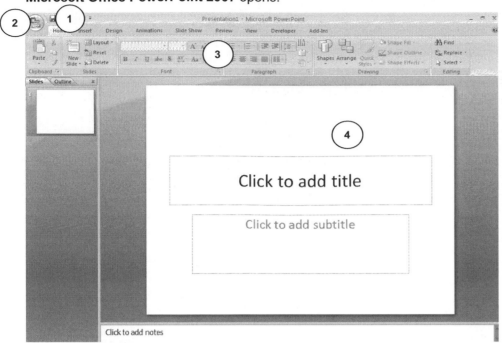

The screen layout will display the following:

①   The Quick Access Toolbar.

②   The Office Button.

③   The ribbon.

④   A new, blank slide.

1.1.2 Closing a Presentation Application (6.1.1.1)

To close PowerPoint, do the following:

* Select the **Office Button**.
* Select **Exit PowerPoint**.
  The **PowerPoint** program will close.

Click **Office Button**

Select **Exit
PowerPoint**

Alternatively, Select the **Close X** button in the
top-right corner of the title bar.

Close X button

1.1.3 Opening a Presentation (6.1.1.1)

To open an existing presentation, do the following:

* Open **PowerPoint**.
* Select the **Office Button**.
* Select **Open**.

Office Button

The **Open** window opens.

- Select the location of the file by clicking the **Look in** arrow and choosing a drive and/or folder.
- Select the file.
- Click **Open**.

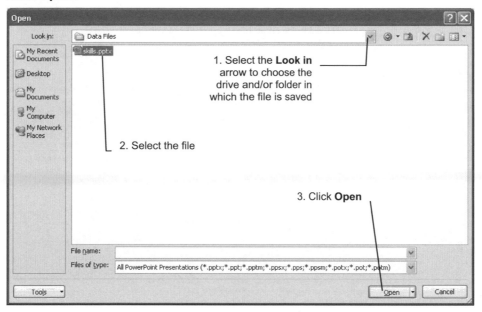

NOTE
To display the Open window, press **CTRL + O**.

Opening Recent Documents

Documents, which have been opened recently, can be accessed more quickly than by using the Open option.

To view recently opened documents, do the following:
- Select the **Office Button**.
- Select the required file from the **Recent Documents** list.

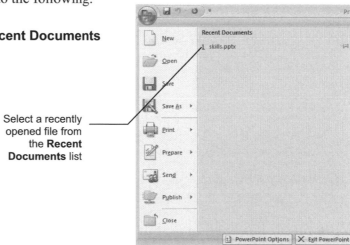

Select a recently opened file from the **Recent Documents** list

To change the number of documents listed in **Recent Documents**, do the following:
- Select the **Office Button**.
- Select **PowerPoint Options**.
- Select the **Advanced** button.
- Enter the number of recent documents that should display in the **Office Button** menu.

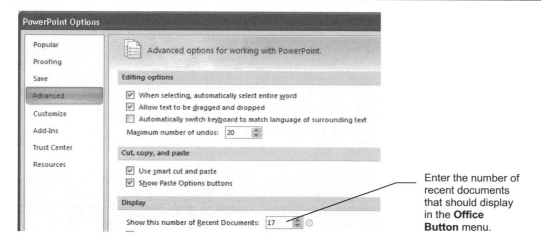

Enter the number of recent documents that should display in the **Office Button** menu.

1.1.4 Closing a Presentation (6.1.1.1)

To close a presentation, do the following:

- Select the **Office Button**.
- Click **Close**.

NOTE

If changes have been made to the file, a message will appear asking if you want to save the file before closing.

- Click **Yes** to save the file.
- Click **No** to close the file without saving.
- Click **Cancel** to cancel the message and return to the presentation.

1.1.5 Creating a New Presentation based on a Default Template (6.1.1.2)

To create a new presentation, do the following:

- Select the **Office Button**.
- Click **New**.
  The **New Presentation** window opens.
- Select **Blank and recent** from the **Templates** list.
- Select **Blank Presentation**.
- Click **Create**.

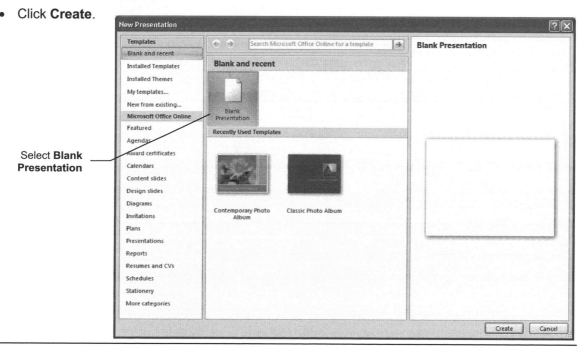

Select **Blank Presentation**

- A new blank slide
  appears with a
  default slide layout
  (**Title Slide** layout).

1.1.6 Saving a Presentation to a Location on a Drive (6.1.1.3)

To save a presentation for the first time, do the following:

- Select the **Office Button**.
- Select **Save**.
  The **Save As** window opens.
- Select the correct drive and/or folder from the **Save in** menu.
- Enter a name in the **File name** box.
- Click **Save**.

1. Select the **Save in**
arrow and choose a
drive and/or folder in
which to save the file

2. Enter a file name in
the box. The default
file name given to a
presentation when
saved for the first time
is **Presentation1**.

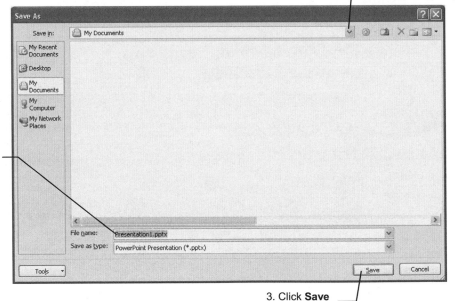

3. Click **Save**

Alternatively, click Save on the Quick Access Toolbar to save a file.

NOTE

When saving a presentation for the first time, clicking **Save** or **Save As** from the **Office Button** menu will result in the **Save As** window opening. Subsequent changes to a presentation can be saved by selecting the **Save** option from the **Office Button**. This will save the presentation with the same name and overwrite the original file.

The keyboard shortcut to save is **CTRL + S**.

1.1.7 Saving a Presentation under Another Name (6.1.1.3)

To save an existing presentation with a different name, do the following:

- Select the **Office Button**.
- Move the mouse over the **Save As** menu option.
  The **Save a copy of the document** sub-menu opens.
- Select **PowerPoint Presentation**.

Select the **PowerPoint Presentation** option to save the file in the default file format

The **Save As** window opens.

- Select the correct drive and/or folder from the **Save in** menu.
- Enter a name in the **Filename** box and click **Save**.

1.1.8 Saving a Presentation as Another File Type (6.1.1.4)

A presentation can be saved in a variety of different formats. See the different formats listed below.

PowerPoint format	Graphic format	Outline/Rich Text format
Presentation (.pptx)	Windows Metafile (.wmf)	Outline/rtf (.rtf)
Design Template (.potx)	GIF (.gif)	
PowerPoint Show (.ppsx)	JPEG (.jpg)	
	PNG (.png)	

Rich Text Format

When a presentation is saved in Rich Text Format, it retains all its formatting features and saves in a format that enables it to be opened and viewed in outline view. This format loses all the **graphical** content that exists in the presentation.

To save the presentation in Rich Text Format, do the following:

- Select the **Office Button** and then move the cursor over the **Save As** menu option.
  The **Save a copy of the document** sub-menu opens.
- Click **Other Formats**.
  The **Save As** windows opens.

Click **Other Formats**

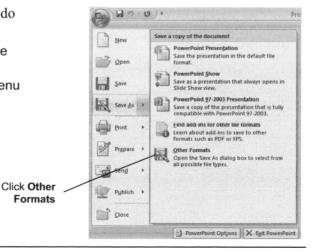

6

- Select the **Save in** arrow and then select the correct drive and /or folder.
- Enter a file name into the **File name** box and then click the **Save as type** arrow.
- Select **Outline/RTF (*.rtf)**.
- Click **Save**.

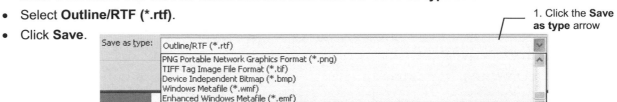

1. Click the **Save as type** arrow

2. Select **Outline/RTF (*.rtf)**

Template

A template contains standard content that will appear on all slides in a presentation. A template can be used repeatedly with other presentations. This saves time and effort when creating a new presentation. Templates are saved with a **potx** file extension and, unless another location is specified, will automatically save in the following location: **C:/Documents and Settings/ Computer Name/Application Data/Microsoft/Templates**

To save a presentation as a template, do the following:
- Select the **Office Button** and then move the mouse over the **Save As** menu option.
  The **Save a copy of the document** sub-menu opens.
- Select **Other Formats**.
  The **Save As** windows opens.
- Select the **Save in** arrow and then select the correct drive and/or folder.
- Enter a file name into the **File name** box.
- Click the **Save as type** arrow.
- Select **PowerPoint Template (.potx)**.
- Click **Save**.

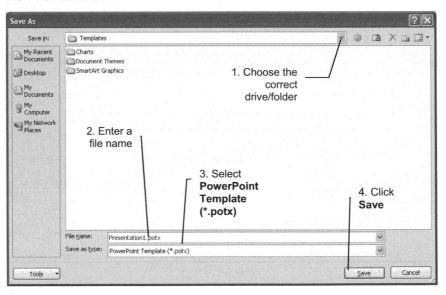

1. Choose the correct drive/folder

2. Enter a file name

3. Select **PowerPoint Template (*.potx)**

4. Click **Save**

NOTE

To save a template in a previous version of PowerPoint, select PowerPoint 97-2003 template (*pot).

Slide Show

A presentation saved in this format will be displayed as a full screen slide show when opened.

To save a presentation as a slide show, do the following:
- Click the **Office Button**.
- Move the cursor over the **Save As** option.

  The **Save a copy of the document** sub-menu opens.
- Select **Other Formats**.

  The **Save As** windows opens.
- Select the **Save in** arrow and then select the correct drive and/or folder.
- Enter a file name into the **File name** box.
- Click the **Save as type** arrow.
- Select **PowerPoint Show (.ppsx)**.
- Select the **Save** button.

Select **PowerPoint Show (*.ppsx)**

> **NOTE**
>
> You can by-pass the **Save a copy of the document** sub-menu by clicking the **Save As** menu command.

Image File Format

A presentation can be saved in a variety of image file formats, such as jpeg, gif, png and wmf.

- A windows metafile (.wmf) image file is a drawn graphic made up of lines rather than picture elements. This means that the picture does not distort when it is resized.

  A bitmap image (such as jpg, gif or png), is a scanned or photographic image that is made up of small dots (or picture elements called pixels). **Jpeg** is an image format used in the compression of photographic images. This format is suitable for on-screen display of low resolution photographs but unsuitable for high resolution commercial printing. **Gif** is an image format used for simple graphics with solid colour and is unsuitable for photographs. This format supports transparency and animation (non-photographic) and is best suited to on-screen display.

  To save a slide for use on the web, save in GIF, JPEG or PNG format.

To save a presentation in image file format, do the following:
- Select the **Office Button**.
- Click **Save As**.

  The **Save As** windows opens.
- Select the **Save in** arrow and then select the correct drive and/or folder.
- Enter a file name into the **File name** box.
- Click the **Save as type** arrow.
- Select an image file format from the menu (i.e. jpg, .gif, .wmf or png).

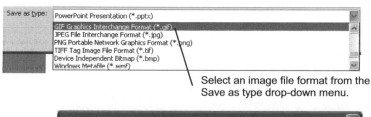

Select an image file format from the Save as type drop-down menu.

- Click **Save**.

  A confirmation window opens.
- To save only the current slide in image file format, select **Current Slide Only**.

Version Number

Each version of PowerPoint has a different number. If the presentation needs to be opened and viewed in a previous version of PowerPoint it can be saved with a different version number.

To check the version number of the software on your computer, do the following:
- Select the **Office Button** and select **PowerPoint Options**.
- Select the **Resources** button.
- Select the **About** button.

about Microsoft Office PowerPoint 2007   About

The **About Microsoft Office PowerPoint** window opens.

This window provides information on the software version currently installed on your computer.

About Microsoft Office PowerPoint

Microsoft® Office PowerPoint® 2007
Part of Microsoft Office Professional Plus 2007

Information about currently installed software will be provided in this window.

- Check the version number – it should be **Microsoft Office PowerPoint® 2007**.
- Click **OK** to close the current window.
- Click **OK** to close the PowerPoint Options window.

To save the presentation with a different version number, do the following:
- Select the **Office Button**.
- Move the cursor over the **Save As** menu command.
  The **Save a copy of the document** drop-down menu appears.
- Select **PowerPoint 97-2003 Presentation** to save a copy of the presentation that is fully compatible with PowerPoint 97-2003.

Save As ► PowerPoint 97-2003 Presentation
Save a copy of the presentation that is fully compatible with PowerPoint 97-2003.

This option ensures that you can open the presentation in an earlier version of PowerPoint

The **Save As** windows opens.
- Select the **Save in** arrow and then select the correct drive and/or folder.
- Enter a file name into the **File name** box.
- Click the **Save as type** arrow.
  The version is selected in the **Save As** type box.
  Alternatively, select the arrow and choose a version number.
- Click **Save**.

PowerPoint 97-2003 is an earlier version of the software

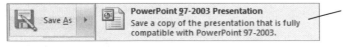

Save as type: PowerPoint 97-2003 Presentation (*.ppt)

Save

NOTE

PowerPoint 2007 does not support saving to PowerPoint 95 and earlier file formats. If you convert your presentation to a 95 or earlier file format, some Office 2007 formatting features may be lost during the conversion.

1.1.9 Switching between Open Presentations (6.1.1.5)

Open presentations will be displayed as tabs on the taskbar.

To switch between open presentations, do the following:

- Select the **View** tab from the ribbon.
- In the **Windows** group, select the **Switch Windows** button.
  A tick will display beside the file name of the currently active presentation.

- Click another file name in the menu to make that the active presentation.

A tick beside the file name indicates that it is the active presentation, currently displayed on screen

Alternatively, open more than one presentation. The presentations will be displayed as tabs on the taskbar at the bottom of the screen. Click a tab to open a presentation.

> **NOTE**
>
> To switch between open presentations, using the keyboard, hold down the **ALT** key and press **TAB**.

1.2 Enhancing Productivity

Productivity can be increased by setting user preferences, such as adding a user name and/or creating a default folder from which to open and in which to save all presentations. Using the Help facility can also aid productivity by providing tips and advice on how to use the program effectively.

In this section, you will learn about the following:
- Setting user preferences.
- Using available Help functions.
- Using magnification/zoom tools.
- Restoring and minimising the ribbon.

1.2.1 Setting User Preferences (6.1.2.1)

User preferences refer to the user name and the default location of opened and saved files. These can be changed as appropriate so that the user name is different or so that files can be opened or saved in another location.

To set user preferences, do the following:

User Name
- Select the **Office Button**.
- Select **PowerPoint Options**.
- Select the **Popular** tab.
- In the **Personalize your copy of Microsoft Office**, position the cursor in the **User name** box and delete the current user name.

- Enter the new user name.
- Click **OK**.

Enter or edit the
User name

Default File Location

- Select the **Office Button**.
- Select **PowerPoint Options**.
- Select the **Save** tab.
- In the **Default File Location** box, enter the required file location of opened and saved files.
- Click **OK**.

Enter the file
location

1.2.2 Using the Help Function (6.1.2.2)

The Help function is available to give advice and help on aspects of the software that you are using. This is useful when you are trying to perform an action and don't know how to proceed further. Just ask the Help function a specific question and then select a relevant topic for the answer.

To use the Help function, do the following:

- Select the **Help** button.
  The **PowerPoint Help** window opens.
- Select a link to a relevant topic.
  A further set of links will appear that correspond with the selected topic.
- Select a relevant link to refine your search.
- Read the information on the chosen topic.
- Use the **Back** button to go back a step or the **Home** button to return to the first window of PowerPoint Help.

Select a topic

Read the information on the chosen topic

- Click **Print** to print a copy of the topic information.

You can also enter specific search criteria into the **Search** box to locate information on specific topics.

To enter search criteria, do the following:
- Enter a question in the **Search** box and click **Search**.
- A list of topic links relating to the search criteria will appear. Click a link to view the topic information.

Enter the search words and click **Search**

A list of topics corresponding to the search criteria will be displayed

Click **Close X** to close the window when finished

Click **Next** to move through the pages or click the page numbers

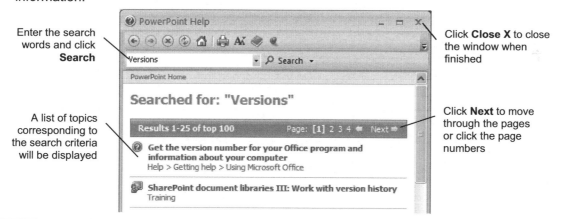

NOTE
Press the **F1** key to display the **PowerPoint Help** window.

1.2.3 Using Magnification (Zoom) (6.1.2.3)
The magnification tools are used to zoom in and out in a presentation.

To use the magification tools, do the following:
- Select the **View** tab from the ribbon.
- In the **Zoom** group, click **Zoom**.
  The **Zoom** window opens.

- Select **Fit** to ensure that the slide will fit the window.

- Select an option button to change the view percentage or use the scroll wheels to increase or decrease the percentage in the **Percent** box.

- Click **OK**.

Select a Zoom to: option button or use the scroll arrows to increase or decrease the percentage

Alternatively, Select the **Zoom Out** button to reduce the view. Select the **Zoom In** button to enlarge the view.

Alternatively, drag the slider towards the Zoom Out or Zoom In buttons to decrease/increase the view.

Zoom Out

Zoom In

Fit slide to current window

Slider

1.2.4 Minimising and Restoring the Ribbon (6.1.2.4)

The ribbon can be minimised and then restored as required.

To minimise or restore the ribbon, do the following:

Minimising the Ribbon

- Right-click the ribbon bar.

- Select **Minimize the Ribbon**.

  The ribbon is hidden and only the tab headers are visible.

Restoring the Ribbon

- Right-click the bar containing the tabs.

- Click **Minimize the Ribbon** (note how a tick is displayed beside the menu command to indicate that it is active).

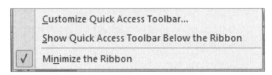

PRACTICE SEQUENCE

1   Open PowerPoint and create a new presentation.

2   Save this presentation as **sale** in the default presentation format.

3   Save another copy of the presentation in **RTF/Outline** format with the filename **saleRTF**.

4   Reopen **Sale** and practise switching between the two presentations.

5   Zoom the **Sale** presentation to **80%** and save.

6   Use the **Help** function to find information on saving a presentation as a template.

7   Close all presentations and exit PowerPoint.

Section 2   Developing a Presentation

A presentation is developed in Normal View. When all slides have been added to the presentation they can be viewed in Slide Sorter view, which will display all slides as thumbnails, or viewed as outline displaying the titles on each slide. It is important that all slides have appropriate titles so that they are distinguishable in outline view. It also helps to have recognisable titles when navigating a presentation in Slide Show view.

2.1   Presentation Views

A presentation can be displayed in a variety of views: Normal, Slide Sorter, Slide Show and Outline. Normal view is displayed as a single slide and is used to create and edit a slide, Slide Sorter view displays miniature, thumbnails of all slides, making it easier to delete and move slides, and Slide Show view is used to view the presentation as a slide show. Outline view displays the titles only, making it easier to view and move slides.

In this section, you will learn about the following:

- Understanding the use of different presentation view modes.
- Recognising good practice in using different titles for each slide to distinguish it in outline view and when navigating in slide show view.
- Changing the presentation view modes.

2.1.1   View Modes (6.2.1.1 and 6.2.1.3)

To change a presentation to Normal, Slide Sorter or Slide Show view modes, do the following:

- Select the **View** tab.
- Select a view mode, such as **Normal**, **Slide Sorter** or **Slide Show**.

Normal View

Normal View enables the user to view an individual slide. The slide can be viewed with different magnification by zooming in or out using the Zoom buttons at the bottom of the screen. This view enables editing and formatting to be carried out on a single slide.

Slide Sorter View

Slide Sorter View enables the user to view all of the slides as thumbnails (miniature slides). This view is used to apply effects or timings to all slides. This view is also useful if you want to move slides to a different position.

Slide Show View

Slide Show View enables the user to view all of the slides as a slide show. In this view, you can navigate the slide show and pause or end the slide show.

To navigate a slide show, do the following:

- Select the **View** tab and **Slide Show**.
- Right-click the slide and a sub-menu will appear displaying options to move onto the next slide or enabling you to choose a specific slide.
- To move to the next slide, click **Next**.
- To select a specific slide, click **Go to Slide** and choose a slide from the list.
- To end the show, click **End Show**.

Outline View

To select Outline view, do the following:

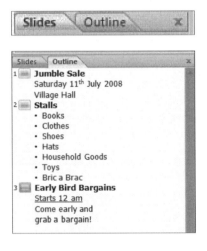

- Selecting **Normal** from the **View** tab.
- Click the **Outline** tab.

  This view will only display the titles and text in each slide, with no the graphical content. This view makes it easier to see the slide content at a glance and to edit the content on each slide. It is also easier to move slides to a different position using this view (more on moving slides later).

> **NOTE**
> The view mode of a presentation can also be changed quickly using the view buttons at the bottom right of the screen.
>
>
>
> Normal View　　Slide Sorter View　　Slide Show View

2.1.2　Slide Titles (6.2.1.2)

It is good practice to use different titles for each slide to distinguish them in Outline view and when navigating a slide show. For example, the following slides display bad practice and would be hard to distinguish when navigating a slide show.

Jumble Sale

Saturday
11 July 2008
Village Hall

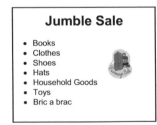

Jumble Sale

- Books
- Clothes
- Shoes
- Hats
- Household Goods
- Toys
- Bric a brac

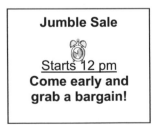

Jumble Sale

Starts 12 pm
**Come early and
grab a bargain!**

When navigating these slides in a slide show, it would be difficult to distinguish between each slide as they would appear with the same title.

To ensure that each slide is easily distinguishable, use appropriate titles for each slide.

When navigating a slide show it is easier to identify slides by their titles if they are relevant to each slide

PRACTICE SEQUENCE

1   Open PowerPoint and then open the **skills** presentation.

2   View the presentation in **Slide Sorter View**.

3   View the presentation in **Outline View**.

4   View the presentation in **Slide Show View** and navigate the show using the **Go to slide** sub-menu:

- Go to slide 3.
- Go to slide 5.
- Go to last viewed slide.
- Go to next slide.

5   Pause the slide show.

6   Resume the show and go to slide 9.

7   End the show.

8   View the presentation in **Standard View**.

9   Close the **skills** presentation.

2.2   Slides

Slides can be formatted with different slide layouts, background colour or design. Slides can be copied and moved within and between presentations.

In this section, you will learn about the following:

- Choosing different slide layouts for a slide.
- Applying design templates to a presentation.
- Changing the background colour on specific slide(s).
- Adding a new slide with a specific slide layout.
- Copying and moving slides in and between presentations.
- Deleting slide(s).

2.2.1 Slide Layouts (6.2.2.1)

The default slide layout in a new presentation is the **Title Slide** layout. This layout can be changed depending on the type of slide layout required. For example, you may want to create a slide to hold a title along with a graphic object, such as a picture or chart. For this you would select the **Title and Content** slide layout.

To change the layout of a slide, do the following:

- Select the **Home** tab from the ribbon.
- Select the **Layout** button.
- Select the required slide layout to match its content.
- The slide layout will be applied to the selected slide.

NOTE

The default slide content for a slide in a new presentation is the **Title Slide**. Subsequent new slides will be inserted with the **Title and Content** slide layout, unless another layout is chosen from the **New Slide** menu.

2.2.2 Applying a Theme (Design Template) (6.2.2.2)

A **theme** is a slide or set of slides that has been formatted with background colour, layout and theme fonts, and then saved as a theme. This theme can be applied to another presentation so that it displays the same formatting. In Office 2007, designs can be applied to a presentation by using a template that uses a customised theme. Themes can be customised to display different colours, fonts and effects and then saved as a custom theme or you can choose from various built-in themes that are available through the **Themes** command in the **Design** tab.

Standard content, such as the title, logo, text and background formatting are all applied to the template – this template can be used repeatedly with content, such as name and date being added to the slide as required

NOTE

Themes have replaced **design templates** used in previous versions of PowerPoint.

Applying a Built-In Theme

To apply a theme to a presentation, do the following:

- Open the presentation.
- Select the **Design** tab in the ribbon.
- The **Themes** group displays the built-in themes available for use with the current presentation. Move the mouse over a theme to see a preview of it applied to the current slide.

These are built-in themes which can be applied to your presentation – move the mouse over a theme to see how it will look when applied

Use the arrows to see more built-in themes or to open the drop-down menu

- The **Themes** menu displays the theme that is applied to the current presentation. The built-in themes are also displayed. More themes can be accessed by selecting **More Themes on Microsoft Office Online**.

Select **Browse for Themes** to find themes or templates with a .potx extension which are stored on your computer

Click **Save Current Theme** to save a customised theme on your computer

Select a built-in theme

- The default theme is the **Office Theme**.
- Select a theme from the **Built-in** section of the menu.

Customising a Theme

The fonts, colours and lines/fill effects can all be changed to customise a theme.

To customise an existing built-in theme, do the following:

- Customise the theme by selecting formatting commands from the **Colors**, **Fonts** and **Effects** menus. The theme colours and fonts are indicated by the bar of colour and the lettering (Aa) on the **Theme** command.

Select a colour scheme or **Create New Theme Colors**

Select a font scheme or **Create New Theme Fonts**

Select a built-in effect

- Click the **Colors** arrow.

  The theme colours currently applied to this theme are indicated by an outline around the menu command.

The theme colours for **Aspect** are highlighted

Theme colours consist of four text and background colours, six accent colours and two hyperlink colours.

To create a new theme colour, do the following:

- Select the **Colors** arrow.

- Click **Create New Theme Colors**.

- The **Create New Theme Colors** window opens.

- Choose the colours for the different elements of the theme and then enter a name for the new theme colour.

- Click **Save**.

  The theme currently applied to your slide displays the new theme colours.

Choose colours for the different elements of the theme

- Click the **Colors** arrow in the **Theme** group to see your custom colour.

The new theme colours are displayed in the **Colors** menu with the saved file name

---

NOTE

To return all theme elements to the original theme colours, select the **Reset** button and then **Save**.

To create New Theme Fonts, do the following:

- Select the **Fonts** arrow.
- Click **Create New Theme Fonts**.

The theme fonts currently applied to this theme is highlighted in the menu.

In this example, the chosen theme uses Verdana theme fonts

- To create new theme fonts, select the **Fonts** arrow and then click **Create New Theme Fonts**.
- Choose the fonts for headings and body text and then enter a name for the new theme font.
- Click the **Save** button.

Choose fonts for the heading and body text

Enter a name for the new theme fonts

A preview of the new theme fonts is provided in the sample box

Click **Save**

- Click the **Fonts** arrow in the **Theme** group to see your custom fonts.

The new theme fonts are displayed in the **Fonts** menu with the saved file name

Theme effects consist of sets of lines and fill effects. To apply an effect, click the **Effects** button and then select an effect.

- The theme effects applied to the current theme is highlighted in the menu.

The chosen theme uses **Aspect Effects**

Saving a Theme

To save a customised theme, do the following:

More button

- In the **Themes** group on the ribbon, click the **More** button.
- Select **Save Current Theme**.

The new theme will save in the **Document Themes** folder.

If you want to save the theme in a different location, do the following:
- Click the **Save in** arrow and select a drive and/or folder in which to save the theme.
- Enter a name in the **File Name** box.

The **Save as type** box will display the file extension associated with themes – Office Theme (*.thmx). If you want to save the theme with a different file type (such as a template (*.potx)), click the **Save as type** arrow and choose a file format.

- Click **Save**.

- Click the **More** button in the **Themes** group to see the customised theme.

NOTE

Click the **All Themes** arrow in the **Themes** menu to change how you view the menu items. You can choose to see all themes, themes only in the current presentation, custom themes which you have created or built-in themes.

Applying a Saved Theme to a Presentation

To apply a theme that is stored on a drive on your computer, do the following:

- On the **Design** tab, in the **Themes** group, click the **More** button.
- Select **Browse for Themes**.
- Select a drive and/or folder from the **Look in** menu.
- Select the theme and then click **Apply** (or double-click the theme to apply it).

2.2.3 Background Colour (6.2.2.3)

The background of a slide can consist of solid colour, gradient colour (using more than one colour), texture or picture. Background colour can be applied to one slide or all slides in a presentation.

To change the background colour, do the following:

- On the **Design** tab, in the **Background** group, click the **Background Styles** arrow.
- Select a colour from the menu or click **Format Background** to see the **Format Background** window.

  The **Format Background** window opens.
- Click the **Solid Fill** option button.
- Click the **Color** arrow.
- Choose a colour from the menu, or click **More Colors**.

Select **Solid Fill** to apply solid background colour

Click the **Color** arrow and then choose a colour

You can also apply gradient, texture or picture fill from this window

Click **More Colors** to see the colour palette

- When **More Colors** is selected, the **Colors** window opens.
- From the **Standard** tab, select shades of different colours or click the **Custom** tab to mix colours together to create a custom colour.

Select a shade...

...or mix colours for a custom shade

- Click **OK**.
- Click **Close** to apply the background colour to the current slide only or click **Apply to All** to apply the background to all slides in the presentation.

NOTE

To return the background to the original background colour, click the **Reset Background** button before you click **Close**. Gradient, texture and picture fills can all be applied from the **Format Background** window.

2.2.4 Adding a New Slide (6.2.2.4)

To add a new slide to a presentation, do the following:

- Select the **Home** tab and then, from the **Slides** group, click the **New Slide** arrow.
- Choose a slide layout to match the intended slide content.

New Slide button

Layout arrow

The two most commonly used slide layouts are **Title Slide** and **Title and Content**.

Title Slide provides placeholders (frames) for a heading and a subheading, **Title and Content** provides a title frame and also a frame to hold bulleted text, tables, spreadsheets and graphical data, such as images and charts

Title Slide

- Select the **Title Slide** layout.

  The slide layout provides a placeholder (frame) for the heading and also a placeholder to hold a subtitle.

- To add a title, click into the placeholder and type the title text. Repeat this to add a subtitle to the subtitle placeholder

Click in the **Click to add title** placeholder and type the title text

Click to add title

Click to add subtitle

Title and Content Slide

- Select the **New Slide** arrow and choose the **Title and Content** slide layout.
- Add a title and then click into the second placeholder to add bulleted text or select one of the content icons.

  When the mouse is moved over an icon, a tag appears, describing its function.

- Double-click an icon to add content and follow the instructions, e.g. enter number of rows and columns for a table.

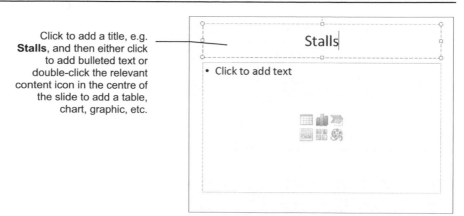

Click to add a title, e.g. **Stalls**, and then either click to add bulleted text or double-click the relevant content icon in the centre of the slide to add a table, chart, graphic, etc.

Bullets

Bullets are used to define lists of information.

To add bulleted text to a slide, do the following:
- Click into the placeholder beside **Click to add text**.
- Enter the text – this will be displayed with the default bullet style.
- Press the **Enter** key to add another line of text – this will also display with a bullet.
- Repeat to add further text to the bulleted list.

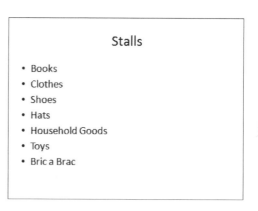

Tables

A table is used to display information in tabular format, i.e. in columns and rows. The intersection of a column and a row is called a cell.

To add a table to a slide, do the following:
- Click inside the placeholder on the slide where the table is to be positioned, e.g. the **Content** section of a **Title and Content** slide.
- Click the **Insert Table** button on the ribbon and select **Insert Table** from the drop-down menu.
  The **Insert Table** window opens.
- Select the number of columns/rows that are required.
- Click **OK**.
  The table appears on the slide.

The **Table Tools** contextual tab appears on the ribbon, holding the **Design** and **Layout** tabs which provide more tools for creating and formatting tables.
- From the **Design** tab, and in the **Table Styles** group, click the **More** button.
- Choose a table style.

Click the **More** button

Move the cursor over the styles to see a tag.

Click the required style to apply it to the table

- Enter text into the first cell of the table.
- Press the **Tab** key on the keyboard to move to the next cell.

NOTE

Pressing the **Tab** key at the end of the final row will insert a new row.

Press the **Shift** and **Tab** key to move to the previous cell in a table.

Helpers

Jane Roberts	Sales
Claire Brennan	Sales
Mary O'Connell	Refreshments
Bill Tyler	Parking
Jack Mason	Parking
Deirdre Brown	Refreshments
Anne Donnelly	Sales
Carrie Bourne	Sales
John Brett	Sales
Dylan Jones	Sales
Cerys Hughes	Sales
Mandy Parker	Sales

Charts

A chart is used to display information in graphical format, i.e. in bars/columns or segments or lines.

To add a chart to a slide, do the following:

- Click inside the placeholder on the slide where the table is to be positioned, e.g. the **Content** section of a **Title and Content** slide.
- Click the **Insert Chart** button on the ribbon.

  The **Insert Chart** window opens.

- Select the type of chart that you want (i.e. column, line, pie).
- Click **OK**.

  The window splits into two sections; one side displays the slide with chart and the second side displays a spreadsheet. The information that you enter into the spreadsheet will create the chart.

Insert Chart button

Note how the contextual **Chart Tools** tab appears on the ribbon, with **Design, Layout** and **Formatting** tabs containing more tools for creating and formatting charts.

- Add the data to the spreadsheet.
- Click **Close X**, in the top-right corner to close the spreadsheet.

6

- The chart will display the data that was entered in the spreadsheet.

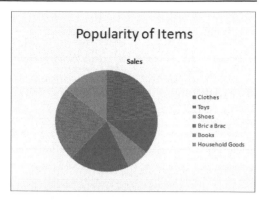

- Data labels and titles can be added to the chart (see sections 4.1.4 and 4.1.5).

NOTE

To display a chart and text on the same slide, click the **Layout** arrow and select the **Two Content** layout from the drop-down list of options. Click inside the required placeholder before inserting the chart and text.

2.2.5 Copying and Moving Slides (6.2.2.5)

Slides can be copied or moved within a presentation or between open presentations.

To copy and move slides, do the following:

In the Same Presentation

- Select the **View** tab and then click **Slide Sorter** from the **Presentation Views** group.
  This view will display all of the slides in the presentation in thumbnail view.

To **copy** a slide, do the following:

- Select the slide and then, from the **Home** tab, select **Copy** from the **Clipboard** group.
- Select the slide that appears *before* the required position and then click **Paste** (slides will be pasted in position *after* the selected slide).
  The duplicated slide will appear in the new position.

To **move** a slide, do the following:

- Select the slide and then, from the **Home** tab, select **Cut** from the **Clipboard** group.
- Select the slide that appears *before* the required position and then click **Paste** (slides will be pasted in position *after* the selected slide).
  The moved slide will appear in the new position.
  Alternatively, use the **Drag and Drop** method of copying and moving slides by dragging the slide to the new position using the mouse. As you drag the slide observe the black vertical line that moves with it. This line should be placed in the required position before releasing the mouse button. To copy, hold down the **CTRL** key whilst dragging to the new position.

Between Open Presentations

- Open the required presentation files. Both files will be displayed as tabs on the taskbar at the bottom of the screen.
- Ensure that the presentation containing the slides to be copied, is the active presentation.
- Select the **View** tab and then click **Slide Sorter** from the **Presentation Views** group.
  This view will display all of the slides in the presentation in thumbnail view.

To **copy** a slide, do the following:

- Select the slide and then, from the **Home** tab, click **Copy** from the **Clipboard** group.
- Click the other presentation on the taskbar or select the **View** tab and **Switch Windows**. Choose the other presentation from the list.
- Ensure that you are viewing this presentation in Slide Sorter View.
- Click the mouse in the required position of the copied slide (a vertical line appears where you click) or click the slide that appears *before* the required position.
- From the **Home** tab, in the **Clipboard** group, click **Paste**.
  The slide will be duplicated in the selected position within the presentation.

To **move** a slide to another presentation, do the following:

- Select the slide and then, from the **Home** tab, click **Cut** from the **Clipboard** group.
- Click the other presentation on the taskbar or select the **View** tab and **Switch Windows**.
- Choose the other presentation from the list.
- Ensure that you are viewing this presentation in Slide Sorter View.
- Click the cursor in the required position of the copied slide (a vertical line appears where you click) or click the slide that appears *before* the required position.
- From the **Home** tab, in the **Clipboard** group, click **Paste**.
  The slide will be moved to the selected position within the presentation.

NOTE

If you want to copy or move more than one slide, select the first slide and then, holding down the **CTRL** key, click the other slides to copied/moved.

The keyboard shortcuts are **CTRL** + **C** to copy, **CTRL** + **X** to cut and **CTRL** + **V** to paste.

2.2.6 Deleting Slides (6.2.2.6)

Selected slides can be deleted within a presentation when they are no longer required.

To delete slides, do the following:

- Select the slide to be deleted (you can do this in Normal, Slide Sorter or Outline view).
- From the **Home** tab, in the **Slides** group, select the **Delete** button.
  The selected slide will be deleted.

NOTE

You can also press the **Delete** key on the keyboard to delete a selected slide.

PRACTICE SEQUENCE

1   Open PowerPoint and the presentation called **sale**.

2   Ensure that the first slide has the **Title Slide** layout and enter the following title: **Jumble Sale**.

3   Enter the subtitle: **Saturday 11th July 2008** on one line and **Village Hall** on a separate line.

4   Create a new slide with the **Title and Content** slide layout and enter the title: **Stalls**.

5   Add the following bulleted text to the slide:
- Books
- Clothes
- Shoes
- Hats
- Household Goods
- Toys
- Bric a Brac

6   Create a new slide with **Title Slide** layout and the title: **Early Bird Bargains**.

7   Enter the subtitle: **Starts 12pm** on one line and **Come early and grab a bargain!** on a separate line.

8   Create a new slide with the **Title and Content** slide layout. Add the title: **Helpers**. Create a table with **9 rows/2 columns**. Add the data below into the table:

Jane Roberts	Sales
Claire Brennan	Sales
Mary O'Connell	Refreshments
Bill Tyler	Parking
Jack Mason	Parking
Deirdre Brown	Refreshments
Carrie Bourne	Sales
Dylan Jones	Sales
Cerys Hughes	Sales

9   Create a new slide with **Title and Content Slide** layout and the title: **Popularity of Items**.

10   Create a pie chart with the following data:

Clothes	10
Toys	5
Shoes	3
Bric a Brac	8
Books	10
Household Goods	6

11   Apply the design template called **blue.potx** to the presentation.

12   Change the background of slide 5 to a light blue solid colour.

13   Copy slide 2 so that the duplicate slide appears before slide 5 (the chart).

14   Move slide 4 so that it is the last slide in the presentation.

15   Delete the duplicated slide (now slide 4). Save the presentation and keep open for the next step.

16   Open a new presentation and copy slides 2 and 5 into it.

17   Save this presentation as **manage** and close.

18   Save and close the **sale** presentation.

2.3 Master Slides

To ensure consistency throughout your presentation, it is advisable to create a master slide, containing standard content and formatting. A presentation can be produced by creating individual slides and applying formatting directly onto each slide. This can be time consuming if the presentation contains numerous slides and a more time effective method is to apply formatting and standard slide content once to a master slide.

In this section, you will learn about the following:

- Inserting a graphical object (picture, image, drawn object) onto a master slide.
- Removing a graphical object from the master slide.
- Entering text into the footer of specific slides and all slides in the presentation.
- Applying automatic slide numbering.
- Applying an automatically updated date and a non-updating date into the footer of specific slides and all slides in a presentation.

2.3.1 Creating a Master Slide

To create a master slide, do the following:

- Select the **View** tab and then, in the **Presentation Views** group, click the **Slide Master** button.
- The master slide opens.

2.3.2 Inserting a Graphical Object into a Master Slide (6.2.3.1)

A graphical object refers to a picture, image or drawn object. If inserted onto a master slide, the graphical object will appear on all slides based on the slide master.

To insert a graphical object onto the master slide, do the following:

- Ensure that **Slide Master** view is selected.
- Select **Slide 1** (the **Master Layout** slide).
- Select the **Insert** tab.
- From the **Illustrations** group, click **Picture**.

  The **Insert Picture** window opens.

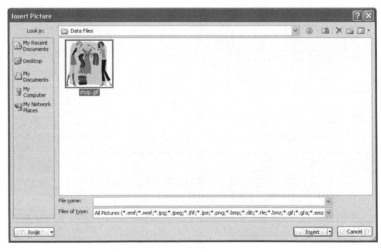

- Click the **Look in** arrow and choose a drive and/or folder.
- Select the picture file.
- Click **Insert**.
- Drag the picture to the required position on the slide.

Resizing a Graphical Object

The picture or drawn object may need to be resized so that it does not overlap text or other items on the slide. It is important that the original proportions of the object are maintained whilst resizing.

To resize a graphical object, do the following:
- Select the object – the object is surrounded by resizing handles.
- Position the mouse arrow over a corner handle (resizing from a corner handle will maintain the original proportions) and then drag in the required direction to either increase or decrease the size of the object.

Resize handles

2.3.3 Deleting a Graphical Object from a Master Slide (6.2.3.1)

Deleting an object from the master slide will also remove it from any slides that are based on the slide master.

To delete a graphical object from the master slide, do the following:
- Select the graphical object.
- Press the **Delete** key on the keyboard.

2.3.4 Inserting a Footer (6.2.3.2)

A footer is an item of data that appears at the bottom of each slide that is based on the master slide. A footer may consist of a company name, the presenter's name or subject specific title.

To insert a footer on the master slide, do the following:
- Ensure that **Slide Master View** is selected.
- From the **Insert** tab, and the **Text** group, select **Header & Footer**.

The **Header and Footer** window opens.

Enter the footer text

Select **Apply to All** to apply the footer to all slides

Select **Apply** to apply the footer to the current slide only

- Click the **Footer** checkbox to add a tick.
- Enter the text that you want to appear in the footer of each slide.
- Ensure that the **Don't show on title slide** tick box is unchecked if you want the footer to appear on all slides, regardless of slide layout.
- Select **Apply to All** to apply the footer to all slides in the presentation or **Apply** to apply the footer to only the current slide.

2.3.5 Inserting Automatic Fields (6.2.3.3)

Automatic fields are items, such as dates and slide numbers, that update automatically. Some fields, such as fixed dates, do not update.

To insert an automatic field on the master slide, do the following:

Slide Numbering

- Ensure that **Slide Master View** is selected.
- From the **Insert** tab, and the **Text** group, select **Slide Number**.

- Select the **Slide Number** checkbox (to add a tick in the box).
- Ensure that the **Don't show on title slide** tick box is unchecked if you want the slide numbers to appear on all slides, regardless of slide layout.
- Select **Apply to All** to apply the slide number to all slides in the presentation or **Apply** to apply a slide number to only the current slide.

Automatically Updated Dates

- Ensure that **Slide Master View** is selected.
- From the **Insert** tab, and the **Text** group, select **Date & Time**.
- Select the **Date and Time** checkbox (to add a tick in the box).
  The **Update automatically** option button should be selected by default.
- Choose a date format from the drop-down list.
- Choose a language by selecting the **Language** arrow and choosing from the list.
- Ensure that the **Don't show on title slide** tick box is unchecked if you want the footer to appear on all slides, regardless of slide layout.

Select a date format and language

- Select **Apply to All** to apply an automatically updating date field to all slides in the presentation or **Apply** to apply a date to the current slide only.

Fixed Dates

- Ensure that **Slide Master View** is selected.
- From the **Insert** tab, and the **Text** group, select **Date & Time**.
- Select the **Date and Time** checkbox (to add a tick in the box).
- Select the **Fixed** option button. This ensures that the date is fixed and will not update when the presentation is reopened on another date.

- The current date will appear in the **Fixed** box.
- Ensure that the **Don't show on title slide** tick box is unchecked if you want the footer to appear on all slides, regardless of slide layout.
- Select **Apply to All** to apply an automatically updating date field to all slides in the presentation or Apply to apply a date to the current slide only.

NOTE

If you want to change the format of the date, delete the date in the **Fixed** box by inserting the cursor to the right of the date and pressing the Backspace key until the date has been deleted. Type the date in the **Fixed** box as you want it to appear on the slide.

2.3.6 Closing the Slide Master

To close the Slide Master, do the following:

- From the **Slide Master** tab, click the **Close Master View** button.
- Ensure that the presentation is saved.

PRACTICE SEQUENCE

1   Open the **sale** presentation.

2   Open the master slide and insert the image **shop.gif**. Position this image in the top right corner of the slide. To ensure that it will not obscure or overlap any other slide items, resize the image.

3   Insert a footer that will appear on every slide in the presentation with your name.

4   Insert an automatically updating date to appear on every slide.

5   Insert slide numbers to appear on every slide in the presentation.

6   Close the master slide and save the presentation with the same name.

7   Close all open presentations.

6

Section 3   Text

When entering text into a presentation, it is good practice to use short concise phrases, bullet points and numbered lists to display data. Bulleted and numbered lists can be indented and line spacing altered to enhance clarity. Text can be entered and edited within a *placeholder* (frame) in either standard or outline view. Editing text consists of deleting, adding and amending text. If you make a mistake whilst entering or editing text, the undo/redo functions enable the user to undo or redo a previous action. Text entered into a placeholder, as a bulleted/numbered list or a table, can be formatted to display with different fonts, sizes, colour and styles and in different alignments, such as left, right and centre. Tables can be further formatted and edited to insert and delete rows and columns and modify row/column height and width. Text can be copied or moved within and between presentations.

3.1   Handling Text

A presentation should contain short concise sentences or text broken down into bulleted or numbered lists. A presentation containing too much text may appear too busy and lose the attention of the audience. Large amounts of information should be summarised into brief sentences or bulleted lists for the benefit of the audience.

In this section, you will learn about the following:

- Recognising good practice in creating slide content: using short concise phrases, bullet points and numbered lists.
- Entering text into a placeholder in standard and outline view.
- Editing text in a presentation.
- Copying and moving text within and between presentations.
- Deleting text.
- Using the undo and redo commands.

3.1.1   Slide Content (6.3.1.1)

Slide content may consist of text entered directly into a placeholder, in the form of titles, subtitles, phrases, bulleted or numbered lists, or entered into a table. The most important point to remember is that slide content should enable an audience to view and understand the information 'at a glance' without the need for reading large amounts of text. Text may be entered in Normal View in either Standard (Slide) or Outline View.

3.1.2   Entering Text in Standard View (6.3.1.2)

Text may be entered in Standard View (Slide View). This view enables the user to see each slide individually.

To enter text in Standard View, do the following:
- Select the **View** tab and then, from the **Presentation Views** group, select **Normal**.

- Ensure that the **Slides** tab is selected.   Slides
- Enter text into the relevant placeholder (frame to hold title or subtitle or bulleted lists).

3.1.3 Entering Text in Outline View (6.3.1.2)

Outline View gives an overview of all slides in the presentation and enables the user to see the titles, subtitles and text within each slide, without viewing the graphical content. This makes it easier to edit slide content.

To enter text in Outline View, do the following:

- Select the **Outline** tab.

  Existing slides will appear in the left hand pane, displaying text only.

- Click the mouse where you want to start typing and enter the required text.

3.1.4 Editing Text in a Presentation (6.3.1.3)

Text can be edited within Standard or Outline View.

To edit text, do the following:

- Position the cursor within the placeholder and then make the necessary adjustments.

  In the example on the right, the text is edited to include the town in the second line of the subtitle text.

3.1.5 Selecting Text

Text must be selected before it can be formatted, copied, cut or deleted. Multiple items of text can be selected, whether adjacent or non-adjacent.

To select text, do the following:

Single Item of Text

- Position the cursor in front of the text and, holding down the left mouse button, drag to highlight the text. The text will display highlighted in blue.

  Alternatively, position the cursor in the text to be selected and double-click the left mouse button.

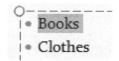

Multiple Adjacent Items of Text

- Select the first item of text and then drag to highlight further items of text on the slide.

Multiple Non-Adjacent Items of Text

- Select the first item of text and then, holding down the **CTRL** key, select further items of text on the slide.

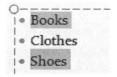

NOTE

Press **CTRL** + **A** to select all items within the selected placeholder.

Press **CTRL**, **SHIFT** + **END** to select all items from the current cursor position.

Hold down the **SHIFT** key and then press a directional arrow to select to the right, left, up or down.

NOTE

You can also select a **placeholder** to format or copy/move the text within it. This method will select all of the text existing within the placeholder. To select a placeholder, click it.

Alternatively, select the **Home** tab and then the **Select** command from the **Editing** group. Select **Selection Pane** and then click the relevant placeholder from the task pane.

To select all items on a slide, click the **Select** command and then click **Select All**.

3.1.6 Copying and Moving Text (6.3.1.4)

Text can be copied or moved within a presentation in Standard or Outline View. It can also be copied or moved between open presentations.

NOTE

The following keyboard shortcut keys can also be used.

Press **CTRL + C** to copy, **CTRL + X** to cut and **CTRL + V** to paste.

In the Same Presentation

- Select the **View** tab and then click **Normal** from the **Presentation Views** group.
- Text can be copied or moved using either Standard View or Outline View.

To copy text, do the following:

- Select the text to be copied and then, from the **Home** tab, click **Copy** from the **Clipboard** group.
- Select the destination slide (the slide to which the text is being copied) and position the cursor where the duplicated text is to be displayed.
- Click **Paste**.
  The duplicated text will appear in the new position.

To move text, do the following:

- Select the text to be copied and then, from the **Home** tab, click **Copy** followed by **Cut** from the **Clipboard** group.
- Select the destination slide (the slide to which the text is being copied) and then position the cursor where the duplicated text is to be displayed.
- Click **Paste**.
  The moved text will appear in the new position.
  Alternatively, use the **Drag and Drop** method of copying and moving text by dragging the text to the new position using the mouse (in Standard View if copying or moving within the same slide or Outline View if copying/moving between slides in the same presentation). As you drag the text, observe the vertical line that moves with it. This line should be placed in the required position before releasing the mouse button. To copy, hold down the **CTRL** key whilst dragging to the new position.

Between Open Presentations

- Open the required presentation files. Both files will be displayed as tabs on the taskbar at the bottom of the screen.
- Ensure that the presentation containing the text to be copied is the active presentation.

To copy text, do the following:

- Select the text.
- From the **Home** tab, click **Copy** from the **Clipboard** group.
- Click the destination presentation on the taskbar or select the **View** tab and **Switch Windows**. Choose the destination presentation from the list.
- Open the required slide in either Standard or Outline View.
- Click the mouse in the required position within the slide.
- From the **Home** tab, in the **Clipboard** group, click **Paste**.
  The text will be duplicated in the selected slide within the presentation.

To move text, do the following:

- Select the text.
- From the **Home** tab, click **Cut** from the **Clipboard** group.
- Click the destination presentation on the taskbar or select the **View** tab and **Switch Windows**. Choose the destination presentation from the list.
- Open the required slide in either Standard or Outline View.
- Click the mouse in the required position within the slide.
- From the **Home** tab, in the **Clipboard** group, click **Paste**.
  The text will be moved to the destination slide within the presentation.

NOTE

If you want to copy or move more than one item of text, select the first item of text and then, holding down the **CTRL** key, click the other items of text to be copied or moved.

To move an entire placeholder within a slide, click within the placeholder and then left-click its border. The cursor will change to a double cross. Holding down the mouse button, drag the placeholder to its new position.

3.1.7 Deleting Text (6.3.1.5)

Text can be deleted in either Standard or Outline View.

To delete text, do the following:
- Select the text to be deleted and then press the **Delete** key on the keyboard.

To delete one character at a time.
- Position the cursor in front of the character(s) to be deleted and press the **Delete** key (alternatively, position cursor behind the character(s) to be deleted and press the **Backspace** key on the keyboard).

To delete whole words without selecting text.
- Position the cursor in front of the word to be deleted and then, holding down the **CTRL** key, press **Delete** (or position cursor behind the word to be deleted and use **CTRL + Backspace**).

3.1.8 Undoing and Redoing (6.3.1.6)

If a mistake is made when entering, editing or deleting text, it can be corrected by using the undo button. To redo the action, the redo button can be used.

To use undo and redo, do the following:

- To undo an action, click the **Undo** button from the **Quick Access Toolbar**.
- To redo an action, click the **Redo** button from the **Quick Access Toolbar**.

To see a list of actions that have been made recently, do the following:
- Click the arrow and select an action from the list.

    Any actions that were completed before the selected action will also be undone.

NOTE

The **Redo** button displays as a repeat button, until the **Undo** button is utilised. When the Undo button is used, the Redo button becomes active.

Select the Undo arrow to see a list of actions

The Redo button displays as the Repeat button until the Undo command is used

---

NOTE

The following keyboard shortcut keys can also be used.

Press **CTRL + Z** to undo and **CTRL + Y** to redo.

PRACTICE SEQUENCE

1   Open the **sale** presentation and edit slide 1 by adding the name of the village **Barton-on-the-Wold** after the text **Village Hall**.

2   Move the text **Come early and grab a bargain** from slide 3 to slide 1 so that it appears beneath the existing subtitle text.

3   Open the presentation called **manage** and create a new slide with the **Title Slide** layout, with the title **Details**.

4   Switch to the **sale** presentation. Copy the text **Saturday 11th July 2008** from slide 1 of the **sale** presentation and paste it into slide 1 of the **manage** presentation so that it appears beneath the title.

5   Switch to the **sale** presentation. Copy the text **Starts 12am** from slide 3 so that it appears beneath the existing subtitle text on slide 1 of the **manage** presentation. Save the **manage** presentation and close.

6   On slide 2 delete the text **Bric a Brac** from the bulleted list.

7   Practise using the **Undo** command to return the text **Bric a Brac** to the bulleted list.

8   Save and close the **sale** presentation.

3.2   Text Formatting

Text formatting includes fonts, sizes, styles, colours, case and alignment. It is good practice to have consistent fonts and styles throughout a presentation; too many different formatting features, such as fonts, sizes and colours can detract from the presentation and appear unprofessional.

In this section, you will learn about the following:

* Changing text formatting: font sizes and font types.
* Applying text formatting: bold, italic, underline and shadow.
* Applying different colours to text.
* Applying case changes to text.
* Aligning text: left, centre and right in a text frame.

3.2.1   Font Types (6.3.2.1)

Font types determine how the type face displays. Fonts can be *serif* or *sans serif.* A serif font is a font with 'tails' on the character.

Times New Roman   This is a serif font – the 'tails' are most apparent on the T and the N.

A sans serif font is a plain unadorned font without 'tails' on the character.

ARIAL   This is a sans serif font – this font is plain and without 'tails'.

There are many serif and sans serif fonts available for use.

To apply font types, do the following:

* Select the text to be changed.
* From the **Home** tab, click the **Font** arrow in the **Font** group.
* Choose a font from the list.

The **Font** arrow

> **NOTE**
> As the mouse is hovered over the font types, the selected text displays the font type. Click to make the selection.

3.2.2   Font Sizes (6.3.2.1)

Font sizes determine how big or small the text appears and should vary for different slide elements. For example, titles should be displayed in a larger font size than subtitles which, in turn, should be a larger font size than bulleted list text or phrases. Font sizes should be consistent throughout the presentation to enhance clarity and provide a professional appearance, i.e. all titles should be the same size.

To change the font size, do the following:

* Select the text to be changed.
* From the **Home** tab, click the **Size** arrow in the **Font** group.
* Choose a size from the list.

The **Size** arrow

> **NOTE**
> As the mouse is hovered over the sizes, the highlighted text displays the currently selected size. Click to make the selection.

6

3.2.3 Font Styles (6.3.2.2)

Font styles can be used to enhance specific items of text within a slide. For example, you may wish to make a certain word stand out by making it **bold**, <u>underlining it</u>, or applying *italic* or shadow to it. Font styles should be used sparingly and be consistent throughout the presentation to enhance clarity and provide a professional appearance.

To change the font style, do the following:

- Select the text to be changed.

- From the **Home** tab, click the required style in the **Font** group.

3.2.4 Font Colour (6.3.2.3)

Font colour can be used to enhance specific items of text within a slide. Font colour should be used sparingly and be consistent throughout the presentation to enhance clarity and provide a professional appearance.

To change the font colour, do the following:

- Select the text to be changed.

- From the **Home** tab, click the **Font Color** arrow in the **Font** group.

  The menu will display the font colours used in the currently applied theme and also the standard colours.

- Select a colour from the menu or choose **More Colors** to see the colour palette.

The **Colors** window opens when **More Colors** is selected.

- From the **Standard** tab, select a colour.

- Click **OK**.

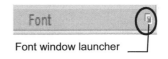

  Alternatively, fonts, sizes, styles and colours can all be applied from the Font window. To open this window, select the Font window launcher in the **Home** tab.

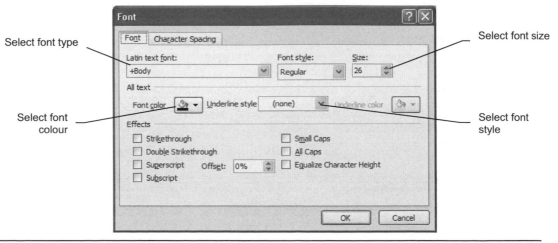

NOTE

Press **CTRL + T** to open the **Font** window.

3.2.5 Changing Text Case (6.3.2.4)

The term **case** refers to the capitalisation of characters. Text can be displayed in lower, upper or sentence case or you can choose to capitalise each word. Another feature is the Toggle case command which displays sentence case in reverse, with the initial letter of a sentence in lower case and the rest in upper case.

See the examples below.

- this is in lower case.

- This is in sentence case (initial character of each new sentence will appear in upper case).

- THIS IS IN UPPER CASE.

- Each Word Is Capitalized.

- tHIS IS TOGGLE CASE (initial character of each new sentence will appear in lower case).

To change the case of text, do the following:

Change case arrow

- Select the text to be changed.

- From the **Home** tab, click the **Change Case** arrow in the **Font** group.

- Select A CASE FROM THE LIST.

NOTE

To 'cycle' through lower, upper and sentence cases using the keyboard hold down the **Shift** key and press **F3**.

3.2.6 Aligning Text (6.3.2.5)

Text can be aligned so that it is displayed on the left, right or centre of the slide.

See the examples below.

This text is left aligned.

This text is centred.

This text is right aligned.

This text is justified which provides a straight edge to both the left and right margins. Justification is only apparent on more than one line of text. The text is stretched so that it matches the line endings of other text in the paragraph.

6

To align text, do the following:

- Select the text to be aligned.

- From the **Paragraph** tab, click the required alignment button.

Left _____   _____ Justify

Centre _____   _____ Right

Alternatively, alignment can be   ed from the **Paragrap**   dow. To open this window, select the Paragraph window launcher in the **Home** tab.

Paragraph

Paragraph window launcher

Select the **Alignment** arrow and choose an alignment from the list

---

NOTE

To change alignment using the keyboard, hold down the **CTRL** key + the following:

L = Left   **R** = Right

E = Centre   **J** = Justify

PRACTICE SEQUENCE

1   Open the **sale** presentation.

2   Format the bulleted list on slide 2 to be **Arial 28**.

3   Apply shadow to the bullet text on slide 2.

4   On slide 1, format the text **Come early and grab a bargain!** to display as bold and italics and with a dark blue font colour.

5   Change the text **Starts 12 pm** on slide 3 so that it displays in upper case and format with an underline.

6   Change the alignment of the tabular data on slide 5 so that it displays in both columns with **Centre** alignment.

7   Save and close the **sale** presentation.

3.3   Bullet and Number Lists

Lists are bulleted or numbered ordered items of text. Bullets and numbers can be formatted to appear with a different symbol/number style and be indented by a specific measurement from the edge of the placeholder. Lists can also be enhanced by increasing or decreasing the line spacing between each line of text.

In this section, you will learn about the following:
- Indenting bulleted text.
- Removing bulleted text.
- Adjusting the line spacing before and after bulleted and numbered lists.
- Switching between different standard bullet and number styles in a list.

3.3.1 Applying and Removing Indents (6.3.3.1)

The default indentation between a bullet and text, using the **Title and Content** layout with the standard Office theme, for a newly inserted bullet is 0.95cm. This can be altered to suit your presentation. Indentation can also be applied to the bullet or number itself so that it displays at a specific measurement from the edge of the placeholder.

To apply and remove indentation from a bulleted list, do the following:
- Select the bulleted/numbered list.
- Click the **Paragraph** window launcher icon. The **Paragraph** window opens.
- Using the **Before text** scroll arrows, select a measurement for the indentation **between** the bullet and text.
- Select the **Special** arrow and choose **Hanging** so that lines of text will indent beneath each other.
- Select the **By** scroll arrows to increase or decrease the measurement (the hanging indent should match the **Before text** indent).
- Click **OK**.

To remove indents, do the following:
- Open the **Paragraph** window.
- Decrease the indent measurements to **0cm**.

Alternatively, in the Paragraph group of the Home tab:
- o Click the Increase List Level button to increase the indent.
- o Click the Decrease List Level button to decrease the indent.
- o Use the Ruler Bar to drag the indent markers to the required measurement.

First line indent

Hanging indent

3.3.2 Adjusting Line Spacing (6.3.3.2)

Line spacing refers to the space before, after or between bulleted lines of text. The default line spacing between lines of text using the standard Office theme is **single**.

To adjust line spacing in a list, do the following:
- Select the bulleted/numbered list to be adjusted.
- Click the **Paragraph** window launcher icon.

The **Paragraph** window opens.

- In the **Spacing** section of the window, use the **Before** scroll arrow to select a measurement for the spacing *before* bulleted text.

- Use the After scroll arrow to repeat this to increase the spacing *after* bulleted text.

- Select the **Line Spacing** arrow and choose an option from the list to change the line spacing *between* lines of bulleted text. If the **Multiple Lines** or **Exactly** options are selected, the **At** list box becomes active to choose a measurement from.

- Click **OK**.

3.3.3 Bullets and Numbering Styles (6.3.3.3)

Bullet and numbering styles can be changed to display a different symbol or number style.

To change bullets and numbering styles, do the following:

Bullet Styles
- Select the bulleted list to be changed.
- Select the **Home** tab.
- Click the **Bullets** arrow in the **Paragraph** group.
- Select a bullet style from the menu or select **Bullets and Numbering** for more options.
- The **Bullets and Numbering** window provides more style options.
  - Click the **Color** arrow and select a different colour for the bullet.
  - Change the size of the bullet by a specified percentage of the text.
- Click **OK**.

Numbering Styles

- Select the numbered list.
- Select the **Home** tab.
- Click the **Numbering** arrow in the **Paragraph** group.
- Select a number style from the menu or select **Bullets and Numbering** for more options.
- The **Bullets and Numbering** window provides more style options. Ensure that the **Numbered** tab is selected.
    o Select a numbering style from the list.
    o Choose a different size for the numbers in relation to the text.
    o Click the **Color** button to change the colour of the numbers.
    o Select **Start at** to change the number sequence.
- Click **OK**.

Numbers arrow

Number size

Number styles

The **Start at** scroll arrows change the numbering sequence

The **Color** arrow makes more colours available

NOTE

The **Mini Toolbar** appears when text is selected. Formatting options such as font, sizes, styles, colour, alignment, indents and bullets can be accessed from this toolbar.

PRACTICE SEQUENCE

1   Open the **sale** presentation.

2   Format the bulleted list on slide 2 so that the text is indented from the bullet with a hanging indent of 1cm.

3   Format the bulleted list on slide 2 so that it displays with a square, pale blue bullet.

4   Format the bulleted list on slide 2 that it displays with **4.5 pt** spacing *before* the bulleted text.

5   Change the line spacing of the bulleted list on slide 2 to **1.5**.

6   Save and close the **sale** presentation.

3.4 Tables

A table displays text in tabular format, in rows and columns. The intersection between a row and a column is called a **cell**. Tables can be formatted to display with or without borders.

In this section, you will learn about the following:

- Entering and editing text in a table slide.
- Selecting rows, columns and an entire table.
- Inserting and deleting rows and columns.
- Modifying column width and row height.

3.4.1 Entering and Editing Text (6.3.4.1)

To enter text in a table, do the following:

- Create a new slide with the **Title and Content** layout.
- Double-click the **Insert Table** icon.
- Choose the number of rows and columns required for the table.
- Click **OK**.
- Enter a title for the slide.
- Position the cursor within the first cell of the table and enter text.
- Press the **Tab** key to jump to the next cell in the same row and enter text.
- Repeat to enter text into the relevant cells (pressing the **tab** key at the end of the final row creates a new row).

To edit text in a table, do the following:
- Position the cursor in the cell and delete/amend text as appropriate (see Section 3.1.4).

3.4.2 Selecting Rows, Columns and an Entire Table (6.3.4.2)
To select a table, or rows or columns in a table, do the following:

To select a row, do the following:
- Position the cursor so that it is pointing at the row. The cursor turns into a black arrow.
- Click to select the row.

To select a column, do the following:
- Position the cursor so that it is above the column. The cursor turns into a black arrow.
- Click to select the column.

To select an entire table, do the following:
- Position the cursor to the left of the first row to see the black arrow.
- Drag the mouse over the remaining rows.
  Alternatively, place the cursor in the table, row or column to be selected and, from the contextual **Table Tools** tab, select the **Layout** tab. Select the **Select** command and then choose **Row**, **Column** or **Table**.

> **NOTE**
> To select rows or columns using the keyboard, hold down the **Shift** key and use the directional arrow keys on the keyboard. To highlight the whole table, press **CTRL + A**.

3.4.3 Inserting and Deleting Rows and Columns in a Table (6.3.4.3)

To insert rows in a table, do the following:

- Select the row *below* or *above* the intended position of the new row.
- From the **Table Tools** tab and the **Layout** tab, click the **Insert Above** or the **Insert Below** command from the **Rows & Columns** group.

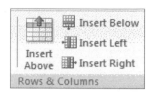

To insert rows in a table, do the following:

- Select a column to the **left** or **right** of the intended position of the new column.
- From the **Table Tools** tab and the **Layout** tab, click the **Insert Left** or the **Insert Right** command from the **Rows & Columns** group.

To delete rows and columns in a table, do the following:

- Select the row or column to be deleted.
- From the **Table Tools** tab and the **Layout** tab, click the **Delete** command from the **Rows & Columns** group.
- Select **Delete Columns** or **Delete Rows**.

3.4.4 Modifying Row Height and Column Width (6.3.4.4)

The rows and the columns in a table can be modified to increase or decrease the height of a row or width of a column. This is useful to ensure that all text is visible within the table.

To modify the height of rows in a table, do the following:

- Select the row or rows to be modified.
- From the **Table Tools** tab and the **Layout** tab, click the scroll arrows on the **Table Row Height** list box to increase or decrease the height of the row (in centimetres) from the **Cell Size** group.

To modify the width of columns in a table, do the following:

- Select the column or columns to be modified.
- From the **Table Tools** tab and the **Layout** tab, click the scroll arrows on the **Table Column Width** list box to increase or decrease the width of the column (in centimetres) from the **Cell Size** group.

NOTE
Column widths and row heights can also be modified by dragging a row/column to increase or reduce size. Position the cursor over the column or row border and the cursor turns into a black cross. Hold down the mouse button and drag to the right to widen a column or drag down to resize a row. Note the column width and row height indicators as you drag, this provides the current measurement as you resize the row or column.

PRACTICE SEQUENCE

1. Open the **sale** presentation.
2. On slide 5 delete the row for **Dylan Jones**.
3. Edit the name **Cerys** to read as **Cheryl**.
4. Insert a new row above **Deirdre Brown** and enter details for **David Black, Sales**.
5. Modify the row height of all rows in the table to **0.75cm**.
6. Modify the column width of both columns in the table to **5cm**.
7. Save and close the **sale** presentation.

Section 4   Charts

Charts are visual graphical representations of numerical data, making it easier to see results 'at a glance'. Charts can be displayed in different formats, such as pie, bar/column and line and formatted with different colours and fonts, sizes and styles. Charts can also be created to display a hierarchical structure, such as organisational charts. This type of chart uses shapes and connecting lines to show the hierarchical relationship existing between different levels.

4.1   Using Charts

To use charts, you need to input data in a spreadsheet. This data is then displayed in chart format in the chart type that you specify. The chart can be modified if required to display a different chart type. Chart titles can also be added or removed as required. The chart data is described by the data labels that are applied. If no labels are applied, the chart is meaningless.

This chart does not contain data labels and so is meaningless

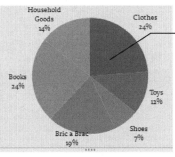

This chart contains category and percentage data labels which describe the segments

In this section, you will learn about the following:

- Inputting data to create built-in charts in a presentation: column, bar, line and pie.
- Selecting a chart.
- Changing the chart type.
- Adding, removing and editing a chart title.
- Adding data labels to a chart: values, numbers and percentages.
- Changing the background colour of a chart.
- Changing the column, bar, line and pie slice colours in a chart.

4.1.1   Creating Charts (6.4.1.1)

To create a chart, do the following:

Insert Chart button

- Create a new slide with the **Title and Content** slide layout.
- Click the **Insert Chart** button on the ribbon.
- Select a chart type, i.e. column, bar, line or pie, in the left hand pane.
- Select a chart sub-type in the right pane.
- Click **OK**.

Chart types

Chart sub-types

- The screen will split so that both the slide and the spreadsheet are displayed.
- Enter data into the spreadsheet.

This example shows data
that will be used to create
a comparison chart

- Close the spreadsheet and return to the chart by clicking Close (X) in the top-right corner.

4.1.2 Selecting Charts (6.4.1.2)

Before a chart can be edited or formatted, it must first be selected. When a chart element is selected, it can be deleted, resized, formatted and moved.

To select a chart do the following:
- Click the chart or chart element to select it.

  Alternatively, select **Chart Tools/Layout** and then, in the **Current Selection** group, click the **Chart Elements** arrow and select a chart element from the list.

  The selected chart element will display with handles surrounding it.

4.1.3 Changing the Chart Type (6.4.1.3)

A chart can be modified to display a different chart type if required.

To change the chart type, do the following:
- Click the chart to select it.

  Alternatively, select **Chart Tools/Layout** and then, in the **Current Selection** group, click the **Chart Elements** arrow and select **Chart Area**.

- Select **Chart Tools/Design**.
- From the **Type** group, click the **Change Chart Type** button.
- Choose a chart type and sub-type.
- Click **OK**.

4.1.4 Chart Titles and Axis Titles (6.4.1.4)

Chart titles help to describe the purpose of the chart. For example, a chart that displays the annual sales figures for a company in 2008 would be entitled: **Annual Sales Figures 2008**. Axis titles can also be used to identify each axis on the chart.

Adding a Chart Title

To add a chart title, do the following:
- Click the chart to select it.

  Alternatively, in the **Chart Tools/Layout** tab, select the **Chart Elements** arrow and select **Chart Area** from the **Current Selection** group.

- Select the **Chart Tools/Layout** tab.
- Click the **Chart Title** command from the **Labels** group.
- From the menu you have the following options:
  - **None** (do not display a chart title).
  - **Centred Overlay Title**.
  - **Above Chart** (this is the usual position).
  - **More Title Options** (to format the chart title).

6

- Select **Above Chart** to add a chart title above the chart.

- Position the cursor within the chart title box, delete the existing text and enter the required chart title text.

Chart title

Editing a Chart Title

To edit a chart title, do the following:

- Position the cursor in the chart title box and amend, or delete, the existing text as necessary.

Formatting a Chart Title

To format a chart title, do the following:

- Click the title to select it.

  Alternatively, select **Chart Tools/Layout** and then, in the **Current Selection** group, click the **Chart Elements** arrow and select **Chart Title**.

- Select **Chart Tools/Layout** tab from the ribbon.

- Click the **Chart Title** command from the **Labels** group.

- Select **More Title Options** from the menu.
  The **Format Chart Title** window opens.

- Select the required formatting options.

- Select the **Home** tab.

- From the **Font** group, select a font, size, style and colour.

- Click **Close**.

From this window you can apply a solid, gradient picture or texture fill, a border with a specific colour and style or shadow effect

You can also apply a 3-D format to the chart title and change the alignment

Removing a Chart Title

To remove a chart title, do the following:

- Click the chart title to select it.

  Alternatively, select **Chart Tools/Layout** and then, in the **Current Selection** group, click the **Chart Elements** arrow and select **Chart Title**.

- Select **Chart Tools/Layout** tab from the ribbon.

- Click the **Chart Title** command from the **Labels** group.

- Select **None**.

  Alternatively, select the chart title and press the **Delete** key.

Axis Titles

The methods above can also be used to add, format or delete axis titles by accessing the **Axis Titles** menu.

- Click the chart to select it.

Alternatively, select **Chart Tools/Layout** and then, in the **Current Selection** group, click the **Chart Elements** arrow and select **Chart Area**.

- Select **Chart Tools/Layout** tab from the ribbon.
- Click the **Axis Titles** command from the **Labels** group.
- Select an axis title option for the horizontal or vertical axis. A sub-menu opens to provide further options.
- Select an option from this sub-menu.
- Position the cursor within the **Axis Title** box.
- Delete the existing text.
- Enter the axis title text into the box.
- Repeat for other axes on the chart.

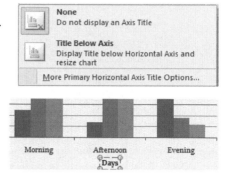

4.1.5 Adding Data Labels (6.4.1.5)

Data labels help to identify the segment, line or column/bar in a chart.

To add data labels, do the following:

Values/Numbers and Percentages

- Click the chart to select it.
- *Alternatively*, select **Chart Tools/Layout** and then, in the **Current Selection** group, click the **Chart Elements** arrow and select **Chart Area**.
- Select **Chart Tools/Layout** tab from the ribbon
- Click the **Data Labels** button from the **Labels** group.
- Select an option from the drop-down list.
  - o Select **None** if you don't want data labels or select one of the display options from the list.
  - o Click **More Data Label Options** to see the **Format Data Labels** window.
- From this window, you can select the type of data label, such as **Value/number**, **Category Name**, **Series Name** or **Percentage**.
- You also have the option of changing the label position.
- Click **Close** when finished.

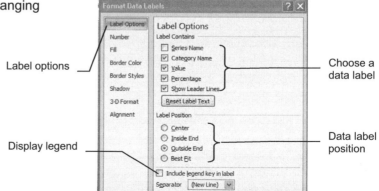

Examples of data labels, all with **Outside End** position.

4.1.6 Background Colour (6.4.1.6)

The background of a chart can be formatted to display a different colour.

To apply background colour, do the following:

- Click the chart to select it.

  Alternatively, select **Chart Tools/Layout** tab and then, in the **Current Selection** group, click the **Chart Elements** arrow and select **Chart Area**.

- Select the **Format Selection** command from the **Current Selection** group.

  The **Format Chart Area** window opens.

- From the **Fill** command, select the **Solid fill** option button.

- Select the **Color** arrow and choose a colour from the palette or click **More Colors** to see a wider choice of colours. You also have the option of formatting the chart area with gradient, picture or texture fill.

- Click **Close**.

Alternatively, select **Chart Tools/Format** tab and then click the **Shape Fill** arrow from the **Shape Styles** group and choose a colour.

4.1.7 Changing a Series Colour (6.4.1.7)

The individual series on a chart can be formatted to display a different colour. For example, you may want to display each column in a column chart as a different colour to differentiate between the series. The individual series are the bar, lines, pie slices or columns that make up a chart.

To change the colour of a series, do the following:

- Click the series to select it.

  Alternatively, select **Chart Tools/Layout** tab and then, in the **Current Selection** group, click the **Chart Elements** arrow and select **Series 'series name'**.

- Select the **Format Selection** command from the **Current Selection** group on the ribbon

  The **Format Data Series** window opens.

- From the **Fill** command, select the **Solid fill** option button.

- Select the **Color** arrow and choose a colour from the palette or click **More Colors** to see a wider choice of colours.

- Click **Close**.

- Repeat this procedure to apply colour to each series in the chart.

NOTE

For pie charts, select the pie chart and then click an individual slice to select it. The slice colour can then be changed in the same way as the colour of columns, bars and lines in other chart types.

PRACTICE SEQUENCE

1   Open the **sale** presentation.

2   Create a new slide with the slide title **Preferred Days** and a **line** chart with the following
     data:

	Weekday	Saturday	Sunday
Morning	2.5	8.5	6.5
Afternoon	1.4	9.2	5
Evening	3.5	1.8	1.2

3   Add the following chart title: **Popularity of Days**.

4   Format the chart title to be Arial, 18, dark blue and italic.

5   Add a vertical rotated axis title: **Voting results**.

6   Add a horizontal axis title: **Days**.

7   Edit the chart title to read: **Preferred Days**.

8   Change the chart type to a column chart.

9   Remove the chart title form the chart.

10   Format each series in a different colour:
     Weekday=dark blue, **Saturday=green**, **Sunday=yellow**.

11   On slide 4, format the pie chart to display category and percentage data labels.

12   Change the background colour of the pie chart to white.

13   Save and close the **sale** presentation.

4.2   Organisation Charts

Organisation charts are used to display a hierarchical structure. This type of chart uses shapes and
connecting lines to show the hierarchical relationship existing between different levels.

In this section, you will learn about the following:

- Creating an organisation chart with a labelled hierarchy by using a built-in organisation chart
  feature of PowerPoint 2007.

- Changing the hierarchical structure of an organisation chart.

- Adding and removing co-workers and subordinates in an organisation chart.

4.2.1 Creating an Organisation Chart (6.4.2.1)

To create an organisation chart, do the following:

- Create a new chart with the **Title and Content** slide layout.

- Add a title for the slide.

- From the Illustrations group on the Insert tab select the **SmartArt** button.
  The **Choose a SmartArt Graphic**
  window opens.

- Select a chart type, such
  as **Hierarchy**.

- Select a chart sub-type.

- Click **OK**.

Select a chart type

The organisation chart displays, ready for inputting data.

Enter data into the chart by clicking into a box and typing

4.2.2 Changing the Structure of an Organisation Chart (6.4.2.2)

An organisation chart can be modified to display a different hierarchal structure if required. For example, a subordinate or co-worker may need to be moved within the structure if they are promoted.

To restructure the organisation chart, do the following:
- Select a level on the organisation chart.
- From the **SmartArt Tools/Design** tab and the **Add a Graphic** group, select **Promote** to increase the level or **Demote** to decrease the level.
  Alternatively, drag a box to the required level and release

Changing Layout
- Select **SmartArt Tools/Design**.
- Click the **More** button in the **Layouts** group.

More button

- Choose a layout from the menu.

Select a layout

Select **More Layouts** for further layout options

- Select **Right to Left** to change the alignment of the chart.
- Select **Text Pane** to add text to the chart (or right-click within a box and select **Edit Text**).

4.2.3 Adding and Removing Levels (6.4.2.3)

An organisation chart can be edited to display or remove specific levels in the hierarchy, such as co-worker or subordinate.

To add or remove levels in an organisation chart, do the following:

Adding Co-workers or Subordinates
- Select a box on the level to which the co-worker will be added.
- Select **SmartArt Tools/Design**.
- Click the **Add a Shape** button in the **Add Graphics** group.
- Choose an option from the menu:
  - **Add Shape After** (to add a co-worker after a selected box).
  - **Add Shape Before** (to add a co-worker before a selected box).
  - **Add Shape Above** (to add a higher level above the selected box).
  - **Add Shape Below** (to add a subordinate below the selected box).
  - **Add Assistant** (to add an assistant to the selected box).

A new box will be added to the chart.

- Right-click the box.
- Select **Edit text**.

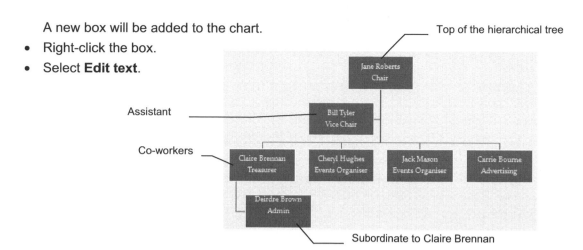

Removing Co-workers or Subordinates

To remove co-workers or subordinates in an organisation chart, do the following:

- Select the co-worker or subordinate to be deleted.
- Press the **Delete** key.

Practice Sequence

1   Open the **sale** presentation.

2   Create a new slide with the slide title **Club Members** and an **organisation chart** slide layout with the data below.

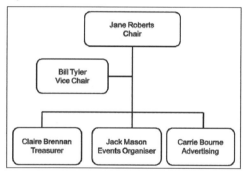

3   Add a co-worker to Claire Brennan with the following details: **Cheryl Hughes**, **Events Organiser**.

4   Add a subordinate to Claire Brennan with the following details: **Deirdre Brown, Admin**.

5   Delete the co-worker **Jack Mason, Events Organiser**.

6   Change the hierarchical structure of the chart so that **Deirdre Brown, Admin** is now co-worker to **Claire Brennan, Treasurer**.

7   The new structure follows the one below.

8   Save and close the **sale** presentation.

Section 5 Graphical Objects

A graphical object refers to an image, picture, drawn object, diagram or chart. Graphical objects can be manipulated by resizing, deleting, rotating and flipping, and by copying and moving between slides and between open presentations. Graphical objects can be aligned in a specified position relative to the slide.

5.1 Inserting and Manipulating Graphical Objects

In this section, you will learn about the following:

- Inserting a graphical object into a slide.
- Selecting a graphical object.
- Copying and moving graphical objects within a presentation and between open presentations.
- Resizing and deleting graphical objects in a presentation.
- Rotating and flipping a graphical object.
- Aligning a graphical object relative to a slide: left, centre, right, top and bottom.

> **NOTE**
>
> In this unit, the term 'picture' refers to a visual representation available from an inbuilt gallery, such the **ClipArt Gallery**. The term 'image' refers to a visual representation that is inserted from a **file**, such as a scanned photograph or drawing. For inserting drawn objects, see Section 5.2.

5.1.1 Inserting a Graphical Object into a Slide (6.5.1.1)

Graphical objects – pictures, images or drawn objects – can be inserted by creating a new slide with a slide layout that enables graphical content or by inserting a graphical object into a slide from a stored location on your computer.

To insert a graphical object into a slide, do the following:

Inserting a Picture Using Slide Layout

- Create a new slide with the **Title and Content** slide layout and double-click the **Insert ClipArt** button.
  The **ClipArt** task pane opens.
- Find a picture in a specific category by positioning the cursor in the **Search for** box and entering a search word.
- Click **Go**.
  Pictures matching the search word will appear.
- Select a picture.

Inserting an Image Using a Slide Layout

- Create a new slide with the **Title and Content** slide layout and double-click the **Insert Picture from file** button.
  The **Insert Picture** window opens.
- Locate the correct drive and/or folder from the **Look in** box.
- Select the image.
- Click **Insert**.

Inserting a Picture onto Any Slide

- Select the **Insert** tab.
- Click the **ClipArt** button in the **Illustrations** group
  The **ClipArt** task pane opens.
- Find a picture in a specific category by positioning the cursor in the **Search for** box and entering a search word.
- Click **Go**.
- Pictures matching the search word will appear.
- Select a picture.

Inserting an Image onto Any Slide

- Select the **Insert** tab.
- Click the **Picture** button in the **Illustrations** group.
  The **Insert Picture** window opens.
- Locate the correct drive and/or folder from the **Look in** box.
- Select the image.
- Click **Insert**.

  Alternatively, locate the required drawn object in the Drawing group on the home tab. Click the drawn object and then click the position where it is to appear on the slide.

Inserting an Drawn Object onto Any Slide

- Select the **Insert** tab.
- Click the **Shapes** button in the **Illustrations** group.
- Select the required drawn object from the drop-down list that appears.
  Note the cursor changes to a cross.
- Click in the placeholder in the required position.

5.1.2 Selecting a Graphical Object (6.5.1.2)

Before a graphical object can be edited, formatted or manipulated, it must first be selected.

To select a graphical object, do the following:
- Click the object.
  Handles appear around the object to indicate selection.
  Alternatively, from the **Home** tab, click **Select** and then **Selection Pane**. Select the picture placeholder from the list of slide elements.

5.1.3 Copying and Moving Graphical Objects and Charts (6.5.1.3)

Graphical objects and charts can be copied and moved in the same presentation or between different presentations.

In the Same Presentation

To copy a graphical object or chart, do the following:
- Select the **View** tab.
- Click **Normal** from the **Presentation Views** group.
- Select the object.
- From the **Home** tab, click **Copy** from the **Clipboard** group.

- Select the destination slide (the slide to which the object is being copied) and click **Paste**.

  The duplicated graphical object or chart will appear in the new position.

To move a graphical object or chart, do the following:
- Select the **View** tab.
- Click **Normal** from the **Presentation Views** group.
- Select the object.
- From the **Home** tab, click **Cut** from the **Clipboard** group.
- Select the destination slide (the slide to which the object is being copied) and click **Paste**.

  The moved graphical object or chart will appear in the new position.

  Alternatively, use the **Drag and Drop** method of copying and moving objects within the same slide by dragging the object to the new position using the mouse. Drag the object to the required position before releasing the mouse button.

  To copy, hold down the **CTRL** key whilst dragging to the new position.

Between Open Presentations

To copy a graphical object or chart, do the following:
- Open the required presentation files.
- Both files will be displayed as tabs on the taskbar at the bottom of the screen.
- Ensure that the presentation containing the objects to be copied is the active presentation.
- Select the object.
- From the **Home** tab, click **Copy** from the **Clipboard** group.
- Click to the other presentation on the taskbar or select the **View** tab and **Switch Windows**.
- Choose the other presentation from the list.
- Open the required slide in standard view.
- Position the cursor in the required position within the slide.
- From the **Home** tab, in the **Clipboard** group, click **Paste**.

  The object will be copied in the selected slide within the presentation.

To move a graphical object or chart, do the following:
- Open the required presentation files.
- Both files will be displayed as tabs on the taskbar at the bottom of the screen.
- Ensure that the presentation containing the objects to be copied is the active presentation.
- Select the object.
- From the **Home** tab, click **Cut** from the **Clipboard** group.
- Click to the other presentation on the Taskbar or select the **View** tab and **Switch Windows**.
- Choose the other presentation from the list.
- Open the required slide in standard view.
- Position the cursor in the required position within the slide.
- From the **Home** tab, in the **Clipboard** group, click **Paste**.

  The object will be copied in the selected slide within the presentation.

> **NOTE**
>
> If you want to copy or move more than one object, select the first object and then, holding down the **CTRL** key, click the other objects to be copied/moved.

5.1.4 Resizing Graphical Objects (6.5.1.4)

Graphical objects can be resized to increase or decrease the size. It is important to ensure that the original proportions of a graphical object are maintained.

To resize a graphical object, do the following:

Using the Mouse

*   Select the object.
    It will be surrounded by handles.
*   Position the cursor over a corner handle.
    The cursor turns into a double headed black arrow.
*   Left-click the mouse.
*   Drag the cursor inwards or outwards to decrease/increase the size.
*   Release the mouse when the object is the required size.

> **NOTE**
>
> Always resize from a corner handle to maintain the original proportions of the image.

Using Picture Tools

*   Select the object.
    It will be surrounded by handles.
    The **Picture Tools/Format** tab becomes available.
*   Click this tab to see the picture formatting tools.
*   Use the scroll arrows on the **Height** and **Width** list boxes to increase or decrease the size of the object.
    Alternatively, click the **Size and Position** window launcher icon.

*   Enter a measurement into the **Height** and/or **Width** boxes.
*   To maintain the original proportions, only change the height or the width and ensure that the **Lock Aspect Ratio** button is selected.
*   Click **Close**.

Change height or width of image ———

Select **Lock Aspect Ratio** to ensure that the width is resized in proportion to the height

5.1.5 Deleting Graphical Objects (6.5.1.4)

To delete graphical objects, do the following:

*   Select the object, it will be surrounded by handles.
*   Press the **Delete** key on the keyboard.

5.1.6 Rotating and Flipping a Graphical Object (6.5.1.5)

To rotate and flip graphical objects, do the following:

- Select the object, it will be surrounded by handles.
  The **Picture Tools/Format** tab becomes available.
- Click this tab to see the picture formatting tools.
- Click the **Rotate** arrow to see a list of rotation and flip commands.

- Select an option from the list or click **More Rotation Options** to rotate by specified degrees.
- Click **Close** when finished.

Use the scroll arrows on the **Rotate** list box to select a specific measurement

Alternatively, objects can also be rotated by using the **Rotate** handle on a selected object. Position the mouse arrow over the rotate handle and drag in the required direction.

Rotate handle

5.1.7 Aligning a Graphical Object (6.5.1.6)

A graphical object can be aligned horizontally on the left, centre or right of the slide, or aligned at the top or bottom of a slide.

To align an object, do the following:

Relative to a Slide
- Select the object to see the handles surrounding it.
  The **Picture Tools/Format** tab becomes available.
- Click this tab to see the picture formatting tools.
- From the **Arrange** group, select the **Align** command to see the menu.
- Select the **Align to Slide** menu option (a tick beside a menu option indicates that it is active).
- The object will align relative to the slide.

Alignment (Left, Right, Centre, Top and Bottom)
- Select the object to see the handles surrounding it.
  The **Picture Tools/Format** tab becomes available.
- Click this tab to see the picture formatting tools.
- From the **Arrange** group, select the **Align** command to see the menu.
- Choose an alignment option from the menu.

PRACTICE SEQUENCE

1   Open the **sale** presentation.

2   Insert a new **Title and Content** slide with the title **Club Meeting.** Enter the bulleted text: **Next meeting 30th December 2008**.

3   Insert a relevant picture from ClipArt.

4   Insert the picture called **sell.gif** into slide 1 so that it displays beneath the title.

5   Resize the picture so that the height is **3cm** and the width will alter proportionally.

6   Insert the picture called **clock.gif** on slide 3 so that it appears on the right side of the subtitle text.

7   Resize the picture so that the height is **5cm** and the width will alter proportionally.

8   Rotate the clock so that it is displayed at **35°** clockwise.

9   Flip the picture horizontally on slide 1.

10   Copy the picture on slide 1 of the **sale** presentation into slide 3 of the **manage** presentation.

11   Save and close the **manage** presentation.

12   Save and close the **sale** presentation.

5.2   Drawn Objects

Drawn objects can be added to a slide in a variety of shapes and sizes. Drawn objects can be formatted with colour, shadow effect, borders and line style. Multiple drawn objects can be ordered so that specific shapes appear in front of or behind other objects or they can be grouped together to create one single object.

In this section, you will learn about the following:

*   Adding different types of drawn object to a slide: line, arrow, block arrow, rectangle, square, oval, circle and text box.
*   Entering text into a text box, block arrow, rectangle, square, oval, circle.
*   Changing the background colour, line colour, line weight, line style of a drawn object.
*   Changing arrow start style and arrow finish style.
*   Applying a shadow to a drawn object.
*   Group and ungroup drawn objects in a slide.
*   Bringing a drawn object one level forward, one level backward, to the front and to the back of other drawn objects.

5.2.1 Drawn Objects (6.5.2.1)

To add a drawn object to a slide, do the following:

Line

*   Select the **Insert** tab from the ribbon.
*   From the **Illustrations** group, click the **Shapes** command.
*   Select the **Line** tool from the **Lines** section of the drop-down menu.

Click the **Line** tool

The cursor turns into a black crosshair symbol (+).

*   Position the crosshair symbol where you want the line to start and then drag the mouse to create the line.

Arrow

- Select the **Insert** tab from the ribbon.
- From the **Illustrations** group, click the **Shapes** command.
- Select the **Arrow** tool from the **Lines** section of the drop-down menu.

Click the **Arrow** tool

The cursor turns into a black crosshair symbol (+).

- Position the crosshair symbol where you want the arrow to start and then drag the mouse to create the arrow.

> **NOTE**
>
> Hold down the **Shift** key to create a line or arrow that is straight.

Block Arrow

- Select the **Insert** tab from the ribbon.
- From the **Illustrations** group, click the **Shapes** command.
- Select one of the **Block Arrow** tools from the **Block Arrow** section of the drop-down menu.

Click a **Block Arrow** tool

The cursor turns into a black crosshair symbol (+).

- Position the crosshair symbol where you want the arrow to start and drag the mouse to create the block arrow.

Rectangle

- Select the **Insert** tab from the ribbon.
- From the **Illustrations** group, click the **Shapes** command.
- Select one of the **Rectangle** tools from the **Rectangles** section of the drop-down menu.

Click a **Rectangle** tool

The cursor turns into a black crosshair symbol (+)

- Position the crosshair symbol where you want the rectangle to start and then drag the mouse to create the rectangle.

> **NOTE**
>
> **Drawing a square**: Follow the instructions to draw a rectangle, but hold down the **Shift** key whilst dragging to create a perfect square.

Oval

- Select the **Insert** tab from the ribbon.
- From the **Illustrations** group, click the **Shapes** command.

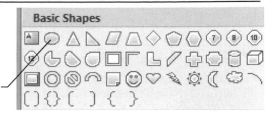

- Select the **Oval** tool from the **Basic Shapes** section of the drop-down menu.

Click the **Oval** tool

The cursor turns into a black crosshair symbol (+).

- Position the crosshair symbol where you want the oval to start and then drag the mouse to create the oval.

> **NOTE**
>
> **Create a circle**: Follow the instructions to create an oval, but hold down the **Shift** key whilst dragging the shape to create a perfect circle.

Text Box

- Select the **Insert** tab.
- From the **Illustrations** group, click the **Shapes** command.
- Select the **Text Box** tool from the **Basic Shapes** section of the drop-down menu.

Shapes

Click the **Text Box** tool

The cursor turns into a black crosshair symbol (+)

- Position the crosshair symbol where you want the text box to start and drag the mouse to create the text box.

Text box

5.2.2 Entering Text into a Drawn Object (6.5.2.2)

Text can be entered directly into a drawn object as required.

To enter text into a drawn object, do the following:

- Click the drawn object to select it.
- The cursor appears within the drawn object ready for text insertion.
- Enter the required text into the drawn object.
- Click outside the drawn object to continue.

What's on offer

> **NOTE**
>
> To edit or format the text in a drawn object, right-click on the object and select Edit Text from the pop-up menu that appears. The cursor appears within the text.

5.2.3 Formatting a Drawn Object (6.5.2.3)

To format an object with background colour, line colour, line weight and line style, do the following:

6

Background Colour

- Select the object.
- From the **Drawing Tools/Format** tab on the ribbon, select the **Shape Fill** command from the **Shape Styles** group.
- Select a colour or choose **More Fill Colors** for a wider choice of colours or select **No Fill** to remove colour.

  From this menu, you also have the choice of formatting the shape with a picture, gradient or texture.

Line Colour

- Select the object.
- From the **Drawing Tools/Format** tab on the ribbon, select the **Shape Outline** command from the **Shape Styles** group.
- Select a colour or choose **More Outline Colors** for a wider choice of colours or select **No Outline** to remove the line.

Line Weight

- Select the object.
- From the **Drawing Tools/Format** tab on the ribbon, select the **Shape Outline** command from the **Shape Styles** group.
- Select **Weight** and choose a weight from the list.

  The weights are displayed in points (pt).
- Select **More Lines** to see more line options.

Line Style

- Select the object.
- From the **Drawing Tools/Format** tab on the tab, select the **Shape Outline** command and then the **Dashes** command from the **Shape Styles** group.
- Select a style or click **More Lines** to see more line options.

  The **Format Shape** window opens.
- Select the **Line Style** command.
- Format the line using the **Line Style** options (width, type, etc.).
- Click **Close**.

5.2.4 Arrow Styles (6.5.2.4)

An arrow can have an arrow shape at the start and/or at the end of the line.

To apply styles to the arrow, do the following:

- Select the arrow.
- From the **Drawing Tools/Format** tab from the ribbon, select the **Shape Outline** command from the **Shape Styles** group and choose **Arrows**.

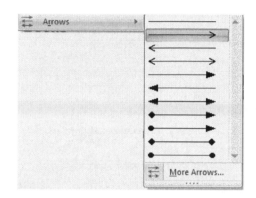

- Select an arrow style from the sub-menu or click **More Arrows** for further formatting options.

  The **Arrow Settings** in the **Format Shape** window enable **Begin** and **End** types to be applied to arrows (a double headed arrow would have both).

- Select a **Begin Type** or **End Type** and then choose a size for the **Begin/End** types.
- Click **Close**.

5.2.5 Applying a Shadow to a Drawn Object (6.5.2.5)

To apply shadow to a drawn object, do the following:

- Select the object.
- From the **Drawing Tools/Format** tab, select the **Shape Effects** command from the **Shape Styles** group.
- Select **Shadow**.
- Select a shadow style from the sub-menu.

5.2.6 Grouping a Drawn Object (6.5.2.6)

Multiple drawn objects can be grouped together into one single object, making it easier to manipulate. The grouped object can be ungrouped when required for editing and modification.

To group or ungroup a drawn object, do the following:

Group

- Select the first object.
- Holding down the **CTRL** key, click the other objects to be grouped.
- From the **Drawing Tools/Format** tab from the ribbon, select the **Group** command from the **Arrange** group.
- Select **Group** from the drop-down menu.

Ungroup

- Select the object.
- From the **Drawing Tools/Format** tab from the ribbon, select the **Group** command from the **Arrange** group.
- Select **Ungroup**.
  The objects will display as individual objects.

Regroup

Objects can be regrouped without selecting each individual object.

To regroup the objects, do the following:
- Select an object (there is no need to select each of the objects to be regrouped).
- From the **Drawing Tools/Format** tab from the ribbon, select the **Group** command from the **Arrange** group.
- Select **Regroup**.
  The objects will display as one single object.

  Alternatively, selected objects can be grouped, ungrouped and regrouped by right-clicking the selected objects and selecting **Group** and then an option from the pop-up menu that appears.

5.2.7 Ordering a Drawn Object (6.5.2.7)

Drawn objects can be ordered so that objects appear in front of or behind specified objects. This is useful when creating a picture consisting of multiple objects.

To order objects, do the following:

Bring Forward One Level
- Select an object.
- From the **Drawing Tools/Format** tab on the ribbon, select the **Bring to Front** command from the **Arrange** group.
- Select **Bring Forward** to bring the selected object forward by one level.

Send Back One Level
- Select an object.
- From the **Drawing Tools/Format** tab on the ribbon, select the **Send to Back** command from the **Arrange** group.
- Select **Send Backward** to send the selected object backward by one level.

Bring to the Front of Other Objects
- Select an object.
- From the **Drawing Tools/Format** tab on the ribbon, select the **Bring to Front** command from the **Arrange** group.
- Select **Bring to Front** to bring the selected object forward to the front of all objects.

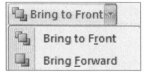

Send to the Back of Other Objects

- Select an object.
- From the **Drawing Tools/Format** tab on the ribbon, select the **Send to Back** command from the **Arrange** group.
- Select **Send to Back** to send the selected object behind all other objects.

Alternatively, selected objects can be ordered by right-clicking the selected objects and selecting **Bring to Front** or **Send to Back** from the pop-up menu, followed by an option from the sub-menu.

PRACTICE SEQUENCE

1   Open the **sale** presentation.

2   Using drawing tools on slide 2, add a block arrow positioned at the right side of the bulleted text. The tip of the arrow should be pointing at the bulleted text.

3   Format the block arrow with a red solid fill colour, a dashed line style with **3pt** weight and grey line colour.

4   Apply a **Perspective** shadow effect to the arrow.

5   Add the following text to the arrow shape: **What's on offer**. Format the text to display with a white font colour and Comic Sans MS, 18, bold.

6   Using the drawing tools create a cloud shape (from Basic shapes) and format with white solid fill colour and a pale grey outline. Position the cloud shape so that it slightly overlaps the end of the block arrow.

7   Add the following text to the cloud shape: **Come rain or shine!**

8   Format the text to display in Comic Sans MS, 18, blue, bold and italic.

9   Using the drawing tools create a sun shape and format with a yellow fill colour and a pale grey outline. Position the sun image on the left side of the cloud.

10   Order the cloud shape so that it displays behind the other shapes.

11   Group the 3 shapes as one object.

12   On slide 1, draw a solid line to separate the title and image from the subtitle text. Format the line to be dark blue with a weight of 4½ pts.

13   Format the line to display as a double headed arrow.

14   On slide 7 insert a text box with the following text: **2008-2009**.

15   Save and close the **sale** presentation.

Section 6   Preparing Outputs

Output refers to the way that the presentation is viewed, either on screen or as printed hard copy. Both types of output require preparation by applying effects and choosing an appropriate output format for slide presentation, such as overhead, handouts or on-screen show. Slides can be hidden as part of a slide show if required and presenter notes can be added to specific slides in the presentation. It is good practice to check spelling and proofread a presentation to ensure it is error free and presented to a professional standard. The layout of a presentation can be altered so that it displays in a different orientation and paper size and then printed in a variety of formats, such as specific slides, handouts, notes pages or Outline View.

6.1   Preparation – Effects and Animation

In this section, you will learn about the following:

- Adding and removing transition effects between slides.
- Adding and removing preset animation effects to different slide elements.
- Adding presenter notes to slides.
- Selecting an appropriate output format for slide presentations, e.g. overhead, handout or onscreen show.

6.1.1 Transition Effects (6.6.1.1)

A transition is the effect that displays between each slide in a slide show. There are a variety of slide transition effects to choose from.

To add or remove a transition effect, do the following:

Adding a Transition

- In **Slide Sorter View**, select the **Animations** tab from the ribbon.
- From the **Transition to This Slide** group, select the **More** button.

The **No Transition** command is selected by default

Click the **More** button to see more transition effects

- Select a transition from the menu.
  The transition effects are grouped by category.
- Use the scroll bar to see all of the transition effects.
- Move the mouse over a transition to see a tag displaying the effect's name.
- Click a transition to select it.
  The transition will be applied to the currently selected slide.
- To apply the selected transition to all slides in the presentation, click the **Apply to All** command.
- Select a speed (slow, medium, fast) from the **Transition Speed** box.

Apply To All

Transition speed

- Automatic transition timings can be set by selecting a time in the **Automatically After** box (or choose to control the slide show by **On Mouse Click**).

- A transition effect is indicated by the following symbol beneath a slide.
- Double-click this symbol to see a preview of the transition effect.

> **NOTE**
>
> A slide show presented by a speaker should be controlled by mouse click. A self-running slide show that is looped to play continuously (such as displaying services in a reception foyer), can be set to play with automatic timings.

Removing a Transition

To remove a transition, do the following:

- In **Slide Sorter View**, select the **Animations** tab from the ribbon.
- From the **Transition to This Slide** group, select the **No Transition** command.
- Select **Apply to All** to remove the transition from all slides in the presentation.

6.1.2 Animation Effects (6.6.1.2)

An animation effect is applied to individual slide elements. The animation effects are displayed when the slide is viewed in Slide Show View.

To add and remove animation effects to slide elements, do the following:

Adding a Preset Animation Effect

- In **Normal View**, select the **Animations** tab from the ribbon.
- Select the slide element(s) to which the animation effect is to be applied.
- From the **Animations** group, select the **Animate** arrow (the default animation effect is **No Animation**).

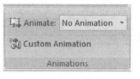

- Select an animation from the menu – the menu items will differ depending on the type of slide element selected.

- Repeat this procedure to apply animation effects to different slide elements.

  Alternatively, animation effects can be applied to slide elements by selecting **Custom Animation**. This will open the **Custom Animation** task pane which provides further animation effects and options to change speed, direction and sequence.

6

Removing a Preset Animation Effect

• In **Normal View**, select the **Animations** tab from the ribbon.

• Select the slide element(s) from which the animation effect is to be removed.

• From the **Animations** group, select the **Animate** arrow and select **No Animation**.

6.1.3 Presenter Notes (6.6.1.3)

Presenter notes are added below a slide and do not display when the slide show is running. Presenter notes can be viewed in standard view and Note Pages view, and can be printed with the slides if required.

To add presenter notes to a presentation, do the following:

• In **Normal View**, select the notes pane beneath the slide.

• Enter the notes text.

Click in the **Notes Area** to
add presenter notes

• To see the full notes pane, select the **View** tab and then **Notes Page**.
  The notes page will appear, displaying the slide above and the notes pane below.

• Enter text as required and format in the same way as normal text.

• Click **Normal View** to close **Note Pages View**.

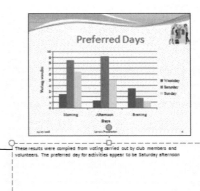

Note Pages View displays the
notes pane beneath the slide

Click in the note pane to add text

6.1.4 Presentation Output (6.6.1.4)

The default presentation output format is **On-Screen Show**. If the presentation is to use overhead transparencies, select the **Overhead** output format. **Handouts** from the presentation can be created and given out to audience members so that they can follow the presentation or be provided for future reference. Handouts can be printed with 1, 2, 3, 4, 6 and 9 slides to a page. The 3 slide handout provides space for the audience to add notes.

To select appropriate output formats for a slide presentation, do the following:

• Select the **Design** tab.

• From the **Page Setup** group, click the **Page Setup** command.
  The **Page Setup** window opens.

Output
format

Orientation for
handouts and
notes

- Select the **Slides sized for:** arrow and choose an option, such as **On-screen Show** or **Overhead** from the list.
- Use **A4 Paper (210 x 297)** to format the slides for A4 paper or select **Custom** if you want to set the measurements yourself.
- Click **OK**.

6.1.5 Hiding and Showing Slides (6.6.1.5)

Specific slides in a presentation can be hidden if required. This is useful when presenting a slide show to different audiences as you can hide certain slides that should only be viewed by a specific audience (for example, sensitive material such as personnel records or accounts).

To hide or show a slide, do the following:

Hiding Slides

- In **Slide Sorter View**, select the slide or slides to be hidden.
- Select the **Slide Show** tab from the ribbon.
- From the **Slide Setup** group, click the **Hide Slide** command.

The hidden slide(s) will display in **Slide Sorter View** with a line through the slide number to indicate it is hidden.

Showing Slides

- In **Slide Sorter View**, select the slide or slides to show.
- Select the **Slide Show** tab on the ribbon.
- From the **Slide Setup** group, click the **Hide Slide** command (this is a *toggle* button, which means that each time it is clicked it turns on/off).

PRACTICE SEQUENCE

1   Open the **sale** presentation.
2   Add a **Dissolve** transition effect to all slides in the presentation.
3   On slide 2, apply a **Wipe (All at Once)** animation effect to the bulleted text.
4   On slide 2, apply a **Fly In** animation effect to the grouped drawn object.
5   On slide 4, apply a **Wipe (By Category)** animation effect to the pie chart.
6   On slide 6, apply a **Fade (By Series)** animation effect to the column chart.
7   On slide 7, apply a **Fly In** animation effect to the title **Club Members**.
8   Add the following notes to slide 6: **These results were compiled from voting carried out by club members and volunteers. The preferred day for activities appears to be Saturday afternoon**.
9   Add the following notes to slide 8: **This meeting is to plan the Spring Fair in March 2009**.
10   Check that the current output format for your slide show presentation is **On-screen Show**.
11   Hide slides 7 and 8.
12   Show slide 7.
13   Save and close the **sale** presentation.

6.2   Checking and Delivering

It is good practice to spell check and proofread your presentation prior to showing or printing, to ensure that it is error free and presented to a professional standard. Slide setup should be modified before printing to ensure that an appropriate orientation and paper size is applied to the presentation. A presentation can be printed as specific individual slides, as handouts (miniature thumbnails), notes or in outline format (this format will only display text but not graphics that appear in the presentation). Once checked, the presentation can be delivered in slide show format. A slide show can be started from any slide and navigated using a shortcut menu.

In this section, you will learn about the following:

* Spell checking a presentation and make changes, e.g. correcting spelling errors and deleting repeated words.
* Changing the slide setup and the slide orientation to portrait or landscape.
* Changing the paper size.
* Printing the entire presentation, specific slides, handouts, notes pages and outline view of slide and choosing the number of copies of a presentation.

6.2.1   Spell Checking a Presentation (6.6.2.1)

It is important before showing or printing a presentation to check the spelling on each slide and correct errors or repeated words.

To check spelling, do the following:

* Select the **Review** tab from the ribbon.
* From the **Proofing** group, click the **Spelling** button.
* Spelling errors will be displayed in the **Not in Dictionary** box and suggestions provided below.

* Select the correct suggestion and click **Change** to correct the spelling.
* Some words that are not in the Spelling dictionary are incorrectly flagged as errors. When this happens, click **Ignore**.

The spelling error is flagged

Suggestions are provided for the correct spelling of the word

Click **Change** to change to the suggested spelling or **Ignore** to retain the current spelling

You are given the opportunity to delete or ignore repeated words.

* Click **Delete** to delete a repeated word or **Ignore** to keep the repeated word and continue the spelling check.

Repeated words are displayed in the **Repeated Word** box

Click **Ignore** to retain the repeated word or **Delete** to delete the repeated word

* When the spell check is complete, a confirmation window opens.
* Click **OK**.

6.2.2 Slide Setup (6.6.2.2)

Slide setup should be performed to change the orientation and paper size before the presentation is printed. Slide orientation refers to portrait or landscape. Portrait is taller than it is wide and landscape is wider than it is tall.

This is orientation is landscape	This orientation is portrait

- Select the **Design** tab on the ribbon.
- From the **Page Setup** group, click the **Page Setup** command.
  The **Page Setup** window opens.

Select the paper size

Select the slide orientation

- Select a slide orientation option button.
  Alternatively, select the **Design** tab and then, from the **Page Setup** group, click the **Slide Orientation** command. Choose **Portrait** or **Landscape**.
- Select a paper size from the **Slides sized for** box.
- Slides can be sized for the various paper sizes.
- Click **OK**.

```
Letter Paper (8.5x11 in)
Ledger Paper (11x17 in)
A3 Paper (297x420 mm)
A4 Paper (210x297 mm)
B4 (ISO) Paper (250x353 mm)
B5 (ISO) Paper (176x250 mm)
```

6.2.3 Printing a Presentation (6.6.2.3)

To print a presentation, do the following:

Entire Presentation

- Select the **Office Button** and then select **Print**.
- From the **Print** sub-menu, select **Print**.
  The **Print** window opens.
- Ensure that the **All** option button is selected in the **Print range** section of the window and that the **Print What** box displays **Slides**.
- Click **OK**.

Name of printer

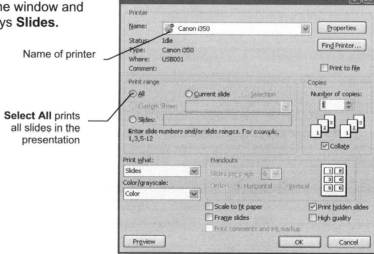

Select **All** prints all slides in the presentation

6

Specific Slides

- Select the **Office Button** and then select **Print**.
- From the **Print** sub-menu, select **Print**.
  The **Print** window opens.
- Select the **Slides** option in the **Print Range** section of the window and enter the slide numbers that you want to print (separate the slides with a comma, i.e. 1, 2, 5).
- Ensure that the **Print What** box displays **Slides**.
- Click **OK**.

Click the **Slides** option button and enter the slide numbers, separated by commas

Click **Current Slide** to print the currently selected slide

Handouts

- Select the **Office Button** and then select **Print**.
- From the **Print** sub-menu, select **Print**.
  The **Print** window opens.
- Select an option in the **Print Range** section of the window.
- Select **Handouts** from the **Print What** box.
- Select the required amount of **Slides per page**.
- Click **OK**.

Select the number of slides per page

Select **Handouts**

Notes Pages

- Select the **Office Button** and then select **Print**.
- From the **Print** sub-menu, select **Print**.
  The **Print** window opens.
- Select an option in the **Print Range** section of the window.
- Select **Notes Pages** from the **Print What** box.
- Click **OK**.

Outline View

- Select the **Office Button** and then select **Print**.
- From the **Print** sub-menu, select **Print**.
  The **Print** window opens.
- Select an option in the **Print Range** section of the window.
- Select **Outline View** from the **Print What** box.
- Click **OK**.

Number of Copies

- Select the **Office Button** and then select **Print**.
- From the **Print** sub-menu, select **Print**.
  The **Print** window opens.
- Use the scroll arrows on the **Number of Copies** list box to increase/decrease the required amount of printed copies.
- Click **OK**.

> **NOTE**
> If you want hidden files to print, select the **Print Hidden Files** checkbox before clicking OK.
> Press **CTRL + P** to open the **Print** window.

6.2.4 Starting a Slide Show (6.6.2.4)
A slide show can be started from any slide in the presentation.

To start a slide show, do the following:

From the Start
- Select the **Slide Show** tab on the ribbon.
- From the **Start Slide Show** group, select **From Beginning**.
  The slide show will start from the first slide in the presentation.

From the Current Slide
- Select the slide from which you want the slide show to start.
- Select the **Slide Show** tab on the ribbon.
- From the **Start Slide Show** group, select **From Current slide**.
  The slide show will start from the currently selected slide.

6.2.5 Navigating a Slide Show (6.6.2.5)
You can navigate between different slides in a slide show by selecting a specific slide title or by selecting the next or previous slide.

To navigate a slide show, do the following:
- Run the slide show.
- Right-click the slide to see a shortcut menu.
- Select **Next** to go to the next slide in the slide show or **Previous** to go to the previous slide. To go to a specific slide, click **Go to Slide** and select a slide title.
- Press **Esc** or click away to close the menu without selecting an option.

PRACTICE SEQUENCE
1   Open the **sale** presentation.
2   Spell check the presentation to ensure that there are no spelling errors or repeated words.
3   Practise changing the orientation of the slides to **Portrait** and **Landscape**. Ensure that the slide orientation is Landscape before continuing the task.
4   Change the paper size to A4 Paper (210 x 297 mm).
5   Print one copy of slides 1, 2, and 5.
6   Print all slides in the presentation in handout format, with 6 slides per page.
7   Print slides 6 and 8 in notes pages format.
8   Print 2 copies of all slides within the presentation in Outline View.
9   Start the slide show from the first slide and navigate to slide 5 **Helpers**.
10   Go to previous slide.
11   Select slide 4 and start the slide show from this slide.
12   Go to slide 8 and end the show.
13   Save and close the **sale** presentation and exit PowerPoint.

Unit 7

Web Browsing
and Communication

Unit 7

Web Browsing and Communication

7

Goals for Unit 7

Unit 7 Web Browsing and Communication is divided into two sections. The first section, Web Browsing, requires the candidate to know about the internet and to use a web browsing application.

The candidate shall be able to:
- Understand what the internet is and common terms associated with it. Be aware of some security considerations when using the internet.
- Accomplish everyday web browsing tasks including changing browser settings.
- Complete and submit web-based forms and search for information.
- Save web pages and download files from the web. Copy web content into a document.

The second section, Communication, requires the candidate to understand some of the concepts of electronic mail (e-mail), to know about other communication options, and to appreciate some security considerations involved in using e-mail.

The candidate shall be able to:
- Understand what e-mail is and know some advantages and disadvantages of its use. Be aware of other communication options.
- Be aware of network etiquette and security considerations when using e-mail.
- Create, spell check and send e-mail. Reply to and forward email, handle file attachments and print an e-mail.
- Be aware of ways to enhance productivity when working with e-mail software. Organise and manage e-mail.

7

Section 1   Web Browsing

1.1   Internet Concepts and Terms

1.1.1   The Internet (7.1.1.1)

The internet facilitates various services, ranging from the transfer of files from one place to another, to e-mail, the world wide web, chat rooms and notice boards, as well as a whole range of online services from shopping to entertainment. In addition, thousands of government, educational and commercial institutions as well as millions of individuals have information that is stored on computer systems and can be accessed over traditional telephone lines, fibre optic cables, satellite communications and almost any other means of telecommunications that is available.

The internet is a global network of computer networks. The computers connected to it communicate with one another and it also provides the infrastructure that converts the information and provides the routes through which the information flows. In the early 1960s, J.C.R. Licklider of the Massachusetts Institute of Technology wrote about a concept he termed Galactic Networks. He envisaged a network of computers on a worldwide scale, across which information would be transferred an idea that eventually became the internet as we know it today.

It is generally accepted that the initial development of the internet was prompted by the Cold War between the US and Russia. To ensure that information could continue to flow should elements of the communications structure be destroyed in a nuclear strike, the US decided to decentralise its information storage and to create a system where information could be accessed through a number of different routes. At the same time, US universities were demanding access to these powerful computers for research purposes. In the late 1960s, super-computers were installed by the military in a number of locations around the US and a network was designed to enable the universities to use its resources.

The main users of this fledgling internet were scientists, engineers and technical experts. During the 1960s and 1970s, US libraries automated their indexes and, over the next decade, made their catalogues available online. Being online was the reserve of technical, scientific and research experts for quite some time as the system was complex to use. As well as the military, the educational community, government bodies and research institutions dominated the internet's use. Mail services emerged in the early 1980s and were predominantly used by educational institutions that engaged at an international level in information exchange.

The growth of accessible databases on the internet grew substantially in the late 1980s and early 1990s and the difficulty of tracking through the huge volume of information prompted the development of catalogues. Throughout the 1990s, the development of systems that could retrieve information links from web-based indexes began to emerge. Parallel to this, technological developments in computing saw greater processing speeds and more user-friendly computer interfaces, telecommunications and cable companies increased capacities and high-speed fibre optic cable networks were being rolled out. The commercial use of the internet did not really begin until the early 1990s and, by the late 1990s, particularly with the commercial provision of internet services, business traffic on the internet was widespread. More recent developments in the internet are attempting to address the challenges presented by even greater capacity demands in the delivery of multimedia, enticing more home users online and an ever increasing growth in online service provision from government, educational and commercial agencies.

7

1.1.2 The World Wide Web (7.1.1.2)

The world wide web (www) is a collection of interlinked documents on the internet. It was conceived by Tim Berners-Lee who wanted to create a virtual space in which information could be shared or exchanged. It required a generic approach to the processing of information from different networks so that different computers could present and locate documents on the **www**. To facilitate this, a code, or computer language, referred to as hypertext mark-up language (HTML) was developed.

The invention of HTML greatly enhanced and eased the access across the web. Typically, clicking a piece of text or an image in a HTML document, called a link, moves to another page, which can be on the same website or a different one entirely. This convenience revolutionised web use, enabling users to browse a myriad of related topics.

1.1.3 Uniform Resource Locators (URLs) (7.1.1.3 and 7.1.1.4)

A **URL**, or **Uniform Resource Locator**, is a text address that uniquely identifies a web page on the internet. URLs are not usually case sensitive. They are made up of a number of different parts separated by dots (full stops) and slash marks.

A typical URL is shown on the right.

- **http** stands for hypertext transfer protocol.
- **www** indicates that this is a world wide web address.
- The **domain name** is a principal part of the address. (A domain is a location or area where the pages are stored.)
- The **top-level domain** often refers to a country or is one of a number of international domains, such as .com (commercial), .net (network), .org (organisation, usually non-commercial), .gov (governmental).

1.1.4 Hyperlink (7.1.1.3 and 7.2.3.1)

As the cursor is moved around a web page, it will occasionally change to a hand with a pointing finger. This indicates that this particular piece of text or graphic is a hyperlink.

A hyperlink is a piece of text, an object or a graphic that acts like a button. Clicking a hyperlink performs an action such as moving to a different part of the same page, displaying a new page or moving to another site altogether.

Anything that changes the cursor to the hand cursor as you move over it is normally a hyperlink. Graphics that include a hyperlink will also change to the hand cursor.

1.1.5 Internet Service Providers (ISPs) (7.1.1.3)

An internet service provider is a business that supplies internet services to individuals, businesses and organisations. Typically, they host websites, provide connectivity services and offer worldwide delivery of e-mails and access to information on the web. There is usually a fee charged for the access facility and setup.

An ISP typically provides the customer with software, a username, a password and a number to enable access through their particular service. With large companies, ISPs often provide direct connection between the company's networks through leased lines. The term internet access provider (IAP) is frequently used for ISP.

1.1.6 Web Browsers (7.1.1.5)

A web browser is an application that enables users to view individual web pages or the collections of linked web pages that comprise websites. These can be accessed on the internet, on a local network or on an individual computer. The browser also facilitates navigating through websites, the use of hyperlinks, and so on. In Microsoft Windows, the most commonly used browser is Internet Explorer, although popular alternatives, such as FireFox and Opera, are also available.

Screenshots and examples in this unit are taken from Internet Explorer Version 7.

1.1.7 File Transfer Protocol (FTP)

File transfer protocol (FTP) is a recognised format that enables users to transfer files between different computers on the internet. FTP works in much the same way as HTTP works for transferring web pages from a server to the user's browser.

- Transferring a file from a remote computer to your own computer is called downloading the file.
- Sending a file to a remote computer is called uploading the file.

1.1.8 An Overview of Search Engines (7.1.1.6)

A **search engine** is a website that helps users to find other websites using a searchable database. Different search engines use different approaches and some concentrate on particular types of search, so it may be possible to find information using one that will not be found using another.

Almost all modern search engines use programs called **spiders** or **automated crawlers** to visit as many other websites as possible, and catalogue their contents to produce a searchable index. When a search engine is used as a result of a user entering a **search term** or terms on the relevant website, powerful **search algorithms** query this index and return results or **hits**.

There are also **meta-search engines** that automatically perform searches against many normal search engines and collate the results together in attempt to provide the largest set of results possible.

Some examples of different search engines are given below.

Automated
Google http://www.google.com.
Microsoft Live Search http://search.live.com.
Yahoo! Search http://www.yahoo.com.
Lycos http://www.lycos.com.

Meta-Search
DogPile http://www.dogpile.com.
IxQuick http://www.ixquick.com.
MetaCrawler http://www.metacrawler.com.

Searching for information involves entering a search term on search engine page. A list of websites that the search engine has determined meet those criteria is then displayed. The individual sites can then be accessed as required. Searching the web is described in detail in Section 1.7 of this unit.

1.1.9 Cookies and Caches

A cookie is a small identifier file. Cookies are placed on the hard disk by the website being visited. When the same website is browsed again later, the cookie notifies the website and often a customised version of the page is returned in response. For example, if a user submits their name and requests information from a web-based book vendor, they will often be presented with a personalised version of the website the next time they return to the site.

Each time a site is visited, the browser saves the contents of the visited pages into a temporary storage area on the hard disk, usually a folder dedicated to temporary internet files called a cache. This speeds up the future downloading of these pages. It is possible to adjust the amount of space used to store these pages, as they can take up large amounts of disk space.

1.1.10 Really Simple Syndication (RSS) Feeds (7.1.1.7)

The large amount of ever-changing content on the web means that it is increasingly difficult for web users to keep up with the various websites and other resources that they may be interested in. Really Simple Syndication (RSS) addresses this problem. Many if not all popular websites now provide one or more feeds or channels that can be subscribed to.

To read this information, an aggregator or feed reader is used. This can be a stand-alone application or integrated into a web browser. The aggregator will handle all RSS subscriptions and automatically check them from time to time, presenting any new items in summary form. This usually happens in the form of small pop-up windows on the screen, which removes the need to check these websites. The summary items can be clicked on to open them and the full item can be read as it appears on the originating website.

Subscribing to an RSS feed can be as simple as visiting a website that is displaying the RSS feed icon although the exact method will vary depending on the application being used as a feed reader.

The illustration on the right shows the **SharpReader** application.

A desktop pop-up appears at the bottom right of the desktop when a new item appears on a feed.

The feed can be opened and items read by clicking the pop-up. In normal operation, the RSS reader window is not visible, and all that will be seen is the occasional pop-up as items come in, enabling users to stay up-to-date but not requiring them to switch applications and check websites constantly.

1.1.11 Podcasts (7.1.1.8)

The term podcast is an acronym for Portable On-Demand Broadcast. Podcasting is an extension of the RSS concept (see Section 1.1.10), where content in any type of file, often music or video, can be subscribed to and automatically downloaded.

In a typical scenario, the following happens:
- Media content, such as episodes of a television show, are made accessible from the internet. Their location is published in a special file called a **feed** which is linked to by a URL.
- Users subscribe to the feed on their computer using a specialised feed reader called a **podcast client** or, sometimes, **podcatcher**.
- The podcast client software takes care of automatically downloading new episodes, files etc. as they become available.
- Users transfer these media files to their portable device for accessing later. Usually, the podcast client software performs this download automatically.

The illustration on the right shows the Juice application with some subscribed feeds.

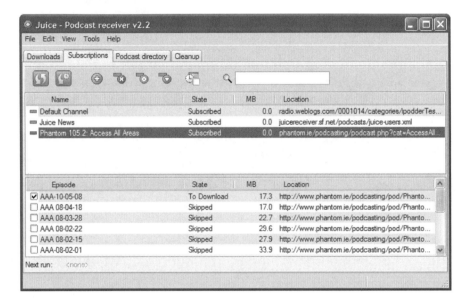

1.2   Security Considerations

1.2.1   Usernames and Passwords (7.1.2.7)

Almost any network, from a home network, to an office or educational establishment network, to the internet itself will require a **username** and **password** to gain access. The use of password security makes it possible to restrict access to authorised entities, and also makes it possible to track user activity. In corporate or educational environments, usernames and passwords are generally issued by IT departments and users are allowed to change their passwords but not their usernames.

It makes sense to choose a strong password, containing a lengthy mixture of upper and lower case letters, numbers and non-alphabetic characters, such as underscores. Many networks will now actively enforce the choosing of strong passwords and require that users change them on a regular basis.

1.2.2 Secure Websites (7.1.2.1)

Buying something online with a credit card or banking online involves using a secure website. These sites employ encryption (see Section 1.2.4) to protect the information being transferred. Web browsers will indicate that a secure section of a website is being viewed.

Internet Explorer shows a padlock icon to the right of the URL.

> **NOTE**
> The URL begins with **https://** rather than the normal http://. This
> indicates that the **secure** version of the HTTP protocol is being used.
>
> https://

Not all parts of a website will be secure. For example, on shopping sites the sections where products are selected are normally unsecured and secure pages only appear at the checkout section, where personal information must be entered.

> **NOTE**
> The Firefox browser will display a padlock icon in the bottom right of the window, and show
> the page URL in yellow in the address
> bar along with another lock icon.   www.amazon.com
>
>

1.2.3 Digital Certificates (7.1.2.2)

When goods are being bought on the internet or when confidential information is being exchanged, there is a need to establish that agencies are authentic and the transfer of data is secure. Digital certificates verify that users are who they claim to be. Digital certificates offer the additional assurance that information sent across the internet between parties is encrypted and that only the authentic person, company or authority has the appropriate mechanism to decode or access the information.

Typically, users will register with an organisation that issues digital certificates. This registration usually requires the checking of confidential information, e.g. credit card numbers and companies, to confirm identity. Companies conducting business across the internet will also register in a similar manner. The certifying authority then facilitates the secure communication between users and the recipient when, for example, a hotel booking is being paid for online.

1.2.4 Encryption (7.1.2.3)

Encrypting files ensure that they cannot be accessed or utilised except by the person for whom the communication is intended. If there is any attempt to intercept a file as it is being transferred across the internet, the encryption offers a high level of security. Encryption is extensively used to protect information such as credit card numbers and sensitive information such as personal data or company secrets.

1.2.5 Malware (7.1.2.4)

The term malware is used to describe a range of unsolicited and usually malicious software programs. They transfer between computers across networks and the internet using various methods – for example from malicious websites and e-mail attachments – by infecting program files or by exploiting security weaknesses in operating systems. Some actively destroy data, some steal passwords and private information, and some remain dormant until they are activated to use the host computer as part of a huge attack on a corporate or government network.

7

They are generally grouped into the headings of **viruses, worms, spyware** and **trojans**.

- **Virus**: This is a type of software that spreads from an infected program to other programs. Generally, viruses can be found in executable programs (.exe files). When the infected executable program is run, the virus spreads to other programs and performs a damaging function. Whatever function the virus performs is known as a **payload**. A payload can be anything that the virus is programmed to do, such as delete data from the hard drive or flash a message on users' screens.

- **Worm**: This is a type of software that spreads across computer networks. Similar to viruses, worms have a payload. One of the most common worm payloads is to use up network bandwidth and slow down the transfer of data across a network.

- **Spyware**: This refers to a range of programs that monitor and collect users' personal information and behaviour. This information is then used for marketing purposes or to redirect users to a specific website. Spyware can also have undesirable effects, such as slowing down an internet connection or a computer's performance in general. Most spyware programs infect a computer by getting users to install them unknowingly, much like Trojan horses.

- **Trojans**: This is a type of program that is designed to resemble another type of software. By deceiving users, a Trojan horse actually gets them to install malicious code on their computers in the belief that they are actually installing a different program. Once installed, the Trojan horse doesn't spread like a virus or worm, but creates what is known as a 'backdoor' that enables access to the infected hard drive without detection.

1.2.6   Antivirus Software (7.1.2.5)

To combat the effectiveness of malware, **antivirus software** can be used. This type of software uses a database of known malware and resides in memory inspecting files as they are accessed on a computer. Problem files can be automatically deleted or placed in **quarantine**. An antivirus application will periodically update its threat database via the internet from a central location – this is vital as new threats appear on a daily basis.

1.2.7   Firewalls (7.1.2.6)

A computer connected to the internet is connected to millions of other computers worldwide. This carries a huge risk of unauthorised access by malicious individuals or criminal organisations. **Firewalls** act as a barrier between individual computers or computer networks and the wider internet, and essentially make them invisible. Firewalls can exist in hardware, for example inside a **broadband router**, or in software. They can be configured to provide **alerts** if someone attempts to intrude.

1.2.8   Risks with Online Activity (7.1.2.8)

Taking part in chat rooms and online discussions can be an engaging and rewarding experience where new friends can be made with people all over the world. Unfortunately, there is an element of risk involved in these types of online activities from cyber-bullies or online predators who seek to gain personal information to harass or cause other types of abuse.

Online harassment might seem rather unlikely because of the anonymous nature of the internet, but it is that anonymity that enables cyber-bullies and online predators to operate successfully. These criminals often masquerade as seemingly harmless people asking normal questions based on genuine interest. In other instances, cyber-bullies and online predators target a specific victim by gathering personal information from online profiles or websites that might contain contact details. Never provide your phone number, postal address or e-mail address on any public profile.

Fortunately, following some simple rules and employing common sense will minimise these risks.

- Use antivirus software and keep it up to date.
- Never reveal your entire name, full date of birth, contact details or other personal information to anyone whose identity you are not absolutely certain of.
- Use strong passwords and change them frequently.

- Ensure the operating system is kept up to date, especially with updates designed to fix security loopholes.

- Never open an unexpected e-mail attachment, even if it appears to be from a known sender.

- Learn to recognise phishing attempts (see Section 2.2.2).

- Where possible and appropriate, avoid entering real personal details, such as name, age, sex or location, into forms on websites. It is necessary, for example, to use correct personal information for banks or where credit card details are needed, but an invented online identity, called an **alias** or **handle** should be used for web forums, etc.

1.2.9   Parental Controls (7.1.2.9)

As computers and high-speed internet connections become increasingly prevalent in homes, so do the dangers posed to younger users. As with the threat from malware, common sense coupled with correct use of the technology can reduce or eliminate these risks.

- **Supervision** of online activity can be effective, perhaps including having the internet computer located in the kitchen or other busy room in the house.

- **Education** is vital for both parents and children. Make sure younger users trust no one outside their own circle of friends, and never release their age, sex or home address in chat rooms, etc. Parents should learn to spot inappropriate behaviour.

- E-mail clients can use a **blacklist** to block e-mails from unwanted senders, or alternatively block all e-mails except those from senders on a **whitelist**.

- As with television, time limits should be established for computer usage and other activities should be encouraged.

- Investigate **parental control software**. This can take the form of stand-alone applications that constantly monitor online activity, or **plug-in** additions to web browsers, such as the free Parental Control Toolbar (http://parentalcontrolbar.org/). These programs sometimes check websites against online blacklists, or search for certain keywords on the site and block based on those.

- **Games** are not just for children, and many contain adult situations and themes. Games software is rated in a similar manner to films by various organisations such as PEGI (http://www.pegi.info). Use the ratings, and search for reviews online to establish a game's suitability.

1.3   First Steps with a Web Browser

Websites on the internet, in offices, on college networks or even individual computers are accessed using an application called a **web browser**, or just **browser**.

1.3.1 Opening and Closing a Web Browser (7.2.1.1)

The first step in accessing the internet is to open the browser.

To open the Internet Explorer browser, do the following:
- Click the **Start** button.
- Select the **All Programs** group, then the **Internet Explorer** option.
  Alternatively, click the Internet Explorer icon on the desktop if it is present.

- If a **broadband** internet connection is being used, the browser window will appear almost immediately.
- If a **dial-up** internet connection is being used, there may be a prompt to use the connection.
  - The **Connect name bar** usually displays the name of your ISP.
  - Your **username** and **password** – received from the ISP upon setup – may be entered automatically. Note that the 'connect' window may vary in its appearance according to connection type and the version of software being used.

- Click **Connect**.

  The computer modem dials the ISP number
  and makes the connection. When the
  connection is successful, the connection
  window closes and Internet Explorer opens
  a preset home page (or start page).

Enter a
username and
password

Click
Connect

The first web page that appears is called the **home page**, initially it is chosen by your computer,
but you can change it to a page that is more relevant for you (see Section 1.4.1).

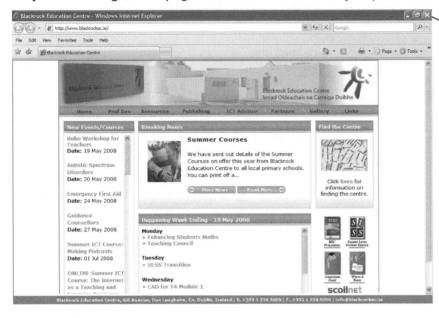

Close X
button

At the end of the browsing session, the browser should be closed.

To close the browser, do the following:
- Click the **Close X** button in the top right of the window.
  Alternatively, select **Exit** from the **File** menu.

NOTE
If a dial-up connection is being used, one of these actions
may or may not close the connection as well.

1.3.2 Displaying a Web Page in a New Window or Tab (7.2.1.3)

New web pages can be viewed in a number of ways. Two of the most useful are by opening a new
window or opening a new tab. Using one of these methods means that it is possible to view more
than one website without having to close one before opening another.

Tabbed browsing enables multiple pages to be open in one Internet Explorer window, but on
separate tabs. This is an invaluable feature that reduces desktop clutter.

Address bar changes to reflect the URL of the active tab.

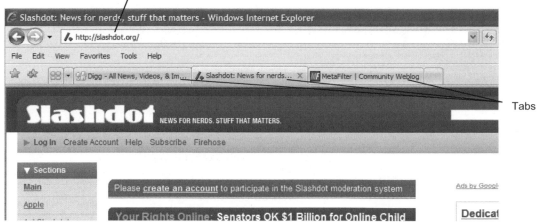

Tabs

In the above image, there are three separate websites open on different tabs. Each tab can be clicked to make it active, and the address bar will change to reflect its URL.

To open a new window in Internet Explorer, do the following:
- Click the **File** menu and select **New Window**.
  Alternatively, use the keyboard shortcut **CTRL + N**.
  A separate Internet Explorer window opens.

To open a new tab, do the following:
- In the **File** menu, select **New Tab**.
  Alternatively, use the keyboard shortcut **CTRL + T**.
  A new tab opens in the current browser.

To open a hyperlink (see Section 1.1.4) in a new window, do the following:
- Right-click the link and select **Open in New Window**.
  A new Internet Explorer window with the linked URL opens.

  A similar procedure is used to open pages in new tabs, except **Open in New Tab** would be chosen.

1.3.3 Stopping a Page from Downloading (7.2.1.4)
Some pages may take a long time to download due to their size, the speed of the internet connection, problems on the website, problems on the internet generally or any combination of the above.

To stop a page from downloading, do the following:
- Click the **Stop** icon on the Internet Explorer menu bar.

Stop button

1.3.4 Refreshing a Web Page (7.2.1.5)

All browsers use caching to some extent, especially if they are being used with a dial-up network connection. This means that pages and images from pages are stored locally on the computer to save downloading them again every time the page is visited. Sometimes, it is necessary to refresh a web page to make sure it is the most up-to-date version, or if the page initially failed to load.

To refresh a page, do the following:
- Click the **Refresh** icon on the Internet Explorer menu bar.
  Alternatively, press **F5**.

Refresh button

1.3.5 Using Help Functions (7.2.1.6)

If you wish to find assistance with different aspects of the browsing application, choose **Help**. This is available to you as you work with the Help function in one of two ways.

- Choose the **Help** menu on the **Menu** bar.
  Alternatively, use the **F1** key on your keyboard.

Using the Help function is described in detail in Section 7 of the Before You Begin unit.

1.4 Adjusting Settings

1.4.1 Setting the Home Page (7.2.2.1)

The first page displayed when the browser is launched is called the home page. In Internet Explorer, this is initially set to an information page stored locally. It is possible to change the home page to something that is more relevant and useful to the individual user, such as a search engine.

To change the home page, do the following:
- Start **Internet Explorer**.
- Go to the web page that is to be set as the new home page.
- From the **Tools** menu select **Internet Options**. The **Internet Options** window opens.
- In the **Home Page** section, click the **Use Current** button.
- Click **OK**.

Click **Use current**

7

Multiple home pages can also be specified, with each opening in a different tab when Internet Explorer is launched.

To set multiple pages, do the following:
- Start **Internet Explorer**.
- Go to the web page that is to be set as the new home page.
- From the **Tools** menu select **Internet Options**. The **Internet Options** window opens.
- In the **Home Page** box, enter the URLs of the pages on separate lines.
- Click **OK**.

Enter URLs

1.4.2 Allowing or Blocking Cookies (7.2.2.4)

Cookies are small files that may be saved on the computer by websites. If personal details are entered in an online form, for example, some may be stored in a cookie so that the next time the website is visited, the information can be filled in again automatically, thus saving time. They can also be used to provide personalised versions of websites.

Cookies can also be used to track what sites have been visited, and this information can be used to target advertising at users. This makes them a potential security concern.

Internet Explorer can be configured to use cookies in various ways.
- Start **Internet Explorer**.
- Click the **Tools** button and select **Internet Options** from the menu. The **Internet Options** window opens.
- Click the **Privacy** tab.
- In the **Settings** section, the slider can be moved up and down to select more or less strict rules for allowing cookies to be stored on the computer.

> **NOTE**
> Higher settings may cause some websites to function incorrectly.

Slider

The cookie settings as described above can be overridden on a site-by-site basis. For example, it might be necessary to always accept cookies from a banking site.

To set this option, do the following:
- Start **Internet Explorer**.
- Click the **Tools** button and select **Internet Options** from the menu. The **Internet Options** window opens.
- Select the **Security** tab.
- Click the **Sites** button.
- The **Per Site Privacy Actions** window opens.
- Enter a website URL in the **Address of website** field.
- Click **Block** or **Allow** for all cookies from that site to be blocked or allowed regardless of the global cookie settings.
- Click **OK**.

Enter the
site's URL

1.4.3   Clearing the Browser Cache and Temporary Internet Files (7.2.2.5)

During normal web browsing, copies of the files that make up the websites visited are sometimes stored in an area of the computer called the cache. These files include any graphics and the HTML or similar files that define the layout of the websites. The reason this is done is to increase performance – if these files are present already on the computer, they do not have to be downloaded every time the website is visited. Similarly, the history of visited sites, the usernames and passwords used, and other items of information are stored in the temporary internet files folder. In Windows XP, this is a hidden folder.

All this stored information takes up disk space, and also creates security and privacy concerns. For this reason, the contents of the cache and the temporary internet files can be deleted.

To delete temporary internet files, do the following:
* Start **Internet Explorer**.
* Click the **Tools** button from the **Command bar**.
* Select **Delete Browsing History** from the menu that opens.
  The **Delete Browsing History** window opens.
* Click the **Delete all ...** button.

Click
Delete all...

1.4.4   Deleting All or Part of the Browsing History (7.2.2.2)

As websites are visited, each address is stored in the browsing history file.

This history can be viewed in Internet Explorer and can be useful in finding sites that have been visited but whose URL has been forgotten.

However, keeping a browsing history means a privacy, and possibly a security, risk is created, so Internet Explorer can be set to clear addresses after a certain number of days.

To set the limit to clear the browsing history, do the following:
* Start **Internet Explorer**.
* From the **Tools** menu, select **Options**.

- In the Browsing history section, click the Settings button. The **Temporary Internet Files and History Settings** window opens.
- In the **History** section, enter the number of days for which the browsing history should be kept.

> **NOTE**
> Enter zero days to disable the history feature completely.

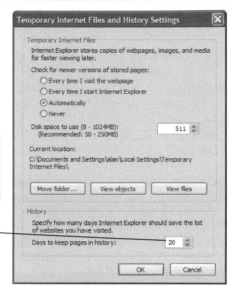

Enter number of days

To manually clear the history completely, do the following:
- Click the **Tools** button on the **Command bar**.
- Select **Delete Browsing History** from the pop-up menu that appears.
  The **Delete Browsing History** window opens.
- Click **Delete History**.
- Click **Close**.

Click **Delete History**

To manually clear a specific website, do the following:
- Click **Favorites**.
  A side bar opens to the right of the window.
- In the **History** tab, right-click the **url/name** of the website to be deleted.
- Click **Delete**.

Click **Delete**

1.4.5 Allowing or Blocking Pop-Ups (7.2.2.3)

Pop-ups are browser windows that automatically appear within the main Internet Explorer window when certain websites are visited. They are often used for intrusive advertising or even the delivery of malware. Internet Explorer version 7 and above has built-in pop-up management capabilities to allow them to be blocked.

Some sites, such as banking sites, however, use pop-ups legitimately to provide a richer user experience, and Internet Explorer can also allow pop-ups where disabling them would make a website unusable.

When a website is visited, Internet Explorer will intercept any attempts by the site to show pop-up windows and display a **pop-up bar** to highlight this.

The bar appears under the Command bar, as below:

Pop-up bar ———

The site used in the above illustration (http://www.popuptest.com) is useful for testing pop-up blocking. In the above example, if the pop-up bar is clicked, a menu opens allowing pop-ups to be enabled for the current site on a temporary or permanent basis.

You can adjust the filter level of the pop-up blocker to regulate what type of pop-ups you want to block. To adjust the filter level, do the following:

- Start **Internet Explorer**.
- In the **Tools** menu, select **Pop-up Blocker**. A sub-menu appears.
- Select **Turn On Pop-up Blocker** from the sub-menu to block pop-ups.
  OR
- Select **Turn Off Pop-up Blocker** from the sub-menu to allow pop-ups.
  The desired setting is applied.

You can adjust the filter level of the pop-up blocker to regulate what type of pop-ups you want to block.

To adjust the filter level, do the following:

- In the **Tools** menu, select **Pop-up Blocker**. A sub-menu appears.
- Select **Pop-up Blocker Settings** from the sub-menu.
  The **Pop-up Blocker Settings** window opens.
- In the **Notifications and filter level** section, select the desired setting from the **Filter level** box.

NOTE

Be sure to select **Show Information Bar when a pop-up is blocked**. Some pop-ups are legitimate features of a web page. If a legitimate pop-up is blocked, you can use the Information Bar to view that pop-up.

1.4.6 Displaying and Hiding Toolbars (7.2.2.6)

By default, Internet Explorer displays various bars such as the **Navigation bar**, **Search bar** and the **Command bar**.

- The **Navigation bar** is where website URLs are entered, and the arrow buttons for navigation are located.
- The **Search bar** to the right enables a search to be performed using the default Search Provider.
- The **Command bar** contains the tabs for any websites that are open, and the Home, Feeds, Print, Page and Tools buttons.

Additional bars such as the **Links bar**, **Menu bar** and **Status bar** can be displayed or hidden by right-clicking on a blank area of the Command bar and ticking or unticking the relevant option on the menu that opens.

NOTE

Toolbars can be displayed or hidden by using the **Menu bar**.

In the **View** menu, click **Toolbars** and select the toolbars to be displayed by ticking or unticking the name in the list.

1.5 Web Navigation

1.5.1 Go to a Uniform Resource Locator (URL) (7.2.1.2)

Every website has a unique address – its Uniform Resource Locator, or URL.

To access a website using its URL, do the following:
- Enter the **URL** in the browser **address bar** (located at the top of the browser window).
- Press **Enter**.
  Alternatively, click the green arrow to **navigate** to that website.

> **NOTE**
> It is not normally necessary to enter the **http://** part, or even the **www**. Entering just **digg.com** in the example above would still connect to the website – and save some typing.

The address bar always displays the URL of the page being viewed. It will change to reflect a change to a new website during browsing.

1.5.2 Accessing Previously Visited URLs (7.2.3.4)

Internet Explorer keeps a history of the locations visited as the browser is used (see Section 1.4.4). This list can be accessed by using the Forward and Backward buttons (see Section 1.5.4) or by clicking the downward arrow to the right of the area where the URL is entered.

Individual URLs in the drop-down list can be clicked to revisit them. Only URLs that were manually typed into the Address Bar are available here – any visited by clicking on hyperlinks are not.

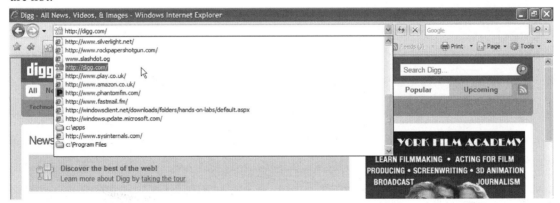

The browsing history can also be permanently displayed in a **History** panel to the left of the Internet Explorer window.

To display the browsing history, do the following:
- Start **Internet Explorer**.
- Click the **Favorites Center** button to the left of the **Command bar**.
  The **Favorites Center** opens to the left of the Internet Explorer window.
- Click the **History** drop-down menu to change to history view.
  The URLs of previously visited websites can
  be accessed.
- Clicking the **Pin** button will cause the
  Favorites Center to be permanently
  locked in place.

Pin button

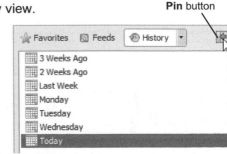

1.5.3 Activating a Hyperlink (7.2.3.1)

The use of **hyperlinks** is one of the things that makes the internet revolutionary. These enable users to move instantly to new pages of information by clicking on special areas in the pages they are currently viewing. This, coupled with the ability to open links in **tabs** (see Section 1.3.2), means an experienced user can browse a huge amount of information very quickly.

Hyperlinks tend to come in two forms.

In a text link the text is underlined in a different colour to the surrounding text, and the cursor changes to a pointing finger icon when moved over it.

Images can also be used as links, and the cursor will change in the same way when moved over them.

Single-clicking a hyperlink will navigate to the **linked location** and display the contents, whether that location is somewhere else on the same page, on a different page on the current website or on a different website altogether. The **linked location** can be displayed either in the current browser window or in a new browser window or a new tab (see Section 1.3.2).

1.5.4 Navigating Backwards and Forwards (7.2.3.2)

In addition to hyperlinks, it is possible to navigate through web pages using the Forward and Backward buttons on the **Navigation bar**.

- The arrow pointing left is the **Backward** button – it goes back to the page that was being viewed before the current one. If the current page was the first to be viewed, this button will be greyed out.
- The arrow pointing right is the **Forward** button. If the Backward button has been used to find previous pages, clicking this button will take the user forward again, through the chain of pages that have been viewed.

In addition, the Backward and Forward buttons both have smaller arrows to the right side. Clicking these arrows will display a menu showing the list of visited locations, enabling one to be clicked on.

1.5.5 Navigating to the Home Page (7.2.3.3)

The home page can be returned to at any time by clicking the home page icon on the Command bar.

1.5.6 Web-Based Forms (7.3.1.1)

Web-based forms are just like real-world forms and are most often used by websites where information must be submitted by the user.

Examples include:
- Booking flights – items such as name, address and contact phone numbers are required.
- Ordering groceries – name, address and a list of items must be supplied.

Web forms often include a variety of **controls** designed for users to enter or select information. All of the common elements that will be encountered are included in the sample form below.

- The **Text Box** enables any text to be entered, for example a name. If a password is being entered, the textbox will display the * character instead of the actual letters, for added security.

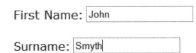

- The **Drop-Down Menu** allows the selection of one item from a list. Only the currently selected item is displayed. The list is 'dropped down' by clicking the arrow, and another item can then be chosen.

- The **List Box** displays a list of items with multiple items being visible at the same time. If there are more items than will fit, a scroll bar will be displayed to the right of the control. Some list boxes allow the selection of multiple items by holding the CTRL key when clicking.

Choose one of the following:

- The **Check Box** is used for simple 'yes or no' choices. Clicking the box will alternate between ticked and unticked states.

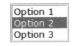 Receive Updates by Email.

- The **Radio** (or **Option**) **Button** presents a range of mutually exclusive choices. At least one must be selected and only one can be selected. Selecting an item will unselect any previously selected item.

◉ Married ○ Single

1.5.7   Submitting a Web-Based Form (7.3.1.2)

When a web-based form has been completed, it can be submitted either by clicking the **Submit** button on the web page or by pressing the **Enter** key on the keyboard.

In some cases, it may be necessary to complete a CAPTCHA before submitting a form. This is a test to verify that the form is being submitted by a human rather than an automated program and is usually a series of slightly distorted letters and numbers that users have to enter into a text field to verify that the submission is authentic.

If the form is either incorrect or incomplete, there is usually a prompt to correct or complete the form before resubmitting it. To reset a web-based form and clear all the fields, either the **Reset** or **Cancel** button can be clicked on the web page.

PRACTICE SEQUENCE

1   Start **Internet Explorer**.

2   In the Address bar, type in the address: **www.becpublishing.com**.

A login box opens, which has to be completed before the website can be accessed.

3   In lower case, type the word **blackrock** in the **username** field.

4   Type **practice** in the **password** box. Remember that these words must be typed in lower case.

5   Click **OK**. The support website window opens.

6   Go to the **Complete a Form** link in the frame to the left-hand side of the page.

7   When the cursor crosses the link, it changes to a hand.

8   Click the left mouse button at this point. The form window will open.

9   Type fictitious information as required into the different boxes.

10   Click **Next** to proceed to the next set of information items.

11   Carry on until a confirmation window opens to indicate the form has been completed.

1.6   Using Bookmarks

1.6.1   Adding Bookmarks (Favorites) (7.2.4.1)

It is convenient to store frequently used URLs so that they do not have to be remembered. This is achieved by creating a **favourite**.

To create a favourite, do the following:
- Browse the website that will be added to the favorites list.
- Click the **Add to Favorites** button.

- Select **Add to Favorites** from the menu that opens.

The **Add a Favorite** window opens.
- The **Name** will have been filled in automatically with the name of the website, but this can be changed if needed.
- Click **Add**.

7

1.6.2 Displaying a Bookmark (Favorite) Web Page (7.2.4.2)
Bookmarks can be viewed in the **Favorites Center** in Internet Explorer.

To display a bookmark, do the following:
- Click the **Favorites Center** button.

The **Favorites Center** opens.
- Click **Favorites** to display the **Favorites** list.
- Click the required bookmark name (website address).

1.6.3 Deleting Bookmarks (Favorites) (7.2.4.1)
To delete favorites, do the following:
- Click the **Add To Favorites** button.
- Select **Organize Favorites** from the menu that opens.
  The **Organize Favorites** window opens.
- Highlight the Favorite to be deleted
  by clicking it once.
- Click **Delete**.
- Click **Close**.

Click the website
to be deleted

Click **Delete**

Click **Close**

1.6.4 Organising Bookmarks (Favorites)

Creating Favorite Folders (7.2.4.3)
If favorites are always added to the main list, the list will soon become very long and unwieldy. It is therefore good practice to group favorites for similar types of websites into folders.

To create a Favorites folder, do the following:
- Click the **Add To Favorites** button.
- Select **Organize Favorites** from the
  menu that opens.
  The **Organize Favorites** window opens.
- Click the **New Folder** on the menu bar.
- A new folder is added to the list.
- Type a name for the new folder.
- Press **Enter**.

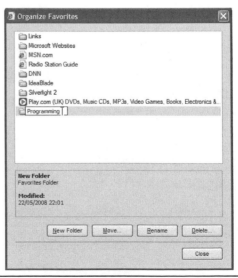

7

Adding URLs to a Favorites Folder (7.2.4.4)

To add websites to a Favorites folder rather than to the main list, do the following:

- Browse to the website to be added to the favorites folder.
- Click the **Add to Favorites** button.

- Select **Add to Favorites** from the menu that opens.

  The **Add a Favorite** window opens.
- Select the correct **Favorites** folder from the **Create In** list.
- Click **Add**.

Deleting a Bookmark Folder (7.2.4.3)

To delete a bookmark folder, do the following:

- In the **Favorites Menu**, select **Organize Favorites**.

  The **Organize Favorites** window opens.
- Click the desired folder to select it.

- The folder is highlighted.
- All web pages contained in the folder are displayed beneath it.
- Click **Delete**.

  A **Confirm Delete** window opens.
- Click **Yes**.
- The selected folder is deleted.
- Click **Close** to close the **Organize Favorites** window.

1.7   Search Engines

1.7.1   Select a Specific Search Engine (7.3.2.1)

A **search engine** is a program that helps you to find information on the web. It stores listings of websites from all over the world and makes them easily available. There are many different search engines associated with the internet, such as AltaVista, Yahoo!, Google and Webcrawler.

To open the Google search engine, do the following:

- Click the **Address bar** with your mouse.
- Type **www.google.ie**.
- Click the **Go** button to right of the Address bar.
  The web page for **Google** will be displayed.

1.7.2   Search by Keyword and Phrase (7.3.2.2)

To perform a general search enter a search word or phrase, also known as a **search term**, in the search box. The number of results returned depends on the words and phrases used and how specific they are.

To search for a phrase, do the following:

- Open **www.google.com**.
- In the search box, enter **blackrock education**.
- Click **pages from Ireland**.
- Click **Google Search**.

The results page will show the number of **hits** – the web pages that the Google search algorithms decide match the words **blackrock** and **education**, with the most relevant listed first.

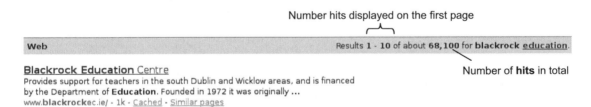

There are various options to select a result.

- Click one of the 10 or 20 most relevant pages that are listed.
- Click a page number in the navigation control at the bottom of the list.

- Click the **Next** or **Previous** links to move back or forwards through the page numbers.

1.7.3 Using Advanced Search Features (7.3.2.3)

Advanced search features work by enabling users to set filters that refine searches and achieve more accurate results. Some common advanced search features include refining searches to match an exact phrase or to exclude certain words in the search. The more precise the keyword or phrase that is used, the more relevant the results found will be. It is also possible to refine searches to match a specific date or file format.

To search for an exact phrase, do the following:
- Open **www.google.com**.
- Click **pages from Ireland**.
- Type **blackrock +education** in the search box.

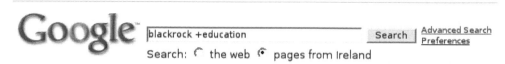

- Typing a **+** sign before a word means that the word must be included in the results.
- Typing a **–** sign means the word must be excluded.
- Click **Search**.
- Fewer pages will be returned than in the original search.
  Alternatively, go to www.google.com.
- Click **Advanced Search**.

Click **Advanced Search**

- The **Advanced Search** page opens.
- In the **Find Results** section, enter the phrase you are searching for in the **with exact phrase** text box.

Find web pages that have...			
all these words:			
this exact wording or phrase:			tip
one or more of these words:	OR	OR	tip
But don't show pages that have...			
any of these unwanted words:			tip

- Click **Google Search**.
  The search results are displayed on the page.

To exclude certain words, do the following:
- Go to **www.google.com**.
- Click **Advanced Search**.
  The **Advanced Search** page opens.
- In the **Find Results** section, enter the phrase you do not want to include in the search in the **without the words** text box.
- Click **Google Search**.
  The search results are displayed on the page.

To match a specific date, do the following:
- Go to **www.google.com**.
- Click **Advanced Search**.
  The **Advanced Search** page opens.
- In the **Date** section, click the arrow to display the drop-down list.
- Select the desired date range from the list.

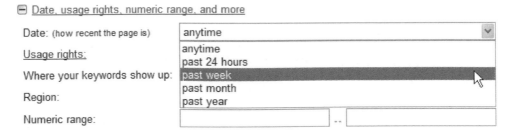

- Click **Google Search**.
  The search results are displayed on the page.

To match a specific file format, do the following:
- Go to **www.google.com**.
- Click **Advanced Search**.
  The **Advanced Search** page opens.
- In the **File Format** section, click the arrow to display the drop-down list.
- Select the desired file type from the list.

- Click **Google Search**.
  The search results are displayed on the page.

Alternatively, you can exclude certain file types by selecting **Don't** from the drop-down list in the **File Format** section.

File Format	Only ∨ return results of the file format	any format ∨
Date	Return web pages first seen in the	anytime ∨

Some tips for using Google are:
- Narrow searches by using + and -.
- To search for an exact phrase, enclose it in double quotation marks. For example, **"blackrock education centre"** will find that exact sequence of words. Searching for **Blackrock education centre** will find pages with the word **Blackrock**, pages with the word **education** and pages with the word **centre**.
- Use wildcards. Searching on **program*** will find **programming, programs, programme**, etc.
- Search on synonyms by using a tilde (~) before the word.
- Google has various conversions that can be performed in addition to searches. Try typing **convert 100 euro to dollars** in the search box for example.
- Google can search images, books and many other specialised areas using the links at the top of the page.

7

1.7.4 Web-Based Encyclopaedias and Dictionaries (7.3.2.4)

Search engines provide generic searching capabilities. There are also online encyclopaedias and dictionaries that can be used in the same way as their printed counterparts.

Encyclopaedias

Wikipedia has become a very popular free online encyclopaedia. To access Wikipedia, do the following:

- Open **Internet Explorer**.
- Browse to **www.wikipedia.org**.
- Enter a search term (in a similar manner to Google – see Section 1.7.1).
- Click the search button and a list of results will be returned.

Enter search term ———

Click the search button

While it provides similar searching functionality to a search engine, the searches in online encyclopaedias are performed against a database of articles rather than web pages.

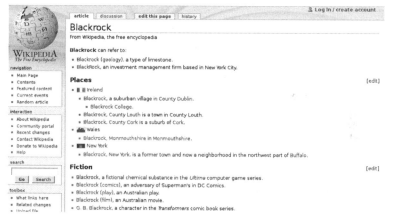

Dictionaries

To use an online dictionary, do the following:

- Go to **www.askoxford.com**.
  A search box is provided to enter a word.
- Enter the word to search, e.g. **heliotrope**.

⦿ **Search the Compact Oxford English Dictionary**

heliotrope   [Go]

Search results

- A search will be performed and the definition returned.

heliotrope

/**hee**lətrop/

• **noun** a plant of the borage family, grown for its fragrant purple or blue flowers.

— ORIGIN Greek *heliotropion* 'plant turning its flowers towards the sun', from *helios* 'sun' + *trepein* 'to turn'.

7

1.8   Saving Files

1.8.1   Saving a Web Page to a Location on a Drive (7.4.1.1)

Web pages can be saved for offline viewing if required. One reason to do this might be if they need to be accessed during periods when an internet connection is not available.

A web page displayed in the browser is built from a variety of files behind the scenes. Any graphics present are not embedded in the page but exist as separate files on the **web server** that the website resides on. When saving, either the page text only can be saved, or the page and all the supporting files that go with it can be saved.

To save a web page in its entirety, do the following:
- Open the website and page that are to be saved.
- On the **Command bar**, click the **Page** button. The **Page** menu opens.

- Select **Save As** from the menu. The **Save Webpage** window opens.
- Browse to the drive and folder to which the page will be saved.
- Ensure the **Save as Type** drop-down menu has **Web Archive, Single File (*.mht)** selected.
- Click **Save**.

NOTE
To save the page text alone, follow the same steps as above but choose **Webpage, HTML Only (*.htm, *.html)** from the **Save as Type** list.

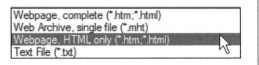

1.8.2   Saving Individual Files from a Web Page (7.4.1.2)

Many websites have files that can be saved, or **downloaded**, to a local computer. They can be in many different formats and, as a result, the relevant software used to open them must be installed on the computer. For example, PDF files require Adobe Acrobat Reader and MP3 files will require a media player application that supports that format.

To practise downloading a text file, image file, sound file and video file, go the website **www.becpublishing.com,** entering the username **blackrock** and password **practice** as required.

Choose the **Download Media Files** link on the web page you access to choose from a variety of information that you can download as practice. Experiment with the different options and files available on the site.

To download an item, do the following:
- Right-click on the link.
- Select **Save Target As** from the menu.

The **Save As** window opens.
- Choose your location in the **Save in** box.
- Choose a name for the file in the **File name** box.
  The options in the **Save as Type** box will reflect the type of file being downloaded.
- Click **Save**.

During the download, a monitoring window normally opens to show the progress of the downloading. Upon completion, you may close the **Download complete** window and proceed according to the choice you made.

1.8.3 Copying Text, Images and URLs to a Document (7.4.1.3)

The majority of material that is accessible on the internet is covered by international copyright, therefore permission must be sought from the copyright owners before any data can be used. A simple e-mail to the owners will usually get a positive response. In order to avoid problems at a later stage, copies of the responses should be kept in a safe location.

Go to www.becpublishing.com to practise (remember the username **blackrock** and the password **practice**).

Follow the steps below to copy text from a web page to a document.
- Click the **Learn About Text** link.
- Highlight the text by dragging the mouse over it.
  There is usually an **Advanced Search** button. Note the links that help with advanced searches.
- Right-click the selected text and select **Copy**.
- Open a word processing document in an application such as Microsoft Word.
- In the **Edit** menu in the word processing document, select **Paste**, or press **CTRL + V**.

To copy an image, do the following:
- Click the **Download Media Files** link.
- Right-click the image.
  A shortcut menu opens.
- Choose the **Copy** command.
- Open a word processing document.
- In the **Edit** menu of the word processing document select **Paste**, or press **CTRL + V**.
  If the Word Processing file is saved, the image will be included in the saved file.

To copy a URL, do the following:
- Click the **Download Media Files** link.
- Right-click on any link and select **Copy Shortcut**.
- Open a word processing document.
- From the **Edit** menu select **Paste**, or press **CTRL + V**.

1.9   Preparing and Printing Web Pages

1.9.1 Preparation

Before printing a web page, it is good practice to preview the output and make any necessary adjustments.

In Internet Explorer, print options are accessed by clicking the **Print** button on the **Command bar**.

1.9.2 Print Preview (7.4.2.2)

To open the Print Preview window, do the following:
- Click the **Print** button on the **Command bar**.
- Select **Print Preview** from the menu that opens.

The **Print Preview** window opens.

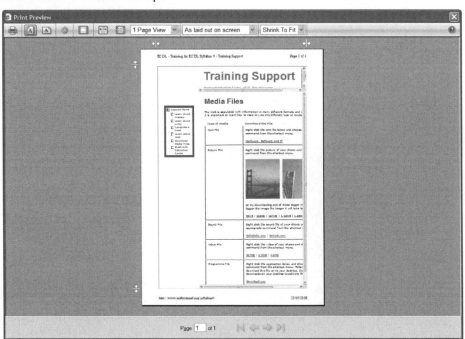

The preview window has a toolbar that provides printing, page set-up and navigation options.

Print   Page Setup

Orientation   View Options

1.9.3   Print Options (7.4.2.1)

To change the print options that are available under the General tab, paper size and so on, do the following:

Changing Orientation

There are two types of page orientation, **Portrait** and **Landscape**. Portrait is a vertical orientation. Landscape is a horizontal orientation.

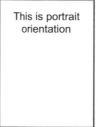

This is portrait orientation

This is landscape orientation

To change the page orientation, do the following:
* Open the desired web page in the browser.
* Click the **Page Setup** button on the **Print Preview** toolbar.
  The **Page Setup** window opens.
* In the **Orientation** section, click **Portrait** or **Landscape**.
* Preview the changes in the top right of the **Page Setup** window.
* Click **OK**.

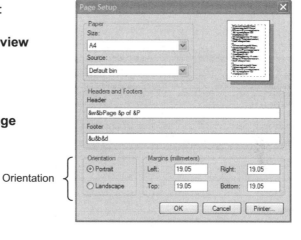

Orientation

Adjusting Margin Settings

Margins refer to the amount of space that appears at the top, bottom, left and right of a page.

To adjust margin settings, do the following:
* Open the desired web page in the browser.
* From the **File menu**, select Page Setup.
  The **Page Setup** window opens.
* In the **Margins** (millimeters) section, type in the desired margins.
* Preview the changes in the top right of the **Page Setup** window.
* Click **OK**.

Margin settings

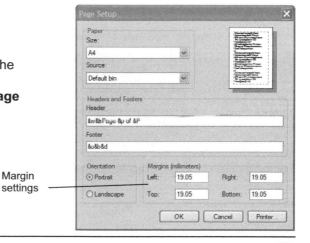

7

Paper Size

To change the paper size, do the following:
- Open the desired web page in the browser.
- From the **File menu**, select **Page Setup**. The **Page Setup** window opens.
- In the **Paper** section, click the box to display the drop-down list.
- Select the desired **Paper size** from the list.
- Click **OK**.

1.9.4 Additional Options (7.4.2.3)

After the page orientation, margins and paper size are specified the page can be printed. This can be done from the Print Preview window by clicking the Print button on the toolbar. This displays the Print window, the main points of which are described below.

General Tab: Select Printer

This area of the window displays printers that are installed in Windows. The printer to be used can be selected by clicking it.

General Tab: Page Range

- **All** – This option prints the entire document.
- **Current Page** – Prints the current page only.
- **Pages** – Allows a range of pages to be printed, for example **1,3,5,6-12** would print pages 1,3,5 and 6, then all pages between 6 and 12.

Select a printer

Specify page range

Specify number of copies

General Tab: Number of Copies

Specify the number of copies to be printed here. If more than one copy of a printout that requires more than a single printed page is specified, the **Collate** options section will become available to allow a collation sequence to be chosen.

Options Tab

Some web pages use **frames**, which are multiple sections each having its own scroll bar and which can be scrolled independently. In effect, they are separate small web pages all displayed on the same screen.

If frames have been used, the **Print Frames** option will be available in the Print window under the Options tab.
- Each frame can be printed on a separate sheet.
- The selected frame can be printed.
- The page can be printed as it appears on screen.

Visit **www.becpublishing.com** for an example of the use of frames. The username **blackrock** and password **practice** are needed.

7

Section 2   Electronic Communication

2.1   E-Mail Concepts and Terms

2.1.1   History

In 1971, Ray Tomlinson, working in a technology company called Bolt, Beranek and Newman, sent the first example of what we would recognise as an e-mail – in other words a message between computers using an address where the recipient's name and their computer were separated by the characteristic @ symbol.

The number of e-mails now sent every day is hard to estimate but at the time of writing in 2008, there could be as many as 62 billion.

2.1.2   Advantages of E-Mail (7.5.3.1 and 7.5.1.1)

Electronic mail, or **e-mail** as it is commonly known, is the most widely used facility available on the internet. Mail programs such as **Microsoft Outlook**, **Outlook Express**, **Netscape Mail**, **Eudora** and **Pegasus Mail**, enable messages to be received locally or internationally for the price of a local telephone call. E-mail is fast, cheap and convenient. You can send an e-mail to an individual or to a group of people at the same time. You can create mailing lists that send mail automatically to particular groups of people. In addition, you can attach files such as spreadsheets, pictures and sounds to your e-mail messages.

E-mail messages can be prepared in advance before you go online or connect via your ISP. This saves on telephone costs when using a dial-up connection. When you are preparing mail without being connected, you are working **offline**. When you are connected, you are **online**.

A different way to use e-mail is by using **webmail**. This provides huge flexibility, because all e-mail is stored on a remote computer belonging to the webmail provider. All that is needed to use it is a web browser, meaning that these e-mails can be read and sent from any location that has a browser and any sort of internet connection – a hotel departures lounge, for example, or a portable device such as an iPhone. There are many webmail providers offering free accounts – examples include **www.googlemail.com** and **www.fastmail.fm**. You should note, though, that mail service providers normally have limitations on the size and number of e-mails you can store.

Traditionally, software applications called **e-mail clients** have been used to receive, store, read, send and organise emails. Some examples are **Windows Live Mail**, **Microsoft Outlook** and **Thunderbird**.

To use e-mail the following are required:

- **An internet connection**: This can be broadband or dial-up. With dial-up, there are considerations to do with the low speed of data transfer involved. It may be easier to compose e-mails when not connected to the internet (offline) and then send them as a batch when connected (or online). Also with dial-up connections, there will be a limit to the size of files that can be attached when sending a message, or that can be received.

- **An e-mail account with an e-mail provider**: Generally the Internet Service Provider (ISP) will allow some e-mail addresses to be set up, and take care of routing messages to and from the customer's computer. In a business or educational establishment, e-mail addresses are usually provided by the IT department.

- **An e-mail client**: E-mail client software must be configured with the details provided by the ISP, including a username and password.

7

2.1.3 Network Etiquette (7.5.3.2)

The development of the internet has created a true global village, bringing together people with varying views, ideas and customs. In order that everyone can communicate without undue misunderstanding, a loosely defined set of rules has emerged to form a convention for online communication, including e-mail and instant messaging. This is known as **netiquette**, a shortening of **network etiquette**.

Some basic guidelines for using e-mail are:
- Use accurate and brief descriptions in subject lines.
- Keep messages brief.
- Reply promptly.
- Don't 'reply to all' unless necessary.
- Spell check outgoing e-mails.
- Remember that tone can be hard to convey, especially to recipients in other cultures. Something said ironically or jokingly may not be read that way. In personal e-mails, use **emoticons** or **smileys** to infer meaning. For example the characters :) look like a smiling face when viewed from the side, and can be used to indicate humour.
- Don't forward chain letter e-mails.
- UPPERCASE IS SHOUTING!

2.1.4 The Structure of an E-Mail Address (7.5.1.2)

An e-mail address is required before email can be sent or received. The address is usually written in lower case letters and contains no spaces. A distinctive feature is the @ symbol that separates the username from the domain part of the address.

In this example, Ethna Boland has an e-mail address in Ireland with Blackrock Education Centre. She has chosen **ethnab** as her username. Her address would be read aloud as 'ethna b at blackrockec dot ie', but written as shown below.

Each e-mail address must be unique. The part after the @ symbol is usually the same for a particular ISP or company, so the person's actual name – before the @ symbol – cannot be duplicated. People often use a variation of their actual name to distinguish them from others with similar names. For example, if Ethna Boland wanted to have the name eboland, she may discover that this particular name has already been taken. She would then have to choose another name.

2.1.5 SMS Messages (7.5.1.3)

The term **SMS** (**Short Message Service**) refers to the technology used to send short (maximum 160 character) text messages across mobile phone networks. Sending SMS messages from mobile phones is commonly referred to as **texting**. Usually, the messages are sent to another mobile phone, although it is possible to send messages to other devices or to send SMS messages from a computer.

> **NOTE**
> Some mobile devices, such as the Blackberry and the iPhone, can send and receive e-mails in the true sense – this is not the same as SMS.

2.1.6 VoIP (7.5.1.4)

VoIP (Voice over Internet Protocol) refers to the use of the internet, and digital equipment connected to it, to transmit voice traffic rather than using a traditional telephone. The advantage is usually cost. A business may have its own private network connecting offices worldwide – if telephone traffic can be transmitted over the same network as data then that business will not have to incur the costs involved if a person in one country calling someone in another country using the normal telephone system. The business will use normal desktop telephones that connect directly into its data network.

The free **Skype** application is popular among home users. Using a headset with a microphone it enables:

- Free voice and video calls to other Skype users worldwide.
- Calls from Skype to normal telephones at much cheaper rates than those offered by telephone companies.

2.1.7 Virtual Communities (7.5.1.6)

Virtual Communities are communities in which people interact with each other in various ways over the Internet, including keeping in touch with their friends, finding new friends, asking advice, playing games, and taking part in discussions and debates.

Some of the most popular examples of virtual communities are **social networking websites** like MySpace and Facebook. On these websites, registered users can add photos and enter personal information to create a unique webpage that represents them to the other members of the community. Users are able to search for people that they know and list them as a friend so that they can easily stay in contact. Users can interact in a variety of ways, including sending e-mails and instant messages, uploading digital photos, music, and videos and playing computer games.

Other types of virtual communities include **internet forums**, where users can ask questions and receive answers or discuss a particular subject. **Chat rooms** are a virtual community where users can send and receive messages, and participate in discussions and private conversations in real time. Internet forums and chat rooms are often controlled by moderators who ensures that no users violate the rules of the community or send abusive or inappropriate messages.

Online computer games often create virtual communities where the members play games against each other. These types of virtual communities can vary in size from a small number of players to a global game involving thousands of players scattered across hundreds of countries. Online computer games are often character-based, role-playing games, but also include games such as chess and tennis as well as even casino games where users can register their credit card details and gamble online.

7

2.1.8 Instant Messaging (7.5.1.5)

Instant messaging (IM) enables computer users to communicate in real time in the form of a 'chat', and is one of the oldest forms of communication using a computer. Messages entered are sent instantly to the other user, who can then reply. It is also possible to transfer files. On a broadband internet connection, there is no cost involved in using IM and it provides an experience closer to a normal conversation than e-mail.

Windows Live Messenger is one such application that is used widely. It provides the user with several facilities including web mail, file sharing online, telephone calls over the web and online chat. The application has a set of convenient icons to display either your own availability or that of others who are on your contact list, e.g. whether you are away from your computer, online and available, and so on.

There are two main ways to use instant messaging.

- **User to User**: This type of instant messaging takes the form of a closed conversation between two users of the same IM network, for example the MSN Messenger network.
- **Chat rooms**: These are virtual rooms that enable many users to connect and chat together at the same time. Normally, chat rooms are based around a topic.

The illustration on the right depicts a chat room used for technical support.

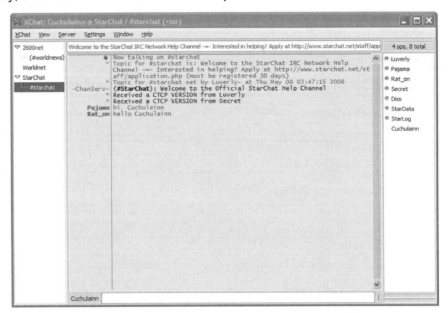

2.2 E-Mail Security Considerations

2.2.1 Fraudulent and Unsolicited E-Mail (7.5.2.1)

E-mail is a popular form of communication and is a powerful tool for targeting advertising messages directly at users. Unwanted e-mail, known as spam or junk mail, has become an increasingly common and controversial way for companies to reach people.

Most e-mail client software applications have a built-in facility for filtering out junk mail. The software will guess whether or not a message is junk based on the contents of the subject line and other indicators. It will then be moved to a junk mail folder if necessary. Periodically, users check the junk mail folder and can either confirm messages as being junk mail or legitimate. In this way, the e-mail client can learn over time to identify unwanted mail. In business and educational networks, this e-mail filtering generally takes place at the point of entry and the individual users may see little or no junk mail at all.

Unsolicited e-mail is a major problem – it has been estimated at times that up to 75 per cent of all e-mails during a given period are spam. Never reply to unsolicited e-mail messages, even those that claim to offer a method of unsubscribing. All this will do is indicate to the sender that they have hit a 'live' e-mail address. Distribute personal and business e-mail addresses extremely carefully. When using online forms supply a fake e-mail address where possible to reduce the risk of the address being harvested for use by spammers.

2.2.2 Phishing (7.5.2.2)

Phishing is in essence impersonation. A user may receive emails supposedly from their bank or major online entities such as PayPal or eBay. The e-mail will detail some reason or other that requires the user to re-enter their username and password, and a link to the bank website will be provided. However, the link will actually go to a different website that has been cloned to look like the real thing. In this way, any usernames and passwords entered are stored away and used for criminal purposes later. Some examples of phishing attempts purporting to be e-mails from eBay are displayed at: http://pages.ebay.com/education/spooftutorial/.

Most modern e-mail clients and web browsers can spot attempted phishing attempts and alert the user, however, these are not foolproof and so it falls on the user to employ caution. Some online banks, for example, will ask for a piece of personal information that a third party could not know, and include this in their e-mails.

No legitimate online entity such as a bank will ever ask for personal details in an e-mail.

The following images illustrate a phishing scam that resembles the Paypal login webpage. Paypal is an internet-based financial service that enables registered users to make secure transactions online. The phishing scam worked by sending e-mails worded to lure recipients into believing the email was from Paypal. The e-mail also stated that the recipient should go to the Paypal site to update their personal details. The e-mail contains a link that appeared legitimate.

https://www.paypal.com/us/cgi-bin/webscr?_cmd=_login-run

However, the actual link differed from the displayed link and, once clicked, took recipients to a website designed to resemble the legitimate PayPal login page.

There are two indications that a link or website is a phishing scam. The first thing to look for is the **link**. The displayed link should be the same as the actual link. In the example, the displayed link is as follows: **https://www.paypal.com/us/cgi-bin/webscr?_cmd=_login-run**.

However, the actual link of the website is as follows:
http://218.246.203/icons/.cgi-bin/paypal/cgi-bin/webscrcmd_login.php.

The second thing to look for is the **lock symbol**. This is perhaps the most important thing to check. The lock symbol will be displayed either to the right of the address bar or at the bottom of the window, not on the page itself – if the lock symbol is displayed on the page, it is not legitimate.

Clicking the lock symbol will display the website's certificate which is designed to authenticate the website's legitimacy. The certificate will display the issuing authority, usually VeriSign, as well as the website the certificate is issued to.

2.2.3 Malware Threats from E-Mail (7.5.2.3)

Malware is an umbrella term that describes a variety of security threats in the form of unwanted programs, including viruses and Trojans. One of the ways that these programs spread is via e-mail. These e-mails will generally come from an unrecognised source, but sometimes they will appear to come from known contacts by using **address spoofing**.

The malicious software will sometimes come in the form of an **executable attachment**, in other words a program that can be saved or run directly from the e-mail. It may appear to be a game, or a joke thus leading the recipient to believe it is harmless but it will in fact introduce malware into the system when executed. Other malware has spread via e-mail by taking advantages of security flaws or bugs in the operating system, for example by including a graphic file that when opened can create a hidden method of entry for an attacker.

Fortunately, the threat of malware spreading via e-mail under Ubuntu is minimal compared to other operating systems because of its secure design. Users should still be careful, however, never to open unexpected executable attachments, even if they are from a known sender.

2.2.4 Digital Signatures (7.5.2.4)

A digital signature is an electronic message or tag that may be used to validate the identity of the source of a message. It also certifies that the original matter of the message or document is intact.

When working with e-mail over the internet, security and privacy are particularly important. Digital signatures associated with reputable sources of information provide a level of guarantee in this regard.

2.3 First Steps with E-Mail

2.3.1 Opening and Closing an E-Mail Application (7.6.1.1)

There are various e-mail clients available that will work with Microsoft Windows. This text will be centred around Microsoft Outlook 2007.

Opening Microsoft Outlook 2007

To open Outlook 2007, do the following:

* Double-click the desktop icon.

  Alternatively, open the Start Menu, click **All Programs** and select **Microsoft Outlook 2007** from the Microsoft Office folder.

When Outlook 2007 opens, it will look similar to the following illustration.

Closing Microsoft Outlook 2007

To close Outlook 2007, do the following:

* Click the **Close X** button in the top-right of the Outlook 2007 window.

2.3.2 Opening E-Mails

E-mails are stored in different folders, which are on the left of the Outlook 2007 window. Incoming messages go to the **Inbox**.

To open an e-mail, do the following,

* Click **Inbox** in the folder list to select it.

  Messages in the Inbox are listed on the right of the window, showing things such as the Sender, Subject and Date.
* Double-click a message to open it.

  The e-mail will open in a new window.

NOTE
Clicking the e-mail once will display the message in the **Reading Pane** (which is normally at the bottom of the Outlook window).

2.3.3 Closing E-Mails

When you are finished with an opened message, it should be closed.

Close X button

To close an e-mail, do the following:

- Click the **Close X** button on the e-mail's title bar.

2.3.4 Using Help Functions

A range of Help options are also available from the Help button on the Standard toolbar in the Outlook window (or of any e-mail message). Clicking the question mark button opens a fully searchable Help file for Microsoft Outlook 2007 and its functions.

Help button

Alternatively, press F1 to open **Outlook Help**.

NOTE
This help is online, so an internet connection is needed.

2.4 Adjusting Settings

2.4.1 Managing Inbox Headings

The column headings at the top of messages in the Inbox can be changed to suit users' particular requirements.

To change these headings, do the following:

- Ensure the **Inbox** is selected in the folder list to the left in the **Outlook 2007** window.
- Right-click any column header in the list of messages.
- Select **Field Chooser** from the pop-up list.

  The **Field Chooser** window opens.

- Drag and drop the required column name to its position in the **Outlook** window.

  Red arrows will indicate where the column will appear in the window.

NOTE
To remove a heading either drag the column header out of the Outlook window or right-click on the header and select Remove this column from the pop-up list.

The results of adding the **Size** column and changing it to be the eighth column are shown below.

2.4.2 Displaying and Hiding Toolbars

The toolbars at the top of the Outlook 2007 window can be displayed or hidden depending on a user's need.

To display or hide toolbars do the following:

- Select **Tools** on the **Standard toolbar**.
- Select **Customize** from the drop-down menu.
  The **Cusomize** window opens.
- On the Toolbars tab, select, or de-select, the required toolbars (add or remove a tick in the box next to the toolbar name).
  The toolbar is added to the top of the **Outlook** window.
- Click **Close**.
  Alternatively, right-click in the toolbar area to select toolbars or to open the Customize window.

In common with most Windows applications, buttons can also be added to and removed from the toolbar.

To add or remove buttons, do the following:

- Click the arrow at the very right of the toolbar to which buttons are to be added or removed.
- Select **Add or Remove Buttons**.

- Select the name of the toolbar (e.g. **Standard**).
- Select or de-select individual buttons in the pop-up menu to display or hide them on the toolbar.

7

Incorrectly spelled words in the message body text or subject lines will be underlined in red.

- Right-clicking the underlined word will display a pop-up menu with suggestions as to the correct spelling.
- Selecting an item from this menu will replace the incorrect word.

Right-click the misspelled word for a range of alternative spellings

Clicking the **Spelling and AutoCorrection** button, opens the **Editor Options** window.

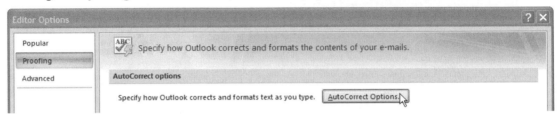

Clicking the **AutoCorrect Options** button in the **Editor Options** window opens the **AutoCorrect** window in which different options can be selected.

- To select them, tick the box next to the option.
- The language of the dictionary used in the spell check can also be set in this window.
- Click **OK** to apply the settings.

NOTE
Individual e-mails can be spell checked at any time by clicking the **Spelling** button in the **Proofing** group of the **Message** tab.

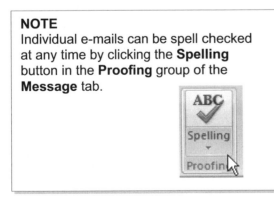

2.7 Attachments

2.7.1 Sending an E-Mail with an Attachment
Files can be attached to e-mails and will be available to all recipients (see Section 2.7.3). As part of this exercise, identify a previously created document file to use as an attachment.

- When the message appears in the recipient's Inbox, there is an indicator (the exclamation mark in the illustration) that it is high priority.

  Different e-mail clients have different ways of indicating the importance of the message.

To send an e-mail with a low priority, do the following:

- Create a new e-mail in Outlook.
- Before sending, click the **Low Priority** button on the New Message window toolbar.

2.5.4 Saving an E-Mail as a Draft

Sometimes, it is necessary to compose an e-mail, but not send it immediately. In this situation, a new message can be saved as a **draft**. It will then be stored in the **Drafts** folder until needed again.

To save a message as a draft, do the following:

- Using Outlook, compose a new e-mail message (see Section 2.6.1).
- Click **Save** on the new e-mail message window Quick Access Toolbar.

  The message will be stored in the **Drafts** folder.

  The message can then be reopened as it is needed and can be amended further and saved as a draft again, or sent.

2.6   Creating and Sending E-Mails

2.6.1 Composing a New E-Mail

It is important to note that the procedure for setting up an e-mail account is not part of the ICDL syllabus. It is assumed that an e-mail account has been set up with an authorised ISP and that Microsoft Outlook 2007 is being used as the default mail application.

To create (or **compose**) a new e-mail, do the following:

- Open **Outlook 2007**.
- Click **New** on the Standard toolbar.

A **New Message** window opens.

- In the **To** field, enter a recipient's e-mail address, e.g. **bec@blackrockec.ie**.
- In the **Subject** field, enter a subject that describes the content of the e-mail.
- Enter the message text, or **body text**, in the main part of the window.

    Additional recipients can be entered in the **To**, **Cc** and **Bcc** fields. Addresses should be separated by semi-colons.

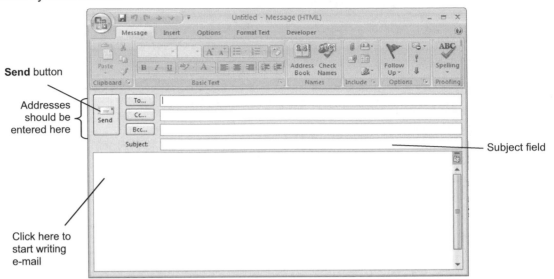

To send the message, do the following:

- Click **Send** on the New Message window toolbar.

2.6.2 Recipients

When composing an e-mail there can be three categories of recipient.

- **To**: The 'To List' contains the main recipients that are affected by the message. In the example above, '5-a-side football' is a mailing list, containing multiple recipients, while 'mike.patton@gmail.com' is an individual recipient.

- **Cc**: The 'Carbon Copy' list is for recipients who may be indirectly affected by the message or that need to be kept 'in the loop'.

- **Bcc**: Recipients in the 'Blind Carbon Copy' list receive the e-mail, but the recipients in the To and Cc lists will not be aware of this. One use of Bcc is for mailings to large numbers of recipients where the identities of the others must be hidden.

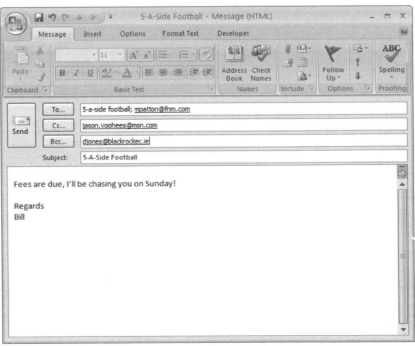

2.6.3 Copying Text from Another Source into an E-Mail (7.6.1.5)

Text can be copied from other documents into an e-mail using the usual cut and paste method.

To copy text from a Microsoft Word document, do the following:

- Open **Outlook 2007** and create a new e-mail message.
- With the new e-mail message still open, start **Microsoft Word** and open the document that contains the text to be copied.
- In **Microsoft Word**, select the text and copy it to the clipboard using **CTRL + C**, or by selecting **Copy** in the **Clipboard** section of the **Home** tab on the ribbon.
- Locate the window for the new e-mail message, and click in the main body text section.
- Press **CTRL + V** to paste the text.
  Alternatively, open select **Paste** in the **Clipboard** group on the **Message** tab.
  The text is copied into the e-mail message.

2.6.4 Replying to E-Mails

An e-mail that is received can be replied to directly, without the need to create a new e-mail and address it to the original sender.

There are two types of reply.

- A normal reply is to just the sender.
- If the message was sent to many recipients, they will not receive the reply.
  A **Reply All** reply will send your reply to all recipients of the original message.

To reply to an email, do the following:
- Select the **Inbox** on the folder list to the left of the Outlook window.
- In the message list, click the message to be replied to once.
- On the toolbar, click either **Reply** or **Reply All**.

A new message window opens.

The e-mail addresses of the original sender will be in the **To** field.
If **Reply All** was clicked, and the original e-mail was sent to multiple recipients, the e-mail addresses for these recipients will also appear in the **To** field.

The subject box will have the text **Re:** and the original subject line.

- Enter the text of the reply in the body section. Whether or not it should be entered above or below the quoted text is the subject of much debate, but for most users entering it above the quoted text is the standard, especially for long messages.
- Click **Send**.

2.6.5 Controlling Original Message Quoting when Replying (7.6.3.2)

When replying to e-mail messages, text of the original message will be automatically quoted in the reply (see Section 2.6.4).

To stop this happening, do the following:

- In the Outlook window click Tools and select **Options** from the drop-down menu.
  The **Options** window opens.
- In the **Preferences** tab, click **E-mail Options**.
  The **E-mail Options** window opens.

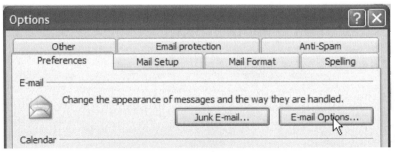

In the **On replies and forwards** section, select **Do not include original message** from the drop-down list.

- Click **OK**.

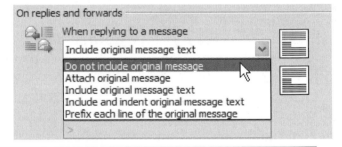

NOTE
Use the E-mail Options window to control quoting the original message when forwarding an e-mail.

2.6.6 Forwarding E-Mails

Forwarding an e-mail involves a person receiving an e-mail and passing that message on to a further recipient who was not included on the original message. It is a very similar action to replying to an e-mail.

To forward an e-mail, do the following:

- Open **Outlook 2007**.
- Select the **Inbox** on the folder list to the left of the Outlook window.
- In the **Message** list, double-click the message to be forwarded to open it.
- In the message window, click the **Forward** button in the **Respond** group of the **Message** tab.

The body text of the original message is quoted in the message to be forwarded.

- Enter a recipient, or recipients, e-mail address in the **To:** box.
- Click **Send**.

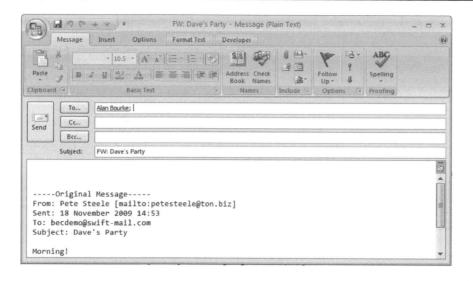

2.6.7 Spell Checking E-Mails

As with any document, it is good practice to spell check e-mails before they are sent. By default, spelling is checked automatically as a message is typed but not before the e-mail is sent.

To set spelling options, do the following:

- In the **Outlook** window click **Tools** and select **Options** from the drop-down menu.

  The **Options** window opens.

- In the **Spelling** tab, select or de-select the options for checking the spelling of e-mails.

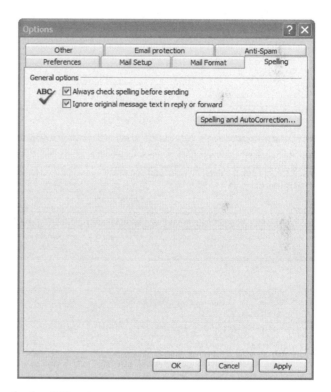

To set the **Check spelling as you type** option, do the following:

- In the Outlook window click Tools and select **Options** from the drop-down menu.
  The **Options** window opens.

- In the **Spelling** tab, click the Spelling and AutoCorrection button.
  The **Editor Options** window opens.

- Ensure the **Check spelling as you type** has been selected in the **When correcting spelling in Outlook** section of the window,

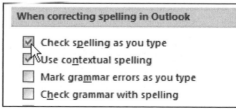

Incorrectly spelled words in the message body text or subject lines will be underlined in red.

- Right-clicking the underlined word will display a pop-up menu with suggestions as to the correct spelling.
- Selecting an item from this menu will replace the incorrect word.

Right-click the misspelled word for a range of alternative spellings

Clicking the **Spelling and AutoCorrection** button, opens the **Editor Options** window.

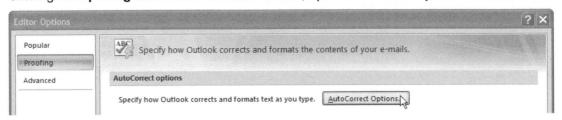

Clicking the **AutoCorrect Options** button in the **Editor Options** window opens the **AutoCorrect** window in which different options can be selected.

- To select them, tick the box next to the option.
- The language of the dictionary used in the spell check can also be set in this window.
- Click **OK** to apply the settings.

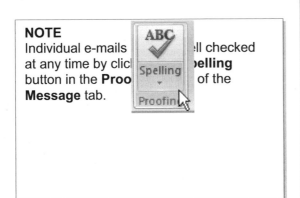

NOTE
Individual e-mails [can be spe]ll checked at any time by click[ing the S]**pelling** button in the **Proo**[fing group] of the **Message** tab.

2.7　Attachments

2.7.1　Sending an E-Mail with an Attachment

Files can be attached to e-mails and will be available to all recipients (see Section 2.7.3). As part of this exercise, identify a previously created document file to use as an attachment.

Inserting an Attachment

To attach the file to an e-mail, do the following:

- Create a new e-mail message in **Outlook 2007**.
- Enter a recipient e-mail address in the **To:** field, and a subject in the **Subject** field.
- Enter some body text.
- Click the **Attach** button in the **Include** group of the **Message** tab.

The **Insert File** window opens.

- Locate the file to attach.
- Click **Insert**.

- The attachment or attachments will be displayed below the subject field.

Removing an Attachment

To remove an attachment, do the following:

- Right-click the attachment in the attachment list.
- Select **Remove** from the menu.

2.7.2 Saving Attachments

When an e-mail with an attachment or attachments is received, the message displayed in the inbox folder will have a paperclip icon indicating that there are attachments.

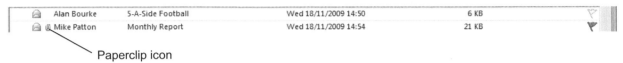

| | Alan Bourke | 5-A-Side Football | Wed 18/11/2009 14:50 | 6 KB | |
| | Mike Patton | Monthly Report | Wed 18/11/2009 14:54 | 21 KB | |

Paperclip icon

To save the attachment so that it can be opened, do the following:

- Open the e-mail message.

- In the message window, the attachments and their size will be displayed in the header area next to a paperclip icon.

  There is one attachment called **report.xlsx** in the illustration on the right.

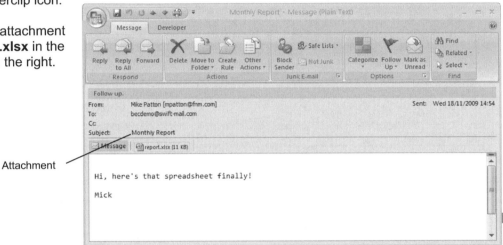

Attachment

- Right-click the attachment.
- Select **Save As** from the menu that opens.
  The **Save Attachment** window opens.
- Choose a location to save the file and give the file a meaningful name.
- Click **Save**.
  When an attachment has been saved, it can be opened in the same way as any file.

When an attachment is received, it can also be opened straight from the e-mail message.

- Right-click the attachment and choose **Open** from the pop-up list.
  The **Opening Mail Attachment** window opens giving options to open the file or save it.
- Click **Open**.
- The file opens in the appropriate application (e.g. Excel or Word).

2.7.3 Considerations when Attaching Files

One of the most powerful features of e-mail is the ability to attach files to messages. However, there are some things that need to be considered to avoid problems with attachments.

- **File size**: Be aware of the size of attachments and the likely types of internet connection used by recipients. It is all too easy for a user in a business, educational or home situation with a high-speed internet connection to attach a multi-megabyte file to an e-mail and send it to multiple recipients without considering the use of bandwidth involved, or that recipients not using a high-speed internet connection may not be able to receive it. If the attachments seem too large, they can be compressed using special software. Image, sound and video files can be created in formats that have compression built in, such as PNG or MP4. The result is much smaller files resulting in much faster transmission via e-mail, but with the same content.

- **File type**: E-mail is a common cause of malware propagation (see Section 1.2.5). As a result, some e-mail clients or e-mail servers may actively strip certain types of attachment out of e-mails due to the security risks they pose. So it may not be possible to send executable attachments to some recipients, for example.

2.8 Mail Management

2.8.1 Efficient E-Mail Management

In Section 2.6.4, the Options window was opened to control the option of including a received message in an outgoing reply. The Options window, also contains other options that can be chosen which help the efficient use of **Microsoft Outlook 2007**.

To choose these settings, do the following:

- In the Outlook window, click **Tools** on the toolbar.
- Click **Options**.
  The **Options** window opens.
- In the Preferences tab, click **E-mail Options**.
  The **E-mail Options** window opens.

  Select or deselect the options you prefer by clicking in the check boxes.

  To activate a choice, click an empty item check box. This will place a check mark in the box, indicating that the option has been activated. Clicking a box that is already checked removes the check mark and deactivates the option.

Some of the options available are as follows.

- **Save copies**: This keeps a copy of all messages that you send.
- **Automatically save**: This automatically saves unsent messages.
- **Close original message**: This ensures an e-mail message window is closed as soon as the **Reply** or **Forward** buttons are selected.

2.8.2 Creating E-Mail Folders

As the **Inbox** and **Sent Items** folders can become cluttered very quickly, messages can be stored in a tidier and more accessible manner using dedicated folders to collect e-mails covering particular subjects. Folders used to collect similarly themed e-mails or e-mails from particular senders should be named appropriately.

To create a new folder in the Inbox, do the following:

- Right-click the Inbox folder in the **Folder** list on the left of the **Outlook** window.

- Select **New Folder**.

A **Create Folder** window opens.

- Enter a name for the folder.

- Click **OK**.

A new sub-folder is created within the **Inbox** folder.

2.8.3 Deleting E-Mail Folders

To remove the folder and all the items in it, do the following:

- Right-click the folder in the folder list that is to be deleted.

Each option contains the name of the folder.

- Select **Delete [name of folder]** from the pop-up menu, e.g. **Delete "5-A-Side"**.
  A confirmation window opens.
- Click **Yes**.

2.8.4 Moving E-Mails to E-Mail Folders

To move a message from the inbox into another folder (e.g. from the **Inbox** to the **5-A-Side** folder created in Section 2.8.2.), do the following:

- Click the message to be moved.
- With the mouse button held down, drag the message to the target folder in the folder list.
  The cursor has a small rectangle attached and the folder will be highlighted.

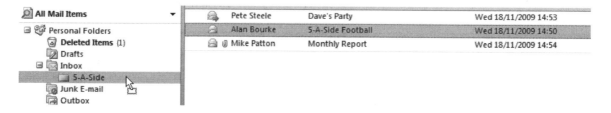

- Release the mouse button.
  The message will disappear from the **Inbox** message list.
- Click the **5-A-Side** folder to view the message.

NOTE

You can also move a message to folders in other ways from the Outlook window.

1.   Using the Edit menu
Select the message to be moved. In the **Edit** menu, click **Move to folder...** from the drop-down list. Choose the folder to which the message should be moved from the **Move Items** window that opens.

2.   Using right-click
Right-click the message to be moved and select **Move to folder...** from the pop-up list that appears. Choose the folder to which the message should be moved from the **Move Items** window that opens.

7

NOTE

If a message has been opened it can be moved to a folder by clicking the **Move to folder** button in the **Actions** group of the **Message** tab. The folder to which the message is to be moved can then be selected from the pop-up menu that opens.

To copy the message instead of moving it, do the following:

- Click the message to be copied so that it is highlighted.
- Hold down the **CTRL** key.
- With the **CTRL** key held down, left-click the message and drag it to the target folder in the folder list.
  The folder will be highlighted.
- Release the mouse button.
  The message will be in both the Inbox and the folder, e.g. in the **5-A-Side** folder.
- Click the **5-A-Side** folder to view the message.

2.8.5 Deleting E-Mails

E-mail builds up quickly and can take up a lot of disk space, especially if large attachments are involved. It is good practice to periodically clear out old messages from e-mail folders.

To delete an e-mail, do the following:

- Click the e-mail to be deleted to highlight it.
- Click the **Delete** button on the toolbar.

The e-mail will be sent to the **Deleted Items** folder in the folder list at the left of the Outlook window.

2.8.6 Restoring Deleted E-Mails

When an e-mail is placed in the **Deleted Items** folder, it is not actually deleted and can still be read and returned back to another folder in the inbox.

To restore a deleted e-mail, do the following:

- Click the **Deleted Items** folder to view the message.
- Drag the message from of the **Deleted Items** folder and drop into the **Inbox** (or other folder).

2.8.7 Emptying the Deleted Items Folder

E-mail is stored in the Inbox and other folders until you decide to delete it. The first step in deleting an e-mail does not remove it altogether, but keeps it in the **Deleted Items** folder.

To delete mail permanently, do the following:

- Right-click the **Deleted Items** folder.
- Select **Empty "Deleted Items" folder** in the pop-up menu that opens.
  A confirmation window opens.
- Click **Yes**.
  Alternatively, open the **Deleted Items** folder and delete the e-mails individually (see Section 2.8.5).

When the **Deleted Items** folder has been emptied, the e-mails are deleted permanently.

2.9   Distribution Lists

Outlook 2007 offers a **Contacts** function, which is a database of e-mail addresses and other information for individual people or groups.

2.9.1   Adding an Address to Contacts

To add a new contact, do the following:

- Click the **Contacts** button at the bottom left of the **Outlook** window.

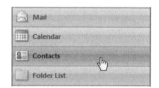

The **Contacts** window opens.

- On the **toolbar**, click **New**.

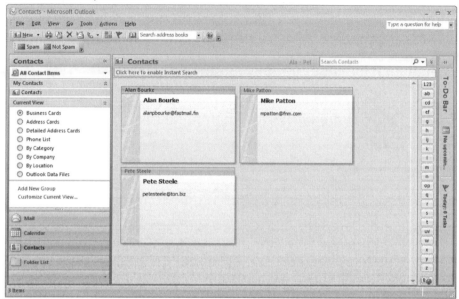

The **Contact** window opens.

- The default view is **General**.

- When all the details have been added, click **Save & Close** to save.

Click **Save & Close**

2.9.2   Deleting a Contact

To delete a contact, do the following:

- Open the main **Contacts** window.
- Select the contact to be deleted.
- Click the **Delete** button on the toolbar.

2.9.3 Updating Contacts with an Addresses from Incoming E-Mails

A contact can be created directly from a received e-mail. This ensures the correct e-mail address is added.

To add a contact from an incoming e-mail, do the following:

- Open the e-mail message from the contact whose details are to be added to **Contacts**.

- Right-click the sender's e-mail address.

- Select **Add to Outlook Contacts** from the menu that opens.

The **Contact** window opens.

- The name and e-mail address of the contact are added automatically.

- Add other details about the contact as required (see **Section 2.9.1**)

2.9.4 Creating Contact Groups

Contact (or Distribution) groups can be used to group contacts together so that a single e-mail can be sent to them as a group, without having to enter each e-mail address individually.

To create a contact group, do the following:

- Open the **Contacts** window.

- Click **New** on the Toolbar.

- Select **Distribution List**.

Index